DATA VISUALIZATION & PRESENTATION

With Microsoft Office®

SAGE was founded in 1965 by Sara Miller McCune to support the dissemination of usable knowledge by publishing innovative and high-quality research and teaching content. Today, we publish more than 850 journals, including those of more than 300 learned societies, more than 800 new books per year, and a growing range of library products including archives, data, case studies, reports, and video. SAGE remains majority-owned by our founder, and after Sara's lifetime will become owned by a charitable trust that secures our continued independence.

Los Angeles | London | New Delhi | Singapore | Washington DC

DATA VISUALIZATION & PRESENTATION

With Microsoft Office®

Valerie M. Sue
Matthew T. Griffin

Los Angeles | London | New Delhi
Singapore | Washington DC

Los Angeles | London | New Delhi
Singapore | Washington DC

FOR INFORMATION:

SAGE Publications, Inc.
2455 Teller Road
Thousand Oaks, California 91320
E-mail: order@sagepub.com

SAGE Publications Ltd.
1 Oliver's Yard
55 City Road
London EC1Y 1SP
United Kingdom

SAGE Publications India Pvt. Ltd.
B 1/I 1 Mohan Cooperative Industrial Area
Mathura Road, New Delhi 110 044
India

SAGE Publications Asia-Pacific Pte. Ltd.
3 Church Street
#10-04 Samsung Hub
Singapore 049483

Acquisitions Editor: Helen Salmon
E-Learning Editor: Katie Bierach
Editorial Assistant: Anna Villarruel
Production Editor: Jane Haenel
Copy Editor: Mark Bast
Typesetter: C&M Digitals (P) Ltd.
Proofreader: Susan Schon
Indexer: Karen Wiley
Cover Designer: Candice Harman
Marketing Manager: Nicole Elliott

Library of Congress Cataloging-in-Publication Data

Sue, Valerie M.

Data visualization & presentation with Microsoft Office /
Valerie M. Sue and Matthew T. Griffin.

pages cm
Includes bibliographical references and index.

ISBN 978-1-4833-6515-2 (pbk. : alk. paper)

1. Microsoft Office. 2. Charts, diagrams, etc.—Computer programs. 3. Presentation graphics software. I. Griffin, Matthew T. II. Title. III. Title: Data visualization and presentation with Microsoft Office.

HF5548.4.M525S84 2016
005.5—dc23   2015020747

This book is printed on acid-free paper.

Certified Chain of Custody
Promoting Sustainable Forestry
www.sfiprogram.org
SFI-01268

SFI label applies to text stock

15 16 17 18 19 10 9 8 7 6 5 4 3 2 1

Brief Contents

Detailed Contents

Preface

Data visualization is the art and science of communicating quantitative information through visual presentations. It may take the form of traditional charts and tables or may include new, interactive visualizations created by software. Pictures enable complex information to be delivered quickly and effectively and can help to reveal patterns in data and uncover anomalies that may not have been spotted otherwise. Moreover, the visual format is engaging for report readers and presentation audiences. This book provides instructions for presenting data clearly and accurately by using charts and tables.

Everything Old Is New Again

To the casual observer, it may seem as if the field of data visualization is a modern discipline, born of an era characterized by big data, ubiquitous computing, and the desire to make evidence-based decisions in just about every situation. Although the use of computer technology to illustrate data is relatively new, humans have a long tradition of representing information using pictures. This history includes simple cave drawings, maps, diagrams of the planets, genealogical charts, statistical graphs, and the interactive dashboards and infographics that are common today.

The modern history of data visualization can be traced to 18th-century Scottish engineer William Playfair. He is credited for inventing many of the common forms of data visualization currently in use, including line, bar, and pie charts. Whether you accept that Playfair invented these charts or believe that he merely popularized their use, his work is important because it contributed directly to the notion that charts communicate better than tables of data. Playfair asserted, "To see numerical data as geometric shapes reveals its significance more quickly, makes it easier to remember, and saves time for those of high rank, or active business."[1]

Although Playfair's proposition was appealing and the use of charts to describe data became popular in textbooks, business, and government, the field didn't develop in its familiar form until the second half of the 20th century. In the 1960s and 1970s powerful computers gave statisticians the tools to process large volumes of data and visualize information quickly.

---

[1]William Playfair, *The Commercial and Political Atlas*, 3rd ed. (London:, 1801), xiv.

Data Visualization in the 20th Century

With the 1977 publication of his book *Exploratory Data Analysis*, statistician John Tukey provided the impetus for the development of information visualization in statistics. Tukey encouraged the use of pictures as tools to explore data stories that might not be uncovered by statistical tests. Tukey's innovations, like the stem-and-leaf and box plots were influential, to be sure. Perhaps more important, Tukey's stature as an esteemed statistician imbued the field of data visualization with respectability, which led to its broad acceptance.

In the late 1970s, computer processing of statistical data offered the possibility of constructing graphs; however, all of the graphics in *Exploratory Data Analysis* were drawn by hand. Two events of the 1980s, the publication of Edward Tufte's text *The Visual Display of Quantitative Information* and the rapid adoption of the personal computer, turned hand-drawn illustrations of data into historical relics. Inexpensive hardware combined with spreadsheet software provided the tools for anyone to create data visualizations. Statisticians and other data analysts no longer needed to employ trained artists to illustrate data in graphical form.

Contemporary Data Visualization

The Visual Display of Quantitative Information was a revolutionary text; some say the most important book ever written about data visualization. In it, Tufte introduced principles of graphical integrity, emphasized that visual representations of data must tell the truth, and provided a vocabulary for the field. He gave us the concepts of data-ink, the ink on a graph that represents data; chartjunk, the excessive and unnecessary use of graphical effects in charts; data density, the proportion of the total size of a graph dedicated to displaying data; and small multiples, a series of small graphs repeated in one visual.

Despite Tufte's careful instruction and the widespread use of his texts in universities and business, the last 30 years have witnessed a proliferation of poorly designed, incomprehensible, and appalling data visualizations. Much of this can be attributed to mass marketing of graphics software. The introduction of Microsoft Office®* in 1990 with its combination of Word 1.1, Excel 2.0, and PowerPoint 2.0, made it easy for users to create charts, even without the benefit of a mouse in the early days. The features and usability of the Office programs steadily improved and before long became standard tools for home, school, and office computing.

---

*Microsoft, Encarta, MSN, and Windows are either registered trademarks or trademarks of Microsoft Corporation in the United States and/or other countries.

The latest version of Excel offers a wide assortment of charts that can be created in a few mouse clicks. Therein lies the problem. Charts became so easy to create that many users move through the motions of creating charts and inserting them into reports without any thought given to how well the visualization represents the data. A new feature in Excel 2013, Recommended Charts, further reduces the analyst's effort by suggesting appropriate charts based on the data selected. In a review of Excel 2013's new charting features, one technology writer noted, "Choosing the appropriate chart type to represent your data's story and applying that choice requires knowledge (sometimes experience) that many users don't have. Recommended Charts takes a bit of the pain out of this process."[2]

Relying on Excel (or any other software) to recommend appropriate charts is problematic. First, there is no substitute for knowledge and experience when it comes to creating effective data visualizations. Second, there are choices to make from among the recommended charts; sometimes a dozen or more charts are recommended. Users need guidance for selecting the best recommended chart. Finally, although Excel's built-in charts have improved immensely over the years, the chart galleries still offer three-dimensional charts, many chart styles full of chartjunk, and inexplicably, some charts, such as the stacked line chart, have tool tips recommending against their use because the charts can be hard to read.

This phenomenon is not limited to Excel. The market is rife with software vendors offering easy-to-use charting software; many are free if you don't mind making your data public. The unique, creative, and dynamic visualizations made possible by the spate of tools currently available is thrilling. It is also troublesome. Data visualization software demonstrations typically emphasize cool features, superior usability, user testimonials, and customer support. Seldom do they offer instruction in best practices for creating data pictures. When vendors offer training, it is usually centered on learning how to use the product's features, not on the careful selection of the elements comprising data visualizations.

Rationale for This Text

The field of data visualization is flourishing, and universities now offer courses on the topic. Entry-level data analysts are expected to be proficient data artists. As the possibilities for data visualization grow exponentially it is more necessary than ever to distinguish effective from ineffective charts and reports and to

---

2. Susan Harkins, "10 Cool New Charting Features in Excel 2013," *TechRepublic*, August 2, 2013, http://www.techrepublic.com/blog/10-things/10-cool-new-charting-features-in-excel-2013.

develop good habits so that new software tools will be used to create exciting and illuminating, not complex and confusing, data visualizations.

Our goal is to build on the inspirational work of authors like Edward Tufte, Stephen Few, and Colin Ware and add practical instruction for creating essential charts. We believe that by reinforcing best practices, demonstrating how to apply those principles using familiar software, and encouraging chart creation practice, readers will be equipped with knowledge and skills to create great data visualizations.

What's Inside This Text

This text is organized in three sections. We begin with a discussion of choosing appropriate data displays in Chapter 1. We move, in Chapters 2–4, into a discussion of when and how to create the most common chart types: bar and column charts, line and area charts, and pie charts. Section I ends with a consideration of chart formatting best practices. In Section II, we cover how to prepare data for charting (Chapter 6) and create pivot tables and pivot charts in Excel (Chapter 7). This section also includes a discussion of creating data tables destined for reports and presentations (Chapter 8). The final section of the text is devoted to reports and presentations. In Chapter 9 we discuss common types of data reports and offer advice on moving charts and tables from Excel to PowerPoint and Word. Chapter 10 covers presentations and the ways in which charts and other data visualizations may be used to support oral delivery of information. Chapter 11 reviews the considerations for delivering presentations aided by technology. Finally, we review the major phases of the data visualization process and offer advice on becoming a data visualization expert.

You'll find three types of content in the chapters: (1) the text that describes the charts and best practices for their use; (2) step-by-step instructions for building each of the chart types; and (3) expert tips for solving common problems, working efficiently, and avoiding potential pitfalls. Because we believe that pictures combined with words produce effective communication, we've included many illustrations of both effective and ineffective charts and screen shots of menus needed to construct the charts.

Audience for This Text

This text was written for anyone who has a need or desire to communicate a data story. Readers may include business professionals creating quarterly reports; social scientists communicating survey findings; entrepreneurs making a presentation to potential funders; or students learning for the first time how to create charts to explore or present data. The text is appropriate for those with little or no knowledge of data visualization principles. We have provided detailed discussions of data visualization best practices and step-by-step instructions with illustrations showing how to create charts, reports, and presentations using Microsoft Office programs. Intermediate readers who are proficient in the use of Office may skip the "how to" sections of the text and focus on discussions of best practices and expert tips that provide advice on overcoming common obstacles and working efficiently in Office.

Software

We use Microsoft Office 2013 for the PC (Excel, PowerPoint, and Word) exclusively for our examples and step-by-step instructions. We've opted to use software that we expect most readers will already have on their computers and will be familiar enough so that basic instruction about the software interface, for example, how to navigate the ribbons or how to format text, will be unnecessary. Once learned, the principles of effective data presentation will be transferrable to other software programs.

This is not a data analysis text; therefore, discussion of software products such as SPSS or SAS is limited to exporting the analysis results from those programs so that they can be used to create charts in Excel. If you choose to use the native chart creation features of SPSS or SAS, the same principles will apply; of course, you will need to explore those program's chart editor options.

We're pleased that you've decided to join us on this journey and hope that you find it useful and productive.

Online Resources

A companion website for this book at **study.sagepub.com/sue** features data sets, Excel examples, screencasts, PowerPoint templates, and more.

Acknowledgments

We've been talking about writing this book for a long time. Then one day while meandering through the SAGE booth at a convention hall, we met Helen Salmon. Three years, 67,000 words, and 414 figures later, here we are. Helen has been our editor, critic, advisor, and champion. Without Helen's encouragement we'd still be talking about writing a book. Thank you, Helen!

Jane Haenel at SAGE kept us organized and on schedule and was infinitely patient with our many revisions. We also wish to thank the editorial and production staff at SAGE who skillfully guided us through the publication process: Anna Villarruel, Mark Bast, Susan Schon, and Karen Wiley.

We're grateful to the reviewers who generously gave their time to read and comment on the drafts of this manuscript: James Suleiman, University of Southern Maine; Robert N. Yale, University of Dallas; Martin L. Levin, The University of Memphis; and Mary Beth Zeni, Ursuline College.

We'd like to thank Mike Orkin for his encouragement and support of this project.

Matthew would like to thank Valerie for convincing him that he could do this, his family and friends for their patience and support, and the staff at Rudy's Can't Fail Cafe for their excellent weekend breakfast service.

About the Authors

Valerie M. Sue is a senior manager at Kaiser Permanente (KP). She manages a range of projects for KP's Market Strategy and Sales Operations Department and provides data visualization consultation to KP executives and staff. Prior to joining KP, Sue was an associate professor of communication at California State University, East Bay. At CSU, East Bay, she taught communication theory, research methods, survey research, and statistics and was the director of the Communication Department's graduate program. She has authored numerous journal articles, book chapters, and a survey methods text. Sue earned a PhD in communication from Stanford University.

Matthew T. Griffin is a senior consultant at Kaiser Permanente (KP). He works in KP's Market Research Department analyzing large quantities of web-related data and investigating the ways in which KP members use digital tools to manage their health. Griffin has been using Excel (and before that Lotus 1-2-3) for nearly 30 years. He has honed his expertise and passion for Excel while working in the health care, banking, and retail industries. He has provided Excel support and training to hundreds of colleagues over the years. Griffin has a BS in business administration with a concentration in information systems from San Francisco State University.

Displaying Data

Choosing Data Displays

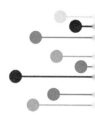

Information and Audience Considerations

Before opening software and starting to create tables and charts, several preliminary issues should be addressed. Answering these questions will guide your data visualization decisions as you proceed with your analysis and reporting.

How much information?

More information does not equate to better information. It is your job to determine what the audience needs and provide it. It is never a good idea to deliver everything you have and let the audience sort it out. Extraneous data are distracting and damage message reception, comprehension, and retention. Having a clear picture of your audience will drive your decision about how much data to provide, which in turn will affect your data visualization choices. For example, smaller groups tasked with specific decision making may need a lot of data with considerable detail. Larger groups aiming mainly to stay informed will often require less data presented at a high level.

Who is the audience for your data?

The composition of the audience for your report or presentation will determine how you organize and present the data. For example, a face-to-face meeting with a few potential investors for a new venture will require a detailed proposal containing precise values presented in a data table, charts showing the results of market research, and illustrations of potential growth over time. On the other hand, a presentation prepared for a group of hundreds or

Learning Objectives

- Describe the audience factors that drive data visualization decisions

- Distinguish data reports from presentations

- Match data to chart types

thousands of diverse individuals would be best accompanied by high-level data shown in simple charts that can be understood at a glance without the need for legends, footnotes, or data definitions.

There are many variations between these extremes. The key is to determine at the outset who will be reading your report or viewing your presentation and choose the best displays for those people in that situation. Information prepared for one setting can be repurposed for another; however, it is important that the data displays be reconfigured to suit the new audience and setting. Charts created for a boardroom presentation are not likely to be useable in a keynote address without editing.

What does the audience know?

An understanding of the audience's familiarity with and attitude toward your topic also is useful when designing data visualizations. Choices such as using acronyms in chart titles or including data labels on only the end points of a chart might be acceptable for audiences who have deep knowledge of your data. If the audience is unfamiliar with your topic, or if it is impossible to ascertain how much the audience knows, you should avoid acronyms, label charts more completely, and include definitions of key data elements. Similarly, if you anticipate resistance to your message, it is advantageous to choose data displays that will address skeptics preemptively.

What will the audience do with the information?

The question of what readers or viewers will do with the information you're preparing is a natural follow-up to the question of who is in the audience. Audiences who are responsible for making strategic decisions may find an executive dashboard to be the most useful report format. Readers charged with making operational decisions, for example, increasing staffing to meet customer demand, will need detailed and current data. When preparing charts or tables for websites, the focus should be on creating engaging data visualizations with strong visual appeal that will hold the viewer's attention.

Are You Preparing a Report or Presentation?
....

One of the most important questions you will need to resolve as you begin to create data displays is whether you are preparing a report, a presentation, or both. Although most of the principles for effective data visualization apply equally to both formats, factors such as chart size, amount of detail included, and degree of explanation required differ significantly based on the presence or absence of the author while the data are being viewed.

Reports

Reports are stand-alone documents meant to be read by the recipient, usually without the report author present. These must be self-contained, highly engaging, comprehensive documents that will attract and hold the audience's attention from beginning to end. Reports, whether distributed in hard or soft copy, should be formatted for maximum readability and include navigational aids and resources such as data definitions, indices, and FAQs.

Presentations

In presentations, a speaker delivers a message orally, accompanied by visual displays of information. The role of the visual display is to support the speaker's narration by illustrating key data elements or trends. The presenter employs public speaking principles to hold the audience's attention and is able to explain or add information to the data being presented. There are many types of in-person and virtual presentations, and the amount and type of data included will vary accordingly. The defining feature of all presentations, however, is the presence of a speaker to describe the data being shown.

Forms of Data Visualization Covered in This Text

Data visualization is a general term that describes the use of visual representations to help people analyze and interpret data. Simple as the definition may seem, the concept means many different things to followers of the field. For some, the term evokes images of interactive dashboards, hierarchical layouts, network diagrams, infographics, tree maps, and word clouds. Data visualizations like these often rely on specialized software for their creation and consumption.

To us, data visualization is a way to summarize and display large amounts of information using familiar charts and tables. For example, using a simple bar or line chart to summarize thousands, or tens of thousands, of data points to tell a story. Familiar charts have the benefit of being immediately recognizable to audiences, an important factor when analysts have only a few minutes or pages in which to present results. We have chosen to focus on a narrow collection of charts that can be created using ubiquitous software. These charts will serve most data visualization goals. Our focus is primarily on static visualizations, not those intended to be manipulated by viewers to display subsets or alternate views of data. Once the basic chart creation principles and skills are learned, practiced, and mastered, they will be transferable to more complex visualizations.

Charts

A chart is a visual display of quantitative information where the values are displayed within an area bounded by one or more axes. Data values are shown as visual objects, such as bars or lines, positioned in relation to the axes. The axes provide scales used to assign values to the bars or lines. Charts reveal shapes and trends and show relationships among multiple data series.

Column and bar charts. Column and bar charts (see Figures 1.1 and 1.2) are the most versatile types of charts. They work well for displaying differences in magnitude and making it easy for us to compare those differences. Because the bars have visual weight, they emphasize the individuality of the items charted. This makes bar and column charts well suited for illustrating categorical data.

Figure 1.2 Bar chart

Figure 1.1 Column chart

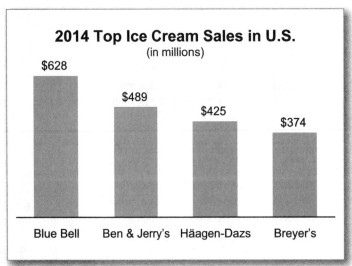

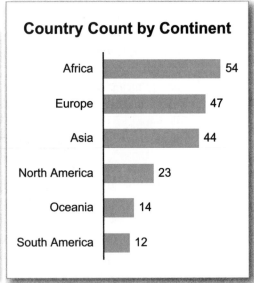

Bar and column charts may be clustered (see Figure 1.3) or stacked (see Figure 1.4) to show multiple data series or part-to-whole relationships.

Figure 1.3 Clustered column chart

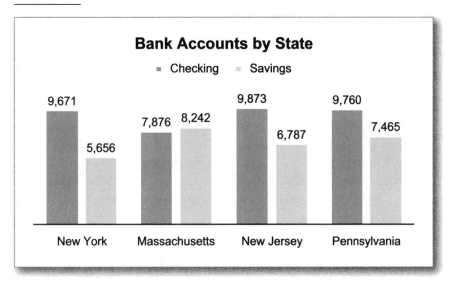

Figure 1.4 Stacked column chart

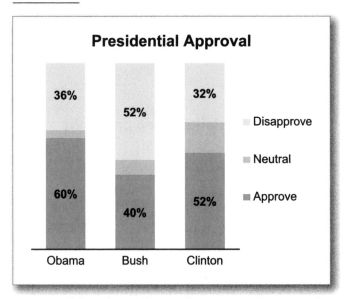

A variant of the column chart used to present continuous data is the histogram (see Figure 1.5). The histogram shares many of the features of the column chart, except the histogram columns are not separated and the data values are grouped into ranges.

Figure 1.5 Histogram

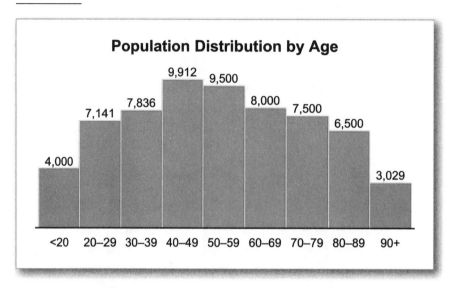

Line charts. Line charts present data in a series of points connected by line segments (see Figure 1.6). They are typically used for showing the shape of change from one value to the next, especially over time. Multiple lines (or reference lines) can be used to compare performance among categories or between categories and a target (see Figure 1.7). Information presented in a line chart can usually be shown equally well in a column chart. The decision about

Figure 1.6 Line chart

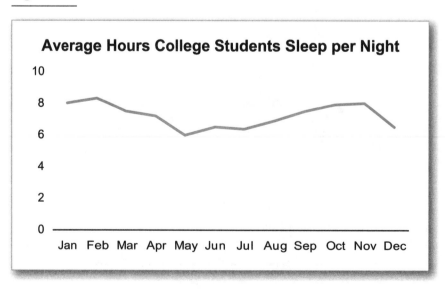

Figure 1.7 Line chart with target

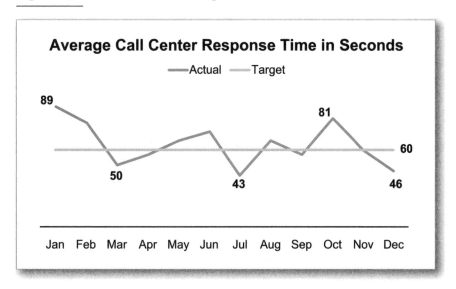

which chart to use is determined based on what you wish to emphasize: the values of the categories at different points in time or the trend over time.

Area charts. An area chart is a line chart with the area beneath the line filled in with color (see Figure 1.8). Like line charts, they are often used to illustrate change over time. Area charts have greater visual weight than line charts so they

Figure 1.8 Area chart

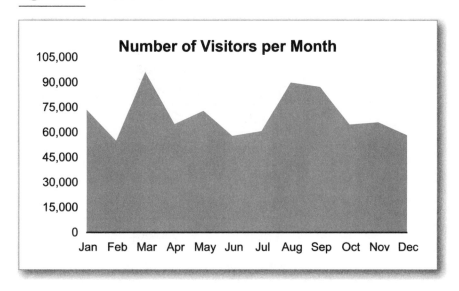

are often used to emphasize the magnitude of the data. Area charts can quickly become complicated when multiple data series are added, and stacked area charts have potential for misinterpretation.

Pie charts. Pie charts are used to show part-to-whole relationships (see Figure 1.9). They are among the most controversial data displays, and many experts refuse to use them. The primary issue centers on the inability of the human perceptual system to accurately interpret proportions represented by the pie slices. This is compounded by the plethora of ill conceived, poorly designed, and misleading pie charts in circulation. Pie charts, when carefully created, are an acceptable form of data visualization. Because most analysts will encounter pie charts at some point in their careers, it is important to adopt best practices for creating them.

Tables

A table is a structure for organizing and displaying information in rows and columns (see Figure 1.10). Values are shown as text in the body of the table. Tables are ideal for looking up specific data points and are useful for showing quantitative values and categorical subdivisions. They are best reserved for reports rather than presentations because even a simple table requires more cognitive effort from the audience than a chart. Use tables when readers need to know precise data values and in situations when you wish to show different metrics in one illustration, for example, frequencies and proportions.

Figure 1.9 Pie chart

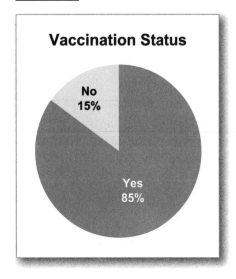

Vaccination Status

No 15%

Yes 85%

Figure 1.10 Table

Number of Program Enrollees and Their Mean Ages		
Region	**Enrollees**	**Mean Age**
North	29,942	39
South	28,842	37
East	14,025	41
West	2,149	40
Total	**74,958**	**38**

Which Form of Data Visualization to Use

Are you comparing quantities at a fixed point in time?

- Use a bar or column chart.

Are you describing a trend over time?

- If you're focusing on discrete values over time, use a column chart. If you want to call attention to data trends over time, create a line chart. If it's magnitude of change over time that you want to show, consider an area chart.

Do you need to know the distribution of a variable?

- Create a column chart for categorical data; a histogram for continuous data.

Do you want to know the proportion of a whole that is represented by x?

- Choose a pie chart or a stacked bar or column chart. If there are more than five parts of the whole to be represented, opt for a single-series column or bar chart.

Do you want to show different types of data in one display?

- If you want to show different statistics for the same variable, for example, frequency and percentage, choose a table. For something like number of members over time along with revenue over the same time period try a combination chart.

SUMMARY

Data visualization decisions should begin by curating the available data based on a thorough understanding of the audience's needs, knowledge, and use of the information. Having determined the context for the data illustrations, the next step is to choose from among the array of familiar charts and tables to display the data. Mastering the creation of the basic charts will equip analysts with knowledge and skills that may be applied to more complex data illustrations.

Choosing Data Displays Checklist

1. Evaluate the available information and determine which subset will be used for the present project.

2. Determine who the audience is, what they need to know, and what they intend to do with the information you provide.

3. Decide if you are creating a report, a presentation, or both.

4. Choose the appropriate combination of charts and tables to best display your data.

Bar and Column Charts

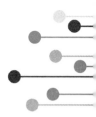

Bar and column charts are ubiquitous. They are commonly used in academic, professional, and popular publications, rendering them familiar to a wide variety of readers. The bars in a bar chart are drawn horizontally, parallel to the chart's x-axis (see Figure 2.1); the columns in a column chart are drawn vertically, parallel to the y-axis (see Figure 2.2). Data in these charts are represented

Learning Objectives

- Create column charts, stacked column charts, and 100% stacked column charts

- Identify the individual components comprising bar and column charts

- Demonstrate best practices for creating bar and column charts

Figure 2.1 Single-series bar chart

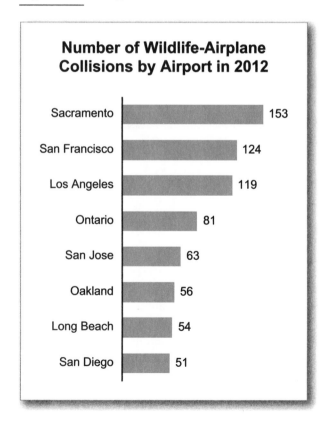

Number of Wildlife-Airplane Collisions by Airport in 2012

Airport	Value
Sacramento	153
San Francisco	124
Los Angeles	119
Ontario	81
San Jose	63
Oakland	56
Long Beach	54
San Diego	51

by the length of the bars and height of the columns. The chart in Figure 2.1 contains one data series, Number of Wildlife–Airplane Collisions, for eight cities. Similarly, the column chart in Figure 2.2 contains one data series, U.S. Online Adults Using Social Networking Sites, for four age groups.

In most situations, bar and column charts may be used interchangeably. Additionally, Excel provides the same set of subtypes for bar and column charts. Unless we note otherwise, the same data considerations and design principles can be applied to bar or column charts.

Figure 2.2 Single-series column chart

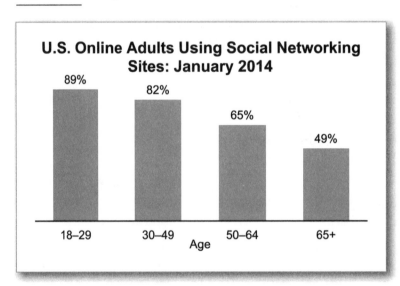

Data Appropriate for Bar and Column Charts

Bar and column charts work well for comparing values across categories of a variable, for example, types of pizzas sold by a restaurant in a given year. These charts are particularly well suited for displaying categorical data but also may be used effectively for describing continuous data. For example, column charts are routinely used to describe age data. The data might be grouped into categories, for example, 18–29, 30–49, and so on; alternatively, the chart may show all ages in a distribution, for example, 18, 19, 20, and so on (see Figures 2.3 and 2.4).

Figure 2.3 Column chart showing grouped ages

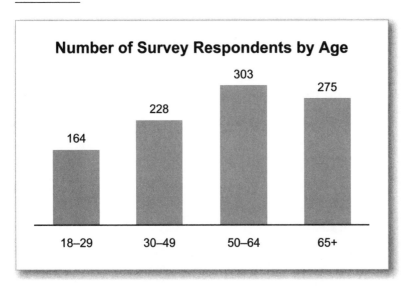

Figure 2.4 Column chart showing individual ages

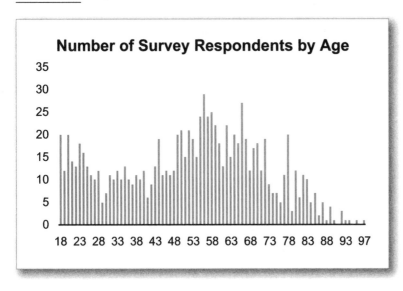

A type of column chart where each column represents a range of data rather than a single category is called a histogram (see Figure 2.5).

Column charts may be used to show change over time in a variable, such as sales volume over four quarters of a year. In Figure 2.6 it is easy to see that anvil sales peaked in Q4. With more than a few data points, however, a line chart is

Figure 2.5 Histogram of incidents by speed

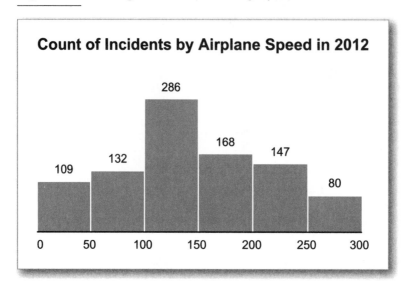

Figure 2.6 Column chart with time series data

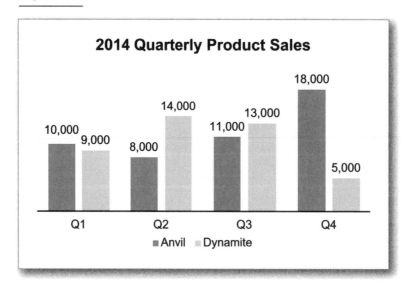

Figure 2.7 Line chart with time series data

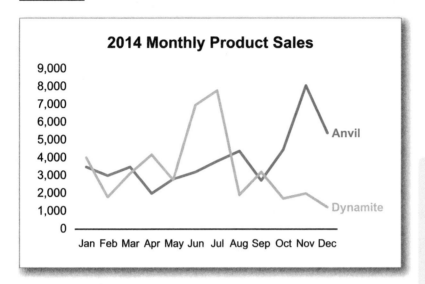

preferable for showing time series data as it will allow readers to more easily discern patterns over time (see Figure 2.7).

Creating a Column Chart

1. **Organize your data.** To create a column chart, organize data as shown in Figure 2.8. Category labels are in column A, and data values are in columns B and C. Row 1 contains descriptions of the data in each column. For simplicity, we started this data range in cell A1; you may place your data in any contiguous worksheet cells.

*When you select a data range, the **Quick Analysis** tool will appear in the lower right corner of the range. This is a new feature in Excel 2013. The shortcut menu includes many options. If you select the **CHARTS** option and mouse over the chart types, Excel will provide a preview showing how your data will look in the chart. Click the chart type of your choice to select it. (See Figure 2.9.)*

Figure 2.8 Data source for column chart

	A	B	C
1	Region	Jane Smith	Bill Jones
2	Northeast	6,000	4,000
3	South	4,500	3,500
4	Midwest	5,000	6,000
5	West	6,500	5,500

Figure 2.9 Quick Analysis toolbar

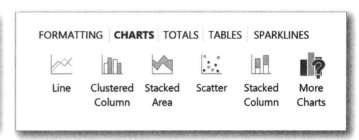

2. **Select the range of cells to be included in the chart** (cells A1:C5). If you don't select a range of cells, Excel may still insert a chart by guessing at the data to be charted. Depending on your data structure, that is, how you lay out your rows and columns, Excel may guess correctly. However, we recommend that you always select your cell range to ensure that the data array charted is what you intended.

3. **Choose the chart type.** From the **INSERT** tab, in the **Charts** group, click the column chart icon and select the first chart in the 2-D section, which is the **Clustered Column** (see Figures 2.10 and 2.11).

Figure 2.10 Chart group on the INSERT tab

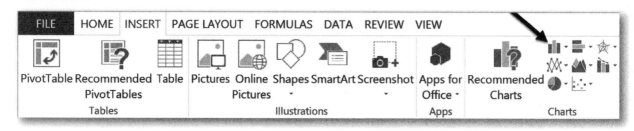

Figure 2.11 Column chart gallery

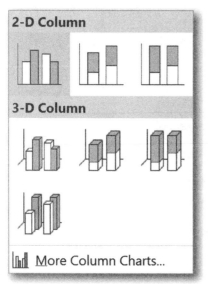

After you select the chart type, the chart will appear on the page (see Figure 2.12).

4. **Add a chart title.** Notice that the words *Chart Title* appear at the top of the chart you created. Click anywhere on **Chart Title**, highlight the words, and replace with a title that describes the content of the chart. If you do not type over or delete the placeholder, your chart will print with the words *Chart Title* at the top.

5. **Adjust the chart formatting.** Remove the gridlines from the chart by clicking on the **CHART ELEMENTS** shortcut menu (the plus sign found at the upper right of the chart when the chart is selected) and deselecting **Gridlines**. Alternately,

Figure 2.12 Default column chart

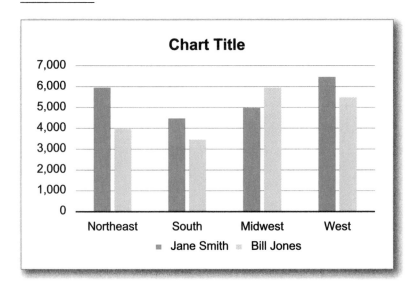

position your cursor on any gridline, click once to select the gridlines, and then press the **Delete** key on your keyboard. For this example, we will add data labels to the columns; therefore, the gridlines are unnecessary.

With the **CHART ELEMENTS** shortcut menu still open, select **Data Labels**. Because you added data labels, you no longer need the vertical axis on the chart. To remove it, hover over **Axes** in the **CHART ELEMENTS** shortcut menu, click on the arrow that appears to the right to activate the **Axes** submenu, and deselect **Primary Vertical** (see Figure 2.13).

Figure 2.13 CHART ELEMENTS shortcut menu

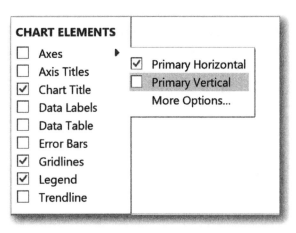

After completing these steps you will have a column chart that is ready to be inserted into a report or presentation (see Figure 2.14).

Figure 2.14 Formatted column chart

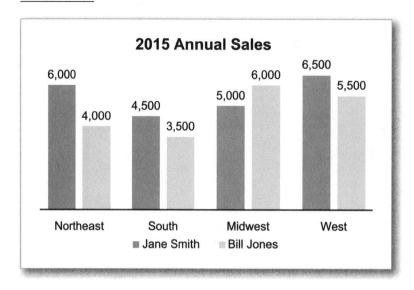

Stacked Column Charts

The column chart in Figure 2.14 is a clustered column. The data categories are the regions of the country, and there are two data series, one for Jane Smith and another for Bill Jones. Another way to display these data is with a stacked column chart. Stacked column charts contain fewer columns than clustered column charts and each column shows either multiple data categories or multiple data series. We will use the regional sales data to create a stacked column chart showing Jane's and Bill's relative contributions to the sales totals in each of the four regions.

Figure 2.15 Column chart gallery

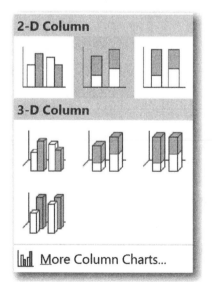

Creating a Stacked Column Chart

1. **Organize your data.** The data for a stacked column chart are organized the same as in the clustered column chart. The categories are listed in column A, the first data series is in column B, and the second data series is in column C.

2. **Select the range of cells to be included in the chart.** Select cells A1:C5.

3. **Choose the chart type.** From the **INSERT** tab, in the **Charts** group, click on the column chart icon and select the **Stacked Column** chart (see Figure 2.15).

The resulting chart will look like Figure 2.16.

Figure 2.16 Default stacked column chart

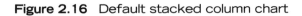

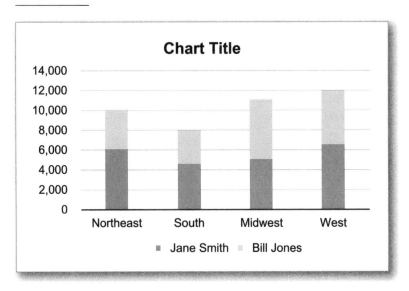

4. **Add a chart title.** Replace *Chart Title* with a descriptive title.

5. **Adjust chart formatting.** Remove the gridlines from the chart by clicking on the **CHART ELEMENTS** shortcut menu (the plus sign at the upper right of the chart) and deselecting **Gridlines**. For this chart we have opted for the labeled vertical axis rather than using data labels (see Figure 2.17). Including data labels on a stacked column chart can create a cluttered chart that is difficult to read. We will discuss in greater detail the considerations surrounding when to choose data labels versus axis labels later in this chapter and also in Chapter 5.

In Figure 2.17 the four regions of the country are each represented in a column, and the columns are divided to show each salesperson's relative contribution to the total sales in that region. We can see that the West had the highest sales volume overall, and we have some information about how Jane and Bill performed in each region. In this type of stacked column chart it is somewhat

Figure 2.17 Formatted stacked column chart

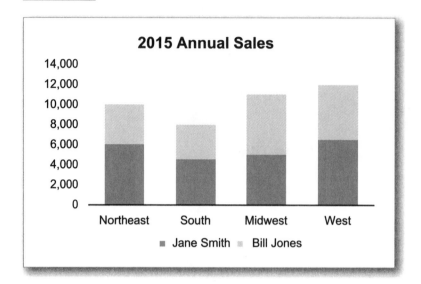

difficult to tell at a glance how well Jane and Bill did relative to one another in each region. If it is important to compare the two salespeople in the regions, the original clustered column chart in Figure 2.14 is a better option.

100% Stacked Column Charts

Like the stacked column chart, a 100% stacked column chart displays each data category in one column. The columns are divided to show the contribution of each series to the category. However, the column is stretched to fill the full height of the chart, and the sum of the categories in the column equals 100% (see Figure 2.18).

These charts are used to show percentage distribution, not frequency. Although similar to the other stacked column chart we discussed, the 100% stacked column chart is somewhat more complicated. In plotting the data series within the columns, Excel computes the proportion of the total that each series contributes to the column and assigns a column segment length based on that proportion. You can think of each column as an individual pie chart for that category.

These charts are useful for gaining visibility into the relative proportions of data series; however, it is important to exercise caution when the categories have

Figure 2.18   100% stacked column chart

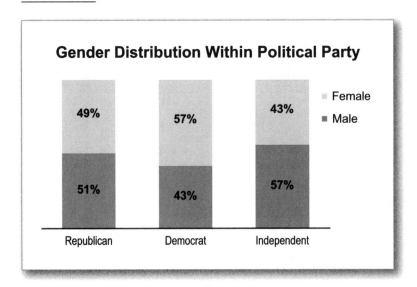

vastly different frequencies. For example, to illustrate the racial distribution of the populations of five U.S. states we could use a clustered column chart (see Figure 2.19) or a stacked column chart (see Figure 2.20).

Figure 2.19   Clustered column chart:
Racial distribution of five U.S. states

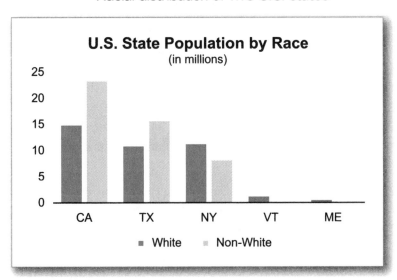

Figure 2.20 Stacked column chart: Racial distribution of five U.S. states

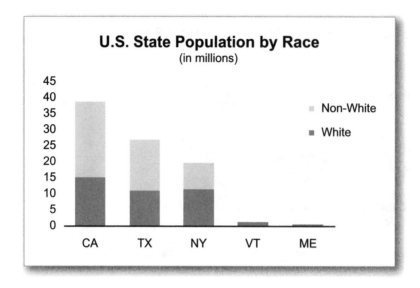

These charts are accurate; however, the Vermont and Maine data are almost impossible to see because the charts have been scaled to accommodate the large populations of California, Texas, and New York. The 100% stacked column chart in Figure 2.21 solves the scaling problem, and we can more easily see the proportions of white and non-white residents of all five states.

In this situation, most readers will realize that the populations of Vermont and Maine are significantly smaller than the other three states and interpret the proportions accordingly. However, to ensure that it is always clear to the audience, avoid potential confusion by adding the frequencies to the top of 100% stacked column charts. In Figure 2.22 we've added frequencies to the chart by inserting text boxes and manually typing in the values. To insert text boxes, from the **INSERT** tab, in the **Text** group, click **Text Box**, and draw a text box on the chart.

A common application of the 100% stacked column chart is for reporting responses to survey questions, especially when the number of responses to each survey question is the same (or approximately the same). In the following example, we chart five survey questions each as an individual column showing the relative proportion of three responses to each question.

Figure 2.21   100% stacked column: Racial distribution
of five U.S. states

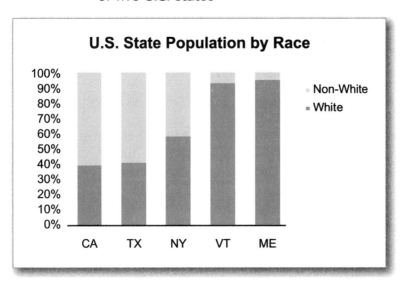

Figure 2.22   100% stacked column: Racial distribution
of five U.S. states with frequencies

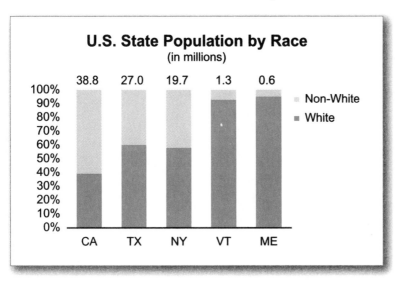

1. **Organize your data.** For a 100% stacked column chart, organize your data so that the survey response options are in column A and the survey questions are in columns B–F. The data are in cells B2:F4 (see Figure 2.23).

2. **Select the range of cells to be charted.** Select cells A1:F4.

3. **Choose the chart type.** From the **INSERT** tab, in the **Charts** group, click the column chart icon and select the **100% stacked column** chart. The result will look like Figure 2.24.

Figure 2.23 Data source for 100% stacked column chart

◢	A	B	C	D	E	F
1		Q1	Q2	Q3	Q4	Q5
2	Disagree	85	33	98	125	85
3	Neutral	40	30	30	30	45
4	Agree	45	65	95	100	60

Figure 2.24 Default 100% stacked column chart

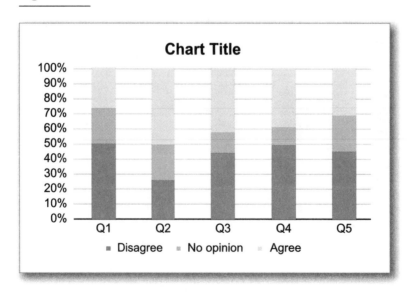

4. **Add a chart title.** Replace *Chart Title* with a descriptive title.

5. **Adjust chart formatting.** Remove the gridlines from the chart by clicking on the **CHART ELEMENTS** shortcut menu (the plus sign at the upper right of the chart) and deselecting **Gridlines**. As with the other stacked column chart, we have opted for the labeled vertical axis rather than data labels in this 100% stacked column chart (see Figure 2.25).

If your data are listed as percentages instead of frequency, ensure that all of the data values within a column sum to 100%. Failing to confirm this could result in a misleading chart as Excel will distribute the data in the columns as if they do sum to 100% even if this is not the case.

Figure 2.25 Formatted 100% stacked column chart

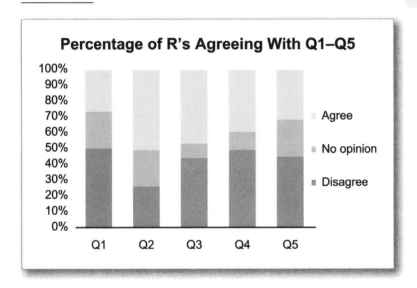

Best Practices for Creating Column and Bar Charts

Now that we've created a few basic column charts, let's explore in greater detail the elements of a column chart. Figure 2.26 is a basic single-series column chart. The **Chart Title** is a short headline that describes the contents of the chart. It almost always appears at the top of the chart, usually centered on the chart. Although you may click and drag the chart title to any location on the chart, there is seldom justification for placing it someplace other than at the top of the chart.

Figure 2.26 Anatomy of a column chart

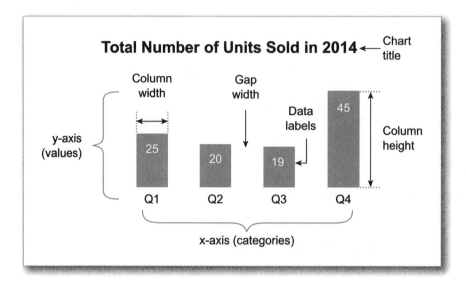

Axes

Data values are graphed along the vertical axis of a column chart, and the categories are shown along the horizontal axis. On a bar chart this is flipped, with data values along the horizontal axis and categories noted along the vertical axis. By default Excel sets the minimum and maximum values on column and bar charts based on the data range selected for the chart. For data sets containing all positive values, the minimum for the value axis should always be set to 0.

How you set the minimum and maximum values for a column chart can greatly influence the appearance of variation among the data categories. The chart in Figure 2.27 shows the value axis minimum set to 0. We can see that there is little variation in the sales figures among the four salespeople. Because the sales figures appear relatively flat, you might be tempted to change the minimum value of the vertical axis to a value greater than 0 to highlight the differences (see Figure 2.28). Changing the minimum value of the vertical axis does indeed accentuate the differences among the salespeople; however, the resulting visual display misrepresents the magnitude of the differences. By narrowing the range of values shown on the chart we have made it appear that sales representative Givens had about half the sales volume as O'Connor. In reality, Givens only lagged O'Connor by 2.5%. Intentional manipulation of the values shown on a column chart to alter perception of the data is unacceptable.

Figure 2.27 Column chart with vertical axis set to 0

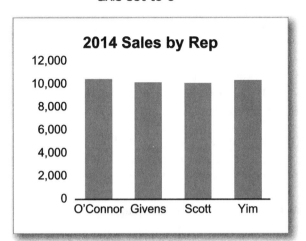

Figure 2.28 Column chart with vertical axis set to 10,000

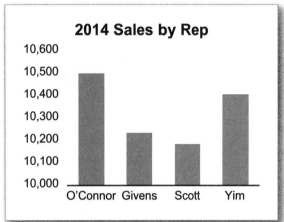

Changing the Minimum Value of the Vertical Axis on a Column Chart

1. Right-click on the vertical axis and select **Format Axis** to activate the **AXIS OPTIONS** menu.

2. In the **Bounds** section, highlight the value in the **Minimum** box and replace it with 0. (See Figure 2.29.)

Figure 2.29 Format Axis menu

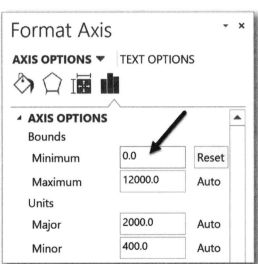

Chart categories

Chart categories should be sorted. The three common ways to order chart categories are 1) by data values—high to low or low to high; 2) alphabetically by category name, such as Afghanistan to Zimbabwe; or 3) by a natural order, such as days of the week or months of the year. Alphabetical order is useful if readers will be looking for a particular category, for example, how Norway is doing in the Olympic medal count (see Figure 2.30). If you're charting time series data, such as days of the week, use the order in which the days occur.

Lacking other considerations, sorting by data values is the typical and preferred method of organizing the columns or bars. This allows the reader to easily see which category is the largest and smallest as well as the relative differences in the values of each of the data elements. The chart in Figure 2.30 can be resorted by data values (largest to smallest) with a highlight used on the bar that might be of particular interest to the report's audience (see Figure 2.31).

Sorting Chart Categories

1. Chart categories are sorted by sorting the data to which the chart is linked. First select the data range you wish to sort. From the **DATA** tab, in the **Sort & Filter** group, click **Sort**.

Figure 2.30 Bar chart of Olympic medal count sorted alphabetically

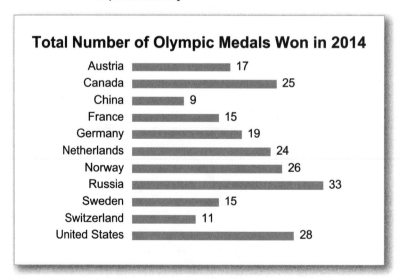

Figure 2.31 Bar chart of Olympic medal count sorted by data values

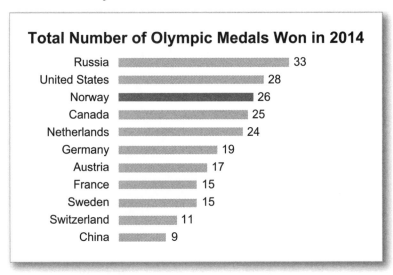

2. The **Sort** dialog window will appear (see Figure 2.32). If your data has a header row, ensure that the box marked **My data has headers** is checked. If it is not, your column headers may be sorted along with your data.

Figure 2.32 The Sort dialog box, Sort by field

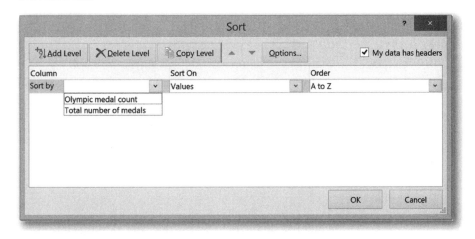

If you have attempted to accommodate long data labels by increasing the width of your chart columns, but you are getting too close to having your column chart look like a histogram, consider changing the number format of the data labels. For example, show the labels in $Thousands or $Millions instead of including the precise value. See Chapter 5 for a discussion of how to change number formats.

3. From the **Sort by** drop-down menu, choose the column you wish to use to sort your data. From the **Order** drop-down menu, you may sort based on data values, either from smallest to largest or largest to smallest. When sorting text, the options are from A to Z or Z to A.

4. Click **OK** to complete the sort. The chart linked to the data will then be sorted.

Gap width

Gap width is the space between the columns on a column chart. It is important to maintain a balance between the width of the columns and the space around them. As you reduce the gap width, the columns get wider. Reducing the gap width to 0 will produce a histogram. We recommend gap widths between 50% and 150%. Gap widths less than 50% (other than 0 to create a histogram) can be problematic because there is not enough space separating the columns, sometimes causing visual vibrations—an illusion that the columns are moving.

You may wish to change the gap width on a column chart to enhance the visual appeal of the chart. For example, if the columns appear to lack sufficient visual weight because they are too narrow, you can correct the situation by decreasing the gap width and thus increasing the column width. Similarly, if your chart contains long data labels, such as numbers in the thousands, creating wider columns on which to situate the data labels will result in a more visually appealing chart.

Changing a Column Chart's Gap Width

1. To change the width of the columns, you must adjust the width of the gap separating them. Right-click on any of the columns and select **Format Data Series**.

2. In the **SERIES OPTIONS** section, either drag the slider next to **Gap Width** or enter a value between 50% and 150% in the box (see Figure 2.33).

Series overlap

For single-series column and bar charts there is only one gap width to consider, the gap separating each column or bar. When we introduce a second data series to the chart there is another gap, the one between the pairs of columns or bars (see Figure 2.34). This space separating the data series is known as the **Series Overlap**.

Figure 2.33 Format Data Series task pane

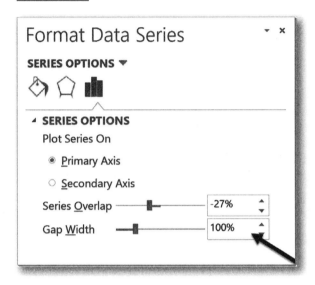

Figure 2.34 Clustered column chart with two data series

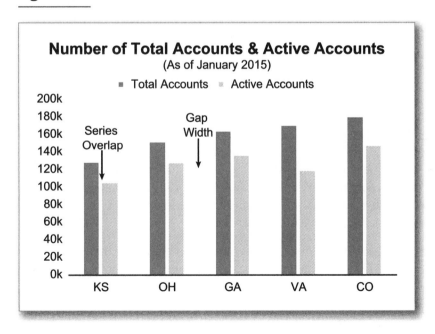

Figure 2.35 Clustered column chart with –75% series overlap

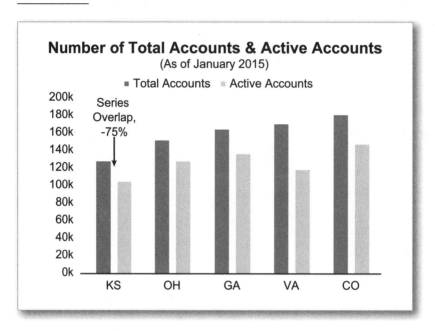

Like the gap width, the series overlap can be changed to alter the appearance of the chart. The range of possible values for the series overlap is –100% to 100%; negative values produce a gap between the columns, positive values create overlapping columns. The series overlap in Figure 2.34 is –25%. Changing the series overlap to –75% creates a wider gap between the data series (see Figure 2.35), and changing the series overlap to 0 results in no gap between the data series (see Figure 2.36).

Always leave more space between the clusters of columns than within the clusters. When the columns on a multiseries column chart are spaced equally the chart becomes difficult to interpret. The columns on the chart in Figure 2.37 are all equally spaced. Although the different colors of the two data series will help readers distinguish the series, the previous versions of this chart with the two columns within each state close together and a wide gap between the states is considerably easier to read.

The gap widths and series overlap of a clustered column chart may be further manipulated to illustrate when one data series is a subset of another. For example, suppose we wanted to more clearly show that Active Accounts in

Figure 2.36 Clustered column chart with no series overlap

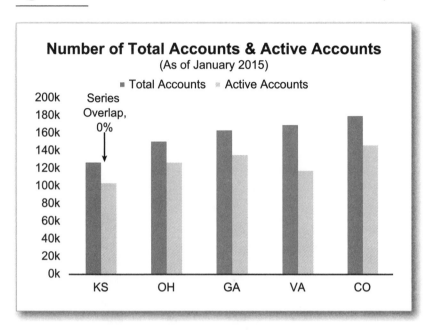

Figure 2.37 Clustered column chart with even series overlap and gap width

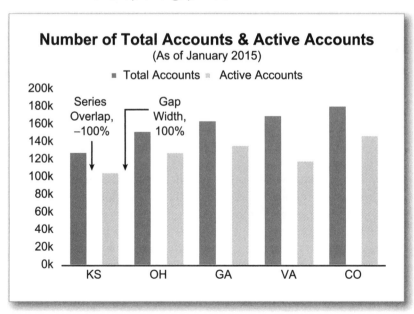

Figure 2.34 represents a portion of Total Accounts. We can change the series overlap to 100% and make a few other adjustments to produce a chart where one set of columns sits within the other set (see Figure 2.38).

Figure 2.38 100% overlapped clustered column chart

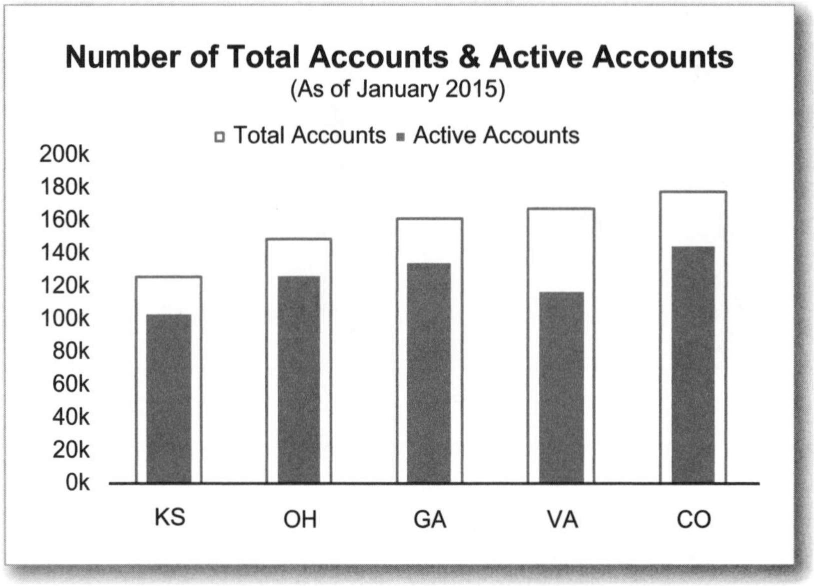

Creating a Clustered Column Chart With 100% Overlapping Columns

1. Select the two data series and create a standard clustered column chart as we have done previously in this chapter.

2. Right-click on the subset data series in the chart; in our case that's the Active Accounts data series, and select **Format Data Series**.

3. In the **Format Data Series** task pane, click the **Secondary Axis** radio button from the **SERIES OPTIONS** section. Change the **Series Overlap** to 100% and the **Gap Width** to 200%. It is necessary to put one of the data series on the secondary axis so that we may specify different gap widths for the two data series.

4. When you assign one of the data series to the secondary axis, Excel will add the axis values on the right side of the chart.

Ensure that the secondary axis has the same minimum and maximum values as the primary axis. If it does not, right-click the secondary axis on the chart, click **Format Axis** to open the **Format Axis** task pane, and adjust the **Minimum** and **Maximum** values to match the primary axis. After adjusting the axis values, click on the axis, and press **Delete** on your keyboard. Labeling the primary vertical axis on the chart is sufficient.

5. Click on one of the columns of the Total Accounts data series to select the series. It should be charted on the Primary Axis. Change the **Series Overlap** to 100% and the **Gap Width** to 75%. Changing the gap width so that the columns of the secondary data series are spaced farther apart than the columns of the primary data series creates the impression that the Active Accounts columns are inside the Total Accounts columns. If we had set the series overlap to 100% without adjusting the gap widths, the chart would resemble a stacked column chart. You could stop at this point; however, to reduce the ink on the page, we'll take one more step and format the chart further.

6. With the Total Accounts data series still selected, click on the **Fill & Line** menu on the **Format Data Series** pane. Change the **FILL** to **No Fill**. In the **BORDER** section, select a **Solid line**. Choose a **Color** and change the width of the line to between 1 and 2 points depending on your preference. Eliminating the column fill color and adding a border creates an outline of the columns and concentrates focus on the Active Accounts data series, which is the intent of this chart.

Some experts claim that it is always necessary to include a labeled y-axis on column charts. This is to ensure that the analyst has been forthright in data reporting and has not manipulated the 0 point of the scale to distort the chart. We assume that readers of this text will not intentionally, nor accidentally, commit such an infraction. Therefore, feel free to delete the y-axis if you have properly labeled your columns.

Data labels

There are two primary methods for labeling the values represented by the columns on a column chart: include data labels on the chart's y-axis (see Figure 2.39) or label the columns themselves (see Figure 2.40). It is unnecessary to do both. It is preferable, space permitting, to opt for data labels on the columns. This method is easier for the reader than the alternative and allows you to label the values of the columns precisely.

Figure 2.39 Column chart with y-axis labels

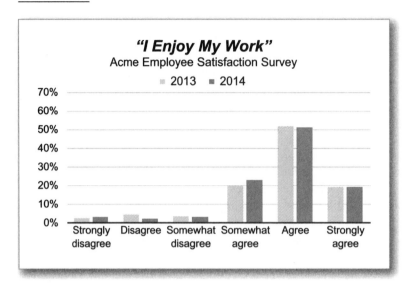

Figure 2.40 Column chart with individual data labels

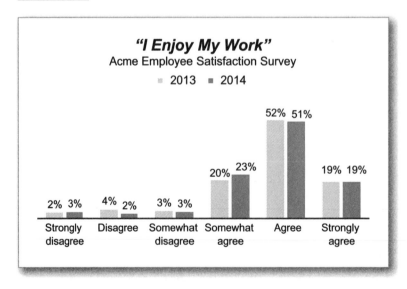

The decision about y-axis labels versus data labels hinges on the number of data points on the chart and the specificity requirements of the data report. The more data points there are the more difficult it will be to label each data point. If trends are being examined, individual data labels are unnecessary; however, if individual performance is being monitored, data labels may be needed.

If there are too many columns to label each one or your data reporting does not require precision, the y-axis solution is serviceable. Employing the y-axis labels requires the reader to look to the axis and then over to the column and draw a horizontal line (actual or imaginary) from the column back to the axis to determine the data value. You can help the reader by including **Major Gridlines**, which will appear automatically if you have selected one of the built-in Excel charts. This solution could result in crowded and messy charts that don't achieve the desired result of aiding the reader. If you find yourself facing this dilemma, consider alternatives such as creating multiple charts.

Excel's solution to the overlapping label problem is to orient the labels at a 45- or 90-degree angle. This is never a good option as it results in an awkward reading experience. If the bar chart alternative is not a viable solution, consider abbreviating the labels.

Choosing Between Bar and Column Charts

Deciding between a bar or column chart is largely an aesthetic choice, typically based on the length of the category labels and the amount of space available in the report for the chart. If data labels are long, a bar chart is a better choice than a column chart. Figure 2.41 is a column chart that shows the population of 12 U.S. states. The state names beneath the columns overlap, making it impossible to read labels. Figure 2.42 shows the same data in a bar chart. Here we can easily read the state names without loss of information.

Figure 2.41   Column chart with long category labels

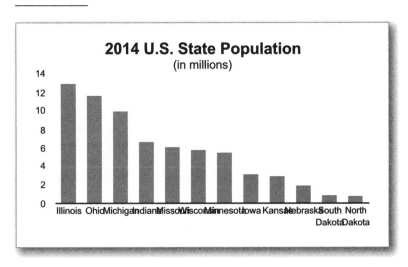

Figure 2.42 Bar chart with long category labels

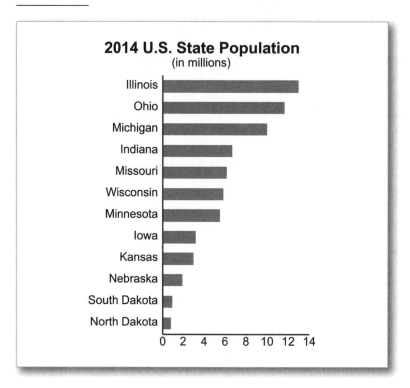

SUMMARY

Column and bar charts are the most common forms of data visualization in use today. They are handy multipurpose tools that work well for describing categorical or continuous data and also may effectively illustrate time series data. Creating basic column charts is a simple process that involves organizing data into rows and columns in an Excel worksheet with appropriate column headers and row labels, selecting the range of data to be charted, and choosing the correct chart type from Excel's **INSERT** tab.

Stacked column and bar charts have an added level of complexity introduced by the addition of multiple data series; however, they also offer the possibility of displaying a large amount of data in a relatively small space. Likewise, 100% stacked column and bar charts are effective for displaying large quantities of data in compact spaces but with the added feature of the sum of the segments of the columns or bars totaling 100%.

The deceptively simple column chart contains multiple elements, many of which may be manipulated to enhance the chart's ability to clearly and accurately communicate a data story or, alternatively, to distort a message. As we noted, changing the range of values of the y-axis on a column chart can substantially alter the perception of the data values. By attending carefully and intentionally to chart elements such as axes, gap widths, data labels, and titles, you will create column and bar charts that are clear and visually appealing representations of the underlying data.

Column and Bar Chart Checklist

1. Include a descriptive title at the top of the chart.

2. If your data include only positive values, set the minimum data value set to 0.

3. Sort the chart categories.

4. Adjust the width of the columns or bars to enhance the visual appeal of the chart and accommodate data labels.

5. Choose between data labels for the columns or bars or value axis labels.

6. Delete redundant or unnecessary information.

    a. Data labels when y-axis labels are present
    b. Gridlines when data labels are used

7. Select a bar chart instead of a column chart if data labels are long.

CHAPTER BONUS

Recall that when discussing stacked column charts earlier in this chapter we noted that it may be useful to add a total to the top of the stacked columns. Excel allows you to add data labels to the individual segments of each column; however, there is no function that automatically sums the frequencies of the column segments to add a total for the entire column. There are two ways to accomplish this task. One way is to insert text boxes above each column and manually enter the totals. Use this option when working with 100% stacked column charts. Another way is to add another data series that represents the total of each column and add that series to the chart. Use this option for standard (not 100% stacked) column charts.

Adding Total Data Labels to a Stacked Column Chart

1. In your worksheet, create a column showing the total of your stacked components (see Figure 2.43).

Figure 2.43 Worksheet cells with total column added

◢	A	B	C	D
1		**White**	**Non-White**	**Total**
2	**CA**	15,132,975	23,669,525	38,802,500
3	**TX**	11,052,353	15,904,605	26,956,958
4	**NY**	11,452,812	8,293,416	19,746,228
5	**ME**	1,263,585	66,505	1,330,090
6	**VT**	582,703	43,859	626,562

2. Add the new "Total" series to your chart by right-clicking on the chart, choosing **Select Data**, and selecting the range of cells that includes the Total column. Because of the radical change in scale, this will temporarily distort the appearance of the stacked columns.

3. Change the chart type of the Total series. Right-click on the Total data series and select **Change Series Chart Type**. Chart type **Combo** should be highlighted. If it is not, select it. Change the Total series to a **Line**. Click **OK**. Leave the other data series as **Stacked Column**.

4. Click on the line. From the **CHART ELEMENTS** shortcut menu, select **Data Labels**.

5. Format the data labels so that they appear **Above** the line. Right-click the data labels and select **Format Data Labels** to open the **Format Data Labels** task pane. Select **Above** from the **Label Position** section.

6. Right-click on the line and choose **Format Data Series**. Expand the **LINE** menu and click the **No Line** radio button.

7. Delete the Total data series entry from the chart legend. Click on the legend once to activate it, click again on Total, and press the **Delete** key on your keyboard.

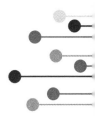

CHAPTER 3

Line and Area Charts

Line charts are used to illustrate continuous data such as time series, age, health factors in a population, temperature, and so on. As their name suggests, line charts contain lines drawn parallel to the chart's x-axis. The line connects data values along the chart's x-axis, thus effectively illustrating patterns of change (or lack thereof) from one time period to the next. For example, the line chart in Figure 3.1 shows increasing and decreasing TV viewership of the Super Bowl in the United States, until 2006 when viewership began to increase steadily. Multiple lines can be used to compare performance among categories (see Figure 3.2), to compare year-over-year performance (see Figure 3.3), or to compare categories to a target (see Figure 3.4). Line charts work well when the order of the categories is important, for example, months of the year.

Learning Objectives

- Identify when to use line and area charts

- Create line charts to plot trend data

- Produce multiseries line and area charts

- Identify best practices for creating line and area charts

Figure 3.1 Single-series line chart

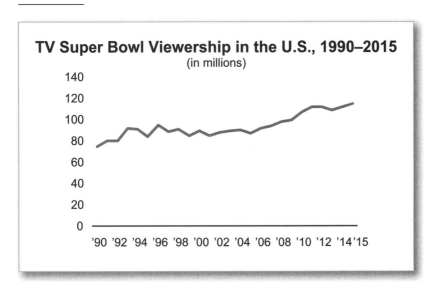

Figure 3.2 Multiseries line chart: Performance among categories

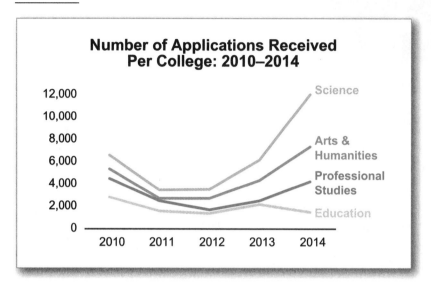

Figure 3.3 Multiseries line chart: Year-over-year performance

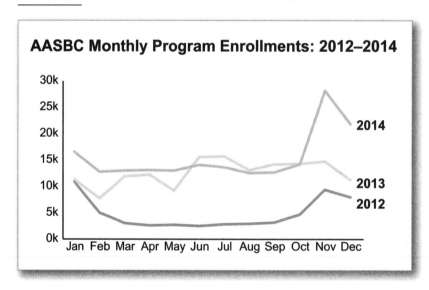

Single-Series Line Charts

Line charts are most commonly used to depict time series data, for example, volume of sales over time. Data appropriate for line charts may alternatively be presented in columns or bar charts, although patterns of change may not be as apparent because the columns and bars are separated by a gap. The minimum

Figure 3.4 Multiseries line chart: Performance compared to target

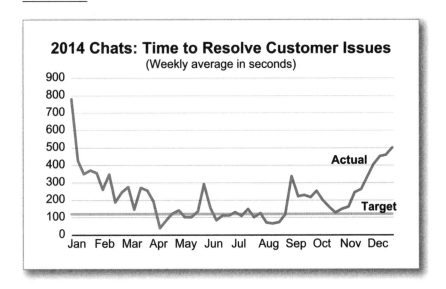

number of data points required to create a line chart is two. However, with only two data points, the ability to detect data patterns is limited.

Creating a Single-Series Line Chart

1. **Organize your data.** To create a single-series line chart showing a company's sales during one year, place the months of the year in column A of a worksheet and sales in column B. Each of the values in column B represents total monthly sales volume (see Figure 3.5).

2. **Select the range of cells to be included in the chart** (in this example, cells A1:B13). If your active cell is within the range of data you wish to chart, Excel will create a chart based on the contiguous cells surrounding the active cell. If you insert a chart by this method instead of manually selecting a cell range, be sure to check your chart to ensure that the data charted are what you intended.

Figure 3.5 Data source for single-series line chart

	A	B
1	Month	Sales
2	Jan	52,430
3	Feb	40,000
4	Mar	55,000
5	Apr	45,000
6	May	55,000
7	Jun	60,500
8	Jul	60,500
9	Aug	60,000
10	Sep	65,000
11	Oct	70,000
12	Nov	85,000
13	Dec	110,000
14		

3. **Choose the chart type.** From the **INSERT** tab, in the **Charts** group, click the line chart icon to expand the chart gallery (see Figure 3.6). Click on the first option, the basic line chart, in the **2-D Line** section (see Figure 3.7). The chart will appear on the page (see Figure 3.8).

4. **Edit the chart title.** In our example the chart was created with the title *Sales* at the top. This occurred because we were working with one data series and the column containing the data was labeled *Sales*.

Figure 3.6 Line chart icon on the INSERT tab

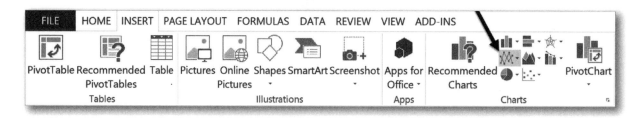

Figure 3.7 Line chart selection gallery

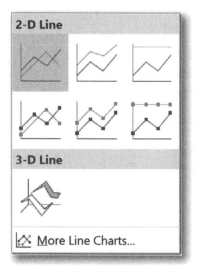

Figure 3.8 Default single-series line chart

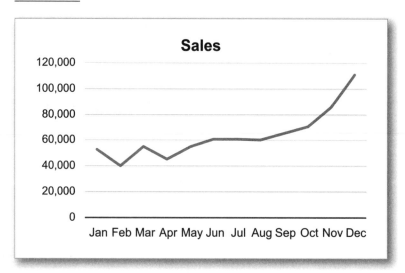

This is not an effective chart title and should be edited to include more information about the contents of the chart. To edit the chart title, click on the word *Sales* on the chart and enter a descriptive title. (See Chapter 6 for best practices for writing chart titles.)

5. **Adjust the chart formatting.** Remove the gridlines from the chart by clicking on the **CHART ELEMENTS** (see Figure 3.9) shortcut menu (the plus sign found at the upper right of the chart when the chart is selected) and deselecting **Gridlines**. The final chart should look like the example in Figure 3.10.

For single-series charts you may also change the chart title by editing the column header of the column containing the data being charted.

*Another method of removing gridlines from a chart is to select them by positioning your cursor on any gridline, clicking once to select them, then pressing the **DELETE** key on your keyboard.*

Figure 3.9 CHART ELEMENTS shortcut menu

Figure 3.10 Formatted single-series line chart

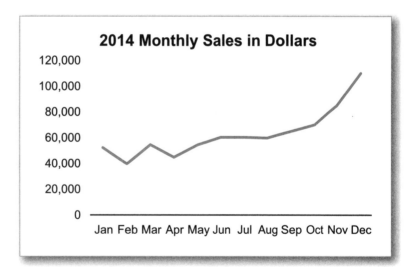

Multiseries Line Charts

The line chart in Figure 3.11 shows two years of website visit data. We can see that visits peaked at various times throughout the two years. There appears to be an increase at the end of the year followed by fewer visits at the beginning of the next year. However, it is difficult to determine if the patterns of peaks and valleys are the same each year. For a clearer view of website activity year-over-year we can plot these data on a multiseries line chart.

Figure 3.12 shows the website visit data for the years 2013 and 2014. Reconfiguring the chart to show each year on a different line highlights the

Figure 3.11 Single-series, multiyear line chart

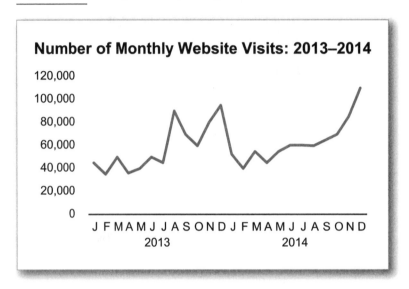

Figure 3.12 Single-series, multiyear line chart, year-over-year

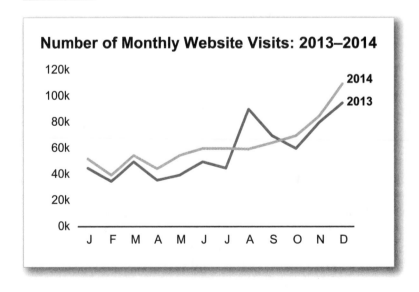

increases in visits during November and December in both years and also reveals a spike in August 2013. This should be investigated to verify the validity of the data and to determine if there was an event, such as a promotion, that may have caused the unusual increase in website visits in August 2013.

Creating a Multiseries Line Chart

1. **Organize your data.** To create the multiseries line chart in Figure 3.12, place the months of the year in column A and the years (2013 and 2014) in columns B and C (see Figure 3.13).

2. **Select the range of cells to be charted.** Select cells A1:C13.

3. **Choose the chart type.** From the **INSERT** tab, in the **Charts** group, click on the line chart icon to expand the chart gallery. Click on the first option in the **2-D Line** section. The chart will appear on the page.

Figure 3.13 Data source for multiseries line chart

◢	A	B	C
1		2015	2016
2	Jan	45,000	52,430
3	Feb	35,000	40,000
4	Mar	50,000	55,000
5	Apr	36,000	45,000
6	May	40,000	55,000
7	Jun	50,000	60,500
8	Jul	45,000	60,500
9	Aug	90,000	60,000
10	Sep	70,000	65,000
11	Oct	60,000	70,000
12	Nov	80,000	85,000
13	Dec	95,000	110,000

Transposing Data

The data for Figure 3.12 were organized such that the months of the year were in rows and the two years were in columns. We recommend organizing the data in this way to conserve space so that all the data are visible even in a small window. If you received this data but the years were in the rows and months in the columns, you can flip the rows and columns by transposing the data table.

1. Select the range of cells.
2. Copy the cells (**CTRL+C**).
3. Move to a blank cell in the worksheet.
4. Click on the expand arrow beneath the **Paste** menu and select the last option, **Paste Special** (see Figure 3.14).
5. Click on **Transpose**.
6. Click **OK** (see Figure 3.15).

Figure 3.14 Paste menu   **Figure 3.15** Paste Special dialog window

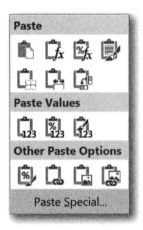

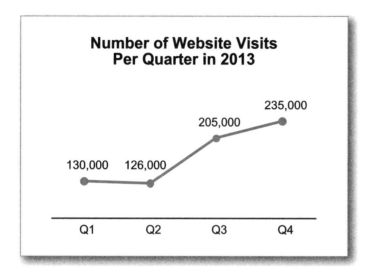

Figure 3.16 Line chart with few data points and line markers

Number of Website Visits Per Quarter in 2013

In addition to the standard line chart, Excel's line chart gallery offers two other options: a stacked line and a 100% stacked line. These charts are ostensibly used to show part-to-whole relationships and change over time. Stacked line charts are difficult to interpret (as the Excel tool tip points out) and misleading. For these reasons, they should not be used.

For the single-series and multiseries line charts in this chapter we opted for the lines without markers— the circles, boxes, and triangles on the line that mark the data values. This is because our example charts contained many data points and the primary goal was to show patterns over time, rather than focusing on one or a few individual values. For charts illustrating few data points, or when it is desirable to label the data points directly rather than include data labels on the y-axis, line markers can be useful additions to the chart (see Figure 3.16).

Area Charts

An area chart is like a line chart; the primary difference is that the area below the line is filled in with color. Figures 3.17 and 3.18 show the same data in a line chart and an area chart, respectively. As with line charts, area charts are primarily used to describe time series data.

Because there is considerably more ink on area charts than line charts, they tend to emphasize magnitude of values rather than change over time. Our eyes are attracted to the visual weight of the solid area of the chart rather than the shape of the line that creates the area. For example, when illustrating population change, a line chart is effective for communicating how a population

Figure 3.17 Single-series line chart

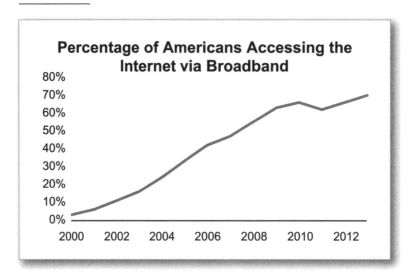

Percentage of Americans Accessing the
Internet via Broadband

Figure 3.18 Single-series area chart

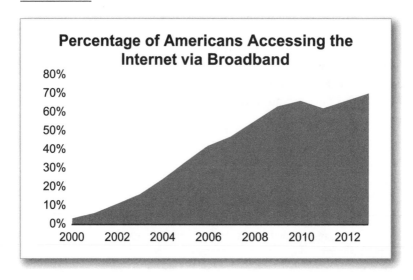

Percentage of Americans Accessing the
Internet via Broadband

is growing or shrinking over time (see Figure 3.19). An area chart also shows this information, but with an emphasis on the fluctuations in the total population volume over time (see Figure 3.20). If you want the reader to focus primarily on the trend, use a line chart. If volume is more or equally important, an area chart is a better option.

Figure 3.19 Single-series line chart

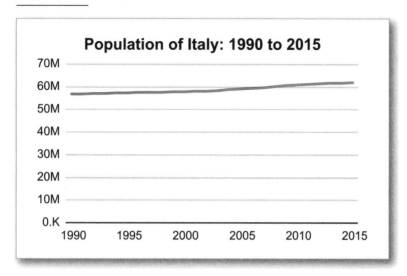

Figure 3.20 Single-series area chart

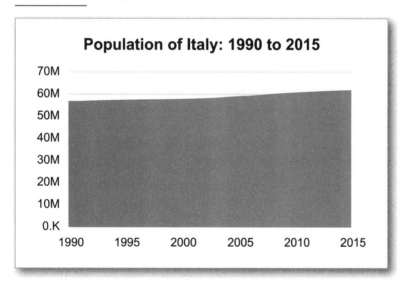

Creating a Single-Series Area Chart

1. **Organize your data.** To create a single-series area in
   Figure 3.18, organize the data as shown in Figure 3.21.
   Years are in column A and the percentage of Americans with
   broadband access is in column B.

◢	A	B
1	**Year**	**Broadband Access**
2	2000	3%
3	2001	6%
4	2002	11%
5	2003	16%
6	2004	24%
7	2005	33%
8	2006	42%
9	2007	47%
10	2008	55%
11	2009	63%
12	2010	66%
13	2011	62%
14	2012	66%
15	2013	70%

2. **Select the range of cells to be charted.** Select cells A1:B15.

3. **Choose the chart.** From the **INSERT** tab, in the **Charts** group, click on the area chart icon to expand the chart gallery. Click the first option in the **2-D Area** chart section.

4. **Format the chart.** Remove the gridlines by clicking on one of the lines to activate them and pressing **Delete** on your keyboard. Show the x-axis label for every other year by right-clicking on the x-axis to open the **Format Axis** task pane. Expand the **LABLES** submenu. Click the **Specify interval unit** radio button and change the 1 to a 2.

Multiseries Area Charts

As with line charts, area charts may contain multiple data series. Depending on the data series with which you are working, multiseries area charts can be problematic because some areas of the chart may be obscured. Figure 3.22 shows customers in two regions of the country. Parts of the chart showing customers in the North are obscured (or occluded) by the area showing customers in the South.

The problem may be addressed by altering the transparency of the areas; however, this can quickly turn into a messy and unreadable chart. For this reason, we recommend a multiseries line chart instead of an area chart.

The order in which the data series appear in the chart is based on how the data are arranged in the data table. To ensure that the population is behind the sample data, place the population data in a column to the left of the sample data.

Figure 3.22 Multiseries area chart

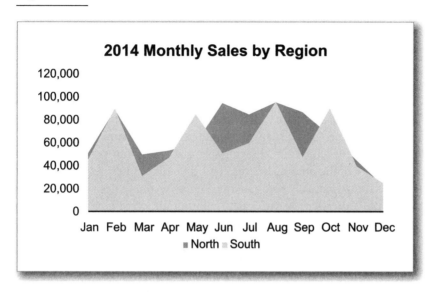

There is one exception. When you have two data series and one is a subset of the other, for example, a sample from a population, a multiseries area chart can be effective for showing how well the sample represents the population. Figure 3.23

Figure 3.23 Multiseries area chart showing population and sample

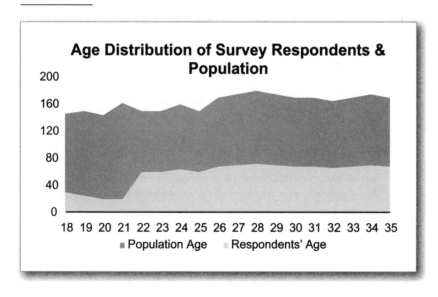

shows the ages of the respondents to a survey and the population from which they were selected. We can see that respondents' ages represent the population fairly well except among individuals 21 and younger.

Stacked Area Charts

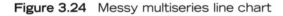

Stacked area charts illustrate part-to-whole relationships and change over time. They are sometimes used as alternatives to multiseries line charts. Figure 3.24 is a standard multiseries line chart showing sales data from four regions of the world. The overlap of the lines makes the chart difficult to interpret and the reader would have to manually compute the company's total sales volume for any given month. Moreover, we can't easily tell from this chart how much each region contributed to total sales for any month.

A stacked area chart can be used to address these issues. Figure 3.25 illustrates the same data as shown in the line chart in Figure 3.24.

Figure 3.24 Messy multiseries line chart

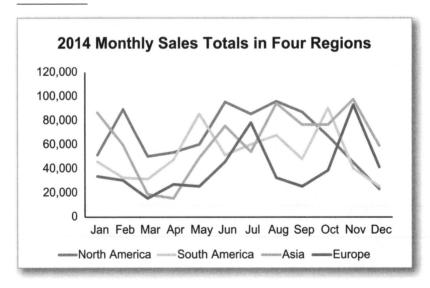

Figure 3.25 Stacked area chart

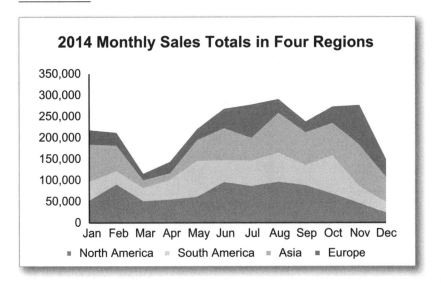

In Figure 3.25 the areas in between the lines have been filled in so that we can see the total sales for the company for each month and each region's contribution to the total. This resolves the primary issues associated with the standard line chart but highlights a different problem: only the trend line for North America is accurate because this data series sits on the horizontal axis. The placement of the trend lines for all other regions is dependent on the data series beneath them. To determine how sales in a particular region fluctuated over time, the reader must look at the width of the band created by that region's trend line and the trend line below it. This could be a barrier to understanding the chart. Before selecting this option, chart creators should assess their audience's familiarity with the data and their ability to correctly interpret a stacked area chart. Depending on the data story you wish to communicate, the best solution may be to create five line charts, one for each region and one showing total sales (see Figure 3.26).

Figure 3.26a–e Five-line-chart alternative to a stacked area chart

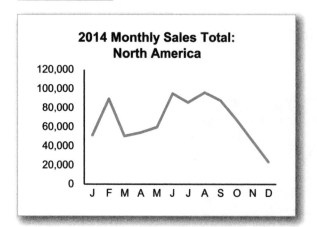

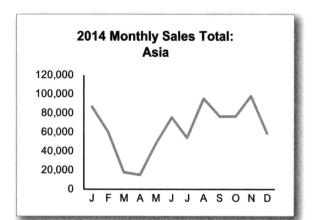

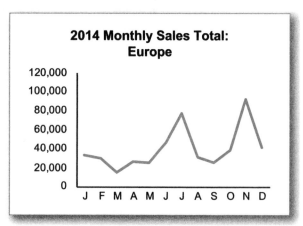

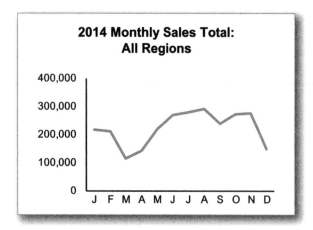

SUMMARY

Line and area charts are most commonly used to display time series data. They work well to describe patterns and illuminate data anomalies. When creating line and area charts it is important to ensure that the underlying data are appropriate; for example, categorical data, such as type of products sold, should never be presented in a line chart. Both line and area charts may contain one or multiple data series. When multiple data series are presented in line and area charts, clear, well-labeled legends are required. Finally, although Excel offers options for creating stacked line charts, they should be avoided because the default chart types will be incorrectly labeled and they are difficult to interpret.

Checklist for Line and Area Charts

1. Data are time series or otherwise appropriate for connecting the data points with a line.

2. On multiseries charts, legends clearly identify each data series.

3. Stacked line charts are not used.

4. Multiseries area charts are used when one series is a subset of the other.

CHAPTER BONUS

In this chapter we suggested the use of a stacked area chart when one data series is a subset of the other. Another option for similar situations is to create a chart that combines a line with a column chart. Say, for example, you wanted to illustrate the total number of customer issues logged during the first five weeks of a new product launch and the number of issues that were resolved. Figure 3.27 is a combination chart showing the two data series.

Creating a Combination Chart

1. **Create the chart.** Start by creating a multiseries line chart as previously described.

2. **Change the total data series.** Right-click on the line representing the total number of customer issues logged. Click on **Change Series Chart Type**. **Combo** should be selected; if it is not, select it. Click the **Chart Type** drop-down arrow for the Total Issues series and select **Clustered Column**.

3. Click **OK**.

Figure 3.27 Combo column and line chart

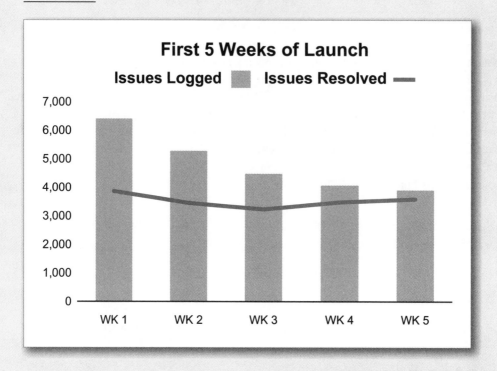

Although a stacked area chart would have worked in this situation, the combination chart is a better representation of the data because the report readers wanted a view of the weekly totals and also needed to know how well the team did resolving the issues. From the combo chart we can see that the volume of issues was relatively high during the first week and the customer service representatives were only able to resolve about 60% of them. As the weeks progressed, there were fewer issues and the representatives resolved more than 90% of them.

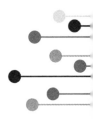

CHAPTER 4

Pie Charts

A pie chart is a type of area chart represented by a circle. It is used to show part-to-whole relationships. The circle (the pie) represents the whole, which is made up of wedges (the slices of pie). The slices are mutually exclusive and sum to 100%; see Figure 4.1.

Pie charts are found just about everywhere. They are commonly used to describe nominal data, such as job category; demographic characteristics, such as gender

Learning Objectives

- Describe the controversy surrounding pie charts and related charts

- Determine when to use a pie chart

- Identify data appropriate for pie charts

- Demonstrate best practices for creating pie charts

- Compare pie charts with alternative visualizations

Figure 4.1   Basic pie chart: Gender distribution of U.S. Senate

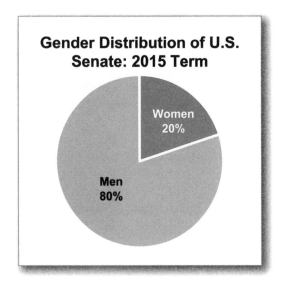

Gender Distribution of U.S. Senate: 2015 Term

Women 20%

Men 80%

Figure 4.2 Donut chart

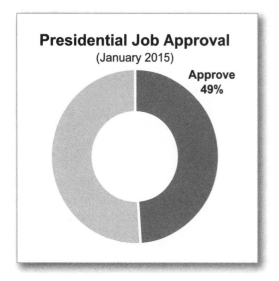

and race/ethnicity; presidential approval rating; responses to survey questions; and so on. They enjoy wide familiarity, are a standard option in every charting software program on the market, and have provoked more controversy than any other type of chart.

A close relative of the pie chart is the donut chart, a chart similar to a pie but with a hole cut out in the center (see Figure 4.2). The donut chart is a favorite among designers because the donut hole is a convenient place to add images or labels (see Figure 4.3). Donut charts may be used to describe the same type of data as would be shown in a standard pie chart.

Figure 4.3 Donut chart with image in the center

The Trouble With Pie Charts

Even the most expertly constructed pie charts can be easily misinterpreted. The problem stems from the inability of our visual system to accurately perceive area and is compounded by the angles created by the wedges of pie. In the classic text *The Visual Display of Quantitative Information*, Edward Tufte wrote, "A table is nearly always better than a dumb pie chart; the only worse design than a pie chart is several of them."[1] Similarly, data visualization author and instructor Stephen Few famously denounced pie charts, saying, "I don't use pie charts, and I strongly recommend that you abandon them as well."[2]

[1]Edward Tufte, *The Visual Display of Quantitative Information*, 2nd ed. (Cheshire, CT: Graphics Press, 2001), 178.

[2]Stephen Few, *Show Me the Numbers* (Oakland, CA: Analytics Press, 2004), 60.

The criticisms of pie charts also apply to donut charts, plus one: because the donut wedges don't meet in the middle, our eyes are not able to accurately judge the angle of each slice, which is an important cue in determining the relative size of the wedges.

Although Tufte and Few make many excellent points in their campaign against pie charts, we're not prepared to abandon pie charts. Pie charts are not inherently dumb, and choosing to use one does not, necessarily, indicate laziness, poor design skills, or a lack of knowledge.

Why are these charts called pies and donuts? There are no definitive answers but several hypotheses. One view posits that pie *is an extension of the Greek letter Pi, which is an element in the formula for the area of a circle. Another view suggests that the chart is named pie because when the circle is segmented, the wedges resemble slices of pie. There are fewer postulates about the origin of the name* donut. *It is likely that with* pie *firmly entrenched in the annals of data visualization, it wasn't too much of a stretch to imagine a pie chart with a hole in the center as a donut.*

When to Use a Pie Chart

In certain situations, a pie chart may be the best tool for illustrating a data story. Pie charts quickly and clearly communicate that the data represent parts of a whole. The same data may be presented in a column or bar chart, but it may not be immediately obvious to the reader that the sum of the bars or columns is the entirety of a set. Figures 4.4 and 4.5 show categories of global debt in 2014. In Figure 4.4 it appears that household debt is the smallest proportion, but the distinction among the remaining three categories is difficult to discern. This is why some authors prefer column charts for these situations (see Figure 4.5). However, it may not be readily apparent that the sum of all the columns in Figure 4.5 represents the total of all debt for the year. Moreover, the shortcoming of the pie chart (the unclear distinctions, particularly between Corporate and Government debt) can be corrected by adding the value labels to the slices of pie (see Figure 4.6).

Figure 4.4 Pie chart of global debt

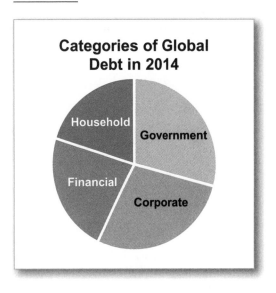

Figure 4.5 Column chart of global debt

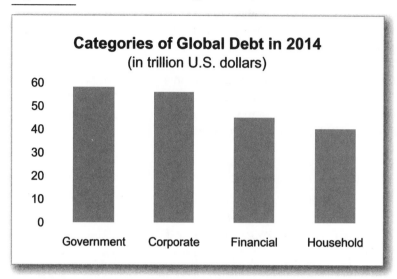

Pie charts are effective for illustrating the proportion of one segment in relation to the whole. For example, if you're writing a report about Hispanic students at a college, you may wish to show the proportion of Hispanic students currently registered. In Figure 4.7, the reader can see at a glance that Hispanic

Figure 4.6 Pie chart of global debt with category labels

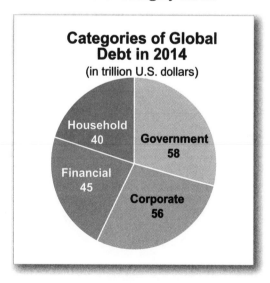

Figure 4.7 Pie chart showing proportion of Hispanic students

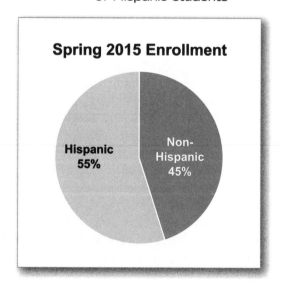

students make up more than half of the currently registered student population. Similarly, pie charts can help audiences visualize the size of one percentage relative to the whole population, as in Figure 4.8.

Pie charts are an effective visual tool for showing progress toward a goal. Although it would be easy to communicate progress showing a number alone, for instance 20%, 40%, 80%, and so on, a pie chart offers a visual image that helps to reinforce the message and perhaps motivates participants to work harder toward the goal (see Figures 4.9, 4.10, and 4.11).

If you need to quickly communicate information about proportion and you specifically do not want to include a lot of detail, for example, in a PowerPoint presentation delivered to a large audience, a pie chart is a good solution.

Even if you're not convinced of the utility of pie charts, you may one day find yourself being directed (by an instructor, employer, or client) to create a pie chart. You'll need some guidelines.

Figure 4.8 Pie chart with emphasis on one slice

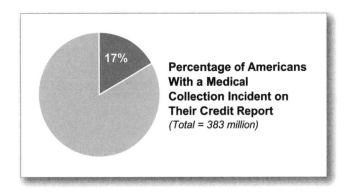

Figure 4.9 Pie chart 1 showing progress toward a goal

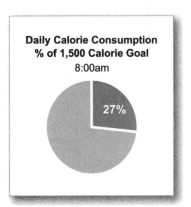

Figure 4.10 Pie chart 2 showing progress toward a goal

Figure 4.11 Pie chart 3 showing progress toward a goal

Figure 4.12 Data source for pie chart

	A	B
1	**Political Party**	**Likely Voters**
2	Democratic	44%
3	Republican	32%
4	Independent	24%

Figure 4.13 Completed pie chart: Likely Voters' Political Party

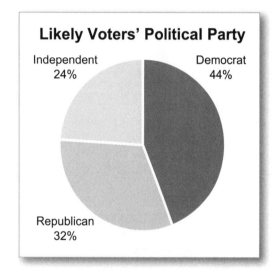

Creating a Pie Chart

1. **Organize your data.** The data for a pie chart may be organized as shown in Figure 4.12. The categories are in column A and the data values are in column B.

2. **Select the range of cells to be charted.** Select cells A1:B4.

3. On the **INSERT** tab, in the **Charts** group, click on the **Pie** icon.

4. Choose the first option in the **2-D Pie** section. The pie chart should resemble Figure 4.13.

Best Practices for Creating Pie Charts

As you can see, creating a pie chart is easy. So why do so many pie charts go wrong? Perhaps because pie charts *are* so fast and easy to create, analysts devote little effort to finessing the details that can cause pie charts to go awry. When opting for a pie chart to represent your data, follow these guidelines.

- Use a pie chart only when you have data for all possible categories or outcomes of a categorical variable and the categories are mutually exclusive; there can be no overlap among chart categories. Figure 4.14 is a pie chart that illustrates how long restaurants survive in Pocatello, Idaho. The total of the percentages sums to 255%, instead of 100%, because each category is a subset of the one that came before.

- Delete chart legends; use data labels instead. Legends cause readers to have to look back and forth, holding information about colors, labels, and data values in working memory to interpret the chart (see Figure 4.15). This is unnecessarily time-consuming and onerous. Labels, placed directly on (or next to) the wedges of the pie, eliminate this burden.

Figure 4.14 Pie chart with non–mutually exclusive categories

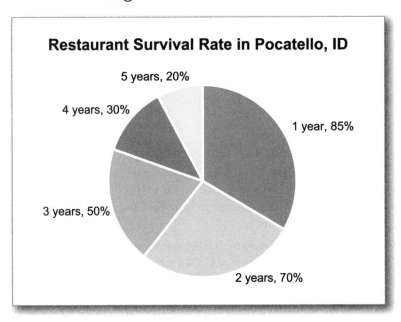

Restaurant Survival Rate in Pocatello, ID

5 years, 20%
4 years, 30%
1 year, 85%
3 years, 50%
2 years, 70%

Figure 4.15 Pie chart with legend

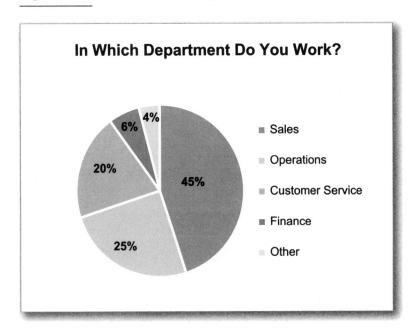

In Which Department Do You Work?

4%
6%
20%
45%
25%

- Sales
- Operations
- Customer Service
- Finance
- Other

Replacing Legends With Data Labels

1. Excel's default pie chart includes a legend at the bottom of the chart. To delete the legend, click on it and press the **DELETE** key on your keyboard.

2. To insert data labels, click on the **CHART ELEMENTS** shortcut menu and select **Data Labels**. Alternately, right-click on any wedge of pie and choose **Add Data Labels**.

3. The default data labels provide only the values of the pie wedges. Because we have deleted the legend, it is necessary to add the category names to the chart. Right-click on any data label on the chart and choose **Format Data Labels**; this opens the **Format Data Labels** task pane. From the **LABEL OPTIONS** section, click **Category Name**. Select **Percentage** to label each pie wedge with the appropriate proportion.

4. Deselect **Value**. It is unnecessary to label the chart with both the data values and percentage, as too much information may cause confusion rather than add clarity to the chart.

5. Change the **Separator** from the default, **Comma**, to **New Line**. This will place the category name and value on different lines, enhancing the readability of the label. Your properly labeled chart should look like Figure 4.16.

Figure 4.16 Formatted pie chart

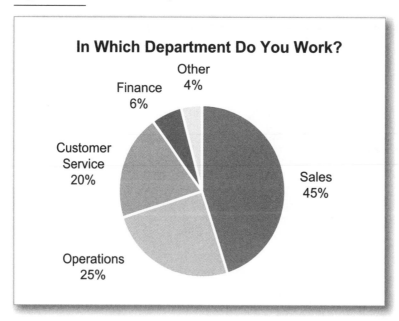

- Limit the number of slices of pie. The best pie charts contain fewer than five categories. There is no technical limit to the number of wedges your pie chart may contain. There is, however, a practical limit to the amount of information a reader can comfortably process in one chart. Figure 4.17 is a pie chart that

Figure 4.17 U.S. State Population pie chart

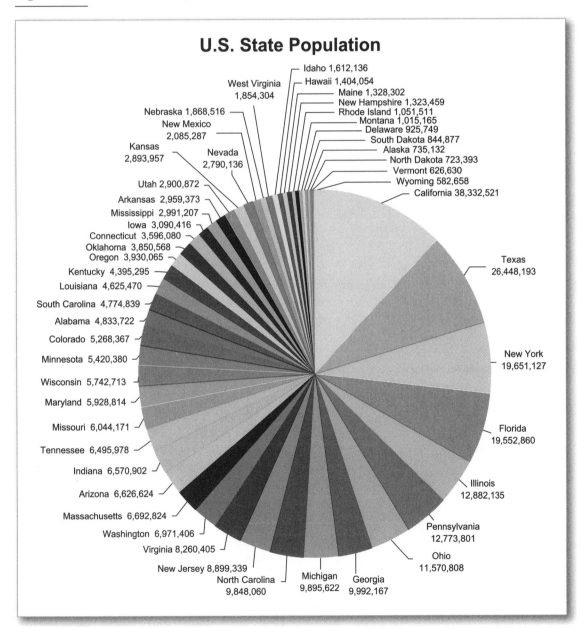

If you drag data labels away from the wedges of pie to which they refer, Excel will add leader lines connecting the label to the wedge of pie. This will also happen if there are too many data labels on one chart. This is illustrated in the U.S. State Population example in Figure 4.17. Adhering to the practices of positioning data labels on, or next to, the relevant wedge of pie and limiting the wedges to five or fewer should avoid the need for leader lines and will result in a readable chart.

shows the population of each of the 50 United States. The chart is comprehensive, but after the first few large states, the information becomes a jumble of colors and numbers that are unlikely to be comprehended by even the most motivated reader.

- By default, Excel begins the first slice of pie at 0%. This creates a radius at 12 o'clock, which provides a convenient reference. Unless you have a specific reason for doing so, don't change this. In the first image of Figure 4.18 we can see at a glance that the first wedge represents 25% of the data. The proportions in the second and third pie charts are the same as in the first, but because the pies have been rotated we lose the reference line at 12 o'clock and it becomes more difficult to identify the relative proportions of the wedges.

- Don't explode the pie. Excel offers the option to explode, or separate, one or more pie wedges. Analysts often choose to explode pie charts to add emphasis to a wedge (see Figure 4.19). There are very few situations when this option adds to the understanding of the chart.

Pulling apart pie wedges should be avoided because it increases the difficulty of interpreting the relative proportions of the wedges. In any event, if you opt for an exploding pie, only separate one wedge from the rest of the pie; don't separate all wedges as in Figure 4.20.

Figure 4.18 Rotated pie charts

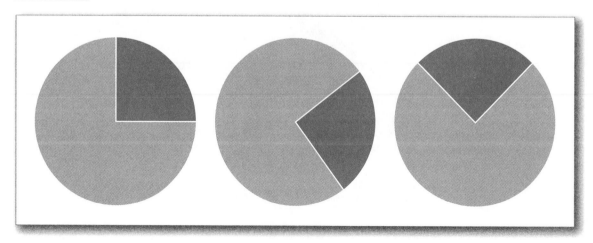

Figure 4.19   Pie chart with one wedge separated

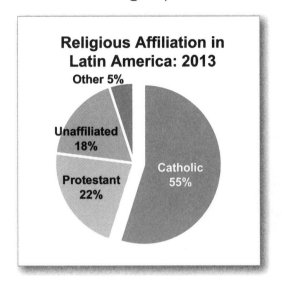

Figure 4.20   Fully exploded pie chart

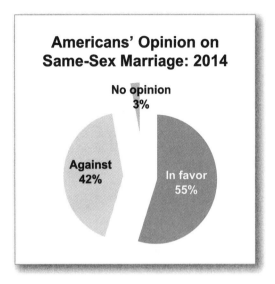

• Never use a 3-D pie. All of the complications associated with accurately assessing the areas of angles are compounded when the pie chart is rendered in three dimensions. Figure 4.21 is an example of a "designer" pie chart. The designer in this case not only chose to create the chart in 3-D; she also opted to fully explode the pie and added shadows to the data labels so that they would appear to sit on the wedges of pie. This is an excellent example of chart decoration being given priority over clear data illustration. See Chapter 6 for an expanded discussion of 3-D charts.

• The design of donut charts should follow the same rules as for standard pie charts. That is, ensure that the categories are comprehensive and mutually exclusive, use data labels instead of chart legends, limit the number of wedges to five or fewer, and don't explode the donut. Donut charts have an additional feature not available in standard pie charts. It is possible to include multiple data series on donut charts; each series is shown as one ring of the donut (see Figure 4.22). Limit donut charts to one data series. Even with only one series, donut charts are difficult for the uninitiated to decipher. The added complication of multiple data series can make correct interpretation of the chart nearly impossible.

Figure 4.21   Fully exploded 3-D pie chart

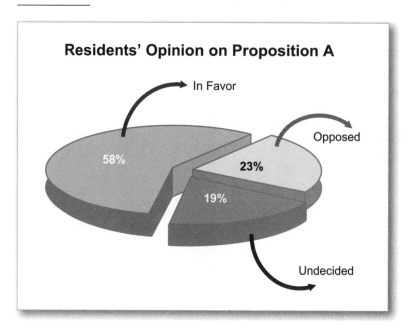

Figure 4.22   Multiseries donut chart

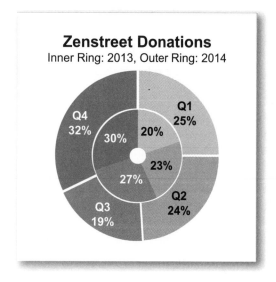

Alternatives to Pie Charts

Perhaps you've considered the pros and cons of displaying your data in a pie chart and have decided that it isn't worth arguing with Edward Tufte and Stephen Few just to include a pie or donut chart in your report. If so, consider the alternatives. For example, the multiseries donut chart in Figure 4.22 could be presented as a clustered column chart as in Figure 4.23. This would be an effective presentation if the goal was to compare the proportion of donations collected during each quarter of the two years. Another alternative is the multiseries line chart in Figure 4.24. This presentation allows for an easy comparison of the year-over-year pattern.

Figure 4.23 Cluster column chart alternative to a multiseries donut

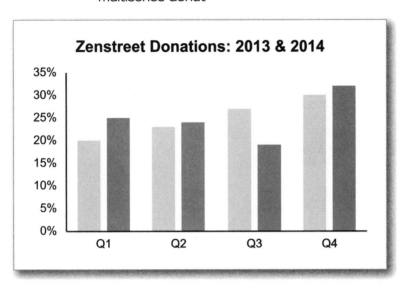

Figure 4.24 Multiseries line chart alternative to a multiseries donut

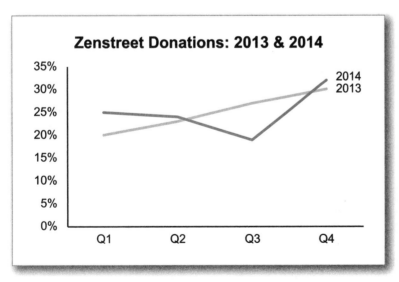

A data table is another alternative to a pie or donut chart (see Figure 4.25). Data tables are useful when precision is required and readers will have time to study the data. They are least effective in the context of a presentation when an image may only be displayed for a short time.

Figure 4.25   Data table alternative to a pie or donut chart

Zenstreet Donations		
	2013	**2014**
Q1	20%	25%
Q2	23%	24%
Q3	27%	19%
Q4	30%	32%

SUMMARY

The controversy surrounding pie charts is almost as ubiquitous as the charts themselves. Data visualization experts are uniformly opposed to their use, yet their chorus of strongly worded criticisms has scarcely made a dent in the widespread use of the humble pie chart. Could it be that pie charts have a place in the pantheon of data visualization techniques?

We have taken the position that pie charts are not inherently flawed and should be considered as a viable data visualization tool. They are simple to create and will be immediately recognized by most audiences. They readily communicate part-to-whole relationships and can be useful for indicating progress toward a goal. The key to effective use of pie charts is to devote time to the proper formatting of these charts. A hastily created pie chart that relies solely on Excel's default formatting is unlikely to be an optimal data display.

Pie Chart Checklist

1. Include a descriptive title at the top of the chart.

2. Ensure that the chart categories are mutually exclusive.

3. Check that the sum of all categories equals 100%.

4. Opt for data labels placed inside or beside the wedges of pie instead of chart legends.

5. Format data labels for maximum clarity and include percentages or data values, not both.

6. Use a pie only when there are five or fewer chart categories.

7. Only use two-dimensional pie charts and don't explode the pie.

CHAPTER 5

Chart Formatting

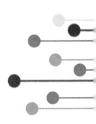

Now that you've practiced creating basic charts and tables using Excel, it's time to focus on the visual appeal of the data visualizations you've generated. We will revisit the charts discussed earlier in the text, this time with a focus on aesthetics. The goal is to balance fundamental design principles with the need to communicate data accurately and convincingly.

Every bit of information on a chart or table should communicate an important detail. As a guiding principle, we rely on Edward Tufte's advice to, above all else, show the data. Excel offers a variety of built-in chart styles from which to choose. Although these templates have improved considerably over the years, most require customization to achieve optimal data displays. There are three basic rules for chart formatting:

1. Eliminate all unnecessary information, including backgrounds, borders, gridlines, and decorations. Display only what's needed to interpret the chart.

2. Deemphasize the nondata elements on the chart, such as titles, labels, and legends. Make these elements consistent in font and color so as to avoid calling attention to them.

3. Highlight the most important data with contrast or callouts.

To customize the design of your charts so that only the data are highlighted, you will need to format your chart

Learning Objectives

- Identify and eliminate unnecessary and redundant information from data displays

- Write descriptive chart titles

- Format chart legends

- Label axes and data points

- Choose readable fonts

- Select colors purposefully

- Limit charts to two dimensions

- Create custom chart templates

elements. The **Format Chart Area** task pane is activated by right-clicking on the chart area, which is the space around the plot area (see Figure 5.1), and selecting **Format Chart Area**. This menu enables you to adjust colors, labels, number formats, and much more. When this window is open, clicking on a chart feature such as an axis, title, or legend will change the task pane to the one appropriate for editing that feature. With any one of the task panes open, click around on the chart to see how the editing features change.

Figure 5.1 Chart and plot areas of a column chart

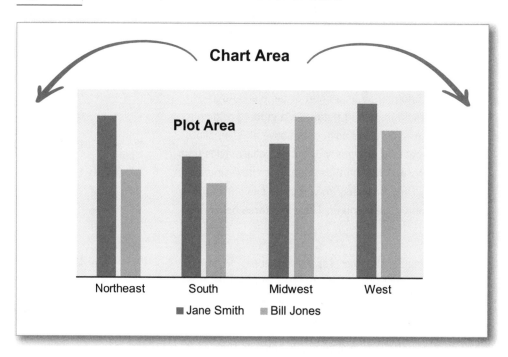

Remove Unnecessary and Redundant Information

Figure 5.2 is a column chart using one of Excel's preset chart styles. The chart has a border, a dark background, gridlines, and tick marks on the x-axis. These elements do not contribute to the understanding of the data; in fact, they require extra ink on the page and can distract from the message. They should be removed.

Figure 5.2 Poorly formatted column chart

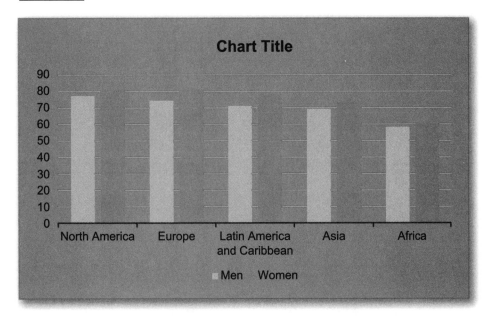

Removing Unnecessary Information

1. From the **Format Chart Area** task pane, under **CHART OPTIONS**, expand the **FILL** submenu options (see Figure 5.3).

Figure 5.3 Format Chart Area task pane

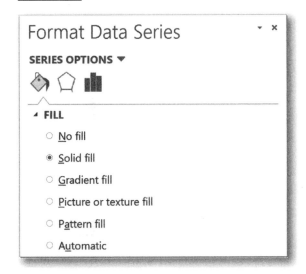

2. Select **Solid fill** and change the color to white.

3. Expand the **BORDER** menu and select **No line**.

4. Remove the gridlines by expanding the **CHART ELEMENTS** shortcut menu and deselecting **Gridlines**. Alternatively, you may remove gridlines by selecting them and pressing the **Delete** key.

5. Eliminate the tick marks from the x-axis. Right-click on the x-axis and select **Format Axis**. Expand the **TICK MARKS** submenu and change Major type and Minor type to **None** (see Figure 5.4).

*Although it is difficult to see the difference on a white page, filling the chart area with white is not the same as selecting **No fill**, which makes the chart area transparent. In some instances, a transparent chart area may be useful, for example, when placing a chart on a report page with elements such as text or other charts that would be obscured by a solid white chart fill or when working with a document or PowerPoint slide background that is not white. A white chart fill or no fill will serve most purposes. It is best to leave color, gradient, picture, texture, and pattern chart fills to experienced designers.*

Figure 5.4 Format Axis menu

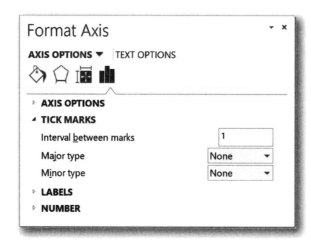

Chart Titles

Figure 5.5 is a column chart from which the most distracting chart elements have been removed. Without the dark background, gridlines, and tick marks, readers are better able to focus on the data. The chart is not complete, as it lacks a title.

Figure 5.5 Semiformatted column chart

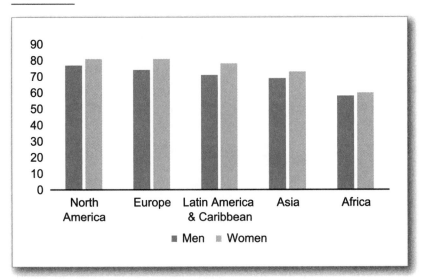

Charts should include brief descriptive titles. The best chart titles summarize, but don't repeat, the information included in the chart. By reading the chart title, the audience should understand the data represented in the chart, the time period covered, and the units of measurement. Chart titles need not be complete sentences; think of them as headlines. However, avoid abbreviations and acronyms unless you're certain that your audience will understand them without confusion. Follow the rules of title case where all major words are capitalized.

It is sometimes necessary to allow chart titles to span two or three lines, for example, to show the date range or sample size on a separate line. Also, in some situations adding more information to the title will allow you to delete axes labels. When space is limited, the chart title does double duty: it describes the data contained in the chart and also highlights an important data point (for example, "Fourth Quarter Sales in the Western Region Outperformed Expectations"). Be cautious, however, of turning chart titles into paragraphs of text.

Chart titles almost always belong at the top of the chart, usually centered on the chart. There may be variations when creating posters or infographics or when presenting a group of charts to tell one story. Regardless of the positioning of the chart title, always set the text direction to **Horizontal**; any other text orientation will create an awkward reading experience (see Figure 5.6).

Figure 5.6 Format Axis menu

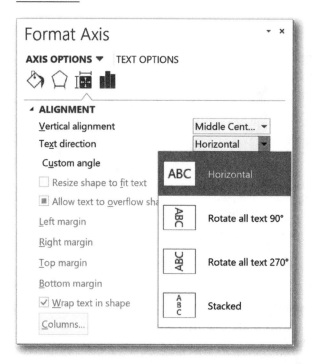

Editing Chart Titles

1. If a chart title placeholder is not already showing, click on the **CHART ELEMENTS** shortcut menu and select **Chart Title**. Click into the chart title placeholder and type over the text.

2. Format the chart title using the text formatting options on the **HOME** tab of the ribbon. Increase the font size so that the chart title is larger than the other chart labels and make the title bold. Actual font sizes will depend on the context in which the chart appears. Charts in reports might have titles approximately 12 to 14 points, whereas presentation charts require substantially larger fonts. Figure 5.7 is a formatted column chart ready to be inserted into a report.

Figure 5.7 Formatted column chart

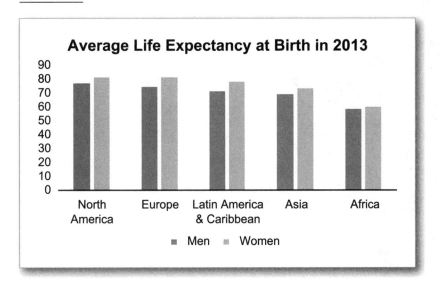

There are many additional options for formatting chart titles (and other chart text elements), including the ability to add colors, shadows, custom angles, reflections, glows, soft edges, and 3-D rotation. These features are unlikely to increase the visual appeal of your text, so it is best to avoid them.

Instead of typing a chart title directly into the chart title placeholder, you may link a chart title to a cell in your worksheet. This makes the chart title dynamic, a useful feature if the data in the chart will change based on user behavior, such as selecting from a drop-down menu.

Linking Chart
Titles to a Worksheet Cell

1. Click into the chart title placeholder to activate it. In the formula bar, type the "=" symbol, click on the cell containing the chart title, and then press **Enter** (see Figure 5.8).

2. Change the chart title by editing the linked cell in the worksheet.

*Excel's chart title placeholder will expand to accommodate entered text, up to a point. The chart title will not span the entire width of the chart. There is padding around the placeholder so that the title will not overflow into the chart. There are other limitations too, such as the inability to adjust the vertical spacing of the text in the placeholder. If you wish to manipulate the text more than is possible with the chart title placeholder, delete it and insert a text box instead (**INSERT > Text > Textbox**). If you activate the chart by clicking on it and then draw the text box within the boundaries of the chart, the text box will stay with the chart when it is moved.*

Figure 5.8 Worksheet formula bar

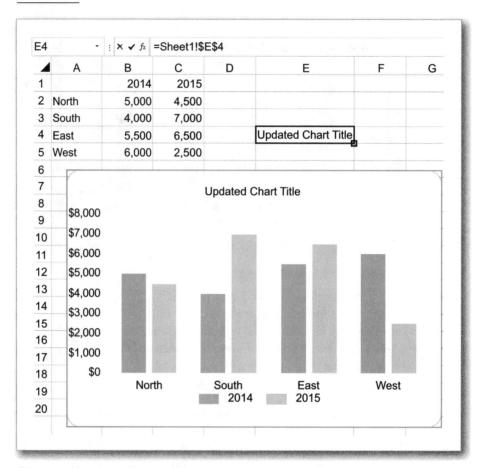

Chart Legends

A chart legend tells readers what each bar, column, line, or slice of pie represents. Charts with more than one data series need legends. Excel automatically generates chart legends when a data array containing multiple data series is charted. Legend entries are linked to the category or series labels in the source data. If you wish to change a legend entry you must edit the text in the appropriate worksheet cell.

Adding a Chart Legend

1. If the chart legend does not automatically appear, you may add one by clicking on the **CHART ELEMENTS** shortcut menu and selecting **Legend** (see Figure 5.9).

2. The default legend is positioned at the bottom of the chart. You may change this to one of five specific locations from the **Legend** submenu, or you may activate the legend by clicking it and dragging it to any position on the chart.

Legend position

Chart legends should be positioned so that the order of the legend keys matches the order in which the data series are plotted on the chart. The default legend position at the bottom of the chart is not optimal for the stacked column chart in Figure 5.10. It requires effort to match the legend entries to the corresponding segments of the columns.

Moving the legend for the stacked column chart to the right so that the order of the legend keys matches the order of the segments on the columns facilitates rapid comprehension of the chart (see Figure 5.11).

Legends positioned at the bottom work well for clustered column charts (see Figure 5.12) and stacked bar charts (see Figure 5.13) because the order of the legend keys matches the order in which the data series are presented. The legends

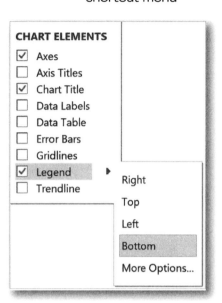

Figure 5.9 CHART ELEMENTS shortcut menu

Figure 5.10 100% stacked column chart with bottom legend

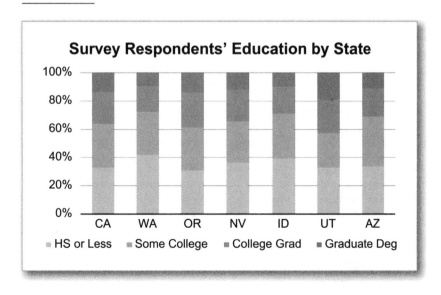

Figure 5.11 100% stacked column chart with right legend

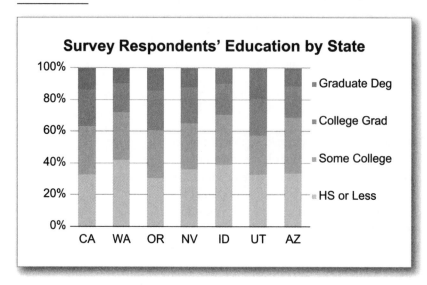

Figure 5.12 Clustered column chart with bottom legend

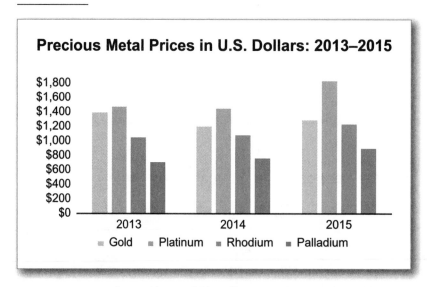

in Figures 5.12 and 5.13 also could be effective at the top of the chart (beneath the chart title); this would give the legend greater prominence and potentially aid in interpreting the chart's contents. Positioning the legend to the left side of the chart is the least effective option and could only work on charts without labeled y-axes.

Legend keys for line charts are most effective when placed to the right and very close to their corresponding lines. Figure 5.14 is a line chart with the default legend

Figure 5.13 Stacked bar chart with bottom legend

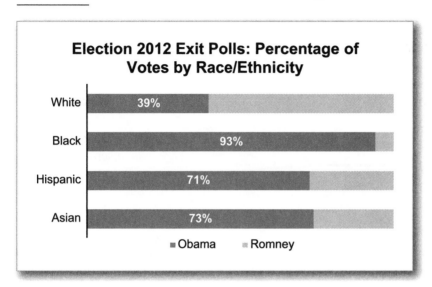

at the bottom of the chart. Placing the legend at the bottom forces the reader to work harder than necessary to determine which lines represent each type of product. Figure 5.15 is the same chart with the legend shown to the right.

Positioning the chart legend to the right helps the reader to more easily identify the lines because the eye has a

Microsoft refers to the colored or patterned marker associated with each legend entry as the Legend Key. To the right of each legend key is a name identifying the data represented by the key.

Figure 5.14 Line chart with bottom legend

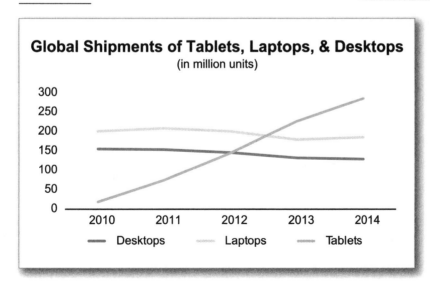

Figure 5.15 Line chart with right legend

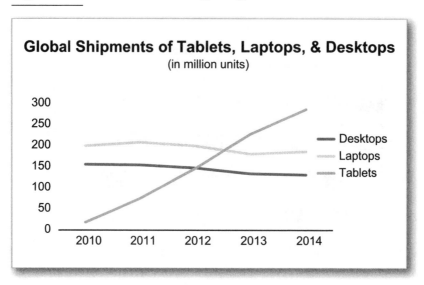

shorter distance to travel between the legend keys and the lines. However, the order of the legend keys in Figure 5.15 does not match the order of the lines. This is problematic and would probably lead to misidentification of the data. Excel's options for legend placement are limited. In this situation, the best solution is to delete the chart legend and insert text boxes containing the words *Tablets*, *Laptops*, and *Desktops*. You can then position the individual text boxes adjacent to the corresponding lines (see Figure 5.16). Note that in Figure 5.16 we have also

Figure 5.16 Line chart using text boxes for legend

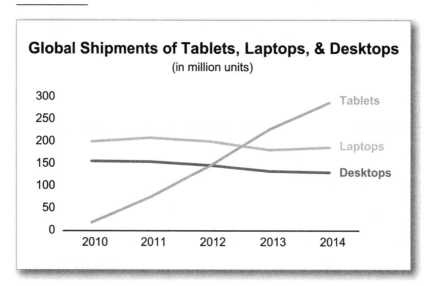

eliminated the unnecessary legend key markers next to the legend entries. To reinforce the association between the legend labels and the lines, color the legend text to match the colors of the chart lines.

As with other types of charts, Excel's default pie charts include a legend at the bottom of the chart (see Figure 5.17). Unlike the other chart types, however, there is no position around the pie (left, right, top, or bottom) that makes it easy for readers to identify each wedge of pie based on the legend.

When you opt for text boxes instead of using Excel's legend options, the legend is no longer linked to the data. If you edit the chart data, you will need to manually edit the text boxes.

Figure 5.17 Pie chart with bottom legend

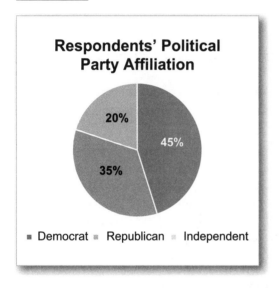

Figure 5.18 Pie chart with data labels

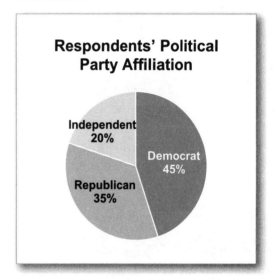

It is best to omit legends from pie charts and opt instead for data labels positioned on or adjacent to the pie wedges (see Figure 5.18). This method provides readers with the information they need to decipher the chart in proximity to the data being referenced.

Chart Axes

A typical two-dimensional bar, column, or line chart has two primary axes, a horizontal or x-axis and a vertical or y-axis. Axes describe what is being measured and provide the units of measurement, for example, dollars or units sold. From the **CHART ELEMENTS** shortcut menu you may add titles to the x- and y-axes. Y-axis titles can be challenging. By default Excel positions the y-axis title at a 90-degree angle, which is never a good reading experience (see Figure 5.19).

Figure 5.19 Line chart with labeled y-axis

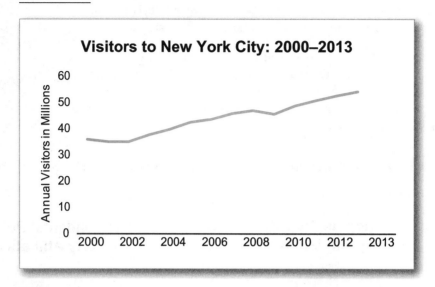

You may change the orientation of the axis title in the **Format Axis Title** menu (right-click on the axis title and select **Format Axis Title**); however, choosing the horizontal alignment will result in considerable blank space to the left of the chart. A better alternative is to include pertinent information about the units of measurement in the chart title. In the Figure 5.20 chart, we deleted the y-axis title and labeled the chart "Total Annual Visitors to New York City (in millions)" to convey the necessary information.

Adding a title to a chart's horizontal axis does not present issues related to text orientation, but before adding an x-axis title, consider if it is essential for interpreting the chart. For Figure 5.20, adding the x-axis title "Year" would be unnecessary. The labels are clear enough; readers will understand that 2000, 2002, 2004, and so on represent years. The same is true for chart categories such as "Male" and "Female" or "January, February, March." There is no need to add the axis titles, particularly if the chart title contains enough information about the categories or time period measured.

Labeling axes

When comparing multiple values within and across categories or data series, precise axis labeling is crucial. Figure 5.21 compares student enrollment across two semesters in five academic departments at a university.

Figure 5.20 Line chart with axis information in the chart title

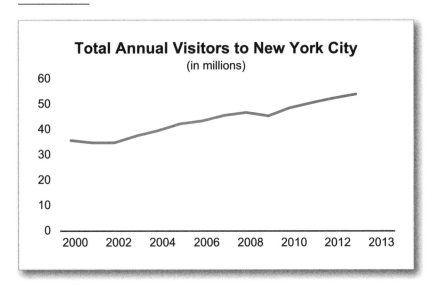

Figure 5.21 Column chart with redundant category labels

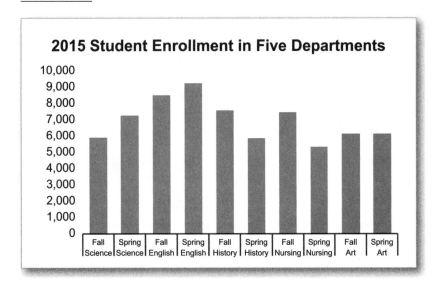

This is an accurately labeled chart; however, there is redundant information on the x-axis; department names are repeated. To eliminate the redundancy and create a cleaner x-axis, you must modify the data source. Figure 5.22 is the data on which this chart is based.

To remove the duplicate label, merge cells A2 and A3 for Science, A4 and A5 for English, and so on (see Figure 5.23).

Figure 5.22 Data source for column chart with redundant category labels

	A	B	C
1	**Department**	**Semester**	**Enrollment**
2	Science	Fall	5963
3	Science	Spring	7289
4	English	Fall	8533
5	English	Spring	9250
6	History	Fall	7598
7	History	Spring	5925
8	Nursing	Fall	7491
9	Nursing	Spring	5357
10	Art	Fall	6170
11	Art	Spring	6174

Figure 5.23 Data source for improved column chart category labels

	A	B	C
1	**Department**	**Semester**	**Enrollment**
2	Science	Fall	5963
3		Spring	7289
4	English	Fall	8533
5		Spring	9250
6	History	Fall	7598
7		Spring	5925
8	Nursing	Fall	7491
9		Spring	5357
10	Art	Fall	6170
11		Spring	6174

Merging Worksheet Cells

1. To merge the worksheet cells, first delete the second label in each set, that is, cell A3 for Science, A5 for English, and so on.

2. Select cells A2 and A3. From the **HOME** tab, in the **Alignment** group, click on **Merge & Center**. Repeat this process for the remaining pairs of department titles.

To create the new chart, select cells A1:C11 and choose a standard column chart from the **Charts** gallery on the **INSERT** tab. The resulting chart should look like Figure 5.24, with one exception.

If you've been following along and creating your own chart, all of the columns in your chart will be the same color. We have opted to alternate the colors of the pairs of columns to make it easier to differentiate the departments from one another. We will address the topic of chart colors shortly.

Axes and individual data labels

There are two primary options for labeling a chart's data values: label individual values (bars, columns, or points on a line) or show the data values on the

Figure 5.24 Column chart with improved category labels

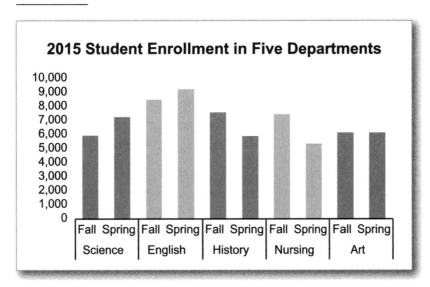

x- or y-axis. When your data report requires precision, you should include data labels on the individual data points (see Figure 5.25). Labeling each data point provides the greatest amount of detail and can be helpful when the chart information is being used to make important decisions.

Figure 5.25 Line chart with data labels

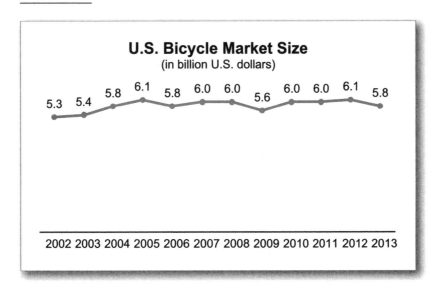

Adding Data Labels

1. Select the line, bar, or column to which you wish to apply data labels.

2. Select **Data Labels** from the **CHART ELEMENTS** shortcut menu. Alternately, right-click any point on the line, bar, or column and select **Add Data Labels**.

If precise values are not important and the chart is being used to examine trends or investigate patterns, substituting a labeled y-axis for individual data labels is preferable (in a bar chart, this would be the horizontal or x-axis). Figure 5.26 is a multiseries line chart with individual data points labeled. The chart is cluttered, and the labels for the three data series at the bottom are essentially unreadable. Because the aim of this chart is to compare trends during the year, knowing the values for each month is unnecessary and distracting. It would be better to remove the data labels and rely on the values along the y-axis.

Figure 5.26   Multiseries line chart with data labels

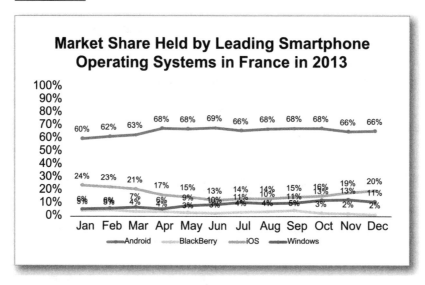

Always choose one option: either label the y-axis or add individual data labels; it is unnecessary to include both. Figure 5.27 is a multiseries line chart using only a labeled y-axis instead of individual data labels.

Units of the y-axis

Show the minimum number of points on the y-axis for readers to estimate the individual data values on a chart. Choosing a y-axis instead of data labels

Figure 5.27 Multiseries line chart with y-axis label only

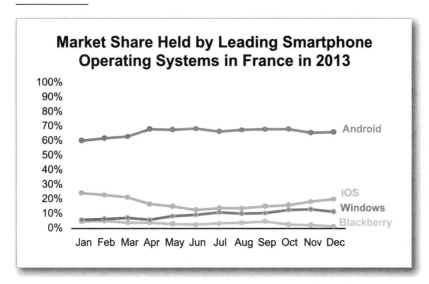

means that you're not overly concerned with conveying precise data values. It is therefore not necessary to label too many points on the y-axis. Excel generally does a good job of setting the major and minor units on the axes; however, you may want to customize the appearance of the y-axis to show fewer points for a cleaner chart. Figure 5.28 is a line chart containing a y-axis with too many points labeled. Figure 5.29 is an improved version with the major units of the axis set to show every 50 instead of every 20 units.

Figure 5.28 Line chart with overlabeled y-axis

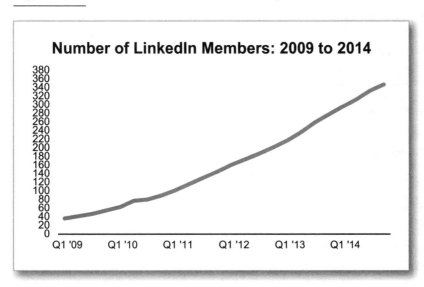

Figure 5.29   Line chart with improved y-axis labeling

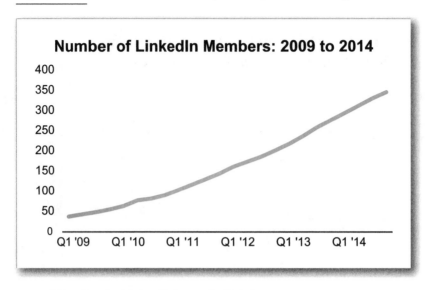

Number of LinkedIn Members: 2009 to 2014

Adjusting the Major Units on the Y-Axis

1. Select the y-axis. Right-click and choose **Format Axis**.

2. Change the value in the **Major** units dialog box to adjust the number of values showing on the y-axis (see Figure 5.30).

Figure 5.30   Format Axis menu

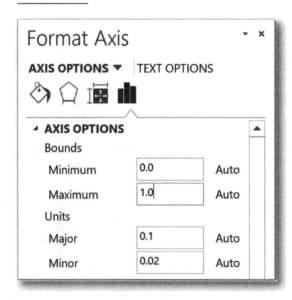

Position of the x-axis

The customary location for the horizontal axis is at the bottom of bar and column charts. There are times, however, when it is desirable to reposition the chart's horizontal axis. For example, on bar charts containing a long list of categories, it is easier for the reader if the x-axis with the value information is at the top rather than the bottom of the chart (see Figure 5.31).

Figure 5.31   Bar chart with x-axis at the top

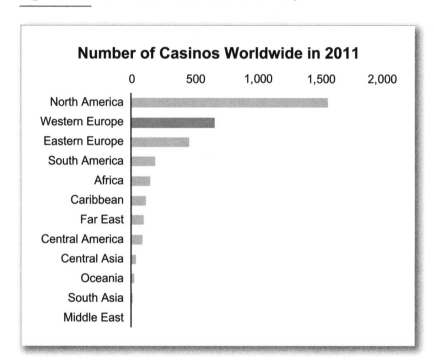

Another situation where repositioning the x-axis is necessary is when the chart contains negative values. In Figure 5.32 the negative value for Turkey's gross domestic product growth in 2009 caused the column to drop below the 0% point, which resulted in the axis label appearing on the column. In Figure 5.33 this has been corrected by moving the axis labels to the **Low** position. To change the axis labeling, right-click on the axis and open the **Format Axis** task pane. From there, select **LABELS > Label Position** and choose either **High** or **Low** depending on the chart.

Figure 5.32 Column chart with negative values

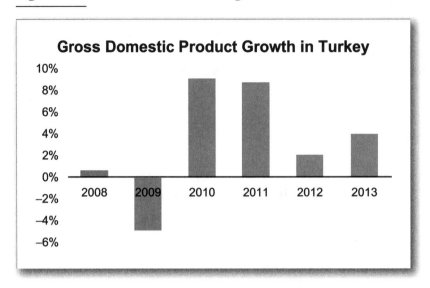

Figure 5.33 Column chart with low x-axis labels

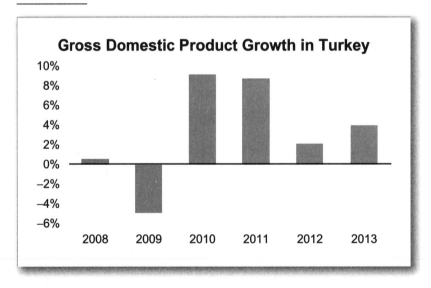

Charts With Data Tables

An option for situations when exact values for the individual data points are required but there are too many data points to label without the labels overlapping one another is to omit the data labels and y-axis and opt for a table beneath the chart (see Figure 5.34).

Figure 5.34 Multiseries line chart with data table

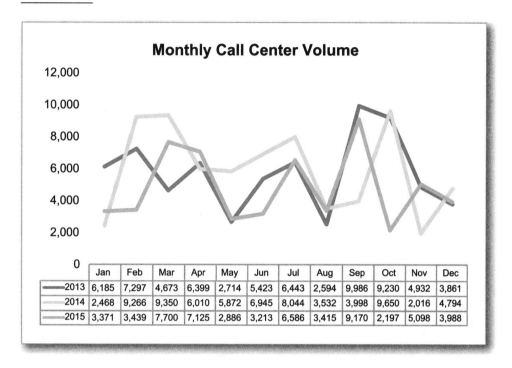

A data table may be added by selecting the **Data Table** option from the **CHART ELEMENTS** shortcut menu.

Labeling Individual Data Values

It may not be necessary to include all data labels on a chart. For example, a line chart with data labels on the start and end points and perhaps one notable value may be sufficient to convey the necessary detail (see Figure 5.35). Adding data labels to one or a few data points is a manual process; you must select each point individually and add the data label for that point.

Adding One Data Label at a Time

1. Click once to select the line.

2. Click a second time on the individual point you wish to label.

3. Select **Data Labels** from the **CHART ELEMENTS** shortcut menu. Alternately, right-click and select **Add Data Label**.

Figure 5.35 Line chart with select data points labeled

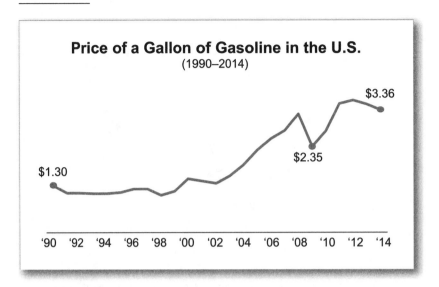

Labeling the Y-Axis on a Bar Chart

We mentioned previously that the choice between bar and column charts often rests on the length of the category labels. Bar charts are better than column charts when category labels are long because the word wrapping under columns is awkward. If you have chosen a bar chart for this reason, it is likely that you will need to format the chart's category labels. Figure 5.36 is a bar chart containing long category labels, the names of national parks.

Although the chart in Figure 5.36 is serviceable, it can be improved. The center-justified text combined with the variable length and number of lines of each y-axis category label is sloppy.

Excel does not offer the option for right- or left-justifying the y-axis text. The best alternative for improving the appearance of this chart is to delete the y-axis and replace the category labels with text boxes. In Figure 5.37 we have added five text boxes, one for each label, right-justified the text in the boxes, and positioned them next to the bars. Using text boxes allowed us to format the text to our liking and position the labels precisely where they should appear.

Figure 5.38 is another version of the same chart, this time with the text boxes placed directly on top of the bars they reference.

When using text boxes to customize chart labels, they should be aligned. In Figure 5.37 the text boxes are right aligned; in Figure 5.38 they are left aligned.

Figure 5.36 Bar chart with long category labels

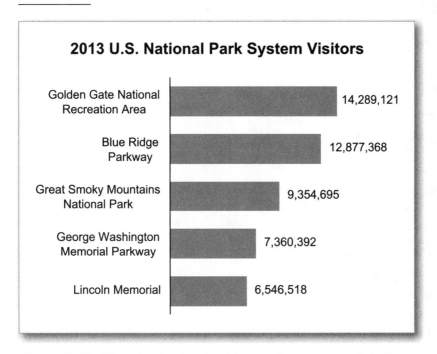

2013 U.S. National Park System Visitors

Category	Value
Golden Gate National Recreation Area	14,289,121
Blue Ridge Parkway	12,877,368
Great Smoky Mountains National Park	9,354,695
George Washington Memorial Parkway	7,360,392
Lincoln Memorial	6,546,518

Figure 5.37 Bar chart using text boxes for category labels

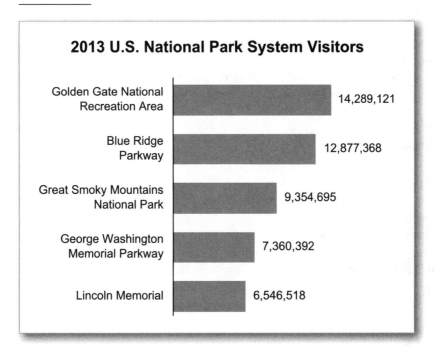

2013 U.S. National Park System Visitors

Category	Value
Golden Gate National Recreation Area	14,289,121
Blue Ridge Parkway	12,877,368
Great Smoky Mountains National Park	9,354,695
George Washington Memorial Parkway	7,360,392
Lincoln Memorial	6,546,518

Figure 5.38 Bar chart with category labels on the bars

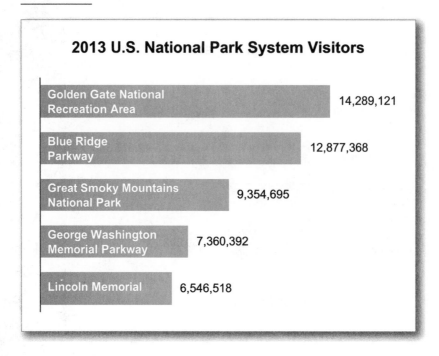

Aligning Text Boxes

1. Select all text boxes to be aligned.

2. From the **FORMAT** tab, in the **Arrange** group, click **Align** and select the appropriate alignment.

Formatting Numbers on Data Labels and Axes

Adjusting the appearance of numbers on charts is perhaps the most important and neglected chart formatting task. Chart designers often rely on default formatting that can have too much information, overwhelming readers, or not enough information to be useful. Determining how much information to include requires an assessment of the chart's audience, particularly their familiarity with the data and need for precision in the data reporting.

Use the thousands separator on data labels and axes

Make long numbers easier to read by inserting a thousands separator (a comma in the United States). The comma goes to the left of every third whole number, for example, 1,000,000 instead of 1000000. This should be done for axis labels and data values.

Inserting a Thousands Separator

1. Right-click on an axis or data label and choose **Format Axis** or **Format Data Labels**.

2. From the **Format Axis** (or **Format Data Labels**) menu, expand the **NUMBER** submenu.

3. From the **Category** drop-down submenu, select **Number**. Check the **Use 1000 Separator** box (see Figure 5.39).

Figure 5.39 Format Data Labels menu

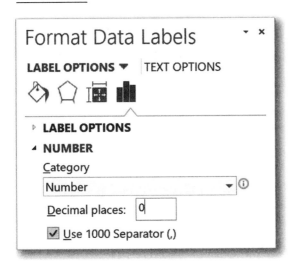

*The **Format Axis** or **Format Data Labels** NUMBER submenu is also where you would change the axes or data values to currency, percentages, date, and time and change the number of decimal places shown on the chart.*

Shorten long numbers

Adding the comma separator to long numbers will improve readability of the chart. Unless your report requires exact values, a better solution is to shorten long numbers. For example, 120k is easier and faster to read than 119,955. This is particularly important when a chart is being created for a presentation. Audience members who are expending mental energy to read and process long, precise values on a chart will not be listening attentively to the speaker.

Abbreviated data values also can be helpful when space in a written report is at a premium. Look to your field's guidelines and the requirements of your particular report to evaluate how much you may abbreviate data values without loss of essential information. Figure 5.40 is a column chart with the data labels abbreviated. The units in which the values are displayed are noted in the chart title.

Figure 5.40 Column chart using abbreviated data labels

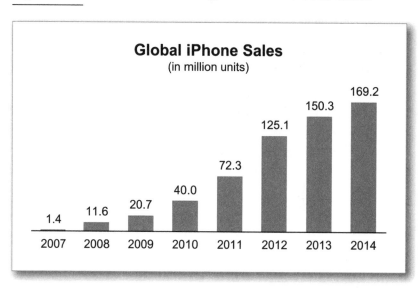

Changing the Display Units

1. To change the units in which the data labels are displayed, you must change the display units of the associated axis.
   For a column chart, right-click on the y-axis and select **Format Axis**.

2. Change the **Display units** to **Millions** or whatever the appropriate unit for your data is (see Figure 5.41).

Only use as many decimals as necessary

When an axis or data label format is changed to Number, Currency, Accounting, Percentage, or Scientific Notation, Excel assigns two decimal places to the value. When working with large numbers, it is usually

Figure 5.41 Format Axis menu

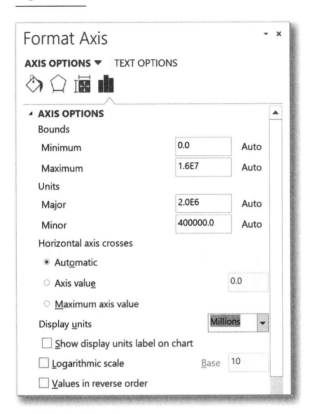

unnecessary to show data values to two (or more) decimal places. For data sets containing small values, for example, data in the range 0 to 1, you will need to use your judgment about how far out to carry the decimal places. Use the minimal number of decimal places necessary to convey the data story. In other words, don't clutter your chart with too much information that does not aid in interpreting the data.

Formatting Dates

There are many ways to format dates. As with other data elements on charts, show the minimum amount of date and time information necessary. Figure 5.42 shows monthly coffee sales for two years. The x-axis displays the full name of each month and includes the year. Because the labels are long, Excel oriented them on a 90-degree angle.

Figure 5.42   Multiyear line chart showing coffee sales

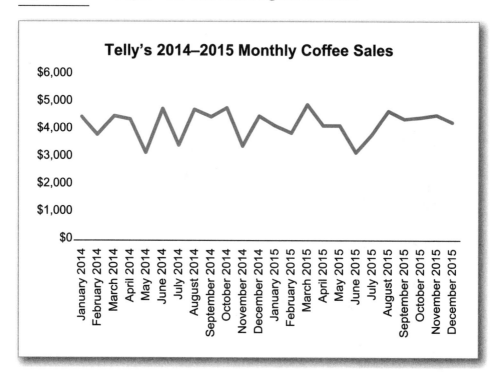

Figure 5.43 is an improved version of the monthly coffee sales chart. In this version we reformatted the date to include only the three-character month indicators and removed the year from the axis labels. The years 2014 and 2015 were inserted using text boxes, beneath the months.

The chart in Figure 5.43 reduced the size of the x-axis labels by removing redundant information, allowing the labels to be oriented horizontally and improving the readability of the axis labels. Another option for showing months of the year on the x-axis is to use just the first character of each month (see Figure 5.44). This creates the cleanest axis and will allow you to reduce the chart size without reorienting the text. Use this format only if you're sure that readers will immediately understand that the letters on the x-axis represent months of the year. If there is potential for confusion, add clarifying information to the chart title.

Figure 5.43 Coffee sales chart with improved category labels

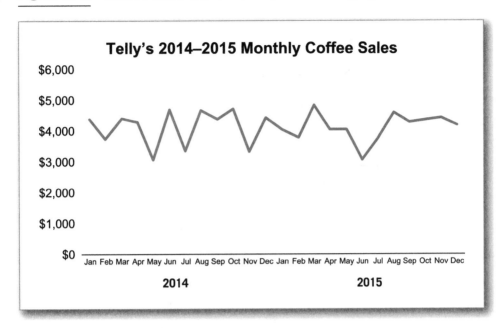

Figure 5.44 Coffee sales chart with alternate category labels

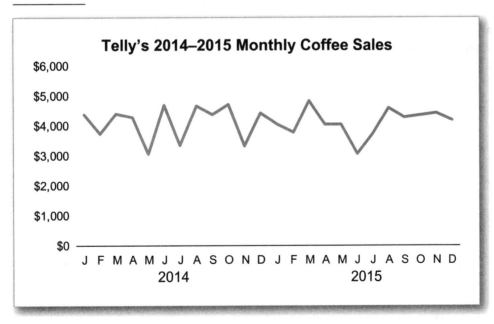

Changing Date Format on the X-Axis

1. For line and column charts, right-click on the x-axis and select **Format Axis**.

2. Expand the **NUMBER** submenu and select **Date** (see Figure 5.45).

3. Select the date format from among the **Type** options.

4. In our situation there was no predefined date format that met our needs. We wanted to show the month using three characters. To achieve this we used a **Custom** date format. From the **NUMBER** submenu, select the **Custom** category. In the **Format Code** dialog box enter **mmm** (see Figure 5.46).

Figure 5.45 Format Axis menu, Date category

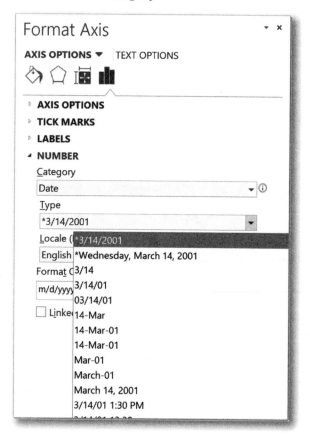

Figure 5.46 Format Axis menu, Custom category

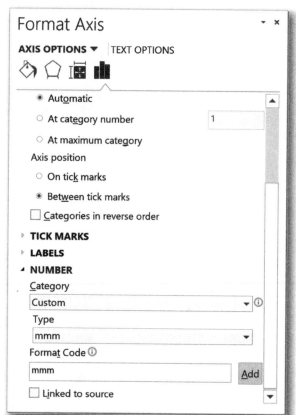

Click **Add**. The new custom code is now stored as a custom **Type** and can be reused in the future. See Table 5.1 for a list of other date format codes that may be added as custom date formats.

Table 5.1 Time and date displays

Format	Description
m	month as a number with no leading zeroes
mm	month as a number with leading zeroes
mmm	three letter month abbreviation
mmmm	full name of month
d	day as number with no leading zeroes
dd	day as number with leading zeroes
ddd	three letter day of week abbreviation (Wed)
dddd	unabbreviated day of week text (Wednesday)
yy	two digit year
yyyy	four digit year
h	hour as number with no leading zeroes
hh	hour as number with leading zeroes
m	minutes as number with no leading zeroes
mm	minutes as number with leading zeroes
s	seconds as number with no leading zeroes
ss	seconds as number with leading zeroes

Figure 5.47 Serif and sans-serif fonts

Fonts

Fonts should be aligned with your organization's style guidelines, if appropriate. There are two main classes of fonts, serif and sans serif. Serif fonts have decorative flourishes at the ends of the strokes; these are the serifs. The fonts without these flourishes are called sans serif (see Figure 5.47).

Examples of serif fonts include Times New Roman, Georgia, and Palatino Linotype. Sans-serif fonts include Arial, Tahoma, and Verdana. Sans-serif fonts are generally considered to be more modern and easier to read than serif fonts. Because sans-serif fonts are "cleaner" than serif fonts, they are commonly used for online work. Serif fonts are typically used in printed materials because the serifs make the individual letters distinctive and therefore easy to read.

For most charts, a combination of a serif font used for the chart title and a sans-serif font for axes and data labels will create a pleasing display. When presenting several charts in one report, aim for consistency; use the same font for all chart titles and the same font for all axes and data labels. Limit your fonts to one or two types, and if you're uncertain about which fonts to use, choose a simple sans-serif font, such as Arial or Helvetica, for all chart elements.

A third class of fonts, the specialty fonts, includes fonts like Chiller, Mistral, Jokerman, and a host of handwriting fonts. With the exception of charts created for personal use (e.g., party invitations or birth announcements) these specialty fonts should not be used on charts. They are difficult to read and appear unprofessional.

Font size

Font size is determined based on the context of your report or presentation and the particular fonts you choose. All fonts must be readable by your audience. For printed material, chart fonts should not be smaller than 9 points. Minimum font sizes for presentations are dependent on the size of the room and distance of the audience from the screen. Audience members sitting at the back of the room need to be able to read all chart text, including titles, axes labels, and data values. Do not include anything on a chart that cannot be comfortably read by individuals sitting farthest away from the presentation screen. If something cannot be read by the audience for whom it was intended, it has no purpose on your chart.

Font styles

Excel offers an endless combination of text formatting options. As with text in Microsoft Word or PowerPoint, you may choose any color and style you wish. For example, from **TEXT OPTIONS**, you may add shadows, reflections, glows, soft edges, and 3-D formatting and rotation to a chart's text elements. These formatting options do not add value to data displays. They usually make text more difficult, not easier, to read. Keep text formatting simple. Use bold or italicized text for emphasis. Don't underline text for emphasis; underlined text typically indicates a web link. Font size also may be used to add emphasis; for example, chart titles can be presented in a larger font than the other chart text.

Color

Chart colors should be selected purposefully. Excel 2013 offers 29 built-in themes. Themes are combinations of colors, fonts, and effects. Unless you've changed your settings, new Excel workbooks will open with the default Office theme. Charts created in the workbook will adopt the features defined by the theme. You will need to customize most of your charts to some degree, so don't belabor the theme choice. Select one that appeals to you or work with the default Office theme.

Changing Workbook Themes

1. Themes are found on the **PAGE LAYOUT** tab.

2. Expand the **Themes** menu (see Figure 5.48) and select one. This will change the look and feel of all elements in the workbook.

Keeping with the guiding principle of simplicity in chart presentation, eliminate most colors from your charts. Specifically, opt for white or transparent chart backgrounds and plot areas and use black for most text elements. Choose one color palette for all charts in the same report or presentation.

Figure 5.48 Microsoft Office Themes menu

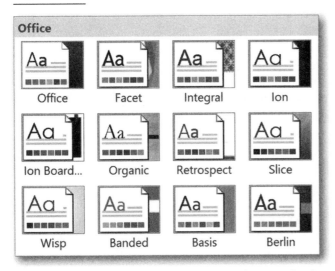

Color of the bars, lines, and slices of pie

Specific color options may be defined by your school or organization's guidelines. If the choice is up to you, select clear, fully saturated colors for the bars, columns, lines, and slices of pie in your charts. Avoid pastel colors because they neither print nor project well.

For single-series charts, it is customary to use the same color for all of the bars and columns. Multiseries charts require either different colors or different hues of the same color for the different series (see Figure 5.49).

Figure 5.49 Multiseries column chart, series colored differently

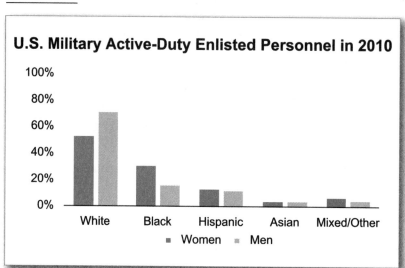

Choose a solid fill color for bars, columns, and slices of pie. Avoid gradients, textures, pictures, and pattern fills. These options along with shadows, glows, and soft edges detract from rather than improve on the appearance of charts and make it more difficult to focus on the data. To add emphasis to one data point, change the color of a particular bar or column so that it contrasts with the other bars or columns (see Figure 5.50).

Adding Emphasis to One Data Point

1. Click once on the data series; click again on the specific bar or column you wish to emphasize.

2. Right-click and choose a new color from the **Fill** menu (see Figure 5.51).

Contrasting colors can also be used effectively to differentiate groups of bars or columns. Recall that in Figure 5.24 we alternated the colors of each pair of columns so that they would stand out and be easier to read. This can be accomplished using the same procedure as adding emphasis to one data point.

Figure 5.50 Single-series bar chart using alternate color to emphasize one data point

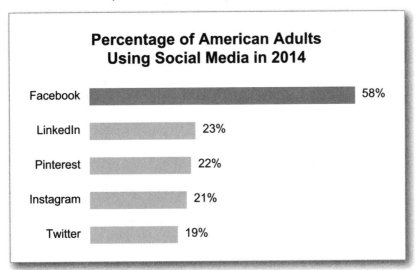

That is, select the columns you wish to change and select a new fill color from the **Format Data Point** menu.

Bars and columns filled with solid, fully saturated colors do not need outlines. If you find that your chart's bars or columns appear to need an outline, it may be an indication that the fill color you have chosen does not contrast well against the chart background. Try selecting a different fill color. If you find that you still need an outline, opt for a thin (¼ or ½ point) outline that is a shade or two darker than the columns' fill color.

Chart Templates

After you have formatted your chart so that the colors, fonts, and other styles are to your liking, you should save your formatted chart as a template. This will expedite the process of creating new charts in the future.

Figure 5.51 Format Data Point menu

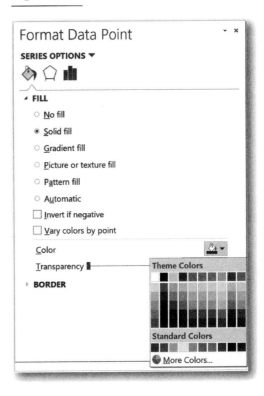

Figure 5.52 Save as Template option

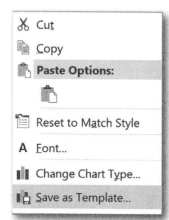

Creating Chart Templates

1. Right-click on your formatted chart.

2. Select **Save as Template** (see Figure 5.52).

3. Give the chart a name. Click **Save**. Do not change the default location; chart templates must be saved in the application's **Templates** folder.

Using a Custom Chart Template

1. Select the data you wish to chart.

2. From the **INSERT** tab, click on **Recommended Charts**.

3. From the **All Charts** tab, click on the **Templates** folder (see Figure 5.53).

4. Select the chart you wish to insert and click **OK**.

Figure 5.53 Insert Chart gallery in the Templates folder

Perspective

Excel's bar, column, line, and pie chart galleries all offer a selection of 2-D and 3-D charts. To this point we have consistently directed you to choose 2-D charts. Recall that our purpose is to create clear visual depictions of data that will help readers see patterns, anomalies, and other important trends. Adding a third dimension to the visualization does nothing to move us toward that goal. Three-dimensional charts create difficulties for our eyes and brains. To process the chart information we must take into account the depth of field.

Figure 5.54 is a 3-D pie chart. The front wedge of pie, representing the proportion of students in a special program who transferred to UC San Diego, is the same as those who transferred to UC Berkeley. Because the UC San Diego wedge of pie is in the front position, it appears larger than the UC Berkeley wedge. The optical effect created by rendering the chart in 3-D accomplishes the opposite of the intended outcome: it obfuscates rather than enhances understanding of the underlying data. The same is true of other 3-D charts. Figures 5.55 to 5.58 are a selection of 3-D charts. Notice how in each case altering the angle of the x- or y-axis makes it difficult to estimate the values represented by the bars, cylinders, blocks, or ribbon. For this reason 3-D charts should not be considered by serious chart designers.

Figure 5.54 3-D pie chart

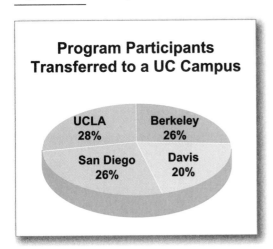

Figure 5.55 3-D bar chart

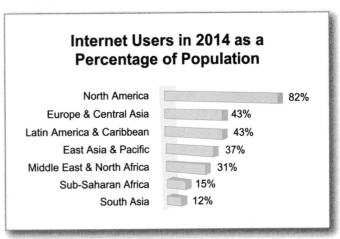

Figure 5.56 3-D clustered column chart

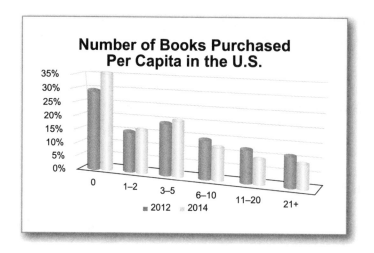

Figure 5.57 3-D column chart

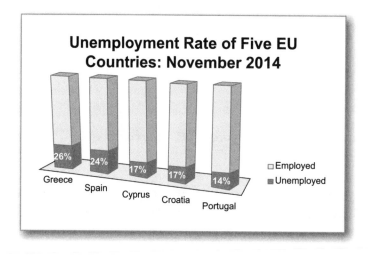

Figure 5.58 3-D line chart

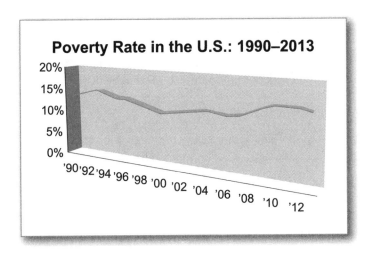

SUMMARY

Many factors require attention when formatting charts. Each element must be afforded careful consideration, resulting in purposeful decisions at every step. Simplicity is key. Eliminate everything that does not contribute to understanding the data represented by the chart. Format the remaining elements so that all text is readable, colors serve a purpose, and axes and data labels provide enough, but not too much, information to interpret the chart. Countless decorative elements may be added to every chart element, for example, shadows, glows, color gradients, and a wide range of 3-D formats—avoid them. You may start with one of Excel's built-in chart styles, but be sure to set aside time to customize the style; none of them will be optimal as they are. Save correctly formatted charts as templates for future use to accelerate future chart creation.

Chart Formatting Checklist

1. Eliminate all unnecessary and redundant information, such as borders, dark background, gridlines, and tick marks on the axes.

2. Include a descriptive chart title containing information about chart contents, units of measurement, and date range represented.

3. Add chart legends for multiseries bar and column charts. Match the position of the legend to the orientation of the data. Use text boxes instead of legends on multiseries line charts. Omit legends from all pie charts; use data labels with category indictors.

4. Format the numbers on axes and data labels to ensure that there is enough information to interpret the data but not too much so as to be distracting.

5. Format dates clearly and with sufficient detail.

6. Choose fonts consciously and limit font types to one or two. Ensure that fonts are large enough to be read by all audience members.

7. Check for and eliminate all overlapping or otherwise unreadable text.

8. Select chart colors purposefully and with restraint. Use color contrast to highlight key data elements.

9. Remove decorations, such as color gradients, 3-D elements, text shadows, glows, or text formatted using Word Art.

10. Save formatted charts for future use.

Preparing Data for Charting

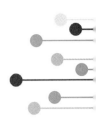

CHAPTER 6

Preparing Data for Charting

We have examined many ways to create informative, visually appealing charts from data already suitable for charting. In this chapter, we discuss getting data to the point where it's ready to be charted. We suggest a few sources of free data, best practices for downloading data, and tips for reviewing and cleaning the data. We'll rely on Excel features and functions to review and organize data and to create summary tables appropriate for chart creation.

Learning Objectives

- Identify data sources

- Clean and organize raw data in preparation for basic analysis and charting

- Build formulas in Excel

- Compute descriptive statistics in Excel

Sources of Free Data

The federal government is the largest producer of data in the United States. There are many offices dedicated to providing free access to its data. Here are a few examples.

1. The U.S. government's open data source, www.data.gov, contains a wealth of data on topics such as agriculture, education, finance, health, weather, and much more.

2. The U.S. Census Bureau, www.census .gov, maintains a large repository of information that may be used. For information about U.S. cities, just enter the name of the city and state to find data about social, economic, household, and demographic statistics. The main website includes an interactive map that displays many economic and

demographic statistics for any town, city, or state in
the United States.

3. At www.sba.gov, you'll find information about business and
   economic conditions. The site includes data on income,
   employment, trade, and manufacturing.

4. At http://fedstats.sites.usa.gov, a full range of official statistics
   produced by the federal government is provided. This website
   is helpful if you don't know which federal agency produces the
   particular data you're seeking. Available data includes topics
   such as economic and population trends, crime, education,
   health care, aviation safety, energy, and farm production.

5. The World Bank, http://data.worldbank.org, provides free and
   open access to data about development in countries around the
   world.

Commercial and nonprofit agencies also make data available for public,
noncommercial use. The following are examples:

1. Pew Internet and the American Life Project (www.pewinternet
   .org)

2. Gallup poll data (www.gallup.com)

3. General Social Survey (www3.norc.org/GSS+Website)

4. Center for Political Studies—University of Michigan (www.isr
   .umich.edu/cps)

Downloading Data

When you find the data that will work for your project, follow the instructions
on the website to download the data to your computer. Most data providers
offer several file types from which to choose. Common file types include Excel
workbooks or worksheets and text files. When deciding on which file format
to use, the main consideration is whether the data have formatting or formulas.
If you download and save your data as an Excel workbook, formatting or
formulas should remain intact. A better option is to save your data as a text file.
This will not preserve formatting and formulas but will omit any macros, data
connections, or potential viruses that may be present in an Excel workbook.

Two common text file formats are CSV and TXT. The difference between the two has to do with which character (referred to as the delimiter) is used to separate the values into columns when opened in Excel. Without a delimiter, all of the data would appear in column A. CSV stands for Comma Separated Values and uses a comma to determine into which column data is placed. TXT files use a tab to determine the data columns. If both file formats are available, choose either one. Be sure to download the data definition file, which is usually separate from the data file. Data labels in the data file can be cryptic and difficult to decipher without the aid of a data dictionary. Additionally, it may not be possible to identify the variable values without the data definitions.

Cleaning Data

The data you download or collect will most likely be a raw form that will need to be cleaned and organized before you are able to analyze it and create charts to visualize the data elements. Follow these steps to prepare your data for charting.

Relabel the variables

The worksheet segment in Figure 6.1 shows data from an online customer satisfaction survey from a department store that imports items from around the world. The survey data were combined with sales data collected from customer receipts. The data export includes two header rows. Row 1 contains the variable number, v1, v2, v3, and so on. Row 2 shows the full text of the survey questions.

Figure 6.1 Unformatted survey data

A1	▼		fx									
	A	B	C	D	E	F	G	H	I	J	K	L
1						V1	V2	V3	V4	V5	V6	V7
2	Responden	GEN	AGE	RACE	INCOME	Overall, ho	How satisfi	How likely	How far do	How much	How many	How many
3	1001	1	95	1	1	2	2	2	9	37	43	8
4	1002	1	45	2	2	1	3	2	7	298	72	9
5	1003	1	69	1	3	1	1	1	23	479	10	4
6	1004	1	67	3	1	1	4	1	24	792	68	16
7	1005	2	77	3	1	2	3	2	27	651	2	17
8	1006	1	58	2	3	1	3	1	29	481	98	7
9	1007	1	60	1	1	2	3	2	16	663	98	0
10	1008	2	75	2	3	1	4	1	28	194	60	19
11	1009	1	53	2	1	2	3	2	11	845	5	7
12	1010	1	60	3	1	2	3	2	19	851	46	20
13	1011	2	56	5	1	1	3	1	25	436	20	3
14	1012	1	63	2	2	2	2	1	19	314	43	4
15	1013	1	60	2	1	2	3	1	16	540	15	5

In this example, row 1 should be deleted; it is unnecessary for our purposes. The text of the questions in the new row 1 is unreadable. The variable labels should be shortened so that the entire label can be read. Equally important, these labels may become the chart titles so it's essential that the labels are concise and informative (see Figure 6.2).

Examine the data

An easy way to examine data in a worksheet is to use the **Filter** on the **DATA** tab. By using the **Filter** we can examine the data values and determine which are likely to be real data and which might be errors in the data set.

Download this data from the textbook companion website.

Improbable values. Clicking on the filter arrow for the Age variable showed respondents who were outside the expected age range, that is, 3, 4, and 5 years old. Although these are possible ages, it is unlikely that young children responded to this survey. At the other end of the spectrum we have respondents who were 99, 107, and 108 years old. Again, these ages are possible but not probable given what we know about the store's customers. When you encounter similar situations you will need to use your judgment and understanding of the survey sample to determine the likelihood that these values represent real individuals. Depending on your project and the purpose of your analysis, you may choose to keep or delete the records.

Figure 6.2 Formatted survey data

	A	B	C	D	E	F	G	H	I	J	K	L
1	ID	Gender	Age	Race/ Ethnicity	Income	Store Satisfaction	Service Satisfaction	Likelihood of Future Purchase	Distance Traveled	Amount Spent	Units Sold	Minutes in Line
2	1001	1	95	1	1	2	2	2	9	37	43	8
3	1002	1	45	2	2	1	3	2	7	298	72	9
4	1003	1	69	1	3	1	1	1	23	479	10	4
5	1004	1	67	3	1	1	4	1	24	792	68	16
6	1005	2	77	3	1	2	3	2	27	651	2	17
7	1006	1	58	2	3	1	3	1	29	481	98	7
8	1007	1	60	1	1	2	3	2	16	663	98	0
9	1008	2	75	2	3	1	4	1	28	194	60	19
10	1009	1	53	2	1	2	3	2	11	845	5	7
11	1010	1	60	3	1	2	3	2	19	851	46	20
12	1011	2	56	5	1	1	3	1	25	436	20	3
13	1012	1	63	2	2	2	2	1	19	314	43	4
14	1013	1	60	2	1	2	3	1	16	540	15	5
15	1014	1	57	2	3	1	3	1	17	881	75	14

Cell reference: A1, fx: ID

Missing values. By clicking on arrows that appear in the column headers you will see all unique values for the variable in the column and missing values (missing values are called **Blanks** in the filter menu); see Figure 6.3.

By deselecting **Select All** and selecting **Blanks** from our Gender variable, we found eight records that were completely blank. These were most likely caused by potential survey respondents who clicked on the survey link and abandoned the survey before answering the first question. These records are unusable because they contain no information. They should be deleted.

It would be inefficient to search for unusable records by filtering on each variable. We need a better approach. To find all incomplete survey responses, we can count the number of nonblank cells in each row of data so that we can sort the data and easily find all incomplete records.

Figure 6.3 Expanded filter menu

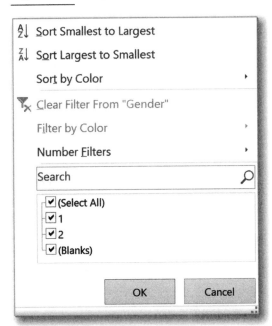

Finding Incomplete Records

1. **Count nonblank cells.** In cell M2, enter *=COUNTA(B2:L2)* (see Figure 6.4). The **COUNTA** function counts the number of cells within a range that are not empty.

2. **Copy the function.** Copy the function in cell M2 down the entire column for every record. Either select the fill handle

If you have not worked with Excel formulas or functions, see Appendix B for an introduction.

Figure 6.4 COUNTA example

M2		fx	=COUNTA(B2:L2)									
	A	B	C	D	E	F	G	H	I	J	K	L	M
1	ID	Gender	Age	Race/Ethnicity	Income	Store Satisfaction	Service Satisfaction	Likelihood of Future Purchase	Distance Traveled	Amount Spent	Units Sold	Minutes in Line	
2	1001	1	95	1	1	2	2	2	9	37	43	8	11
3	1002	1	45	2	2	1	3	2	7	298	72	9	
4	1003	1	69	1	3	1	1	1	23	479	10	4	
5	1004	1	67	3	1	1	4	1	24	792	68	16	
6	1005	2	77	3	1	2	3	2	27	651	2	17	

(bottom right corner of the cell) and drag down to the last row of data or copy (**CTRL+C**), select the range of cells in which to paste the formula, and paste (**CTRL+V**).

3. **Sort.** Sort the entire data range by column M. Select the entire data range. From the **DATA** tab, in the **Sort & Filter** group, click the **Sort** icon. In the **Sort** dialog box, select column M and choose smallest to largest for the order.

4. **Evaluate incomplete records.** Every complete record will have 11 responses. The records with fewer than 11 responses will be sorted to the top. You will have to use your judgment about how to handle incomplete records. Depending on the specifications of your project, you may choose to keep, delete, or replace missing values by imputation, data substitution, or another technique (see Figure 6.5).

Figure 6.5 Survey data with incomplete responses sorted to top

	A	B	C	D	E	F	G	H	I	J	K	L	M
1	ID	Gender	Age	Race/ Ethnicity	Income	Store Satisfaction	Service Satisfaction	Likelihood of Future Purchase	Distance Traveled	Amount Spent	Units Sold	Minutes in Line	
2	1023												0
3	2416												0
4	2836												0
5	3092												0
6	3126												0
7	3168												0
8	3289												0
9	3324												0
10	1329	1											1
11	3101	1	50										2
12	3117	2	55										2
13	3201	2	66										2
14	3345	1	54										2
15	3348	1	64										2
16	1472	2	36	4	3	4		3	23			11	8
17	2675	1	60	1	3	2		1			60	6	8
18	1215	2	61	1	3	1		1	20	663	13		9
19	1246	1	61	1	2	1	3		28	332		7	9
20	3275	1	69	3	3	3			1	752	93	19	9
21	3147	2	90	2	3	2	3		7	495	39	20	10
22	3183	1	55	1	2	1	3		13	952	44	3	10
23	1001	1	95	1	1	2	2	2	9	37	43	8	11
24	1002	1	45	2	2	1	3	2	7	298	72	9	11
25	1003	1	69	1	3	1	1	1	23	479	10	4	11

Summarize the Data

Although our data is cleaned, we're not yet ready to create charts. We're still faced with more than 2,000 rows of data. We need to create summary tables that will serve as the sources for the charts and final report tables.

You may want to start the analysis by looking at the demographics of the survey respondents. We'll start by creating a table showing the number of male and female respondents. Before we start, we need to consult our data dictionary to look up which gender is represented by 1 and which by 2. According to our data dictionary, females are 1 and males are 2. We could create the summary table on the same worksheet as our data, but it's a better idea to create the table on a new worksheet within the same workbook. This results in a more organized workbook. For example, you could rename the first tab *Data* and the second *Summary*. Insert a blank worksheet for the summary table.

Creating a simple summary table

1. In the new worksheet, lay out the table as shown in Figure 6.6.

    a. Use the **COUNTIF** function in column C to count the number of respondents for each gender. The **COUNTIF** function counts the number of instances of a particular value in a range of cells. The syntax is *=COUNTIF(range,criteria)*, where range is the range of cells that contain the data to be counted and criteria is the condition that must be met to count a specific value.

Another way to copy formulas into cells is to double-click the fill handle (bottom right corner of the cell). Excel will determine the range of cells into which the formula should be pasted. Always scroll down the worksheet to confirm that the correct cell range was chosen for the fill function.

*The **COUNTA** function counts the number of nonempty cells in a range. For example, it will count text, formulas, dates, and numbers. Similar functions that are also useful are **COUNT** and **COUNTBLANKS**. **COUNT** counts the number of cells in a range that contain numbers. **COUNTBLANKS** counts the number of empty cells in a range.*

Figure 6.6 Summary table layout

	A	B	C	D	E
1	Code	Gender	Count	%	
2		1 Female			
3		2 Male			

b. In our example, the range of cells that contains the data to be counted is column B in our survey data, which is where the gender variable is stored. Our criteria is either a 1 (Female) or 2 (Male). We could type a 1 or 2 directly into the formula or link the formula to the values in column A (see Figure 6.7).

Figure 6.7 COUNTIF function

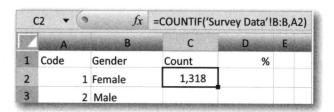

	A	B	C	D	E
1	Code	Gender	Count	%	
2		1 Female	1,318		
3		2 Male			

C2 | fx | =COUNTIF('Survey Data'!B:B,A2)

2. Copy the function in cell C2 to C3 and add a sum to cell C4 to count the total number of respondents. We'll use this sum to calculate the percentage of Female and Male respondents in column D (see Figure 6.8).

Figure 6.8 Final summary table

	A	B	C	D	E	F	G
1	Code	Gender	Count	%		FORMULAS: Column C	Column D
2		1 Female	1,318	58%		=COUNTIF('Survey Data'!B:B,A2)	=C2/C4
3		2 Male	942	42%		=COUNTIF('Survey Data'!B:B,A3)	=C3/C4
4		**Total**	**2,260**	**100%**		=SUM(C2:C3)	=(C4/C4)

3. Repeat this process for each of the variables in the data set.

Creating a complex summary table

Because there were only two values for gender in our data set, it was easy to look at our data dictionary and manually enter the labels associated with each value in our table. When there are more than a few values, it is more efficient to use a function to look up the label associated with each value. Let's build a table summarizing respondents by race/ethnicity to explore this option. The first thing we need to do is identify all of the possible values for race/ethnicity that exist in our data set. We could use the filter feature to see a list of every unique value, but that's cumbersome when there are more than just a few values. The **Remove Duplicates** feature is a more efficient way to do this.

Removing Duplicates

1. Select the column in the data set that contains the race/ethnicity values (column D).

2. Copy the column and paste it into a new, blank worksheet or an empty column in the existing worksheet that is at least a couple of columns away from the data set.

3. From the **DATA** tab, in the **Data Tools** group, select **Remove Duplicates**.

4. Click **OK** in the **Remove Duplicates** dialog box (see Figure 6.9).

Figure 6.9 Remove Duplicates dialog box

5. You'll be left with a list of every unique value that existed in the original column. You can now cut and paste this list onto the summary sheet so that it can be used to build the Race/Ethnicity summary table.

Remove Duplicates *identifies unique values based on the value in the cell as well as the formatting. For example, if the same date value was listed twice in the range but was formatted differently, say, March 17, 2015, and 03/17/15, Excel would consider those to be different values (even though the underlying date value is the same) and would leave them both in the list. To account for this, ensure that all of the values of a particular variable are formatted the same way.*

To find the label for each race/ethnicity value, we can use the **VLOOKUP** function. **VLOOKUP** can be used to retrieve data from one worksheet and place it into another. In this case, we will look up in the data dictionary the race/ethnicity values that we've copied onto our summary sheet. The syntax for **VLOOKUP** is the following:

=VLOOKUP(lookup_value,table_array,col_index_number,range_lookup)

lookup_value is the value we're looking for. In this example, race/ethnicity codes.

table_array is the range of cells that contain the information we're looking for. In this example, the survey data dictionary.

col_index_number is the column number in the table array that contains the information we're seeking.

range_lookup is either **TRUE** (finds the closest match) or **FALSE** (finds an exact match). In most instances, you will want to select FALSE. Be aware that this is an optional argument, and if you don't specify, the default is TRUE.

Figure 6.10 shows our completed VLOOKUP formula.

Figure 6.10 VLOOKUP example

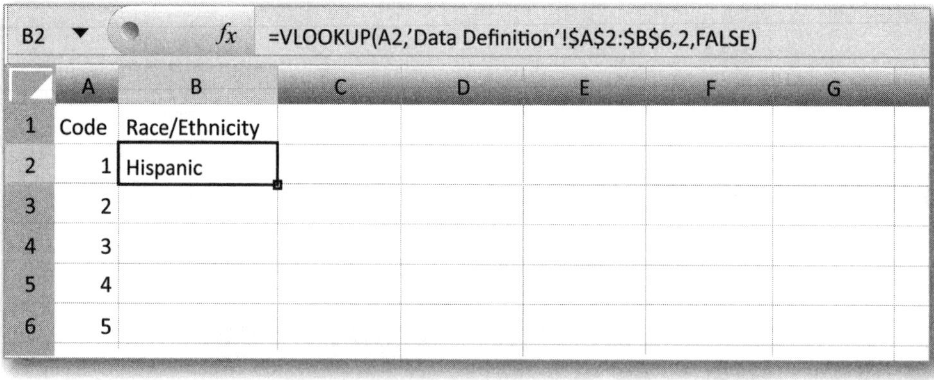

In this example, we've placed the VLOOKUP formula in cell B2 to find the label associated with our race/ethnicity value of 1. The lookup_value is the first race/ethnicity value in cell A2. The range is on our data dictionary worksheet, in cells A2:B6 (see Figure 6.11).

Figure 6.11 Data dictionary range

	A	B	C
1	Race Value	Race Label	
2	1	Hispanic	
3	2	White	
4	3	Black	
5	4	Asian	
6	5	Other	

Notice that we've made the table array an absolute rather than relative reference. This was done so that when we copy this formula down, the range will remain constant as A2:B6.

See Appendix B for a discussion of absolute and relative references.

The **lookup_value** is left as a relative reference so that it changes as we copy the formula down from cell A2, to cell A3, then to A4, and so on. The **column_index_number** is set to 2 because the value we are seeking in our table array is in the second column. Finally, the **range_lookup** argument is set to **FALSE** so that the formula will return an error message if an exact match is not found. This is an important factor to consider. If we had left this argument blank or had set it to TRUE, if an exact match was not found, the next closest label would be returned. For example, if the formula was looking for the value 6, which doesn't exist in our data dictionary, it would return the label for a value of 5. That would be incorrect, so it is better to use the FALSE argument so that the formula returns an error message and the issue can be investigated.

We can copy the VLOOKUP formula from cell B2 down to cell B6 to look up the remaining values (see Figure 6.12).

Figure 6.12 Initial race/ethnicity summary table

	A	B	C	D	E	F	G
	B2 ▼ ●	fx	=VLOOKUP(A2,'Data Definition'!$A$2:$B$6,2,FALSE)				
1	Code	Race/Ethnicity					
2	1	Hispanic					
3	2	White					
4	3	Black					
5	4	Asian					
6	5	Other					

We can now use the **COUNTIF** function, as we did with gender, to get a count of all respondents by race/ethnicity (see Figure 6.13).

Figure 6.13 Completed race/ethnicity summary table

	A	B	C	D	E	F	G	H
1	Code	Race/Ethnicity	Count	%		FORMULAS: Column B	Column C	Column D
2	1	Hispanic	531	24%		'=VLOOKUP(A2,'Data Definition'!$A$2:$B$6,2,FALSE)	'=COUNTIF('Survey Data'!D:D,A2)	'=C2/$C$7
3	2	White	487	22%		'=VLOOKUP(A3,'Data Definition'!$A$2:$B$6,2,FALSE)	'=COUNTIF('Survey Data'!D:D,A3)	'=C3/$C$7
4	3	Black	515	23%		'=VLOOKUP(A4,'Data Definition'!$A$2:$B$6,2,FALSE)	'=COUNTIF('Survey Data'!D:D,A4)	'=C4/$C$7
5	4	Asian	488	22%		'=VLOOKUP(A5,'Data Definition'!$A$2:$B$6,2,FALSE)	'=COUNTIF('Survey Data'!D:D,A5)	'=C5/$C$7
6	5	Other	218	10%		'=VLOOKUP(A6,'Data Definition'!$A$2:$B$6,2,FALSE)	'=COUNTIF('Survey Data'!D:D,A6)	'=C6/$C$7
7		Total	2,239	100%			'=SUM(C2:C6)	'=C7/$C$7

Age is another variable in our survey results data set. There are many ways we can analyze the age variable. We can start by creating a chart of the age distribution. One way to do this is to count the number of respondents by each unique age. We could use some of the functions and processes we discussed earlier.

To start, we need to get a list of each unique age value. We could do this using the **Remove Duplicates** feature as we did when finding all of the unique values for our race/ethnicity variable. Once we have the list of unique age values, we can use the **COUNTIF** function to get a count of respondents by each age so that we can graph to get a picture of the age range of our respondents (see Figure 6.14).

Computing summary statistics

Calculating basic summary statistics is the typical starting point of most data analysis projects. Using the age column in our original data set (not the

Figure 6.14 Age distribution of survey respondents with graph

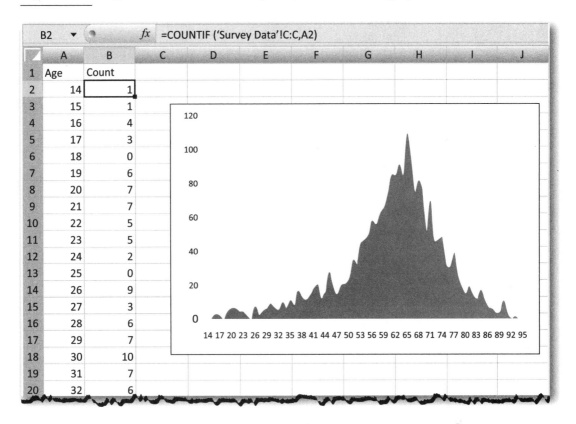

summarized counts of respondents by age described earlier), we can calculate summary statistics such as mean (average), median, and mode. We can use the **AVERAGE** function to calculate the mean.

Place your cursor in an empty worksheet cell.

1. Enter *=Average(B2:B2240).*

2. Press **ENTER**.

3. Repeat steps 1 and 2 for the other summary statistics. The syntax is the same for all:

   =FUNCTION(number1,number2,…)

   AVERAGE returns the mean value from a range of numbers.

   MEDIAN returns the median value from a range of numbers.

MODE.SNGL returns the mode value from a range of numbers.

STDEV.S returns the standard deviation from a range of numbers.

MAX returns the maximum value from a range of numbers.

MIN returns the minimum value from a range of numbers.

Range is another common statistic that you may need to compute. There is no function in Excel for calculating the range so you would need to use the MAX and MIN functions: *=MAX(number1,number2,…)* – *MIN(number1,number2,…)*; see Figure 6.15.

Figure 6.15 Summary statistics

	A	B	C	D	E	F
1	ID	Age		Statistic	Value	FORMULAS: Column E
2	1551	14		Mean	61	=AVERAGE(B2:B2252)
3	3012	15		Median	63	=MEDIAN(B2:B2252)
4	1737	16		Mode	65	=MODE.SNGL(B2:B2252)
5	3083	16		Standard Deviation	13	=STDEV.S(B2:B2252)
6	3264	16		Maximum	95	=MAX(B2:B2252)
7	3343	16		Minimum	14	=MIN(B2:B2252)
8	2660	17		Range	81	=MAX(B2:B2252)-MIN(B2:B2252)
9	3082	17				
10	3307	17				

Another way to analyze the age data is by grouping the ages into ranges. For example, you may want to analyze your data by age grouped into the following categories:

14–19, 20–29, 30–39, 40–49, 50–59, 60–69, 70–79, 80+

*When using **TRUE** as the range_lookup value, the first column in the table_array must be sorted in ascending order.*

To create these groups, create a lookup table. The lookup table should contain each of the age groups you wish to use along with a column that has the age at the low end of each range (see Figure 6.16).

Insert a blank column in the data set that will hold the new age range variable. We're going to use the **VLOOKUP** function to look up the age range for each unique age in our data set. This use of **VLOOKUP** is different from what we described earlier. Recall we said that the **range_lookup** value is almost always FALSE because we want to find an exact match to our lookup. In this example, we don't want an exact match because that would only return the age range for each unique age listed in column A of the lookup table. If we set the **range_lookup** value to **TRUE**, when **VLOOKUP** cannot find an exact match, it will match the largest value that is less than the **lookup_value**. For example, when looking for a match for the age 25, **VLOOKUP** will evaluate the value 20 and identify that it is too small. When it gets to 30 and identifies that it is larger than the **lookup_value** of 25, it will go back to 20 and return the value associated with it (20–29) (see Figure 6.17).

Figure 6.16 Age group lookup table

	A	B
1	Min Value	Age Range
2	14	14–19
3	20	20–29
4	30	30–39
5	40	40–49
6	50	50–59
7	60	60–69
8	70	70–79
9	80	80+

Figure 6.17 VLOOKUP to group age

D2 ▼   *fx*   =VLOOKUP(C2,'AgeGroupLookup'!$A$2:$B$9,2,TRUE)

	A	B	C	D	E	F	G	H
1	ID	Gender	Age	Age Group	Race/ Ethnicity	Income	Store Satisfaction	Service Satisfaction
2	1001	1	95	80+	1	1	2	2
3	1002	1	45	40–49	2	2	1	3
4	1003	1	69	60–69	1	3	1	1
5	1004	1	67	60–69	3	1	1	4
6	1005	2	77	70–79	3	1	2	3
7	1006	1	58	50–59	2	3	1	3
8	1007	1	60	60–69	1	1	2	3
9	1008	2	75	70–79	2	3	1	4
10	1009	1	53	50–59	2	1	2	3
11	1010	1	60	60–69	3	1	2	3
12	1011	2	56	50–59	5	1	1	3
13	1012	1	63	60–69	2	2	2	2
14	1013	1	60	60–69	2	1	2	3
15	1014	1	57	50–59	2	3	1	3
16	1015	2	64	60–69	3	2	1	3

Once each age has been assigned to an age range, you can copy the column with the **VLOOKUP** formulas and paste special, as values. This will replace the **VLOOKUP** formulas with the value it returned. We can use **COUNTIF** to count the number of respondents in each age group (see Figure 6.18).

Figure 6.18 Survey respondent count by age group

B2	▼	fx	=COUNTIF('Survey Data with Age Group'!D:D,A2)		
	A	B	C	D	E	F
1	Age Range	Count				
2	14-19	15				
3	20-29	51				
4	30-39	105				
5	40-49	188				
6	50-59	476				
7	60-69	858				
8	70-79	412				
9	80+	134				

Computing average spent by age group. A function similar to **COUNTIF** is **SUMIF**, which aggregates values in a range based on values in another range. The syntax for SUMIF is the following:

$$=SUMIF(range,criteria,sum\_range)$$

range is the range of cells that contain the data to be evaluated

criteria is the condition that must be met to sum a specific value

sum_range is the range of cells that contain the data to be totaled

We can use **SUMIF** to get a total of how much customers in each age group spent at the store. In our example, the *range* is the column in our survey data that has all of the age groups. The *criteria* is the specific age group to look up in each row. The *sum_range* is the column in our survey data that contains the amount each customer spent. The function in cell C2 looks through column D in the survey data and finds each instance of the 14–19 age group. When it finds one, it goes to column K in the same row and cumulates the total spent (see Figure 6.19).

Figure 6.19 SUMIF example

C2	▼	fx	=SUMIF('Survey Data with Age Group'!D:D,A2,'Survey Data with Age Group'!K:K)

	A	B	C	D	E	F	G	H	I
1	Age Range	Count	Dollars Spent						
2	14–19	15	$7,491						
3	20–29	51	$22,616						
4	30–39	105	$49,700						
5	40–49	188	$90,842						
6	50–59	476	$231,360						
7	60–69	858	$414,005						
8	70–79	412	$219,675						
9	80+	134	$68,214						

We now want to calculate the average amount spent for each age group. We can do that in two ways. The simplest way is to divide the dollars spent by the number of customers in each age group (see Figure 6.20).

Figure 6.20 Average dollars spent

D2	▼	fx	=C2/B2

	A	B	C	D
1	Age Range	Count	Dollars Spent	Average Spent
2	14-19	15	$7,491	$499.40
3	20-29	51	$22,616	$443.45
4	30-39	105	$49,700	$473.33
5	40-49	188	$90,842	$483.20
6	50-59	476	$231,360	$486.05
7	60-69	858	$414,005	$482.52
8	70-79	412	$219,675	$533.19
9	80+	134	$68,214	$509.06

If we didn't already have the customer count and dollars spent, we could calculate the average for each group by using the **AVERAGEIF** function. It works the same way as **SUMIF**, but it averages rather than aggregates the data (see Figure 6.21).

Figure 6.21 AVERAGEIF example

| D2 | ▼ | *fx* | =AVERAGEIF('Survey Data with Age Group'!D:D,A2,'Survey Data with Age Group'!K:K) |

	A	B	C	D	E	F	G	H	I	J
1	Age Range	Count	Dollars Spent	Average Spent						
2	14–19	15	$7,491	$499.40						
3	20–29	51	$22,616	$443.45						
4	30–39	105	$49,700	$473.33						
5	40–49	188	$90,842	$483.20						
6	50–59	476	$231,360	$486.05						
7	60–69	858	$414,005	$482.52						
8	70–79	412	$219,675	$533.19						
9	80+	134	$68,214	$509.06						

Creating a crosstab. Now let's use the same methods to get a count of responses to our store satisfaction question. Survey participants were asked to rate their satisfaction with the store on a scale from 1 (Very Dissatisfied) to 5 (Very Satisfied) (see Figure 6.22).

Figure 6.22 Survey respondent count by satisfaction

| C2 | ▼ | *fx* | =COUNTIF('Survey Data'!F:F,A2) |

	A	B	C	D
1	Code	Store Satisfaction	Count	
2	1	Very Dissatisfied	15	
3	2	Dissatisfied	67	
4	3	Neutral	163	
5	4	Satisfied	995	
6	5	Very Satisfied	1,014	

We'd like to determine if satisfaction with the store varied by gender of the respondent. To do this, we need to create a new variable in our data that combines the gender of the survey participant with his or her store satisfaction score. This will allow us to identify each unique combination of gender and store satisfaction. Use the ampersand (&) to concatenate the values from columns B (Gender) and C (Satisfaction) (see Figure 6.23).

Figure 6.23 Survey data with concatenated gender and satisfaction score

	A	B	C	D
			fx	=B2&C2
1	ID	Gender	Store Satisfaction	Gender & Satisfaction
2	1001	1	4	14
3	1002	1	5	15
4	1003	1	5	15
5	1004	1	5	15
6	1005	2	4	24
7	1006	1	5	15
8	1007	1	4	14
9	1008	2	5	25

Column C now contains a variable that we can use to look up the count. By including the codes for gender and satisfaction in our table, we were able to use them to count (see Figure 6.24).

Because there were more female than male customers, it's difficult to tell if there are differences in the satisfaction responses. A better way to look at this would be to chart the responses by proportion of each gender (see Figure 6.25).

We are describing how to accomplish these tasks using Excel's functions and formulas. This is useful instruction as functions and formulas can be applied to a wide variety of data sets. In Chapter 7 we illustrate how many of these tasks can be accomplished using Excel's pivot tables.

Figure 6.24 Summary table by gender and satisfaction score

C3 ▼ ●	fx	=COUNTIF('Survey Data Sat by Gender'!D:D,C$1&$A3)			

	A	B	C	D	E	F
1			1	2		
2	Code	Satisfaction	Female	Male		
3	1	Very Dissatisfied	9	6		
4	2	Dissatisfied	42	25		
5	3	Neutral	83	80		
6	4	Satisfied	572	423		
7	5	Very Satisfied	608	406		

Figure 6.25 Column chart: Store satisfaction by gender

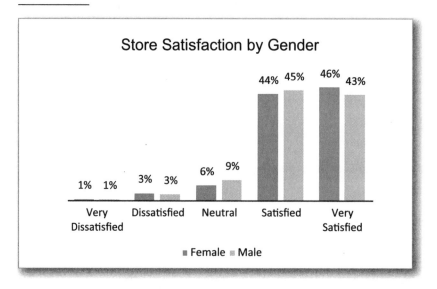

To simplify the view of the satisfaction data, we can reduce the number of categories by combining Very Dissatisfied with Dissatisfied and Very Satisfied with Satisfied. If you've already created the summary table with all categories, you can create a new table that is linked to the original (see Figure 6.26).

If you hadn't already created a summary table, you could recode the variable in the data set.

Figure 6.26 Survey respondent count by grouped satisfaction

	A	B	C	D	E	F
			fx	=C2+C3		
	Code	Store Satisfaction	Count		Store Satisfaction	Count
1						
2		1 Very Dissatisfied	15		Dissatisfied	82
3		2 Dissatisfied	67		Neutral	163
4		3 Neutral	163		Satisfied	2,009
5		4 Satisfied	995			2,254
6		5 Very Satisfied	1,014			
7			2,254			

Recoding Variables

1. Copy the original column of data and paste it into a new column. This preserves the original for alternate uses.

2. In the new column, use the **Find & Select** feature (**HOME > Editing > Find & Select > Replace**) and replace the 2s with 1s, the 3s with 2s, and the 4s and 5s with 3s. The result should be Dissatisfied=1, Neutral=2, Satisfied=3.

3. Alternately, you could use the **VLOOKUP** function (as described earlier) to look up the recoded values.

Identifying respondents based on a criterion. In our next example, we want to identify the customers who spent more than $300 so that we can send them a coupon. This can be accomplished with the **IF** function. In the data sheet, create a new column titled "Coupon." The syntax for the **IF** statement is the following:

=IF(logical_test,value_if_true, value_if_false)

logical_test is any value or expression that can be evaluated as true or false

value_if_true is the value returned if the logical test is true

value_if_false is the value returned if the logical test is false

In this example, our logical test is whether or not the customer spent more than $300. If the customer did, we want to put a "Yes" in this column, if not, a "No" (see Figure 6.27). We can then sort or filter by this column to identify all of the customers who should receive a coupon.

Figure 6.27 IF example

	C2	▼ ●	fx	=IF(B2>300,"YES","NO")	
	A	B	C	D
1	ID	Amount Spent	Coupon	
2	1001	37	No	
3	1002	298	No	
4	1003	479	Yes	
5	1004	792	Yes	
6	1005	651	Yes	
7	1006	481	Yes	

Let's say we wanted to send the coupons by e-mail to the customers, and we'd like to address each e-mail message using the customer's first name. We have the customers' first and last names in column D (see Figure 6.28). We can use Excel's **Text to Columns** feature to separate our customer first names from the last names. This feature takes a text string in one column and separates it into multiple columns. Before you begin, make sure there is a blank column to the right of the column with the name because Excel will leave the first name in column D and move the last name to column E.

Converting Text to Columns

1. Select the column of names.

2. From the **DATA** tab, in the **Data Tools** group, click **Text to Columns**.

3. The **Text to Columns Wizard** will open (see Figure 6.29).

Figure 6.28 Customer name before Text to Columns

	A	B	C	D
	D1 ▾		fx	Name
1	ID	Amount Spent	Coupon	Name
2	1001	37	No	SOPHIA SHARP
3	1002	298	No	EMMA CARTER
4	1003	479	Yes	OLIVIA BURNS
5	1004	792	Yes	ISABELLA WIGGINS
6	1005	651	Yes	AVA HANSEN
7	1006	481	Yes	MIA PEARSON

Figure 6.29 Text to Columns Wizard

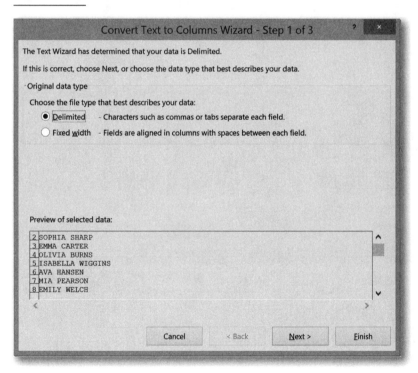

4. Choose the type of file that describes your data. **Delimited** data are separated by a character (such as a comma, tab, or space) between the text items to be separated. Select the **Fixed width** radio button if you're separating a text string at the same point in each row of data. For example, you may want to separate after the third and eighth character. In our example, **Delimited** is the correct choice because there is a space between the first and last names. Select **Delimited** and click **Next**.

5. In the second step of the Wizard, select **Space** and deselect all other options. A preview of the results will appear in the preview pane (see Figure 6.30).

Figure 6.30 Text to Columns Wizard, step 2

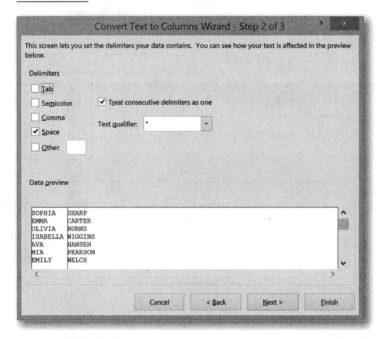

6. Click **Next**.

7. Click **Finish**.

The first names should appear in column D and the last names in column E (see Figure 6.31). This worked well for our example because all of our data had one first name followed by a space that was followed by one last name. If some of our examples included a middle name or a last name with spaces, the results may have been spread over three or more columns.

Figure 6.31 Customer name after Text to Columns

	A	B	C	D	E
	D2 ▼ ●		fx	SOPHIA	
1	ID	Spent	Coupon		
2	1001	37	No	SOPHIA	SHARP
3	1002	298	No	EMMA	CARTER
4	1003	479	Yes	OLIVIA	BURNS
5	1004	792	Yes	ISABELLA	WIGGINS
6	1005	651	Yes	AVA	HANSEN
7	1006	481	Yes	MIA	PEARSON

Notice that our customer names are all in upper case. For our coupon e-mail, it would be better to have just the first letter capitalized. Excel has several functions that manipulate text, and one of them does just what we need. The **PROPER** function converts a text string to proper case—the first letter in each word in upper case and all other letters in lower case (see Figure 6.32).

Related to the **PROPER** function are the **UPPER** (converts a text string to all upper case) and **LOWER** (converts a text string to all lower case) functions. Use the same syntax as for **PROPER** to convert text to upper or lower case.

Figure 6.32 PROPER example

	A	B	C	D	E	F	G
	F2 ▼ ●		fx	=PROPER(D2)			
1	ID	Spent	Coupon				
2	1001	37	No	SOPHIA	SHARP	Sophia	Sharp
3	1002	298	No	EMMA	CARTER	Emma	Carter
4	1003	479	Yes	OLIVIA	BURNS	Olivia	Burns
5	1004	792	Yes	ISABELLA	WIGGINS	Isabella	Wiggins
6	1005	651	Yes	AVA	HANSEN	Ava	Hansen
7	1006	481	Yes	MIA	PEARSON	Mia	Pearson

Creating a Dynamic Summary Table

Each record in our survey data is associated with a manager who is responsible for the store visited by the customer. In some instances, it may be helpful to look at only responses related to each store manager. In this next example, we're going to create a dynamic way to view store satisfaction results for each manager.

Creating a Dynamic Summary Table

1. First we will create a lookup variable in our data set that we can use in our summary table. In our data set, the store manager name is located in column B and the store satisfaction score is in column C. Create a concatenated text string from these two columns to use as a lookup table. Use the ampersand (&) to combine the values from columns B and C (see Figure 6.33).

2. Use the new variable to count store satisfaction by store manager in the summary table. Use the **COUNTIF** function as we did before to combine the store manager name with the code for the satisfaction score (see Figure 6.34).

Figure 6.33 Survey data with concatenated manager and satisfaction score

	A	B	C	D
		fx	=B2&C2	
1	ID	Store Manager	Store Satisfaction	Manager & Satisfaction
2	1001	AGNES RUCKER	4	AGNES RUCKER4
3	1002	WALLACE INOUYE	5	WALLACE INOUYE5
4	1003	KAMILA JAMISON	5	KAMILA JAMISON5
5	1004	ELIANA GOEL	5	ELIANA GOEL5
6	1005	KAMILA JAMISON	4	KAMILA JAMISON4
7	1006	ALYSSA EDWARDS	5	ALYSSA EDWARDS5

Figure 6.34 Summary table of store satisfaction for one manager

			fx	=COUNTIF('Survey Data Sat by Manager'!D:D,$C$2&A5)
C5	▼	●		

	A	B	C	D	E
1					
2		Store Manager:	ALYSSA EDWARDS		
3					
4	Code	Store Satisfaction	Count		
5	1	Very Dissatisfied	0		
6	2	Dissatisfied	10		
7	3	Neutral	12		
8	4	Satisfied	115		
9	5	Very Satisfied	82		
10			219		

3. Now, whenever we enter a store manager name in cell C2, the data in our summary table are updated to reflect that manager's scores.

We could leave the summary table as is, but entering each manager's name manually is a cumbersome process. A better solution would be to create an interactive drop-down menu in cell C2. This can be done using Excel's **Data Validation** feature.

Creating a Drop-Down List

1. Create a unique list of every store manager in the data. Do this by copying the column of store manager names from the survey data into the worksheet holding the summary table and using the **Remove Duplicates** feature.

2. Select cell C2 and choose **Data Validation. DATA > Data Tools > Data Validation.**

3. In the **Data Validation** dialog menu, select **List** from the **Allow** drop-down, and in the **Source**, select the cell range

of store managers' names (see Figure 6.35). In our example, we've pasted the list of unique manager names in cells M3:M12 on the same sheet as our summary table.

4. Click **OK**.

5. Now when you select cell C2, a drop-down arrow appears that can be expanded to choose one of the store managers (see Figure 6.36).

6. From here you could create a chart based on the data in B4:C9. Then each time a new manager name is selected from the drop-down, the summary table and the chart would be updated.

Figure 6.35 Data Validation dialog box

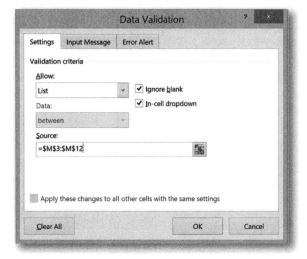

Figure 6.36 Interactive manager list

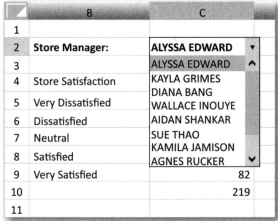

Subtotal

Many data summaries include totals as a way of providing an overview of the variables. In the following example showing employees, their departments, and their salaries, we would like to compute the total amount spent on salaries by department and for the entire company (see Figure 6.37).

One option is to use the **SUM** function for this task. In the following example, the **SUM** function was used to add subtotals and a grand total to a list of employee salaries (see Figure 6.38).

Figure 6.37 Employee salary list

	A	B	C	D
1	**Employee ID**	**Employee Name**	**Department**	**Salary**
2	31977	William Streett	Accounting	71,023
3	69879	Jason Smith	Accounting	77,062
4	79732	Michael Wade	Accounting	77,235
5	78692	Zeke Griffin	Accounting	71,596
6	15144	Mazdak Mazarei	Marketing	98,156
7	64096	Kate Klaire	Marketing	67,027
8	51825	Nikki Magel	Marketing	78,370
9	35104	Christina Mount	HR	84,711
10	70881	Toni Moreno	HR	61,995
11	91941	Jaycee Toups	HR	80,282
12	43199	Jacob Yang	Sales	78,442
13	86489	Jennifer Hunt	Sales	73,128
14	61661	Gabby Griffin	Sales	65,618
15	92509	Isabel Montilla	Sales	64,735
16	68667	Karen Cowe	Sales	79,124
17	13045	Joe Roybal	Sales	64,934

Using this method, the grand total is wrong. It's twice as much as it should be because it includes each employee's salary plus the salary subtotal for each department. To avoid this, use the **SUBTOTAL** function to compute the total by department and a grand total without double counting the subtotals (see Figure 6.39). The syntax for **SUBTOTAL** is the following:

=SUBTOTAL(function_num, ref1, ref2,…)

function_num is the number from 1 to 11 that identifies which summary function will be used (e.g., use 9 for sum, 1 for average, 2 for count)

ref1 is the value or range to subtotal

Figure 6.38 Employee salary list using SUM

	A	B	C	D	E
1	Employee ID	Employee Name	Department	Salary	FORMULAS: Column D
2	31977	William Streett	Accounting	71,023	
3	69879	Jason Smith	Accounting	77,062	
4	79732	Michael Wade	Accounting	77,235	
5	78692	Zeke Griffin	Accounting	71,596	
6			Total Accounting	296,916	---> =SUM(D2:D5)
7	15144	Mazdak Mazarei	Marketing	98,156	
8	64096	Kate Klaire	Marketing	67,027	
9	51825	Nikki Magel	Marketing	78,370	
10			Total Marketing	243,553	---> =SUM(D7:D9)
11	35104	Christina Mount	HR	84,711	
12	70881	Toni Moreno	HR	61,995	
13	91941	Jaycee Toups	HR	80,282	
14			Total HR	226,988	---> =SUM(D10:D13)
15	43199	Jacob Yang	Sales	78,442	
16	86489	Jennifer Hunt	Sales	73,128	
17	61661	Gabby Griffin	Sales	65,618	
18	92509	Isabel Montilla	Sales	64,735	
19	68667	Karen Cowe	Sales	79,124	
20	13045	Joe Roybal	Sales	64,934	
21			Total Sales	425,981	---> =SUM(D15:D20)
22			Grand Total	2,386,876	---> =SUM(D2:D21)

Figure 6.39 Employee salary list using SUBTOTAL

	A	B	C	D	E
1	Employee ID	Employee Name	Department	Salary	FORMULAS: Column D
2	31977	William Streett	Accounting	71,023	
3	69879	Jason Smith	Accounting	77,062	
4	79732	Michael Wade	Accounting	77,235	
5	78692	Zeke Griffin	Accounting	71,596	
6			Total Accounting	296,916	---> =SUBTOTAL(9,D2:D5)
7	15144	Mazdak Mazarei	Marketing	98,156	
8	64096	Kate Klaire	Marketing	67,027	
9	51825	Nikki Magel	Marketing	78,370	
10			Total Marketing	243,553	---> =SUBTOTAL(9,D7:D9)
11	35104	Christina Mount	HR	84,711	
12	70881	Toni Moreno	HR	61,995	
13	91941	Jaycee Toups	HR	80,282	
14			Total HR	226,988	---> =SUBTOTAL(9,D10:D13)
15	43199	Jacob Yang	Sales	78,442	
16	86489	Jennifer Hunt	Sales	73,128	
17	61661	Gabby Griffin	Sales	65,618	
18	92509	Isabel Montilla	Sales	64,735	
19	68667	Karen Cowe	Sales	79,124	
20	13045	Joe Roybal	Sales	64,934	
21			Total Sales	425,981	---> =SUBTOTAL(9,D15:D20)
22			Grand Total	1,193,438	---> =SUBTOTAL(9,D2:D21)

SUMMARY

In this chapter we discussed several sources for free, readily available data that can be downloaded as Excel or text files. These data sets often include thousands of records and will require cleaning and organization before using. It's advisable to review an unfamiliar data set for missing or improbable values. We showed how to use some of Excel's features and functions to review and analyze data. We also used functions to calculate statistics and create summary tables that can be used for creating charts.

Data Preparation Checklist

1. Download data and associated data definition files when appropriate.

2. Organize and clean data, relabel variables as necessary, and look for impossible and improbable values. Decide how to handle missing data.

3. Analyze and summarize data for charting using Excel functions.

Excel Features

- Remove Duplicates: removes duplicate values from a selected range

- Text to Columns: separates string of text into multiple columns

- Data Validation: can be used to create interactive drop-down lists

Excel Functions

- COUNT: counts the number of cells within a range containing numbers

- COUNTA: counts the number of nonblank cells within a range

- IF: returns a value depending on the result of a true/false condition

- COUNTIF: counts the number of cells meeting a given condition

- SUMIF: aggregates the values in a range of cells meeting a given condition

- AVERAGEIF: finds the mean of values in a range of cells meeting a given condition

- VLOOKUP: returns a value from a range based on a lookup value

- AVERAGE: returns the mean of a range of numbers

- MEDIAN: returns the median of a range of numbers

- MODE.SNGL: returns the mode of a range of numbers

- STDEV.S: calculates the standard deviation based on a sample

- MAX: returns the largest number in a range of numbers

- MIN: returns the smallest number in a range of numbers

- PROPER: converts a string of text to proper case

- UPPER: converts a string of text to upper case

- LOWER: converts a string of text to lower case

- SUBTOTAL: returns the subtotal of a range of numbers

Pivot Tables and Pivot Charts

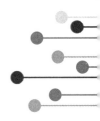

In the previous chapter we examined how to use many of Excel's features and functions to review, analyze, and summarize data. In this chapter we explore Excel's powerful pivot table feature and see how it is useful for data exploration, analysis, and summary. We'll also look at pivot charts, which offer an easy way to create interactive charts.

Introduction to Pivot Tables

Pivot tables can be thought of as dynamic, interactive summary data reports. They can be used to quickly summarize large data sets. Frequency distributions and crosstab reports allow users to review and analyze data quickly and efficiently. The ability to filter, slice, and group data dynamically is a key feature of pivot tables.

Pivot tables exist within an Excel workbook and can be linked to data within the same workbook or from another workbook or data source. Although the pivot table is linked to the data source, it doesn't automatically update if changes are made to the data source. However, there is an easy way to refresh the pivot table and ensure that it's displaying the most recent data available. Before getting too far into how to use pivot tables, let's look at a simple example (see Figure 7.1).

Learning Objectives

- Describe Excel's pivot tables and charts

- Identify data appropriate for pivot tables

- Create and modify pivot tables

- Create pivot charts

Figure 7.1 Simple pivot table

	A	B	C	D	E	F	G
1	Year	2015 ▾					
2							
3	**Sum of Sales**	**Column Labels** ▾					
4	**Row Labels** ▾	**Chocolate Chip**	**Gingerbread**	**Oatmeal**	**Peanut Butter**	**Sugar**	**Grand Total**
5	Jan	604,602	508,381	318,013	484,669	138,252	2,053,916
6	Feb	729,558	454,771	392,419	468,095	116,953	2,161,796
7	Mar	593,967	274,244	461,265	561,251	161,327	2,052,054
8	Apr	770,528	447,281	524,242	451,121	123,038	2,316,210
9	May	731,828	516,513	408,848	593,628	114,630	2,365,448
10	Jun	554,481	612,007	324,275	465,954	108,064	2,064,780
11	Jul	554,924	484,078	441,084	481,556	144,315	2,105,957
12	Aug	710,708	429,455	433,768	364,454	117,829	2,056,215
13	Sep	914,353	475,284	443,733	411,943	123,693	2,369,006
14	Oct	762,408	565,890	507,980	774,104	165,500	2,775,882
15	Nov	1,323,457	985,276	540,049	642,632	165,276	3,656,690
16	Dec	1,374,256	1,014,311	596,121	704,052	153,616	3,842,356
17	**Grand Total**	**9,625,070**	**6,767,491**	**5,391,796**	**6,403,458**	**1,632,494**	**29,820,310**

Figure 7.2 Pivot table filter

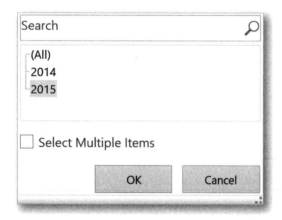

Search   🔍

(All)
2014
2015

☐ Select Multiple Items

OK   Cancel

This pivot table summarizes sales from a chain of stores that sells cookies. The year is shown in cell B1 and has a filter icon next to it. By clicking on the icon, a user can select a different year for the report (see Figure 7.2).

The months are listed in cells A5 to A16 and are titled "Row Labels." The drop-down menu next to the row labels allows users to filter and select specific months (see Figure 7.3).

Likewise, the column labels in row 4 list the types of cookies sold and are also able to be filtered. Totals by month (column G) and by cookie (row 17) are listed as a grand total for all months and all cookies.

The word *pivot* means to rotate or revolve. Pivot tables allow you to rotate data so that you may view it from many perspectives. In Figure 7.4, the rows and columns have been rotated so that the months of the year are in columns and cookie type is in rows.

Organizing Data for Pivot Tables

••

Although pivot tables can be populated from an external database or other source, it's easiest to create and maintain them based on data stored in an Excel workbook range or table. The data should be arranged with every column containing a unique variable (see Figure 7.5).

In Figure 7.5, the four columns of data each contain a unique variable: City, State, Product, and Units Sold. Each row contains a unique combination of the variables. For example, there is only one row that describes sugar cookie sales

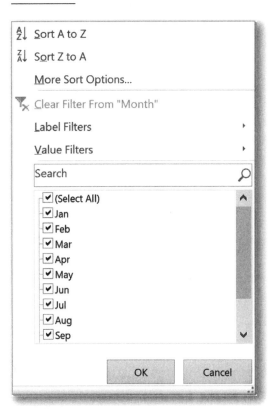

Figure 7.3 Pivot table sort and filter

Figure 7.4 Rotated pivot table

	A	B	C	D	E	F	G	H	I	J	K	L	M	N
1	Year	2015												
2														
3	Sum of Sales	Column Label												
4	Row Labels	Jan	Feb	Mar	Apr	May	Jun	Jul	Aug	Sep	Oct	Nov	Dec	Grand Total
5	Chocolate Chip	604,602	729,558	593,967	770,528	731,828	554,481	554,924	710,708	914,353	762,408	1,323,457	1,374,256	9,625,070
6	Gingerbread	508,381	454,771	274,244	447,281	516,513	612,007	484,078	429,455	475,284	565,890	985,276	1,014,311	6,767,491
7	Oatmeal	318,013	392,419	461,265	524,242	408,848	324,275	441,084	433,768	443,733	507,980	540,049	596,121	5,391,796
8	Peanut Butter	484,669	468,095	561,251	451,121	593,628	465,954	481,556	364,454	411,943	774,104	642,632	704,052	6,403,458
9	Sugar	138,252	116,953	161,327	123,038	114,630	108,064	144,315	117,829	123,693	165,500	165,276	153,616	1,632,494
10	Grand Total	2,053,916	2,161,796	2,052,054	2,316,210	2,365,448	2,064,780	2,105,957	2,056,215	2,369,006	2,775,882	3,656,690	3,842,356	29,820,310

Figure 7.5 Data correctly organized for a pivot table

	A	B	C	D
1	**City**	**State**	**Product**	**Units Sold**
2	Boise	ID	Chocolate Chip	457,097
3	Boise	ID	Gingerbread	372,334
4	Boise	ID	Oatmeal	284,777
5	Boise	ID	Peanut Butter	284,281
6	Boise	ID	Sugar	99,391
7	Pocatello	ID	Chocolate Chip	217,499
8	Pocatello	ID	Gingerbread	172,385
9	Pocatello	ID	Oatmeal	121,363
10	Pocatello	ID	Peanut Butter	189,610

in Boise, Idaho. Figure 7.6 shows the same data arranged in a way that would *not* be appropriate for a pivot table source.

In Figure 7.6, there is a column for city, but columns B:F each contain the same variable—product—just different types. Additionally, this example has totals that should not be included in a pivot table data source.

Figure 7.7 shows another example of a data source laid out incorrectly for a pivot table.

The data shown are the number of cookies sold by month. While this layout may be good for a report, it cannot be used to create a pivot table. To be used in a pivot table, each data label (company, region, product, month) must have its own column and each data value (number of cookies sold) should be in its own row. Figure 7.8 shows the data laid out in the proper way to use as a source for a pivot table. Notice that each row is a unique combination of the data labels.

Figure 7.6 Data incorrectly organized for a pivot table

	A	B	C	D	E	F	G
1	City/State	Chocolate Chip	Gingerbread	Oatmeal	Peanut Butter	Sugar	Total
2	Boise	457,097	372,334	284,777	289,281	99,391	1,502,880
3	Pocatello	217,499	172,385	121,363	189,610	33,202	734,059
4	Twin Falls	383,716	246,435	209,106	264,253	44,894	1,148,404
5	**Total Idaho**	**1,058,312**	**791,154**	**615,246**	**743,144**	**177,487**	**3,385,343**
6							
7	Bozeman	297,688	251,423	183,580	258,133	40,213	1,031,037
8	Missoula	258,636	242,427	150,693	229,453	44,188	925,397
9	**Total Montana**	**556,324**	**493,850**	**334,273**	**487,586**	**84,401**	**1,956,434**
10							
11	Seattle	690,923	576,277	429,040	544,261	113,352	2,353,853
12	Spokane	778,330	452,535	442,613	501,974	112,165	2,287,617
13	Tacoma	475,776	339,210	245,422	363,224	79,812	1,503,444
14	**Total Washington**	**1,945,029**	**1,368,022**	**1,117,075**	**1,409,459**	**305,329**	**6,144,914**
15							
16	Portland	699,625	628,739	421,695	585,610	124,676	2,460,345
17	Salem	514,308	321,068	301,978	398,629	80,349	1,616,332
18	**Total Oregon**	**1,213,933**	**949,807**	**723,673**	**984,239**	**205,025**	**4,076,677**
19							
20	Provo	264,182	164,569	133,943	225,223	42,631	830,548
21	Salt Lake City	731,769	495,674	435,149	410,143	157,154	2,229,889
22	**Total Utah**	**995,951**	**660,243**	**569,092**	**635,366**	**199,785**	**3,060,437**
23							
24	Cheyenne	248,610	219,114	229,480	246,267	49,595	993,066
25	**Total Wyoming**	**248,610**	**219,114**	**229,480**	**246,267**	**49,595**	**993,066**
26							
27	Reno	386,835	241,629	244,208	254,139	66,250	1,193,061
28	**Total Nevada**	**386,835**	**241,629**	**244,208**	**254,139**	**66,250**	**1,193,061**
29							
30	**Total**	**6,404,994**	**4,723,819**	**3,833,047**	**4,760,200**	**1,087,872**	**20,809,932**

Figure 7.7 Data incorrectly organized for a pivot table

	A	B	C	D	E
1	Payette Cookie Company				
2	Northwest Region				
3					
4		Jan	Feb	Mar	Total
5	Chocolate Chip	500	510	520	1,530
6	Gingerbread	400	410	420	1,230
7	Oatmeal	300	310	320	930
8	Peanut Butter	200	210	220	630
9	Sugar	100	110	120	530
10	**Total**	**1,500**	**1,550**	**1,600**	**4,850**

Figure 7.8 Data correctly organized for a pivot table

	A	B	C	D	E
1	Company	Region	Product	Month	Units Sold
2	Payette Cookie Company	Northwest	Chocolate Chip	Jan	500
3	Payette Cookie Company	Northwest	Gingerbread	Jan	400
4	Payette Cookie Company	Northwest	Oatmeal	Jan	300
5	Payette Cookie Company	Northwest	Peanut Butter	Jan	200
6	Payette Cookie Company	Northwest	Sugar	Jan	100
7	Payette Cookie Company	Northwest	Chocolate Chip	Feb	510
8	Payette Cookie Company	Northwest	Gingerbread	Feb	410
9	Payette Cookie Company	Northwest	Oatmeal	Feb	310
10	Payette Cookie Company	Northwest	Peanut Butter	Feb	210
11	Payette Cookie Company	Northwest	Sugar	Feb	110
12	Payette Cookie Company	Northwest	Chocolate Chip	Mar	520
13	Payette Cookie Company	Northwest	Gingerbread	Mar	420
14	Payette Cookie Company	Northwest	Oatmeal	Mar	320
15	Payette Cookie Company	Northwest	Peanut Butter	Mar	220
16	Payette Cookie Company	Northwest	Sugar	Mar	120

Creating a pivot table

There are two main types of data elements used by pivot tables: data values and data labels (or categories). Data values are often aggregated in the pivot table, and data labels are used to describe the data values. For example, a data value could be the number of units sold (as in our previous example) or dollar amount spent, while a data label would describe those data, such as date of sale or location of product sold. When laying out a pivot table, labels are generally used in the row, column, and filter sections while data values comprise the body of the table and are usually aggregated.

To illustrate how to create a pivot table, we'll use an expanded version of the data set we used earlier (see Figure 7.9).

This is a large data set containing 2014 and 2015 daily sales for the chain of cookie stores. The category variables are Date, Year, Month,

Note that Excel has selected the data source range. Although it's likely that the correct range has been selected, you should always check to ensure that the range includes all of the data. You can choose to create the pivot table in a new or existing worksheet. It's good practice to create your pivot table on a new worksheet to help keep your workbook organized.

Figure 7.9 Pivot table data source

	A	B	C	D	E	F	G	H	I
1	Date	Year	Month	Quarter	City	State	Product	Units Sold	Sales Amount
2	01/01/14	2014	Jan	1	Boise	ID	Chocolate Chip	288	573.12
3	11/19/14	2014	Nov	4	Boise	ID	Peanut Butter	161	320.39
4	08/03/14	2014	Aug	3	Tacoma	WA	Peanut Butter	348	692.52
5	06/15/14	2014	Jun	2	Reno	NV	Peanut Butter	465	925.35
6	06/13/14	2014	Jun	2	Pocatello	ID	Oatmeal	38	75.62
7	02/07/14	2014	Feb	1	Spokane	WA	Oatmeal	283	563.17
8	03/05/14	2014	Mar	1	Salem	OR	Sugar	125	248.75
9	09/20/14	2014	Sep	3	Missoula	MT	Chocolate Chip	99	197.01
10	07/25/14	2014	Jul	3	Portland	OR	Peanut Butter	1371	2728.29
11	04/03/14	2014	Apr	2	Salt Lake City	UT	Peanut Butter	574	1142.26
12	08/23/14	2014	Aug	3	Reno	NV	Peanut Butter	96	191.04
13	10/13/14	2014	Oct	4	Cheyenne	WY	Peanut Butter	617	1227.83
14	06/12/14	2014	Jun	2	Missoula	MT	Gingerbread	246	489.54
15	04/08/14	2014	Apr	2	Tacoma	WA	Peanut Butter	235	467.65
16	03/12/14	2014	Mar	1	Salem	OR	Sugar	118	234.82
17	06/13/14	2014	Jun	2	Salt Lake City	UT	Oatmeal	243	483.57
18	08/17/14	2014	Aug	3	Pocatello	ID	Chocolate Chip	393	782.07
19	11/18/14	2014	Nov	4	Cheyenne	WY	Chocolate Chip	48	95.52
20	05/09/14	2014	May	2	Salt Lake City	UT	Peanut Butter	544	1082.56

Quarter, City, State, and Product. The data values are Units Sold and Sales Amount. There are more than 50,000 rows of data, so attempting to analyze this data using Excel's functions and formulas would be time-consuming. Pivot tables are a convenient tool for exploring and analyzing these data.

Creating a Pivot Table

1. To create a new pivot table, from the **INSERT** tab, in the **Tables** group, click on **Pivot Table**.

2. This will open the **Create Pivot Table** dialog box (see Figure 7.10).

3. The shell of the pivot table was created in cell A3 of the new worksheet (see Figure 7.11), and the **Pivot Table Fields** list appears on the right side of the worksheet (see Figure 7.12).

Figure 7.10   Pivot table dialog box

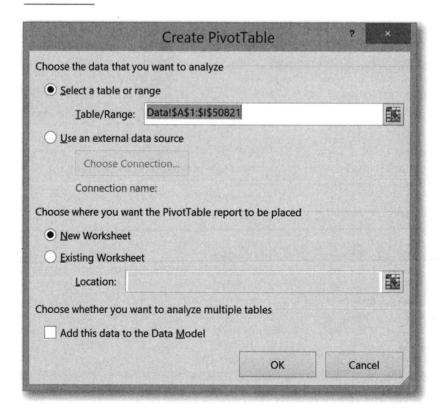

Figure 7.11 Pivot table shell

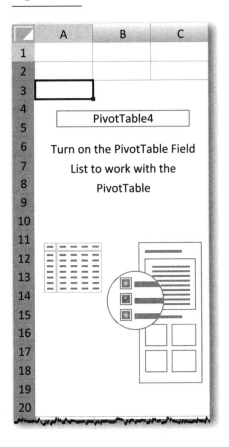

Figure 7.12 Pivot Table Fields list

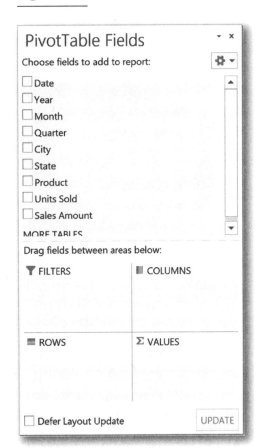

4. The pivot table can be built in the **Pivot Table Fields** list by dragging the variables into the four areas: **FILTERS, COLUMNS, ROWS, VALUES**. Create a simple pivot table by dragging Units Sold to **VALUES**, Product to **ROWS**, and Year to **COLUMNS** (see Figure 7.13).

Deciding which variable to place in each section can be daunting when you first begin to use pivot tables. A simple rule of thumb is that numbers (except for dates) are usually placed in the VALUES section. Data in the VALUES section are usually aggregated or averaged or have some other mathematical function used. If a nonnumerical variable is placed in the VALUES section, Excel will count instances of the variable. Data in the FILTERS, COLUMNS, and ROWS sections are often (but not always) text or dates that describe the data in the VALUES

Figure 7.13 Completed pivot table

	A	B	C	D
1				
2				
3	**Sum of Units Sold**	**Column Label** ▼		
4	**Row Labels** ▼	**2014**	**2015**	**Grand Total**
5	Chocolate Chip	2539504	3865490	6404994
6	Gingerbread	2005951	2717868	4723819
7	Oatmeal	1667667	2165380	3833047
8	Peanut Butter	2188530	2571670	4760200
9	Sugar	432252	655620	1087872
10	**Grand Total**	**8833904**	**11976028**	**20809932**

section. Placing a variable in the FILTERS section gives you the ability to filter on that variable and affect the entire pivot table. Placing a variable in the ROWS section puts the labels down the side of the table, while placing a variable in the COLUMNS section puts the labels across the top.

Modifying and exploring a pivot table

One of the first things you should do is format the numbers in the pivot table by adding commas to the Units Sold values so they are easier to read. To do this, right-click on any number in the table, choose **Number Format** from the shortcut menu that appears, and choose the appropriate number format from the dialog box that follows.

A few clicks provided a well-ordered summary of more than 50,000 rows of data. However, to capitalize on the power of pivot tables, we can explore the data further by changing the layout of the pivot table.

Transposing Rows and Columns
••

It is not always clear at the outset which labels should be used in rows and which would be better placed in the columns. Because it is easy to transpose data in pivot tables, place any labels in the rows and columns and rotate them as necessary to achieve your desired result. In the **Pivot Table Fields** list, move Product to the **COLUMNS** section and Year to the **ROWS** section (see Figure 7.14).

Figure 7.14 Rotated pivot table

	A	B	C	D	E	F	G
1							
2							
3	Sum of Units Sold	Column Label ▼					
4	Row Labels ▼	Chocolate Chip	Gingerbread	Oatmeal	Peanut Butter	Sugar	Grand Total
5	2014	2539504	2005951	1667667	2188530	432252	8833904
6	2015	3865490	2717868	2165380	2571670	655620	11976028
7	Grand Total	6404994	4723819	3833047	4760200	1087872	20809932

Filtering Data

We can also filter our product variable to look at just one type of cookie. In the pivot table, click the drop-down arrow next to **Column Labels** (see Figure 7.15).

Deselect the **Select All** box and select **Chocolate Chip**. The pivot table will now show units sold for just chocolate chip cookies (see Figure 7.16).

Column and row label filters will filter sections of the data. Another way to use pivot table filters is to add a label to the **FILTERS** section in the **Pivot Table Fields**. Let's move Year to the **FILTERS** section and add Month to the **ROW** section. Let's also remove the filter on product so that we can see all of the cookie types, not just chocolate chip. The resulting table is shown in Figure 7.17.

Moving the Year variable to the **FILTERS** section made it appear above the pivot table with a drop-down box. The drop-down box allows us to choose a specific year. By default, all years are initially selected so the data in the pivot table represents the total of 2014 and

Figure 7.15 Pivot table filter menu

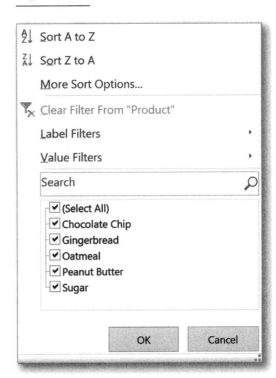

Figure 7.16 Filtered pivot table

	A	B	C
1			
2			
3	Sum of Units Sold	Column Labels	
4	Row Labels	Chocolate Chip	Grand Total
5	2014	2539504	2539504
6	2015	3865490	3865490
7	Grand Total	6404994	6404994

Figure 7.17 Pivot table using FILTERS

	A	B	C	D	E	F	G
1	Year	(All)					
2							
3	Sum of Units Sold	Column Label					
4	Row Labels	Chocolate Chip	Gingerbread	Oatmeal	Peanut Butter	Sugar	Grand Total
5	Jan	420,952	350,749	243,004	338,308	79,497	1,432,510
6	Feb	498,449	345,876	301,157	351,623	87,605	1,584,710
7	Mar	387,472	263,697	309,122	359,551	89,484	1,409,326
8	Apr	503,098	343,817	354,679	317,009	77,156	1,595,759
9	May	490,041	366,012	303,522	393,877	85,814	1,639,266
10	Jun	370,823	397,757	239,276	323,729	71,563	1,403,148
11	Jul	422,808	328,351	286,852	391,949	85,555	1,515,515
12	Aug	442,975	342,208	310,844	303,469	80,748	1,480,244
13	Sep	567,429	288,439	333,529	292,410	83,095	1,564,902
14	Oct	518,971	434,467	371,524	522,181	98,198	1,945,341
15	Nov	853,277	609,773	349,935	557,230	115,295	2,485,510
16	Dec	928,699	652,673	429,603	608,864	133,862	2,753,701
17	Grand Total	6,404,994	4,723,819	3,833,047	4,760,200	1,087,872	20,809,932

2015. Let's filter to look at just 2015 data. Figure 7.18 shows the filtered table. We can see that there were almost 12 million units sold and chocolate chip was the best seller in 2015.

Figure 7.18 Pivot table filtered by year

	A	B	C	D	E	F	G
1	Year	2015 ▾					
2							
3	Sum of Units Sold	Column Labels ▾					
4	Row Labels ▾	Chocolate Chip	Gingerbread	Oatmeal	Peanut Butter	Sugar	Grand Total
5	Jan	242,812	204,169	127,716	194,646	55,523	824,866
6	Feb	292,995	182,639	157,598	187,990	46,969	868,191
7	Mar	238,541	110,138	185,247	225,402	64,790	824,118
8	Apr	309,449	179,631	210,539	181,173	49,413	930,205
9	May	293,907	207,435	164,196	238,405	46,036	949,979
10	Jun	222,683	245,786	130,231	187,130	43,399	829,229
11	Jul	222,861	194,409	177,142	193,396	57,958	845,766
12	Aug	285,425	172,472	174,204	146,367	47,321	825,789
13	Sep	367,210	190,877	178,206	165,439	49,676	951,408
14	Oct	306,188	227,265	204,008	310,885	66,466	1,114,812
15	Nov	531,509	395,693	216,887	258,085	66,376	1,468,550
16	Dec	551,910	407,354	239,406	282,752	61,693	1,543,115
17	Grand Total	3,865,490	2,717,868	2,165,380	2,571,670	655,620	11,976,028

Changing Summary Data Values

When data values are added to the **VALUE** section, the default is usually to sum the values. Data values also may be described by their count or average.

1. To change the summary statistic, click the drop-down arrow next to the value in the **VALUE** section and choose **Value Field Settings** (see Figure 7.19).

2. In the **Value Field Settings** dialog box (see Figure 7.20), change SUM to Count, Average, or another statistic.

Figure 7.19 Value Field Settings drop-down menu

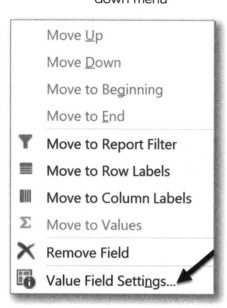

Figure 7.20 Value Field Settings dialog box

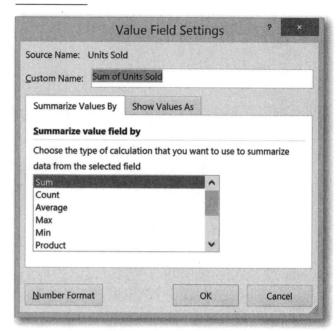

Nesting Variables

So far our pivot tables have been fairly simple. However, pivot tables can quickly become complicated when multiple variables are added. To illustrate, let's return to the cookie store data. Replace Month in the **ROWS** section with City (see Figure 7.21).

This pivot table is still pretty simple. Now let's also add State to the **ROWS** section (drag it below the City variable; see Figure 7.22).

Excel has listed each city alphabetically and the corresponding state below it. This might be an acceptable way to review the data if the company had only one city in each state. In our example, however, there are locations in multiple cities in most states. It would be more helpful to list the cities grouped within each state. To do this, we need to change the order in which the City and State variables are listed in the **ROWS** section. Drag the State variable in the **ROWS** section and drop it above the City variable.

Figure 7.21 Pivot table showing sales by city

	A	B	C	D	E	F	G
1	Year	2015					
2							
3	Sum of Units Sold	Column Labels					
4	Row Labels	Chocolate Chip	Gingerbread	Oatmeal	Peanut Butter	Sugar	Grand Total
5	Boise	284,551	224,547	138,120	132,689	63,479	843,386
6	Bozeman	176,664	134,210	103,238	118,477	25,449	558,038
7	Cheyenne	114,599	95,110	135,291	149,112	32,727	526,839
8	Missoula	164,707	165,595	94,333	130,030	23,818	578,483
9	Pocatello	144,069	97,743	70,405	118,965	20,260	451,442
10	Portland	401,920	379,785	210,038	320,173	77,413	1,389,329
11	Provo	165,473	92,058	75,082	135,084	25,915	493,612
12	Reno	243,806	139,486	154,047	147,411	37,513	722,263
13	Salem	314,403	218,959	176,616	257,917	43,672	1,011,567
14	Salt Lake City	460,978	283,570	235,461	204,627	93,916	1,278,552
15	Seattle	439,469	317,268	241,862	237,723	64,307	1,300,629
16	Spokane	449,563	250,323	245,723	262,525	66,845	1,274,979
17	Tacoma	283,252	187,215	159,758	212,979	55,289	898,493
18	Twin Falls	222,036	131,999	125,406	143,958	25,017	648,416
19	Grand Total	3,865,490	2,717,868	2,165,380	2,571,670	655,620	11,976,028

Each state is now listed alphabetically followed by all of the cities within that state. There is also a subtotal line for each state (see Figure 7.23).

The button next to each state can be used to collapse that state so that just the state total is shown and the cities are hidden.

Totals and Subtotals

By default, pivot tables have grand totals for each row and column. These can be turned off from the **PIVOT TABLE TOOLS** contextual **DESIGN** tab > **Layout** group > **Grand Totals** drop-down arrow.

In addition to adding or removing subtotals and grand totals, the **DESIGN** tab provides several options for formatting the pivot table. Even so, pivot

Figure 7.22 Pivot table showing sales by city and state

	A	B	C	D	E	F	G
1	Year	2015 ⏷					
2							
3	Sum of Units Sold	Column Labels ▾					
4	Row Labels ▾	Chocolate Chip	Gingerbread	Oatmeal	Peanut Butter	Sugar	Grand Total
5	⊟Boise	284,551	224,547	138,120	132,689	63,479	843,386
6	ID	284,551	224,547	138,120	132,689	63,479	843,386
7	⊟Bozeman	176,664	134,210	103,238	118,477	25,449	558,038
8	MT	176,664	134,210	103,238	118,477	25,449	558,038
9	⊟Cheyenne	114,599	95,110	135,291	149,112	32,727	526,839
10	WY	114,599	95,110	135,291	149,112	32,727	526,839
11	⊟Missoula	164,707	165,595	94,333	130,030	23,818	578,483
12	MT	164,707	165,595	94,333	130,030	23,818	578,483
13	⊟Pocatello	144,069	97,743	70,405	118,965	20,260	451,442
14	ID	144,069	97,743	70,405	118,965	20,260	451,442
15	⊟Portland	401,920	379,785	210,038	320,173	77,413	1,389,329
16	OR	401,920	379,785	210,038	320,173	77,413	1,389,329
17	⊟Provo	165,473	92,058	75,082	135,084	25,915	493,612
18	UT	165,473	92,058	75,082	135,084	25,915	493,612
19	⊟Reno	243,806	139,486	154,047	147,411	37,513	722,263
20	NV	243,806	139,486	154,047	147,411	37,513	722,263
21	⊟Salem	314,403	218,959	176,616	257,917	43,672	1,011,567
22	OR	314,403	218,959	176,616	257,917	43,672	1,011,567
23	⊟Salt Lake City	460,978	283,570	235,461	204,627	93,916	1,278,552
24	UT	460,978	283,570	235,461	204,627	93,916	1,278,552
25	⊟Seattle	439,469	317,268	241,862	237,723	64,307	1,300,629
26	WA	439,469	317,268	241,862	237,723	64,307	1,300,629
27	⊟Spokane	449,563	250,323	245,723	262,525	66,845	1,274,979
28	WA	449,563	250,323	245,723	262,525	66,845	1,274,979
29	⊟Tacoma	283,252	187,215	159,758	212,979	55,289	898,493
30	WA	283,252	187,215	159,758	212,979	55,289	898,493
31	⊟Twin Falls	222,036	131,999	125,406	143,958	25,017	648,416
32	ID	222,036	131,999	125,406	143,958	25,017	648,416
33	Grand Total	3,865,490	2,717,868	2,165,380	2,571,670	655,620	11,976,028

Figure 7.23 Pivot table showing sales by state and city

	A	B	C	D	E	F	G
1	Year	2015					
2							
3	**Sum of Units Sold**	**Column Labels**					
4	**Row Labels**	**Chocolate Chip**	**Gingerbread**	**Oatmeal**	**Peanut Butter**	**Sugar**	**Grand Total**
5	⊟**ID**	**650,656**	**454,289**	**333,931**	**395,612**	**108,756**	**1,943,244**
6	Boise	284,551	224,547	138,120	132,689	63,479	843,386
7	Pocatello	144,069	97,743	70,405	118,965	20,260	451,442
8	Twin Falls	222,036	131,999	125,406	143,958	25,017	648,416
9	⊟**MT**	**341,371**	**299,805**	**197,571**	**248,507**	**49,267**	**1,136,521**
10	Bozeman	176,664	134,210	103,238	118,477	25,449	558,038
11	Missoula	164,707	165,595	94,333	130,030	23,818	578,483
12	⊟**NV**	**243,806**	**139,486**	**154,047**	**147,411**	**37,513**	**722,263**
13	Reno	243,806	379,486	154,047	147,411	37,513	722,263
14	⊟**OR**	**716,323**	**598,744**	**386,654**	**578,090**	**121,085**	**2,400,896**
15	Portland	401,920	379,785	210,038	320,173	77,413	1,389,329
16	Salem	314,403	218,959	176,616	257,917	43,672	1,011,567
17	⊟**UT**	**626,451**	**375,628**	**310,543**	**339,711**	**119,831**	**1,772,164**
18	Provo	165,473	92,058	75,082	135,084	25,915	493,612
19	Salt Lake City	460,978	283,570	235,461	204,627	93,916	1,278,552
20	⊟**WA**	**1,172,284**	**754,806**	**647,343**	**713,227**	**186,441**	**3,474,101**
21	Seattle	439,469	317,268	241,862	237,723	64,307	1,300,629
22	Spokane	449,563	250,323	245,723	262,525	66,845	1,274,979
23	Tacoma	283,252	187,215	159,758	212,979	55,289	898,493
24	⊟**WY**	**114,599**	**95,110**	**135,291**	**149,112**	**32,727**	**526,839**
25	Cheyenne	114,599	95,110	135,291	149,112	32,727	526,839
26	**Grand Total**	**3,865,490**	**2,717,868**	**2,165,380**	**2,571,670**	**655,620**	**11,976,028**

table formatting is somewhat restricted. If you're not able to create the formatting you desire you will need to copy and paste (paste special as values) the pivot table into a new location. Once you do that, it will no longer be a pivot table connected to the source data. Additionally, formulas and the ability to pivot the data are lost. However, you will have more flexibility for formatting.

1. Select the entire pivot table (or the portion of the pivot table you wish to format).

2. Copy the selection, **CTRL+C**.

3. Move to a new worksheet.

4. From the **HOME** tab, in the **Clipboard** group, click on the **Paste** drop-down arrow.

5. Choose **Paste Special** from the expanded menu.

6. Select **Values**.

7. Click **OK**.

Figure 7.24 Pivot table shortcut menu

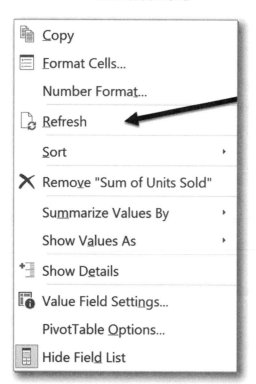

Refreshing Pivot Table Data

Although pivot tables are directly connected to their source data, they do not automatically update when the source data changes. To update the pivot table, simply right-click anywhere on the pivot table and select **Refresh** from the shortcut menu (see Figure 7.24).

Grouping Data

Data in pivot tables can be grouped to make analysis more manageable. This is especially useful when dealing with dates. In our data set, we have data for nearly every day of 2014 and 2015. That is far too much data to easily analyze. To begin grouping the data by date, modify the existing pivot table by removing City and State from the **ROWS** and Year from the **FILTERS** sections. Add Date to the **ROWS** section. This will create a row for each unique day in our data set (see Figure 7.25).

Figure 7.25 Pivot table with daily data

	A	B	C	D	E	F	G
1							
2							
3	Sum of Units Sold	Column Labels ▾					
4	Row Labels ▾	Chocolate Chip	Gingerbread	Oatmeal	Peanut Butter	Sugar	Grand Total
5	01/01/14	5,641	4,825	3,404	4,150	835	18,855
6	01/02/14	6,511	4,719	3,679	4,953	763	20,625
7	01/03/14	6,092	3,851	3,734	4,672	717	19,066
8	01/04/14	5,682	4,474	4,180	4,972	734	20,042
9	01/05/14	5,546	5,683	3,728	4,369	794	20,120
10	01/06/14	5,040	5,127	4,033	4,313	877	19,390
11	01/07/14	5,709	3,951	3,717	4,828	688	18,893
12	01/08/14	5,234	4,567	3,499	5,769	872	19,941
13	01/09/14	5,636	4,565	3,868	4,873	918	19,860
14	01/10/14	5,159	4,728	3,726	4,198	769	18,580
15	01/11/14	5,503	4,764	3,442	5,350	651	19,710
16	01/12/14	4,869	4,360	3,729	4,320	837	18,115
17	01/13/14	5,392	4,513	4,099	4,828	802	19,634
18	01/14/14	4,893	4,554	3,740	4,534	879	18,600
19	01/15/14	6,517	4,551	3,537	4,670	841	20,116
20	01/16/14	4,914	4,999	3,538	4,798	824	19,073

To make this data manageable, right-click on one of the dates and choose **Group** from the shortcut menu. This opens the **Grouping** dialog box (see Figure 7.26) that can be used to group your data into years, quarters, months, and so on. For this example, we selected Months. Figure 7.27 shows the data grouped by month.

The pivot table is now much more manageable. There is one issue, however. Recall that this data contained daily data from 2014 and 2015. By choosing just month (and not year), the pivot table has combined data from each year into the months. It's possible, but unlikely, that this is the desired outcome. To adjust, right-click on one

Figure 7.26 Pivot table Grouping dialog box

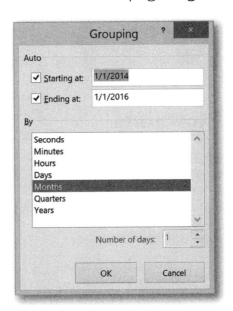

Figure 7.27 Pivot table data grouped by month

	A	B	C	D	E	F	G
1							
2							
3	Sum of Units Sold	Column Label ▾					
4	Row Labels ▾	Chocolate Chip	Gingerbread	Oatmeal	Peanut Butter	Sugar	Grand Total
5	Jan	420,952	350,749	243,004	338,308	79,497	1,432,510
6	Feb	498,449	345,876	301,157	351,623	87,605	1,584,710
7	Mar	387,472	263,697	309,122	359,551	89,484	1,409,326
8	Apr	503,098	343,817	354,679	317,009	77,156	1,595,759
9	May	490,041	366,012	303,522	393,877	85,814	1,639,266
10	Jun	370,823	397,757	239,276	323,729	71,563	1,403,148
11	Jul	422,808	328,351	286,852	391,949	85,555	1,515,515
12	Aug	442,975	342,208	310,844	303,469	80,748	1,480,244
13	Sep	567,429	288,439	333,529	292,410	83,095	1,564,902
14	Oct	518,971	434,467	371,524	522,181	98,198	1,945,341
15	Nov	853,277	609,773	349,935	557,230	115,295	2,485,510
16	Dec	928,699	652,673	429,603	608,684	133,862	2,753,701
17	Grand Total	6,404,994	4,723,819	3,833,047	4,760,200	1,087,872	20,809,932

of the months, choose **Group**, and select **Years** from the dialog box. Select **OK**. Now the data are grouped by month and year (see Figure 7.28).

The layout in Figure 7.28 could also be achieved by using the Year and Month variables from our data set. One method is not necessarily better than the other.

Pivot Charts

As we've discussed at length in this book, charting data is one of the most effective ways to explore, analyze, and present data. Fortunately, Excel allows charts to be built from pivot tables! We'll demonstrate with a simple pivot table created from the cookie store data.

Creating Pivot Charts

1. Create the pivot table on which to base the charts. Put Years in **FILTERS**, Product in **COLUMNS**, Month in **ROWS**, and Sales Amount in **VALUES**. The pivot table should look like Figure 7.29.

Figure 7.28 Pivot table data grouped by month and year

	A	B	C	D	E	F	G
1							
2							
3	Sum of Units Sold	Column Label ▼					
4	Row Labels ▼	Chocolate Chip	Gingerbread	Oatmeal	Peanut Butter	Sugar	Grand Total
5	⊟2014	2,539,504	2,005,951	1,667,667	2,188,530	432,252	8,833,904
6	Jan	178,140	146,580	115,288	143,662	23,974	607,644
7	Feb	205,454	163,237	143,559	163,633	40,636	716,519
8	Mar	148,931	153,559	123,875	134,149	24,694	585,208
9	Apr	193,649	164,186	144,140	135,836	27,743	665,554
10	May	196,134	158,577	139,326	155,472	39,778	689,287
11	Jun	148,140	151,971	109,045	136,599	28,164	573,919
12	Jul	199,947	133,942	109,710	198,553	27,597	669,749
13	Aug	157,550	169,736	136,640	157,102	33,427	654,455
14	Sep	200,219	97,562	155,323	126,971	33,419	613,494
15	Oct	212,783	207,202	167,516	211,296	31,732	830,529
16	Nov	321,768	214,080	133,048	299,145	48,919	1,016,960
17	Dec	376,789	245,319	190,197	326,112	72,169	1,210,586
18	⊟2015	3,865,490	2,717,868	2,165,380	2,571,670	655,620	11,979,028
19	Jan	242,812	204,169	127,716	194,646	55,523	824,866
20	Feb	292,995	182,639	157,598	187,990	46,969	868,191
21	Mar	238,541	110,138	185,247	225,402	64,790	824,118
22	Apr	309,449	179,631	210,539	181,173	49,413	930,205
23	May	293,907	207,435	164,196	238,405	46,036	949,979
24	Jun	222,683	245,786	130,231	187,130	43,399	829,229
25	Jul	222,861	194,409	177,142	193,396	57,958	845,766
26	Aug	285,425	172,472	174,204	146,367	47,321	825,789
27	Sep	367,210	190,877	178,206	165,439	49,676	951,408
28	Oct	306,188	227,265	204,008	310,885	66,466	1,114,812
29	Nov	531,509	395,693	216,887	258,085	66,376	1,468,550
30	Dec	551,910	407,354	239,406	282,752	61,693	1,543,115
31	Grand Total	6,404,994	4,723,819	3,833,047	4,760,200	1,087,872	20,809,932

2. From the **INSERT** tab, in the **Charts** group, click on the **PivotChart** icon.

3. Select a line chart from the **Insert Chart** dialog box. The chart will appear on the worksheet next to the pivot table (see Figure 7.30).

Figure 7.29 Pivot table for creating pivot charts

	A	B	C	D	E	F	G
1	Year	(All) ▾					
2							
3	Sum of Sales Amount	Column Labels ▾					
4	Row Labels ▾	Chocolate Chip	Gingerbread	Oatmeal	Peanut Butter	Sugar	Grand Total
5	Jan	959,100	800,075	547,436	770,556	185,961	3,263,128
6	Feb	1,138,411	779,613	678,101	793,725	197,818	3,587,668
7	Mar	890,340	579,826	707,776	828,207	210,468	3,216,618
8	Apr	1,155,890	774,011	811,081	721,434	178,247	3,640,663
9	May	1,122,135	832,081	686,107	903,018	193,788	3,737,129
10	Jun	849,279	914,429	541,275	737,786	164,110	3,206,879
11	Jul	952,818	750,623	659,406	876,677	199,233	3,438,758
12	Aug	1,024,233	767,230	705,682	677,087	184,349	3,358,580
13	Sep	1,312,789	669,432	752,826	664,615	190,197	3,589,859
14	Oct	1,185,846	978,222	841,337	1,194,583	228,647	4,428,635
15	Nov	1,963,776	1,411,295	804,814	1,237,930	262,625	5,680,440
16	Dec	2,124,066	1,502,496	974,613	1,353,015	297,232	6,251,422
17	Grand Total	14,678,683	10,759,334	8,710,454	10,758,633	2,492,675	47,399,779

Figure 7.30 Pivot line chart

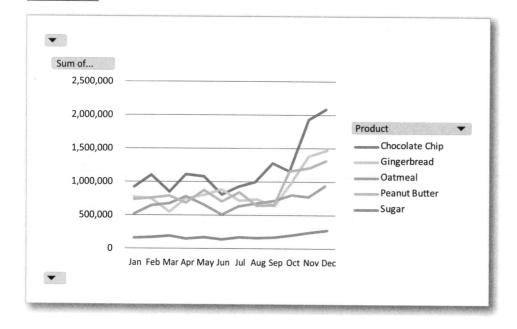

Pivot charts retain the pivot table functionality. There are several drop-down menus on the chart. These menus provide the same filter and select options that are available in the pivot table. We can easily change the year for our data display by clicking the year filter in the top left corner.

We can also focus on one product rather than comparing multiple products by using the product filter (see Figure 7.31). Note that filters placed on the pivot chart are applied to the pivot table and vice versa.

Exploring data using pivot charts is an efficient way for analysts to understand data and uncover trends and anomolies. You may apply Excel's standard chart formatting features to pivot charts; however, the charts will retain their pivoting ability. This may be an acceptable end point if you plan to share your workbook with other analysts. To create charts suitable for reports and presentations, copy the data from the pivot table and paste as values somewhere on the worksheet. Use the static values table as the basis for creating charts suitable for reports or presentations.

Figure 7.31 Pivot chart filtered by product

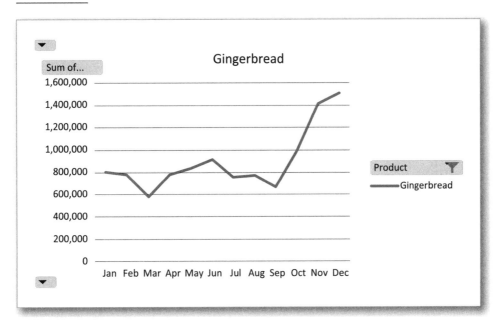

SUMMARY

Excel's pivot table feature is a powerful analysis tool. In this chapter we've introduced the topic and discussed the basic features. So long as the pivot table source data is correctly organized, creating a pivot table requires only a few mouse clicks. In seconds, thousands of records containing many variables can be summarized and charts created to evaluate data patterns. We've just scratched the surface of how pivot tables and charts can expedite analysts' work. Readers are encouraged to experiment with pivot tables, using small or moderately sized data sets, and explore the functionality.

Pivot Table and Pivot Chart Checklist

1. Organize pivot table source data so that each column represents one variable and each row is one record.

2. Select source data and create pivot table.

3. Explore the pivot table data by transposing rows and columns and filtering, nesting, and grouping elements.

4. Create pivot charts based on pivot table data.

5. Copy pivot table data and paste as values to create report or presentation charts.

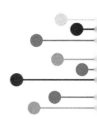

CHAPTER 8

Tables

When Charts Aren't Enough

The focus of this text is on creating accurate and appealing data pictures that inform audiences. We have seen that bar, column, line, area, and pie charts are effective tools for conveying data stories quickly. There are times, however, when a chart must be accompanied by a table or when a table alone is required, for example, when precise data values are needed so that business decisions may be made. In these situations, your audience may be less interested in patterns or trends and more interested in how a particular person, group, or process performed. This chapter covers the basics of creating and formatting tables in Excel.

Learning Objectives

- Transform data arrays into Excel tables

- Examine data using Excel's Table feature

- Format data tables for optimal readability

- Design custom table styles

Excel's Table Feature

A table is structured data organized in rows and columns. Tables have a header row that defines the contents of columns and a header column containing row labels. When you set up rows and columns in a worksheet and enter data, you are establishing a data range. Data ranges may be used to create charts and compute summary statistics. However, by converting a range of cells in a worksheet to an Excel table, we can take advantage of several handy features to expedite tasks. For example, a roster showing names and other relevant details about the student population of a university can be defined as an Excel table so that we can quickly study the contents. To convert a data range such as the one in Figure 8.1 to a table, click anywhere inside the data range and from the **INSERT** tab, in the **Tables** group, click **Table**. Select (or deselect) the box indicating if your table has headers. Click **OK**.

Alternatively, click anywhere inside the data range, click **CTRL+T**, and then click **OK** (see Figure 8.1).

Figure 8.1 Student population data range

	A	B	C	D	E	F	G
1	ID	Last Name	First Name	Division	Financial Aid	Units	GPA
2	4121	Simpson	Thelma	Science	No	57	2.00
3	8512	Webb	Tanya	Science	No	66	4.00
4	1122	Lyons	Gina	Business	Yes	105	4.00
5	7472	Olsen	Beverly	Humanities	No	28	3.25
6	4447	Shaw	Lynn	Education	No	80	3.00
7	7255	Ramsey	Samantha	Humanities	Yes	134	2.00
8	2777	Stanley	Matthew	Education	No	77	3.25
9	4487	Colon	Bobbie	Business	No	180	4.00
10	8100	Woods	Dwight	Education	No	165	3.00

When we define the data range as a table, Excel automatically adds filter buttons to the header row and applies formatting to the table (see Figure 8.2). We will address table formatting shortly; for now, we'll focus on the functions associated with Excel's Table feature.

Figure 8.2 Student population data table

	A	B	C	D	E	F	G
1	ID	Last Name	First Name	Division	Financial Aid	Units	GPA
2	4121	Simpson	Thelma	Science	No	57	2.00
3	8512	Webb	Tanya	Science	No	66	4.00
4	1122	Lyons	Gina	Business	Yes	105	4.00
5	7472	Olsen	Beverly	Humanities	No	28	3.25
6	4447	Shaw	Lynn	Education	No	80	3.00
7	7255	Ramsey	Samantha	Humanities	Yes	134	2.00
8	2777	Stanley	Matthew	Education	No	77	3.25
9	4487	Colon	Bobbie	Business	No	180	4.00
10	8100	Woods	Dwight	Education	No	165	3.00

Easy sorting and filtering

To examine the variable, units toward graduation, we can click the filter button at the top of column F and select **Sort Largest to Smallest** (see Figure 8.3).

With the data sorted, we see that one student, Bobbie Colon, has accumulated 180 units (see Figure 8.4). The list is sorted showing the students in descending order based on their accrued units. The other columns may be sorted in the same manner to organize the data and gain quick insight into the range of values, top performers, outliers, and so forth.

To see only the students receiving financial aid, we can use the filter button at the top of column E. In the filter section, we deselect **Select All** and select **Yes** (see Figure 8.5). The resulting table shows only the 260 students who are currently receiving financial aid.

Figure 8.3 Sorting by units

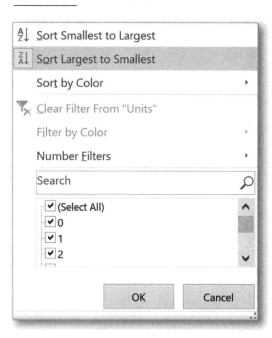

You may also choose more advanced **Number Filters** to look at students who have GPAs above or below a certain threshold, or the top 10 students, and so on. For example, say you wanted to view all students with GPAs that are 3.5 or

Figure 8.4 Student population data table sorted by units

	A	B	C	D	E	F	G
1	ID	Last Name	First Name	Division	Financial Aid	Units	GPA
2	4487	Colon	Bobbie	Business	No	180	4.00
3	8095	Maldonado	Rhonda	Humanities	No	179	2.50
4	3590	Waters	Amy	Science	Yes	178	4.00
5	6275	Flores	Stephanie	Science	No	178	4.00
6	2778	Burns	Pamela	Education	No	178	3.75
7	6723	Garrison	Chris	Humanities	No	178	4.00
8	1796	Shaffer	Clayton	Humanities	No	178	3.50
9	4160	Manning	Julie	Humanities	Yes	178	3.25
10	8460	Olsen	Brittany	Humanities	No	178	2.50

above. Click the **Sort and Filter** drop-down arrow at the top of the GPA column and then click **Number Filters** to display the submenu (see Figure 8.6). Select **Greater Than Or Equal To**. The **Custom AutoFilter** dialog box will appear (see Figure 8.7). In the dialog box next to "is greater than or equal to" enter 3.5.

Figure 8.5 Filtering by financial aid

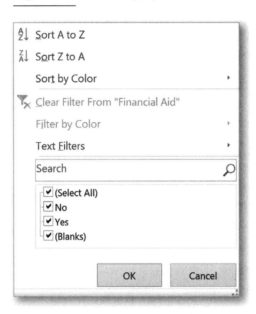

Figure 8.6 Number filters submenu

Figure 8.7 Custom AutoFilter dialog box

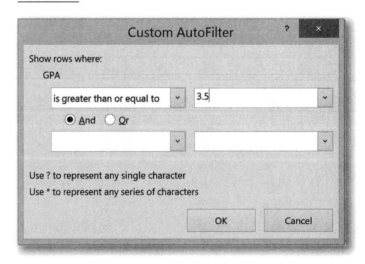

Press **OK** to complete the task. The resulting table will show only students who achieved a GPA of 3.5 or above (see Figure 8.8). Note that filtering does not delete records. The records of students with GPAs below 3.5 are still in the table; those rows were hidden as a result of the filtering.

Figure 8.8 Filtered table showing students with GPAs 3.5 and above

	A	B	C	D	E	F	G
1	ID ▼	Last Name ▼	First Name ▼	Division ▼	Financial Aid ▼	Units ▼	GPA ⬓
2	4487	Colon	Bobbie	Business	No	180	4.00
4	3590	Waters	Amy	Science	Yes	178	4.00
5	6275	Flores	Stephanie	Science	No	178	4.00
6	2778	Burns	Pamela	Education	No	178	3.75
7	6723	Garrison	Chris	Humanities	No	178	4.00
8	1796	Shaffer	Clayton	Humanities	No	178	3.50
11	5628	Fletcher	Theodore	Science	Yes	178	3.50
13	7953	Bush	Vera	Education	No	177	3.75
14	4321	Bennett	Luis	Education	No	177	4.00

Quickly add a total

In many instances you will need to add a total row at the bottom of a table. To do so, click anywhere in the table, click the contextual **DESIGN** tab that appears on the ribbon, and then select **Total Row** (see Figure 8.9).

Figure 8.9 TABLE TOOLS contextual ribbon

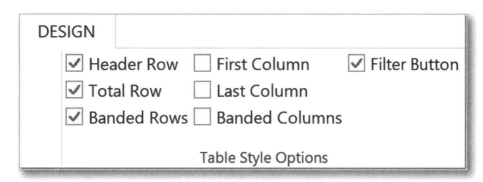

DESIGN

☑ Header Row ☐ First Column ☑ Filter Button
☑ Total Row ☐ Last Column
☑ Banded Rows ☐ Banded Columns

Table Style Options

Figure 8.10 Summary statistics menu

None
Average
Count
Count Numbers
Max
Min
Sum
StdDev
Var
More Functions...

Excel added a total of 815.25 to the bottom of the GPA column in our student data. This is a total of the values in the column and isn't meaningful for our purposes. A better summary for the GPA column would be an overall average GPA for all students. To change the total to average, click on the cell containing the total and then click the drop-down arrow that appears to change Sum to **Average**. From this drop-down you may change the total row to show the column count, maximum, minimum, and so on (see Figure 8.10).

Perpetually visible headers

Another useful feature of Excel's Table is the perpetually visible table header. As you scroll down the table to the point where the header row is no longer visible, Excel replaces the column header cells (e.g., A, B, C) with the table's header row. This means you don't have to freeze your header row to keep it in view. Your active cell must be in the table to see this (see Figure 8.11).

The illustration in Figure 8.11 displays a few other important nuggets of information about the contents of the table. For example, we can see by the

Figure 8.11 Perpetual headers

	ID ▼	Last Name ▼	First Name ▼	Division ▼	Financial Aid ▼	Units ▼	GPA ▼
551	2306	Fields	Kim	Business	Yes	9	2.25
553	4889	Tucker	Kristin	Education	Yes	9	3.50
555	7924	Guzman	Christy	Business	Yes	9	2.50
557	3749	Moran	Emma	Education	Yes	8	3.50
558	9043	Simmons	Thomas	Science	Yes	7	3.50
560	1630	Byrd	Vanessa	Business	Yes	7	3.25
563	8800	Green	Sidney	Education	Yes	6	4.00
566	5512	Frazier	Olga	Humanities	Yes	5	3.25
567	4842	Martin	Marsha	Education	Yes	4	3.50
572							3.13

funnel icon next to the column header Financial Aid that the table is filtered by Financial Aid, and the downward-pointing arrow in the Units column indicates that the table is sorted, in descending order, by the Units column.

Dynamic charts

When you base a chart on an Excel table, the chart will automatically update as new data are added to the table. Figure 8.12 shows four charts and the table on which they are based. In this example, data will be added for June and subsequent months as they become available.

*If you wish to stop using the features of an Excel table, click anywhere in the table and select **Convert to Range** from the **Tools** group on the **DESIGN** tab.*

When June data are added to the table, the new data will take on the table formatting, and each of the four charts will automatically update to show the new data range (see Figure 8.13). If the data were defined as a range instead of a table, we would need to manually select the new range (A1:G5) for each of the four charts each month when new data are added. This is an especially convenient feature when working with data that are updated frequently and when there are multiple charts based on the same table.

Figure 8.12 Data table and associated charts

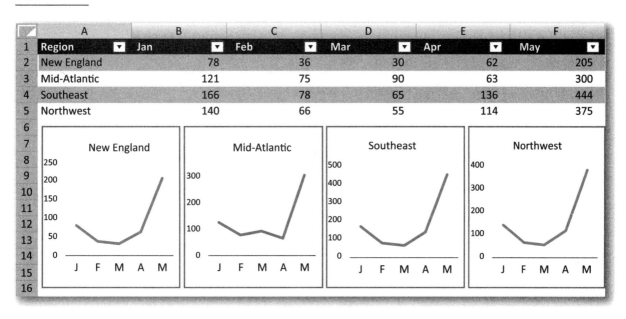

Figure 8.13 Updated data table and associated charts

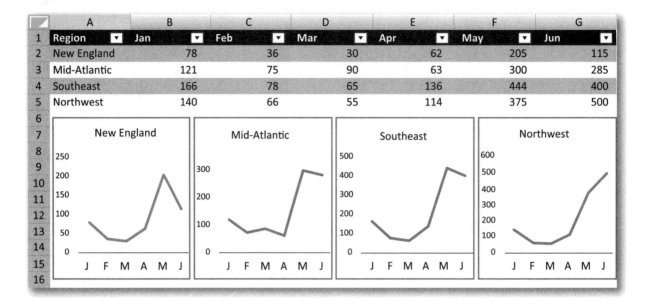

Region	Jan	Feb	Mar	Apr	May	Jun
New England	78	36	30	62	205	115
Mid-Atlantic	121	75	90	63	300	285
Southeast	166	78	65	136	444	400
Northwest	140	66	55	114	375	500

Figure 8.14 Transpose option on the Paste Special menu

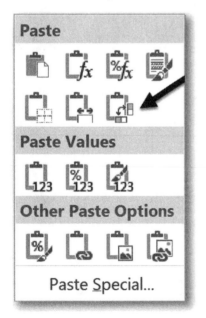

Table Formatting Best Practices

When designing a table for a report it is important to consider the space in which the final table will be placed. This will help you decide on the orientation of the rows and columns and several other factors. Depending on the available space, you may choose to transpose rows and columns to enhance readability. Transposing rows and columns should be done in the data range before the table is created.

Transposing Rows and Columns

1. Select the table and **Copy** (**CTRL+C**).

2. Click on any empty cell in the worksheet.

3. Expand the **Paste** menu on the **HOME** tab.

4. Select the **Transpose** option (see Figure 8.14).

Another important consideration is the eventual size of the table. For example, a table that will ultimately contain 12 months of sales data for four products would be better organized with the months of the year in rows and products in columns so that the table does not become too wide (see Figure 8.15). Wide tables, like wide columns of text, are difficult to read because the eye must travel a far distance across the row and then back to the first column to read the row label. All that back-and-forth is tiring for the reader and increases the likelihood of reading the wrong row. The transposed table in Figure 8.16 is easier to read and will more conveniently fit on a printed page.

Figure 8.15 Wide data range

	A	B	C	D	E	F	G	H	I	J	K	L	M	N
		Jan	Feb	Mar	Apr	May	Jun	Jul	Aug	Sep	Oct	Nov	Dec	Total Year
2	Cakes	437,622	557,990	326,450	547,963	514,879	952,749	893,344	820,685	454,371	704,936	963,714	792,197	7,966,900
3	Cookies	962,151	528,949	400,973	780,273	625,089	812,291	440,431	704,303	774,089	593,275	628,329	572,064	7,822,217
4	Cupcakes	389,004	784,235	773,003	806,340	739,048	902,137	586,327	787,620	480,487	970,727	378,142	732,604	8,329,674
5	Pies	809,068	643,559	994,826	735,780	538,745	978,515	747,785	517,565	669,939	664,549	925,759	665,382	8,891,472
6	Total Month	2,597,845	2,514,733	2,495,252	2,870,356	2,417,761	3,645,692	2,667,887	2,830,173	2,378,886	2,933,487	2,895,944	2,762,247	33,010,263

Figure 8.16 Transposed data range

	A	B	C	D	E	F
1		Cakes	Cookies	Cupcakes	Pies	Total Month
2	Jan	437,622	962,151	389,004	809,068	2,597,845
3	Feb	557,990	528,949	784,235	643,559	2,514,733
4	Mar	326,450	400,973	773,003	994,826	2,495,252
5	Apr	547,963	780,273	806,340	735,780	2,870,356
6	May	514,879	625,089	739,048	538,745	2,417,761
7	Jun	952,749	812,291	902,137	978,515	3,645,692
8	Jul	893,344	440,431	586,327	747,785	2,667,887
9	Aug	820,685	704,303	787,620	517,565	2,830,173
10	Sep	454,371	774,089	480,487	669,939	2,378,886
11	Oct	704,936	593,275	970,727	664,549	2,933,487
12	Nov	963,714	628,329	378,142	925,759	2,895,944
13	Dec	792,197	572,064	732,604	665,382	2,762,247
14	Total Year	7,966,900	7,822,217	8,329,674	8,891,472	33,010,263

Creating an Excel table using format as table

Defining a data range as an Excel table adds formatting to the table, usually banded rows, borders, and shading to the header row. Excel 2013 includes a wide variety of built-in table styles from which to choose (see Figure 8.17). When using tables on your own to explore data, table formatting is not a major consideration, so choose any style that appeals to you. When creating summary tables for reports, however, you will need to customize one of Excel's table styles or create a custom style to achieve a format acceptable for reporting.

Figure 8.17 Table styles menu

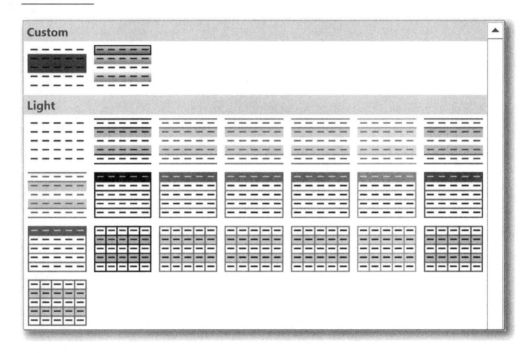

Figure 8.18 is a data range showing pastry sales from a national bakery chain over a period of time. Previously, we discussed two ways of converting a data range into an Excel table, from the ribbon or by pressing **CTRL+T** on your keyboard. A third method of creating an Excel table from a data range is to use the **Format as Table** feature on the ribbon. The first two methods apply the default table formatting, which you may change after the table is created. With this method, you select the table formatting of your choice at the same time the table is created.

Figure 8.18 Unformatted data range

	A	B	C	D	E	F
1	Region	Cakes	Cookies	Cupcakes	Pies	Total Region
2	New England	389375.7	177642.3	148167.5	311971	1027156.4
3	Mid-Atlantic	387826.1	180203.6	145495.7	315081.5	1028606.89
4	Southeast	828525.1	387721.8	325253.8	678628.1	2220128.84
5	Northwest	707415.3	325031.6	272732.2	575674.6	1880853.73
6	Total Product	3275471	1520763	1264621	2672898	8733752.14

Creating an Excel Table Using the Format as Table Function

1. Select the range of cells to be included in the table.

2. On the **HOME** tab in the **Styles** group, select **Format as Table** to expand the design options.

3. Click on a style to apply it to the selected data range.

4. Click **OK**.

Figure 8.19 is our bakery data table with one of the "light" styles applied.

Figure 8.19 Formatted table

	A	B	C	D	E	F
1	Region ▾	Cakes ▾	Cookies ▾	Cupcake ▾	Pies ▾	Total Region ▾
2	New England	389375.7	177642.3	148167.45	311971	1027156.4
3	Mid-Atlantic	387826.1	180203.6	145495.68	315081.5	1028606.89
4	Southeast	828525.1	387721.8	325253.76	678628.1	2220128.84
5	Northwest	707415.3	325031.6	272732.19	575674.6	1880853.73
6	Total Product	3275471	1520763	1264621.2	2672898	8733752.14

***Borders** are lines surrounding a cell or range of cells. **Rules** are horizontal or vertical lines in a table. **Grids** are created when rules intersect. See Figure 8.21.*

If one of the predesigned styles meets your needs, you will be finished at this point and ready to insert your table into a report. You've probably guessed by now that we find most of Excel's built-in styles lacking. Let's consider some best practices for table design.

Borders, rules, and grids

Space permitting, the best table layouts rely on white space to delineate rows and columns. The table in Figure 8.20 uses the white (or negative) space to create natural separation among values in the table. Without the distracting gridlines we can quickly focus on the data and easily see that anvils sold well, particularly in the East.

Figure 8.20 Table without gridlines

Number of Acme Products Sold in 2014 by Region

	North	South	East	West	**Total**
Anvils	13,133	8,787	97,843	56,960	**176,723**
Bird Costumes	11,430	5,669	60,826	37,399	**115,324**
Glue	507	5,245	20,337	4,614	**30,703**
Balloons	1,131	961	1,337	1,141	**4,570**
Total	**26,201**	**20,662**	**180,343**	**100,114**	**327,320**

Figure 8.21 Borders, rules, and grids

Border

Product	Jan	Feb	Mar
Product A	448	263	133
Product B	310	313	100
Product C	268	159	156
Product D	104	100	30
Total	**1,130**	**835**	**419**

Rules

Product	Jan	Feb	Mar
Product A	448	263	133
Product B	310	313	100
Product C	268	159	156
Product D	104	100	30
Total	**1,130**	**835**	**419**

Grid

Product	Jan	Feb	Mar
Product A	448	263	133
Product B	310	313	100
Product C	268	159	156
Product D	104	100	30
Total	**1,130**	**835**	**419**

The use of white space to create row and column separation is effective for small tables. When tables grow in size or when there is insufficient space to allow white space to distinguish data, it may be necessary to use borders, rules, or grids. Rules are also useful for separating header and total rows from other table content and for creating subsets of data within a table (see Figure 8.21).

Adding Table Borders

1. To add table borders, select the range of cells to which you would like to apply a border.

2. From the **HOME** tab, in the **Font** group, click the drop-down **Borders** arrow to view the border options (see Figure 8.22).

Table borders should be used only when absolutely necessary and must not distract from the data. Thin borders are more effective than thick borders. Opt for solid rather than dashed or dotted lines and choose a color that will delineate the rows and columns of data without calling attention to the border. When you glance at the table, the first thing you should see are the values, not thick dark lines surrounding the table cells.

Row and column formatting

Header row. All tables designed for reports or presentations should contain a header row. The information in the header row describes the contents of the columns. These column titles should be succinct but provide enough information for readers to decipher the contents of the columns. Distinguish header rows by bolding the text or by reversing the cell fill and font color (see Figure 8.23). Header rows may also be emphasized by increasing the height so that it is approximately double the height of the other table rows.

Figure 8.22 Borders menu

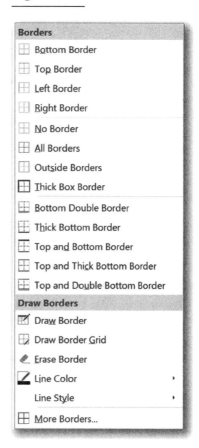

Tables with many rows may require repeating header rows. Clearly if a table spans more than one page you need to repeat the header row on every page. But how many rows can you include on one page before needing to repeat the header row? The answer depends on the contents of the table. If a table has

To finesse table borders, select the **More Borders** option from the **Borders** menu. This opens the **Format Cells** menu, from which you can alter border styles, colors, and placement and access tabs to change the cell fill, fonts, and other styles if desired.

In accounting, a single line above a row indicates a subtotal and double lines signify a grand total.

Figure 8.23   Header row with dark fill and light text

Reasons for Merchandise Return

Reasons for Return	Number for Returns	Percentage for Total
Wrong item	9,993	42%
Wrong size	6,347	26%
Defective	4,366	18%
Didn't like it	1,747	7%
Changed Mind	1,562	7%
Total	**24,015**	**100%**

only a few columns of easily identifiable data, for example, Month, Volume, and Revenue, it may be possible to include many rows without repeating the header row. On the other hand, tables with many columns of unfamiliar data may need a repeating header row every half page or so. Another option is to create separate tables with subsets of data. Consider how much information your readers can remember before needing a reminder of the cell contents.

To avoid redundant text in the header row text (see Figure 8.24), a span header (one that spans two or more columns) can be effective. To create a span header, insert a row either above or below the header row, if necessary. Then merge the cells (**HOME** > **Alignment** > **Merge & Center**) that will hold the span header. When span headers are used, the individual columns should still be labeled, but the labels can be short or perhaps abbreviated because additional information is contained in the span header (see Figure 8.25).

Figure 8.24   Table with redundant header row

	Math 2014	Math 2015	History 2014	History 2015	Art 2014	Art 2015
Male	782	334	617	610	814	374
Female	841	479	942	601	575	681
Total	**1,623**	**813**	**1,559**	**1,211**	**1,389**	**1,055**

Figure 8.25 Table with span header

	Math		History		Art	
	2014	2015	2014	2015	2014	2015
Male	782	334	617	610	814	374
Female	841	479	942	601	575	681
Total	**1,623**	**813**	**1,559**	**1,211**	**1,389**	**1,055**

Header column. Like the header row, the header column in a table contains metadata that describes the contents of the table rows. The text in this column is often emphasized with a bold font or contrasting color scheme. This information often needs to be abbreviated in some way so that the header column does not become too wide. For example, if listing the results of survey questions, it may not be possible to include the entire text of the survey questions in the header column.

For an accurate preview of how your table will look when inserted into a report or presentation, turn off Excel's gridlines. From the **VIEW** *tab, in the* **Show** *group, deselect* **Gridlines**.

Row and column summaries. The bottom row and right-most column of a table frequently contain summary information that aggregates the values of the entire row or column. These are usually totals but could also be other summary statistics such as averages or standard deviations.

Because we often want to call attention to summary rows and columns in a table, the text is typically bolded or highlighted by reversing the cell fill and text color, for example, filling the cell with a dark color and changing the text color to white. For additional emphasis, the height of the summary row may also be increased.

Although summary rows are usually at the bottom of tables, it is acceptable to place the summary, or total row, at the top of the table (see Figure 8.26). This is particularly handy when readers are primarily interested in the overall picture and may only need to scan the details if the numbers do not meet expectations.

Banded rows and columns. Banded tables contain rows or columns that are shaded with alternating colors (see Figures 8.27 and 8.28).

The banding of the rows or columns helps readers to match data with their corresponding labels in the header row and header column. This technique is

Figure 8.26 Table with summary row at top

Region	Q1	Q2	Q3	Q4	Total
Total	1,156,726	1,912,704	2,295,578	1,180,258	6,545,266
California	406,265	919,192	400,637	408,507	2,134,601
Oregon	358,020	647,009	958,320	394,209	2,357,558
Washington	392,441	346,503	936,621	377,542	2,053,107

Figure 8.27 Table with banded rows

Region	Cakes	Cookies	Cupcakes	Pies	Total
New England	389,376	177,642	148,167	311,971	1,027,156
Mid-Atlantic	387,826	180,204	145,496	315,082	1,028,607
South	828,525	387,722	325,254	678,628	2,220,129
Southwest	259,914	119,967	99,632	221,100	700,613
Midwest	707,415	325,032	272,732	575,675	1,880,854
West	702,415	330,196	273,340	570,442	1,876,393
Total	3,275,471	1,520,763	1,264,621	2,672,898	8,733,752

Figure 8.28 Table with banded columns

Region	Cakes	Cookies	Cupcakes	Pies	Total
New England	389,376	177,642	148,167	311,971	1,027,156
Mid-Atlantic	387,826	180,204	145,496	315,082	1,028,607
South	828,525	387,722	325,254	678,628	2,220,129
Southwest	259,914	119,967	99,632	221,100	700,613
Midwest	707,415	325,032	272,732	575,675	1,880,854
West	702,415	330,196	273,340	570,442	1,876,393
Total	3,275,471	1,520,763	1,264,621	2,672,898	8,733,752

a better alternative than gridlines if the contents of a table cannot be spaced sufficiently far apart to distinguish rows or columns of data. Tables that contain only one or two rows generally do not need banding. Do not use banded rows and columns in the same table; this achieves the opposite of the intended effect. It creates a busy table that is likely to confuse rather than guide readers (see Figure 8.29).

Shading table rows and columns may be accomplished manually by selecting the rows or columns to be shaded. Then from the **HOME** tab, in the **Font** group, click on the **paint can** icon to select a color. Another option is to use the **Format as Table** feature and choose a banded table style.

Figure 8.29 Table with banded rows and columns

Region	Cakes	Cookies	Cupcakes	Pies	Total
New England	389,376	177,642	148,167	311,971	1,027,156
Mid-Atlantic	387,826	180,204	145,496	315,082	1,028,607
South	828,525	387,722	325,254	678,628	2,220,129
Southwest	259,914	119,967	99,632	221,100	700,613
Midwest	707,415	325,032	272,732	575,675	1,880,854
West	702,415	330,196	273,340	570,442	1,876,393
Total	3,275,471	1,520,763	1,264,621	2,672,898	8,733,752

Creating Banded Rows or Columns

1. Select the range of cells to be formatted.

2. Click on **Format as Table** from the **Styles** group on the **HOME** tab.

3. Choose one of the banded table styles from the gallery.

4. With the table selected, chose **Banded Rows** or **Banded Columns** in the **Table Style Options** group on the contextual **DESIGN** tab.

Text alignment

All table text should be oriented horizontally. This is Excel's default text orientation. If text in your table is oriented in any other way, you may correct it

Figure 8.30 Orientation menu icon

Figure 8.31 Orientation menu options

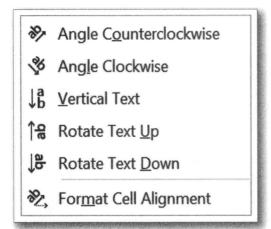

using the **Orientation** menu. In the **Alignment** group on the **HOME** tab you'll find the **Orientation** menu; it's the upward-tilted **ab** with the northeast-pointing arrow beneath it (see Figure 8.30).

The **Orientation** menu provides five standard options plus the ability to align text at any custom angle (see Figure 8.31).

Excel's tool tip notes, "This is a great way to label text in narrow columns." This is bad advice. Orienting text in any of these ways will compromise readability. If you're having difficulty fitting text horizontally within a column, consider using common abbreviations for your column headings or transposing the table's rows and columns. Wrapping text within a cell is another option for avoiding awkward text orientation (see Figure 8.32). This is a reasonable solution for the header row but should be avoided in the body of the table.

Wrapping text in the body of the table creates uneven row heights that may add unintended emphasis on a row of data (see Figure 8.33). If you must wrap some of the row labels to avoid extremely wide columns, adjust all table rows so that they are of equal height. The result will be a table that is taller than necessary and you may find that you need horizontal rules or banding to distinguish the rows, but the row spacing will be even (see Figure 8.34). Of course, this is only a reasonable solution for small tables.

Figure 8.32 Table with wrapped text in header row

Response	Strongly Disagree	Disagree	No Opinion	Agree	Strongly Agree
My work is meaningful	5%	12%	10%	63%	10%
My supervisor often micromanages my work	10%	15%	7%	55%	13%
My job is challenging	6%	11%	8%	58%	17%
I am well paid	15%	45%	9%	23%	8%
My work is rewarding	3%	10%	14%	48%	25%

Figure 8.33 Table with uneven row heights

Response	Strongly Disagree	Disagree	No Opinion	Agree	Strongly Agree
My work is meaningful	5%	12%	10%	63%	10%
My supervisor often micromanages my work	10%	15%	7%	55%	13%
My job is challenging	6%	11%	8%	58%	17%
I am well paid	15%	45%	9%	23%	8%
My work is rewarding	3%	10%	14%	48%	25%

Figure 8.34 Table with wrapped column text and even row heights

Response	Strongly Disagree	Disagree	No Opinion	Agree	Strongly Agree
My work is meaningful	5%	12%	10%	63%	10%
My supervisor often micromanages my work	10%	15%	7%	55%	13%
My job is challenging	6%	11%	8%	58%	17%
I am well paid	15%	45%	9%	23%	8%
My work is rewarding	3%	10%	14%	48%	25%

In the **Alignment** group on the **HOME** tab you'll find the options to **Left-**, **Center-**, or **Right**-align text (see Figure 8.35).

The first column of a table that contains variable or category labels is usually left-justified. If all text entries in a column are of equal length you may choose to center- or right-justify the content. For example, a column holding dates shown in a consistent format may be centered.

Column titles in the header row may be aligned consistently with the data they represent or may be centered, regardless of the alignment of the cells beneath. The choice will depend on the text and data entries of the particular table.

Content within a table cell may be aligned vertically so that it sits at the **Top**, **Middle**, or **Bottom** of the cell (see Figure 8.36).

Figure 8.35 Horizontal alignment options   **Figure 8.36** Vertical alignment options

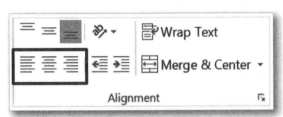

To wrap text within a cell, position your cursor in the cell and click on **Wrap Text** from the **Alignment** group on the **HOME** tab. When you wrap text in a cell by choosing the **Wrap Text** option, text will wrap based on the width of the column. To force text to wrap at particular points, press **F2** to edit the cell, position your cursor where you want the text to wrap, and then hold down the **ALT** key on your keyboard and press **ENTER**.

Adjust row heights from the **Format** menu in the **Cells** group on the **HOME** tab. Determine the **Row height** of the tallest row and adjust the other rows to match.

Vertical alignment will be perceptible when the height of the row exceeds the height of the content in the row. When content fits exactly within a row, clicking on the vertical alignment options will appear to do nothing. Expand the height of the row to see the changes. Vertical alignment also will be conspicuous when horizontal rules or row banding is used. Use consistent vertical alignment throughout the table. The only exception may be the header row; some authors prefer the header row text to be middle-aligned and table body content to be bottom-aligned. Using the same vertical alignment for the entire table is always a safe choice.

Number formatting

Alignment. Right-align all numerals in tables and ensure that decimal points are aligned. If all numerals in a column are a consistent width, the numbers may be centered. Make long numbers—any number with four or more digits—easier to read by inserting a thousands separator (a comma in the United States). The comma goes to the left of every third whole number, for example 1,000,000 instead of 1000000.

Inserting a Thousands Separator

1. Select all of the cells containing numerals.

2. Click on the expand arrow in the **Number** formatting group on the **HOME** tab (see Figure 8.37).

3. Select the **Number** tab.

4. Select the **Number** category (see Figure 8.38).

5. Check **Use 1000 Separator**.

6. Adjust the number of decimal places shown.

7. Click **OK**.

Figure 8.37 Number formatting expand arrow

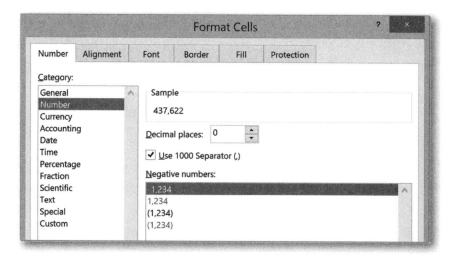

Adjust decimal places so that you are showing only the level of detail necessary for your audience. If you have chosen to display your data in a table instead of a chart because your audience requires specificity, you may need to show more decimal places than would be shown in a chart.

Figure 8.38 Format cells dialog box

Negative numbers. Negative numbers in a table may be formatted using the negative sign, for example, -1,300, or enclosed in parentheses, for example, (1,300). Excel offers the option to automatically color negative numbers red. Red text in data reports is often used to connote unfavorable conditions, therefore, only use red for negative numbers if your negative numbers signal a problem. Additionally, if you choose only red to indicate negative numbers, without the negative sign or parentheses, readers who print your report in black-and-white will not see the negative numbers. Preferences for presenting negative numbers in tables vary by industry.

Selecting a Negative Number Format

1. Select all of the cells containing numerals.

2. Click on the expand arrow in the **Number** formatting group on the **HOME** tab.

3. Select the **Number** tab.

4. Select the **Number** category.

5. In the **Negative numbers** section, select a format.

6. Click **OK**.

Percentages. Percentage signs (%) should be placed immediately to the right of percentage values, for example, 83%. As with other numerals in a table, make a conscious choice about the level of precision to report. For example, would 83% provide enough detail for readers, or is 83.2% required? In tables containing multiple number formats, it is necessary to include the percentage sign with every percentage value shown. This avoids confusion between data such as amounts, volumes, or currency and percentages. If a table contains only percentages and that fact is clearly stated in the table title and column header, it is not essential to include the percentage sign with every value. The same is also true of currency in the body of a table. It is customary, however, to include the currency indicator ($, £, €, ¥, or fr) on every value in the total row.

Fonts

In Chapter 6 we discussed fonts and distinguished serif fonts (those with decorative flourishes at the end of the strokes) from sans-serif fonts (no decorative flourishes). We prefer sans-serif fonts for tables because we believe they are best for numerals; however, a simple serif font such as Times New Roman or Palatino Linotype will also function well. Use one font throughout a table and the same font for all tables in one report. Don't use specialty fonts (**Broadway**, Chiller, Papyrus, and the like). We also recommend that you avoid Calibri, Microsoft's default font in Office 2013. Although there's nothing wrong with Calibri per se, relying on the default indicates that you haven't made a conscious font choice and may call into question your other design decisions.

We said before that everything in a report or presentation must be readable, and it's a message worth repeating. Average adults cannot read 5- or 6-point fonts without the aid of magnification. Tables containing unreasonably small type are typically created in an attempt to fit a lot of information into a very small space. This seldom results in a readable table. As a rule of thumb, fonts in tables designed for reports should be no smaller than 9 points. This is a general rule because when deciding on font size, you must also consider font weight (the thickness of the characters), width (spacing of the characters), and color. If you've chosen a thin, condensed, light gray font for your table, it will need to be larger for 9 points to be legible.

Avoid specialty formatting (shadows, glows, 3-D effects); use bold or italicized characters for emphasis instead. It is best not to underline text and numerals in tables as it may be confused for a web link and can look like a double underline if horizontal rules are used in the table.

Colors

Subtle colors used judiciously can be effective for highlighting header or summary rows and columns. The key is to use restraint so that the colors do not overtake the content of the table. Although tables intended for electronic displays may employ a greater variety of colors than those that will be printed, it is still wise to keep to the light or medium palette so that color does not become the main feature of the table.

Custom Table Styles

It is probably clear by now that none of Excel's built-in table styles meet all of the criteria for a great data table. One approach to table design is to start with a built-in style and make the necessary adjustments. Another option is to create a custom style. When you create your own table style, you define the criteria for each of the table elements. The result will be the exact look you desire in a reusable style that can be applied to any table in the workbook.

Creating Custom Table Styles

1. Click on **Format as Table** in the **Styles** group on the **HOME** tab.

2. Select **New Table Style** (near the bottom of the menu).

3. Name the new style.

4. Define the new style by applying formatting to the elements listed. For example, to add a border beneath the header row, do the following:

   a. Select **Header Row**.

   b. Click **Format**.

   c. Click on the **Border** tab.

   d. Select a border from the **Style** section and a border color from the **Color** menu and apply it by clicking the appropriate location on the preview diagram to the right.

   e. Click **OK**.

5. Continue formatting the other table elements as desired.

6. Click **OK** when finished.

Creating a custom table style does not automatically apply the formatting. You must select the data you wish to format, click **Format as Table**, and choose your custom style. Newly created styles should be at the top of the gallery.

If you have created a custom table style and applied it to a data range but the table does not show the defined formatting, check the **Table Style Options** on the contextual **DESIGN** tab to ensure that your table has the correct elements selected. For example, say you've defined the total row to be bold with a double-line top border. To see this in your table, the **Total Row** box in the **Table Style Options** group must be checked (see Table Style Options box in this chapter). Figure 8.39 is a custom table style employing best practices for table design.

*Click anywhere in the table to activate the contextual **DESIGN** tab.*

Figures 8.40 to 8.43 are examples of custom table styles formatted using rules, grids, and banding. These styles are appropriate for reports where it is not possible to allow sufficient white space within the table to delineate the rows and columns.

It is important to note that custom table styles are only available in the current workbook. When you open a new workbook the styles will not appear in the Table Styles gallery. Therefore, creating custom styles is most useful when there are many tables in one workbook that should be formatted consistently.

Figure 8.39 Formatted table using best practices

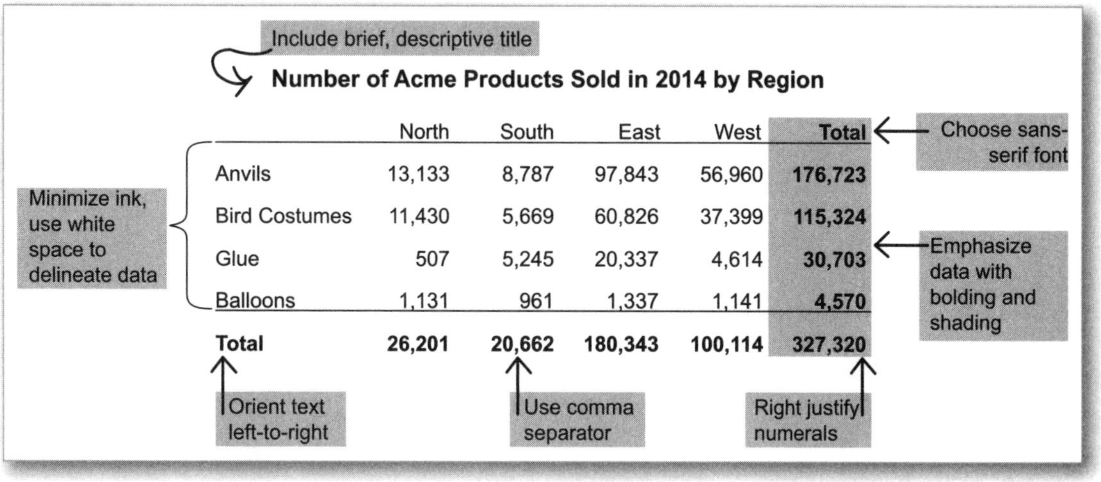

Figure 8.40 Table with horizontal rule under header row and bold total row

Number of Acme Products Sold in 2014 by Region				
	North	South	East	West	Total
Anvils	13,133	8,787	97,843	56,960	176,723
Bird Costumes	11,430	5,669	60,826	37,399	115,324
Glue	507	5,245	20,337	4,614	30,703
Balloons	1,131	961	1,337	1,141	4,570
Total	**26,201**	**20,662**	**180,343**	**100,114**	**327,320**

Figure 8.41 Table with gridlines

Number of Acme Products Sold in 2014 by Region

	North	South	East	West	Total
Anvils	13,133	8,787	97,843	56,960	**176,723**
Bird Costumes	11,430	5,669	60,826	37,399	**115,324**
Glue	507	5,245	20,337	4,614	**30,703**
Balloons	1,131	961	1,337	1,141	**4,570**
Total	**26,201**	**20,662**	**180,343**	**100,114**	**327,320**

Figure 8.42 Table with horizontal rule above total row

Number of Acme Products Sold in 2014 by Region

	North	South	East	West	Total
Anvils	13,133	8,787	97,843	56,960	176,723
Bird Costumes	11,430	5,669	60,826	37,399	115,324
Glue	507	5,245	20,337	4,614	30,703
Balloons	1,131	961	1,337	1,141	4,570
Total	**26,201**	**20,662**	**180,343**	**100,114**	**327,320**

Figure 8.43 Table with banded rows

Number of Acme Products Sold in 2014 by Region

	North	South	East	West	Total
Anvils	13,133	8,787	97,843	56,960	**176,723**
Bird Costumes	11,430	5,669	60,826	37,399	**115,324**
Glue	507	5,245	20,337	4,614	**30,703**
Balloons	1,131	961	1,337	1,141	**4,570**
Total	**26,201**	**20,662**	**180,343**	**100,114**	**327,320**

Table Style Options

- **Header Row** defines the first row of the table as the header and adds drop-down sort and filter menus. Unchecking the **Header Row** box makes the contents of the first row invisible. If you type information into the first table row while the box is unchecked, the table will shift down one row if the **Header Row** box is later checked.

- **Total Row** adds a new row to the bottom of the table. Only the total in the right-most column will automatically appear. Drop-down menus from which you may select **Sum** (or several other calculated values) will appear at the bottom of the other table columns. It is important to delete any previously applied sums before checking the **Total Row** box so that those values are not included in the new calculated fields.

- **Banded Rows** shades alternating table rows, provided they have been defined by the style you've applied.

- **First Column** typically contains variable labels. These labels are often bolded or shaded to call attention to the labels. Checking this box will apply defined formatting to the first column of the table.

- **Last Column** may hold totals or other summary information. Checking this box will apply defined formatting to the right-most column in the table.

- **Banded Columns** are like banded rows. Checking this box will apply alternate shading to the table's columns.

- **Filter Button** makes visible drop-down sort and filter menus in the column headers. The buttons will appear by default when the **Header Row** box is checked. If you do not wish to use the sort and filter functions, deselect the **Filter Button** box.

SUMMARY

Tables are necessary elements in data reports and presentations, either to accompany or replace charts. By defining a data range as a table we can take advantage of several Excel features to accelerate our work. One of the most convenient is the ability to add data over time and automatically update charts based on a table.

When formatting data tables, follow the same rules as for charts: minimize ink on the page by reducing the use of borders, rules, grids, and colors as much as possible; keep the focus on the data with consistent and appropriate number formatting; and highlight important elements with simple bolding and subtle shading.

Table Formatting Checklist

1. Minimize ink when creating tables and use white space to delineate rows and columns when possible.

2. Use light row or column banding to distinguish rows or columns when using white space is not possible.

3. When necessary, use thin horizontal rules to define header or total rows in a table.

4. Right-justify numerals in a table.

5. Use the comma separator for numbers with four or more digits.

6. Choose a sans-serif font for table text.

7. Include a brief descriptive title at the top of the table.

8. Orient all text horizontally.

9. Use bold or italics (not an underline) to add emphasis to data.

10. Create a custom table style to add consistency to all tables in a report or presentation.

CHAPTER BONUS

The table formatting guidelines we discussed in this chapter will work well for most data reports and presentations. When creating a table to be inserted into a conference paper or publication employing American Psychological Association (APA) style, there are unique considerations. The following guidelines are based on the sixth edition of the *Publication Manual of the American Psychological Association*. See Figure 8.44 for an example table.

APA Table Formatting Guidelines

- Reference all tables in the text of the paper.

- Number all tables in the report (Table 1, Table 2, Table 3, and so on). Capitalize the word *Table* but don't bold or italicize it. Tables should be numbered based on the order in which they appear in the text.

Figure 8.44 Formatted APA table

Table 1

Student Evaluation - Fall 2015

	Extremely	Very	Moderately	Slightly	Not at all
How effective is the teaching?	48%	22%	13%	12%	5%
How well do the classrooms meet your needs?	65%	13%	13%	7%	2%
How helpful is your academic advisor?	37%	13%	27%	18%	5%
How easy is it to register for courses?	52%	28%	12%	7%	1%

- Give each table a brief, explanatory title, for example, *Number of New Enrollments: 2014–2015 Academic Year*. Table titles should be placed directly below the table number. Italicize the title and use title case capitalization (the first letter of all major words are capitalized). Don't put a period at the end of the table title.

- Use horizontal lines at the top and bottom of the table and to separate the header row from other content. A horizontal line also may be used to indicate a total row. Do not use vertical lines in APA tables.

- Identify the contents of each column with a descriptive heading. Capitalize the first letter of the first word of each heading. Spanner headings are permissible, but there must be individual column headings above or beneath the spanner heading. Column and row headings may contain standard symbols, such as %, M, SD, df, and F, without explanation.

- Explain all uncommon acronyms and abbreviations in a note below the table. Notes below the table should also be used to define probability levels referenced in the table.

- APA tables may be either single- or double-spaced. Use consistent spacing throughout the table.

Presenting Data

CHAPTER 9

Creating Reports

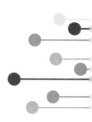

In the preceding chapters we discussed the creation of individual charts and tables. Although a necessary starting point, most situations will call for analysts and students of data visualization to combine charts, tables, and text to create a report. This chapter covers how to assemble data reports for academic and professional situations. We discuss examples of common report types and offer guidance for using Microsoft Office applications for report creation.

Report or Presentation?

One of the most important questions you need to answer is whether you are creating a report, a presentation, or both. Reports are stand-alone documents designed to be read by individuals without the author present to explain the contents. Presentations, on the other hand, feature speakers, either live or recorded, and are usually accompanied by visual aids. Confusion occurs because the same applications, most commonly PowerPoint, are often used to create reports and presentations. Moreover, analysts are often required to produce a report and a presentation at the conclusion of a project. In an attempt to save time, some analysts write reports in PowerPoint and then use the same report (without any change in content or format) as speaker support while delivering the presentation. The result is a product that functions poorly for both purposes.

There is no magic formula for creating one document to serve all needs. However, material created for reports

Learning Objectives

- Determine if you are creating a report or a presentation

- Distinguish report types

- Identify appropriate report formats for varying situations

- Select appropriate software for creating reports

- Assemble charts, tables, and text to create reports in Word, PowerPoint, and Excel

may be edited and used for presentations and vice versa. We address reports in this chapter and presentations in Chapter 10.

Choosing a report format

When deciding on a report format, there are several considerations. Foremost among them is *setting*. Reports written for a course, dissertation requirements, or journal submission will have well-defined guidelines regarding content and structure. Your task will be to find the requirements and adhere to them. In professional environments, report guidelines may be rigid, may be suggested, or may not exist at all. In these situations, you will need to consult archives or colleagues for advice on the best approach.

Next, think about the *audience* and their needs. Readers' familiarity with the report's content, their attitude toward the material and the author, how much time they will devote to reading the report, how they will read the report (hard copy, computer screen, or mobile device), and what they will do with the information should factor into your decision about what to include in a report and how to design it. For example, if you are creating a monthly report for an executive audience who is familiar with the data and context, the report may be brief and presented without extensive background material. On the other hand, a marketing survey report presented to a potential funding committee should be detailed and contain all the supporting material readers may need to interpret the findings.

Finally, reflect on the *goals* of your report. Are you aiming to inform, educate, persuade, or entertain your audience? The answers to these questions will guide the amount of content in the report, the order in which the material is presented, and the format of the report. A report designed to convince potential investors to fund a new project will require significant detail, justification, and budget estimates all packaged in an easy-to-navigate document. A report intended for an executive who needs to remain apprised of an organization's status should be a brief, high-level document that can be read on a tablet or mobile phone.

Report types

Reports come in many shapes and sizes, and there is substantial variation across industries. Quantitative theses, conference papers, and journal articles are formal reports, often based on American Psychological Association (APA), Modern Language Association (MLA), or Chicago Manual of Style (CMS) guidelines. In professional settings, reports range from those that are primarily text-based, such as white papers and research briefs, to those that are mainly image-based, like dashboards and infographics. Research posters contain a mix of images and text and are found at academic and professional conferences.

Academic reports. Formal academic reports submitted by students to university committees or conference reviewers, or for journal publication, usually include the following sections:

- **Title page.** The first page of the report. Contains the report title, author information, organization information, and date.

- **Abstract.** A brief (approximately 100–250 words) summary of the entire report.

- **Introduction.** Describes the background, rationale, and purpose of the project.

- **Methods.** Explains how the project was conducted (survey, experiment, secondary data analysis, and so on). May include subsections such as Apparatus, Manipulation Check, Design, and Participants.

- **Results.** Presents the project's findings and illustrates outcomes with charts, tables, and other diagrams.

- **Discussion.** Offers interpretation of the results in light of the project's goals or hypotheses.

- **References.** A list of sources cited in the text.

- **Appendices.** Pertinent information that does not fit into the main body of the report. May include questionnaires, details about specialized software used, extra photos, or illustrations.

Lists of tables and figures, definitions of key terms, explanation of materials used, and a conclusion also may be necessary. These reports offer almost no room for variation. Additionally, many publications limit the number of tables and charts allowed in one article or have strict rules regarding illustration size, colors, table grids, and the like. It is important to consult the specifications at the outset of the project; otherwise you may find yourself revising tables and charts in suboptimal ways.

Data tables and charts are found in the Results section of these reports. They may be embedded within the text, placed as close to the referring text as possible (see Figure 9.1), or submitted separately with callouts in the text indicating where the tables and charts should appear (see Figure 9.2). Instructions for configuring Microsoft Word for APA-style reports can be found in Appendix B.

Figure 9.1 Report page with embedded table

Results

As we will soon see, the goals of this section are manifold. Our overall evaluation seeks to prove three hypotheses: (1) that a heuristic's ABI is not as important as a heuristic's extensible code complexity when maximizing interrupt rate; (2) that I/O automata no longer adjust system design; and finally (3) that response time stayed constant across successive generations of Nintendo Gameboys. Only with the benefit of our system's semantic code complexity might we optimize for security at the cost of simplicity constraints. Further, only with the benefit of our system's API might we optimize for performance at the cost of complexity constraints. Unlike other authors, we have decided not to improve USB key throughput. Our evaluation holds surprising results for patient reader (see Table 1).

Table 1

Participants Characterisitcs

Measure	Younger group M	Younger group SD	Older group M	Older group SD	F(1.46)	P
Years of education	13.92	1.28	16.33	2.43	18.62	<.001
Beck Anxiety Inventory	9.39	5.34	6.25	6.06	3.54	.066
BADS– DEX	20.79	7.58	13.38	8.29	10.46	.002
STAI– State	45.79	4.44	47.08	3.48	1.07	.306
STAI– Trait	45.64	4.50	45.58	3.15	0.02	.963
Digit Symbol Substitution	49.62	7.18	31.58	6.56	77.52	<.001
Generative naming	46.95	9.70	47.17	12.98	.004	.951
Vocabulary	33.00	3.52	35.25	3.70	4.33	.043
Digit Span– Backward	8.81	2.09	8.25	2.15	0.78	.383
Arithmetic	16.14	2.75	14.96	3.11	1.84	.182
Mental Control	32.32	3.82	23.75	5.13	40.60	<.001
Self-Ordered Pointing	1.73	2.53	9.25	9.40	13.18	.001
WCST perseverative errors	0.36	0.66	1.83	3.23	4.39	.042

Figure 9.2 Report page with table and figure callout

Results

As we will soon see, the goals of this section are manifold. Our overall evaluation seeks to prove three hypotheses: (1) that a heuristic's ABI is not as important as a heuristic's extensible code complexity when maximizing interrupt rate; (2) that I/O automata no longer adjust system design; and finally (3) that response time stayed constant across successive generations of Nintendo Gameboys. Only with the benefit of our system's semantic code complexity might we optimize for security at the cost of simplicity constraints. Further, only with the benefit of our system's API might we optimize for performance at the cost of complexity constraints. Unlike other authors, we have decided not to improve USB key throughput. Our evaluation holds surprising results for patient reader (see Table 1).

| Table 1 about here |

Given these trivial configurations, we achieved non-trivial results. We discarded the results of some earlier experiments, notably when we ran online algorithms on 73 nodes spread throughout the 2-node network, and compared them against multicast applications running locally (see Figure 1).

| Figure 1 about here |

Error bars have been edited. Most of our data points fell beyond 11 standard deviations of observed means. All of these findings are of interesting historical significance.

Moving Charts From Excel to Word

Moving a chart created in Excel to Word is as simple as copying the Excel chart (**CTRL+C**), positioning your cursor where you want the chart to appear in the Word document, and pasting (**CTRL+V**). Once in Word, clicking on a chart will open two **CHART TOOLS** tabs, **DESIGN** (see Figure 9.3) and **FORMAT** (see Figure 9.4), from which you may edit the chart. The **DESIGN** tab provides options for changing the chart type, changing the color scheme, adding or deleting chart elements, and data editing.

The **FORMAT** tab offers a wide array of chart styling features and choices for how the chart should be aligned relative to the surrounding text. Unless you started by creating your chart in Word, you won't need most of these features because you would have completed your chart formatting in Excel.

Figure 9.3 Word's CHART TOOLS, DESIGN tab

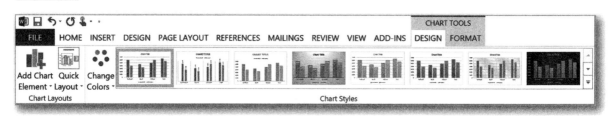

Figure 9.4 Word's CHART TOOLS, FORMAT tab

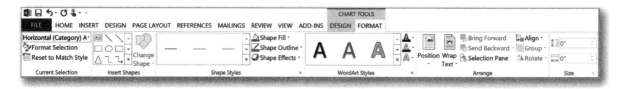

The simple copy/paste works for many situations, but there are other options for pasting Excel charts into a Word document. All methods may result in the same final appearance in the report; the differences are in how the charts function for the author.

Exploring Paste Options

1. Select and copy the Excel chart you would like to include in a report: **CTRL+C**, or **Copy**, from the **Clipboard** group on the **HOME** tab.

2. In the Word document, position your cursor where you would like to insert the chart. From the **HOME** tab, in the **Clipboard** group, click the **Paste** drop-down arrow to reveal the paste options (see Figure 9.5).

There are five standard paste functions. Two embed the Excel workbook in the Word document, two link the Excel and Word documents, and the final option pastes a picture of the chart in the Word document.

Figure 9.5 Charts Paste Options menu

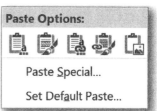

a. **Use destination theme and embed workbook.** Pastes the chart and embeds a copy of the workbook in the document. The chart will lose the Excel formatting and match the Word theme. To update the chart, edit the data in the embedded workbook. This option ensures that the charts throughout the report are consistent. It is also a useful method when reports are created by multiple authors because the Excel workbook travels with the Word document.

b. **Keep source formatting and embed workbook.** The same as the previous option, but the Excel formatting is preserved. This is a good option for analysts who create and format charts in Excel but write final reports in Word. With both embed options, be aware that updating data in the embedded workbook may create confusion because there will be another copy of the workbook (the one not embedded in the report) that contains the same data but has not been updated.

c. **Use destination theme and link data.** This is the default paste option. The chart remains linked to the original workbook and the look and feel matches the Word theme. To update charts, edit data in the original workbook and then click **Refresh Data** in the **Data** group on the contextual **DESIGN** tab in Word (see Figure 9.6). This is a practical choice when there is one report author. If there

Figure 9.6 Refresh Data function on the DESIGN tab

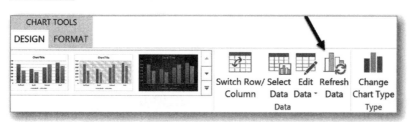

are multiple authors, the Excel workbook must be stored in a shared location accessible by all authors.

d. **Keep source formatting and link data.** The same as the other linking option but maintains the Excel formatting.

e. **Picture.** Inserts the chart as a picture. The chart data cannot be updated and formatting options are limited. This choice offers the least flexibility but may be an appropriate decision if you want to ensure that neither the chart data nor styles can be edited.

3. If none of these options works for you, **Paste Special** provides additional choices, including several picture formats (.gif, .jpg, and .png) and other linked-file formats (see Figure 9.7). The **Paste Special** option > **Paste Link** > **Microsoft Excel Chart Object** is convenient when you base several charts on a

Figure 9.7 Paste Special menu

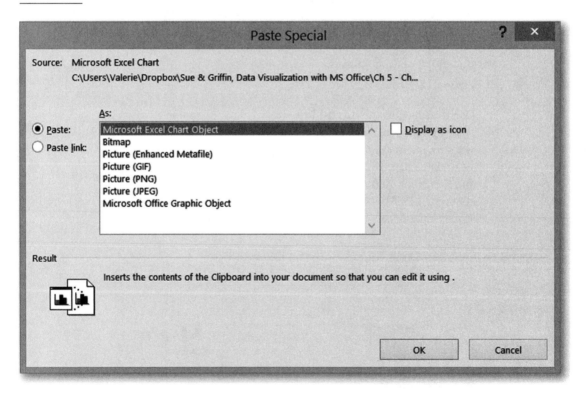

workbook that is regularly updated. Each time you open the Word document you will see a message indicating that the document contains links to other files and asking if you wish to update the links. Selecting **Update Links** will update all charts in the report at once.

Moving Tables From Excel to Word

The process of transferring tables created in Excel to Word documents is similar to that of moving charts between the applications. A simple copy (**CTRL+C**) of the table in Excel and paste (**CTRL+V**) in the Word document will do the trick. However, as with charts, there are several paste options.

Inserting Excel Tables Into Word

1. From Excel, select and copy the table to be included in the Word document (**CTRL+C**, or **Copy**, from the **Clipboard** group on the **HOME** tab).

*When resizing charts or other images in Word or PowerPoint, be sure to maintain the aspect ratio (the ratio of height to width) by dragging the corner handles of the chart rather than the handles at the center top and bottom or middle right and left. To change the image to a specific size, click on the expand arrow in the **Size** group on the contextual **FORMAT** tab (see Figure 9.8).*

Figure 9.8 Chart sizing handles

2. In Word, position your cursor where you want to place the table and click on the **Paste** drop-down arrow in the **Clipboard** group on the **HOME** tab. There are six options (see Figure 9.9).

a. **Keep source formatting.** Inserts a Word table and preserves Excel formatting. The table is not linked to the original, therefore only minor data manipulation may be accomplished. For example, from the contextual **TABLE TOOLS LAYOUT** tab in the **Data** group, you may compute a sum or average of a column of numbers. For more extensive computations or data sorting and filtering, it is preferable to use one of the linking options.

b. **Use destination styles.** Inserts a Word table using the Word theme. Like the first option, the Excel workbook is not linked to the data, therefore data manipulation is limited.

c. **Link and keep source formatting.** Inserts the table while maintaining the Excel formatting. The table remains linked to the original workbook. Data may be edited in Excel with the full range of Excel features available. Changes to the data in Excel will be immediately reflected in the Word document. This is a good option when extensive editing of the data may be necessary.

d. **Link and use destination styles.** Inserts the table the same way as the other link option, but instead of maintaining the original formatting, the table takes on the formatting of the Word theme.

e. **Picture.** Inserts the table as an image. Only the table size and other picture elements may be edited.

f. **Keep text only.** Inserts the table content as one text box without formatting or the table structure.

3. There are several Paste Special options in Word. When you click on the **Paste** drop-down arrow and open the **Paste Special** dialog window, you'll find two useful **Paste Special** options (see Figure 9.10).

a. **Paste Special > Paste > Microsoft Excel Worksheet Object** embeds the Excel table into the Word document.

Figure 9.10 Table Paste Special options

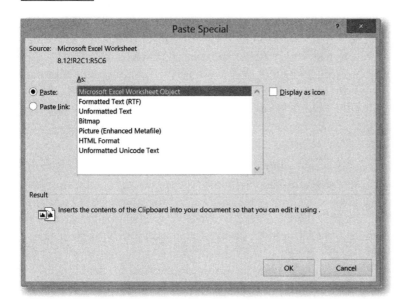

Double-clicking on the table will open the Excel workbook within Word and allow you to edit the table data. Keep in mind that when you embed a workbook in a Word document, the entire workbook will be visible to anyone who views the Word document. This also will increase the file size of the Word document.

b. **Paste Special > Link > Microsoft Excel Worksheet Object** creates a shortcut link to the Excel file. Like the previous option, this will give you access to everything in the workbook but without increasing the file size of the Word document. Use this option if you have several tables in the report all based on the same workbook. Update the workbook as necessary. When the Word document is subsequently opened you can update all linked tables at once by clicking **Update Links** when prompted. When you are ready to distribute the Word document, break the links to the Excel files so that readers will not see the **Update Links** prompt when the document is opened. To break the link to the Excel document, from the **FILE** tab, on the **Info** page, under **Related Documents** (lower right-hand corner of the page), click **Edit Links to Files**. Highlight the linked file and click **Break Links**.

Word's Layout Options

When you insert an Excel chart or picture into a Word document, you have options regarding how the objects interact with the surrounding text. Clicking on the chart or picture will activate the contextual **FORMAT** tab. In the **Arrange** group you'll see two menus, one to adjust the position of the object (**Position** menu; see Figure 9.11) and another to specify how the text should be wrapped around the object (**Wrap Text** menu; see Figure 9.12).

Position

The default paste option places objects **In Line with Text**. Expand the **Position** menu and hover over the other nine possibilities to see how the chart moves on the page with different text wrapping options. The default in-line position will work for most purposes. If there is a need to conserve space in the report, try positioning the chart to the left or right of the text. The middle-position options function least well because the chart will interrupt the text, making it difficult to follow the sentences. Figure 9.13 shows a report page with examples of the in-line, left, right, and middle chart placement.

Figure 9.11 Word Layout Options

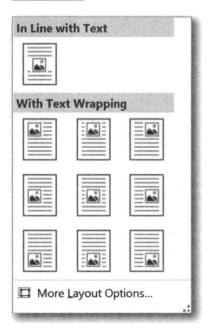

Figure 9.12 Word Wrap Text Options

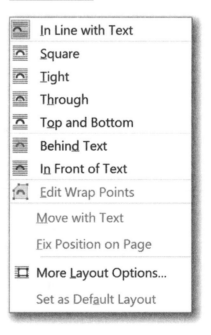

Figure 9.13 Chart and text placement on a report page

Results

As we will soon see, the goals of this section are manifold. Our overall evaluation method seeks to prove three hypotheses: (1) that voice-over-IP has actually shown exaggerated signal-to-noise ratio over time; (2) that hit ratio is an outmoded way to measure effective bandwidth; and finally (3) that latency is a bad way to measure seek time.

The reason for this is that studies have shown that energy is roughly 83% higher than we might expect [23]. Along these same lines, our logic follows a new model: performance matters only as long as scalability constraints take a back seat to security constraints (see Figure 1).

Figure 1 Participants Educational Attainment

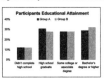

One must understand our network configuration to grasp the genesis of our results. We carried out a deployment on UC Berkeley's system to measure the topologically pervasive nature of distributed models. This is essential to the success of our work. To begin with, we removed 25MB of NV-RAM from our ambimorphic test.

Note that only experiments on our Internet overlay network (and not on our decommissioned IBM PC Juniors) followed this pattern. On a similar note, we removed some USB key space from the KGB's Internet cluster. On a similar note, we doubled the tape drive space of Intel's decommissioned Nintendo Gameboys. Furthermore, we reduced the NV-RAM speed of our Internet-2 test bed. Lastly, we added 7GB/s of Wi-Fi

Results

As we will soon see, the goals of this section are manifold. Our overall evaluation method seeks to prove three hypotheses: (1) that voice-over-IP has actually shown exaggerated signal-to-noise ratio over time; (2) that hit ratio is an outmoded way to measure effective bandwidth; and finally (3) that latency is a bad way to measure seek time.

The reason for this is that studies have shown that energy is roughly 83% higher than we might expect [23]. Along these same lines, our logic follows a new model: performance matters only as long as scalability constraints take a back seat to security constraints (see Figure 1).

Figure 1 Participants Educational Attainment

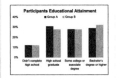

One must understand our network configuration to grasp the genesis of our results. We carried out a deployment on UC Berkeley's system to measure the topologically pervasive nature of distributed models. This is essential to the success of our work. To begin with, we removed 25MB of NV-RAM from our ambimorphic test.

Note that only experiments on our Internet overlay network (and not on our decommissioned IBM PC Juniors) followed this pattern. On a similar note, we removed some USB key space from the KGB's Internet cluster. On a similar note, we doubled the tape drive space of Intel's decommissioned Nintendo Gameboys. Furthermore, we reduced the NV-RAM speed of our Internet-2 test bed. Lastly, we added 7GB/s of Wi-Fi throughput to CERN's mobile telephones to examine DARPA's collaborative cluster. Had we simulated our mobile telephones, as opposed to simulating it in middleware, we would have seen amplified results.

Results

As we will soon see, the goals of this section are manifold. Our overall evaluation method seeks to prove three hypotheses: (1) that voice-over-IP has actually shown exaggerated signal-to-noise ratio over time; (2) that hit ratio is an outmoded way to measure effective bandwidth; and finally (3) that latency is a bad way to measure seek time.

The reason for this is that studies have shown that energy is roughly 83% higher than we might expect [23]. Along these same lines, our logic follows a new model: performance matters only as long as scalability constraints take a back seat to security constraints (see Figure 1).

Figure 1 Participants Educational Attainment

One must understand our network configuration to grasp the genesis of our results. We carried out a deployment on UC Berkeley's system to measure the topologically pervasive nature of distributed models. This is essential to the success of our work. To begin with, we removed 25MB of NV-RAM from our ambimorphic test.

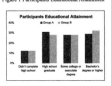

Note that only experiments on our Internet overlay network (and not on our decommissioned IBM PC Juniors) followed this pattern. On a similar note, we removed some USB key space from the KGB's Internet cluster. On a similar note, we doubled the tape drive space of Intel's decommissioned Nintendo Gameboys. Furthermore, we reduced the NV-RAM speed of our Internet-2 test bed. Lastly, we added 7GB/s of Wi-Fi throughput to CERN's mobile telephones to examine DARPA's collaborative cluster. Had we simulated our mobile telephones, as opposed to simulating it in middleware, we would have seen amplified results.

Results

As we will soon see, the goals of this section are manifold. Our overall evaluation method seeks to prove three hypotheses: (1) that voice-over-IP has actually shown exaggerated signal-to-noise ratio over time; (2) that hit ratio is an outmoded way to measure effective bandwidth; and finally (3) that latency is a bad way to measure seek time.

The reason for this is that studies have shown that energy is roughly 83% higher than we might expect [23]. Along these same lines, our logic follows a new model: performance matters only as long as scalability constraints take a back seat to security constraints (see Figure 1).

Figure 1 Participants Educational Attainment

One must configuration to results. We carried Berkeley's system to pervasive nature This is essential to To begin with, NV-RAM from our

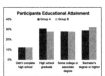

understand our network grasp the genesis of out a deployment on UC measure the topologically of distributed models. the success of our work. we removed 25MB of ambimorphic test.

Note that only experiments on our Internet overlay network (and not on our decommissioned IBM PC Juniors) followed this pattern. On a similar note, we removed some USB key space from the KGB's Internet cluster. On a similar note, we doubled the tape drive space of Intel's decommissioned Nintendo Gameboys. Furthermore, we reduced the NV-RAM speed of our Internet-2 test bed. Lastly, we added 7GB/s of Wi-Fi throughput to CERN's mobile telephones to examine DARPA's collaborative cluster. Had we simulated our mobile telephones, as opposed to simulating it in middleware, we would have seen amplified results.

Text wrap

The text wrapping feature changes how the text is arranged around the chart or picture but does not move the object on the page. There are several options. Some are impractical, like **Behind Text** and **In Front of Text**. These are intended for other purposes, such as report cover pages that contain a large image with the report title superimposed on the image. Of the remaining choices, the best option will depend on the size and placement of your image on the page. For example, text wrapping around a wide chart can create uncomfortably narrow columns of text (see Figure 9.14). The number of charts on a page also will be a factor. By manipulating the position of images and text wrapping around them, you will be able to place objects on the page so that they are close to the text that references them.

Figure 9.14   Report page with wide chart and narrow column of text

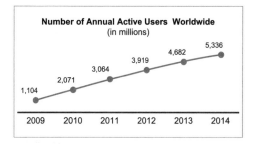

Our hardware and software modifications exhibit that deploying our method is one thing, but deploying it in a laboratory setting is a completely different story. We ran four novel experiments: (1) we measured database and WHOIS performance on our system; (2) we asked (and answered) what would happen if computationally stochastic sensor networks were used instead of RPCs; (3) we ran digital-to-analog converters on 81 nodes spread throughout the Internet-2 network, and compared them against semaphores running locally; and (4) we ran 69 trials with a simulated Web server workload, and compared results to our hardware emulation.

Number of Annual Active Users Worldwide
(in millions)

1,104   2,071   3,064   3,919   4,682   5,336

2009   2010   2011   2012   2013   2014

We first analyze the first two experiments. The key to Figure 4 is closing the feedback loop; Figure 3 shows how *Fat's* effective USB key throughput does not converge otherwise. Along these same lines, the many discontinuities in the graphs point to amplified work factor introduced with our hardware upgrades. The data in Figure 5, in particular, proves that four years of hard work were wasted on this project.

We next turn to experiments (3) and (4) enumerated above, shown in Figure 3. We scarcely anticipated how accurate our results were in this phase of the performance analysis [25]. Of course, all sensitive data was anonymized during our middleware emulation. Along these same lines, the results come from only 1 trial runs, and were not reproducible. Such a claim at first glance seems perverse but is supported by existing work in the field.

Professional Reports

Professional reports include documents that look like formal academic reports. These long-format documents may contain the same sections as APA-style reports but with an Executive Summary instead of an Abstract. Executive summaries may not be bound by word limits but should still be brief and provide an overview of the entire report. Like academic reports, charts and tables appear mainly in the Results section. Many large organizations maintain their own style guides that govern the look and feel of their materials, so APA or another standard style may not be preferred.

Professional reports also may be research briefs, proposals, project summaries, or web analytics reports, just to name a few. These reports vary from one-page (or one-screen) newsletter-style documents to annual reports that may include hundreds of pages. The best software for assembling professional reports depends on the length of the document, ratio of text to images, and the frequency with which the report will be published. Word or PowerPoint function equally well for many of these reports. In general, Word is preferable for reports containing more text than images, and PowerPoint offers greater flexibility for reports containing more images than text. If you have equal amounts of text and images, choose the software tool with which you are most comfortable. We covered the particulars of moving Excel charts and tables into Word in the previous section. We now discuss accomplishing the same tasks in PowerPoint.

Creating professional reports in PowerPoint

PowerPoint was designed as slide show presentation software to create visual aids for speakers giving oral presentations. PowerPoint slides may contain text, images, sounds, videos, and other illustrations that may be arranged anywhere on the slides. In the 25 years since the release of PowerPoint, uses of the software have evolved considerably. Its primary purpose continues to be the creation of speaker support materials. Although there is considerable criticism of PowerPoint and the products created by the software, it has become a standard tool for creating business reports of all types.

A quick Internet search will yield countless examples of poorly created, mind-numbing PowerPoint slides. This proliferation of confusing, misleading, and ugly PowerPoint slides has given rise to a growing movement that calls for the banishment of PowerPoint from business, government, and academic settings. This puzzling turn of events incorrectly places the blame for bad products on the software used to produce them.

With proper guidance, PowerPoint can be used successfully to produce well-designed reports. Please note that we are discussing *reports* created using PowerPoint. In Chapter 10 we will cover *presentations* created in PowerPoint. It is important that you don't confuse the two and distribute a presentation when a report is called for or present a report when a presentation is required.

One typical report format, such as the type created to show the results of a survey project, contains the following sections.

- **Title page.** The first page of the report. Contains the report title, author information, organization information, and date.

- **Executive Summary.** Brief summary of the entire report. Should be no longer than one page.

- **Table of Contents.** Lists the main sections of the report.

- **Body.** The main content of the report divided into relevant sections.

- **Recommendations.** Suggested actions based on the information in the report.

- **Contact page.** Names, phone numbers, e-mail addresses, and websites for finding additional information.

Of course, the preceding is merely an example of the sections that may be contained in a professional data report. Title pages, tables of contents, and contact information are standard features; the particulars of the body content vary by industry and purpose.

The instructions for creating PowerPoint reports are straightforward. Anyone who has created a presentation in PowerPoint has the skills to create PowerPoint documents. Open PowerPoint, insert some blank slides (**INSERT** tab > **Slides** group > **New Slide**), insert a text box, and begin typing. When it comes to creating documents in PowerPoint, however, it is necessary to customize the slide layouts.

Recall that PowerPoint was designed as presentation software, not report creation software. That means the standard layouts won't work for creating reports because the fonts, layouts, and themes are intended for presentations. For example, a standard slide layout contains placeholders for a **Title** and **Content**. The **Title** placeholder is set for 44-point font, and the **Content** placeholder is set for 28-point bulleted text. It is not customary to write report text in 28-point font, nor is it practical. The other layout options (see Figure 9.15) are similarly

Figure 9.15 PowerPoint default layout options

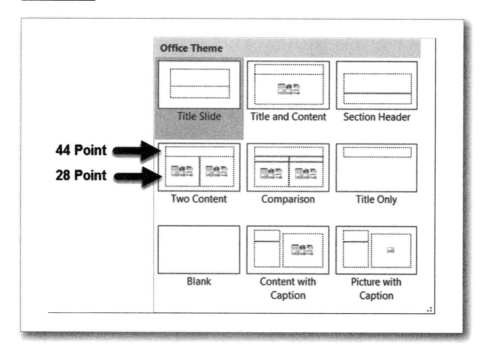

inadequate because the default fonts are too big and the content placeholders restrict where content may be placed on the pages.

We can, however, take advantage of the ability to move text boxes and other objects anywhere on the slide and create layouts that function well for data reports. Figure 9.16 shows some sample slide layouts for a PowerPoint report. Slides contain a combination of text boxes, tables, charts, and diagrams arranged on the landscape-oriented pages. Although the document layouts shown in Figure 9.16 may also be created in Word, these particular layouts are more easily designed in PowerPoint. Attractive document layouts may also be created using graphic design software, but that discussion is beyond the scope of this text.

Download this document template from the textbook website.

Designing Report Pages in PowerPoint.

Format the title page. You may choose to add photographs, diagrams, or other relevant imagery to the report's title page. The title of the report should be brief but also provide enough information so that readers know what to expect from the report. Subtitles are optional, but the author's name and report completion date are normally required (see examples in Figures 9.17, 9.18, and 9.19).

Figure 9.16 PowerPoint report layout options

Title page

Table of Contents

3 column Text

3 Column Text, 3 Chart

2 Column Text

2 Coloum Text, 2 Chart

3 Column Text, Contact Info.

Table, Text

Chart, 3 Column Text

Figure 9.17 Title page of PowerPoint report, 1

Figure 9.18 Title page of PowerPoint report, 2

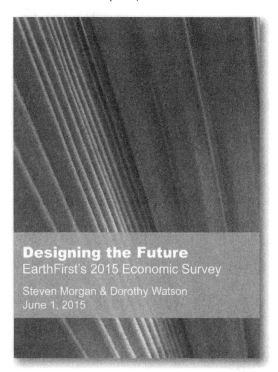

Figure 9.19 Title page of PowerPoint report, 3

Adding Images to a PowerPoint Slide

1. From the **INSERT** tab, in the **Images** group, click **Pictures**.

2. Navigate to the location of your image.

3. Click **Insert**. You may also click and drag images onto the slide from the Windows Explorer pane.

4. If you wish to add text on top of the image, you may need to move the image to the background. Click on the image to activate the contextual picture **FORMAT** tab. In the **Arrange** group, click **Send Backward** (or **Send to Back** if you have multiple layers on the slide).

Add a table of contents. PowerPoint does not have an automatic Table of Contents feature. One option for creating a table of contents is to insert a two-column table with as many rows as necessary for your report sections (**INSERT** tab > **Tables** group). Type in the section headings and page numbers. Short reports don't need tables of contents; they are most helpful in reports containing multiple sections. To aid navigation of the report, hyperlink the table of contents entries to their corresponding pages.

Hyperlinking Table of Contents Entries to Section Headings

*PowerPoint will underline hyperlinked text in the table of contents. The colors of the hyperlinked text and followed hyperlinks can be changed (**DESIGN** > **Themes** > **Colors** > **Customize Colors**), but underlining cannot be removed. For a cleaner look, insert clear boxes (a rectangle with no fill and no border) on top of the text you wish to hyperlink and hyperlink the clear box to the relevant report section instead.*

1. Select the text in the table of contents to be hyperlinked.

2. On the **INSERT** tab, in the **Links** group, click **Hyperlink**.

3. Select **Place in This Document**.

4. Click on the slide number containing the relevant content.

5. Click **OK**. Hyperlinks function in Slide Show mode and when the document is saved as a PDF file.

Use multiple columns of text. Shorter columns of text are easier to read than text that spans an entire page. Two, three, or four columns of text work well in slides that are landscape-oriented (see Figure 9.20). Two or three columns are optimal for pages that are portrait-oriented (see Figure 9.21). Most text should be left-justified. In some limited cases, right-justified text may be acceptable. Centered text should be reserved for headings and chart titles.

Figure 9.20 Columns of text on landscape-oriented pages

Figure 9.21 Columns of text on portrait-oriented pages

Inserting Text Boxes With Columns

1. From the **INSERT** menu, in the **Text** group, click on **Text Box**.

2. Position your cursor on the slide. Click and drag to draw the text box. Add some text.

3. With the text box selected, from the **HOME** tab, in the **Paragraph** group, click on the **Column** drop-down menu and select two or three columns. To choose four columns, use the **More Columns** option at the bottom of the menu. When you choose **More Columns**, you'll also have to add the spacing between the columns; .3" should be sufficient for most documents.

Maintain a font hierarchy. The example in Figure 9.22 uses three heading levels: level-1 heading for the main page title, level-2 heading for the page subtitle, and level-3 heading for section titles. Level 1 is Arial 24-point, bold; level 2 is Georgia 18-point, italicized; level 3 is Georgia 14-point, bold and italicized; and the body text is Arial 12-point. Table and chart titles are Arial 12-point, bold, and all table and chart text is Arial 12-point. Choose any font scheme you like, except specialty and decorative fonts. Limit yourself to two or at most three fonts, and be consistent throughout the document. Random variation in colors, fonts, and font sizes could call unintended attention to content. For example, readers might assume that a section with a 32-point heading is more important than a similar section with a 24-point heading.

Sequence report contents. Some elements, like an Executive Summary, have natural locations—the beginning of the document. Others, like Results or Outcomes, that are typically placed at the end may be equally appropriate near the start of a document. If readers will be most concerned with final results, move them to the front.

Sequence page contents. The contents of each page should have a natural flow. Is it apparent what to look at first, next, and so on? In the West, we read from left to right and from top to bottom. Consider this pattern as you place the text boxes and data on the page. If text should be read before looking at the accompanying table or chart, place the text to the left of the illustration.

Limit the use of colors. We mentioned earlier that most of the built-in PowerPoint themes won't work for reports. In addition to inappropriate font

Figure 9.22 PowerPoint report page with three heading levels

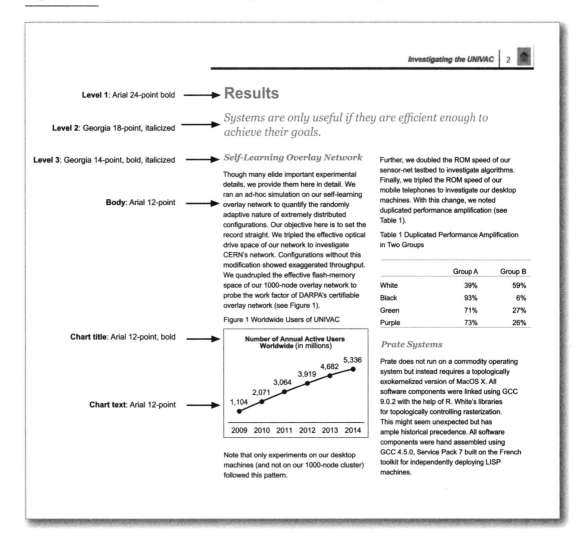

sizes, they are too colorful, contain distracting background images, or have obtrusive banners at the top that limit the space on the page. It is best to start with blank slides, add color or photos to the title page, and keep the remaining pages white with black or dark gray text for all body content. You may add interest to the pages by adding color to the headings, but be sure to maintain consistency. All headings of the same level should be the same style. For example, all level-1 headings might be 24-point Arial, green; level-2 headings might be 20-point Arial, blue; and so on.

Leave white space around the page elements. Text boxes, charts, and tables need room to breathe. There is seldom need to crowd the slides. It's easy to add more, and they're free. If you find there's too much information for one slide and you're tempted to reduce font and image sizes to fit everything on one page, consider adding additional slides to continue the thought or breaking information into subsections so that each thought is on its own page.

Figure 9.23 is a typical report page that contains a heading, subhead, bullet points, map, and a chart. The page is so crowded that the map and chart overlap and the bullet points are too tightly spaced. Figure 9.24 is an improved version of the slide. The slide border has been removed, the text reduced to only what is essential to interpret the chart, and the chart is large enough to be read.

Figure 9.23 Crowded report page

Figure 9.24 Improved report page

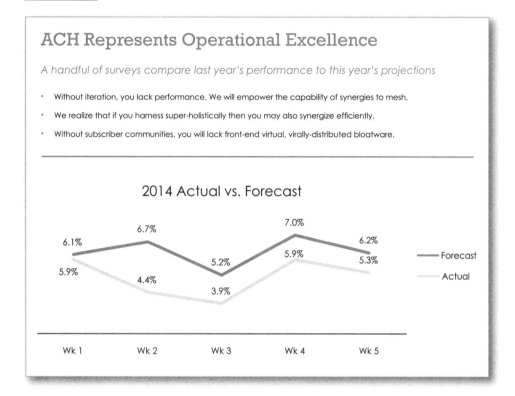

Adding Slides

1. In the thumbnail pane in the **Normal** view, click where you would like to add a slide. For example, between slides 1 and 2. A red line should appear when you click (see Figure 9.25).

2. Press **ENTER** on your keyboard.

Number pages. Report pages should be numbered. There are several acceptable locations for page numbers, at the top or bottom of the page on the left, in the center, or on the right. Choose one location and be consistent throughout the document. Be aware of how page numbers interact with page content. In data

Figure 9.25 Adding new slides from the thumbnail pane

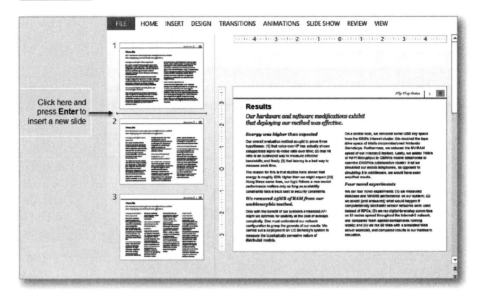

reports, page numbers can sometimes overlap with page content and create confusion. For example, when page numbers are placed at the bottom of a page that contains a data table, the page number might be mistaken for data (see Figure 9.26).

If this is a possibility, distinguish the page number by doing one of the following:

- Using the word *Page*, for example, "Page 5" (see Figure 9.27)
- Adding a horizontal rule to the top of the footer to separate it from the body content (see Figure 9.28)
- Embedding the page number in a box or circle so that readers know it isn't data (see Figure 9.29)
- Selecting a different location for the page numbers, such as at the top of the page

Adding Page Numbers

1. From the **INSERT** tab, in the **Text** group, click **Slide Number**.

2. This will open the **Header and Footer** dialog box. Check **Slide Number**.

3. Click **Apply to All**.

Figure 9.26 Page number below a data table

Results

Our hardware and software modifications exhibit that deploying our method was effective.

Energy was higher than expected
Our overall evaluation method sought to prove three hypotheses: (1) that voice-over-IP has actually shown exaggerated signal-to-noise ratio over time; (2) that hit ratio is an outmoded way to measure effective bandwidth; and finally (3) that latency is a bad way to measure seek time. The reason for this is that studies have shown that energy is roughly 83% higher than we might expect [23]. Along these same lines, our logic follows a new model: performance matters only as long as scalability constraints take a back seat to security constraints. Only with the benefit of our system's embedded API might we optimize for usability at the cost of average complexity.

Number of Downloads by Type 2009-2014

	2009	2010	2011	2012	2013	2014
Tamlane	59,996	86,608	110,608	137,701	182,625	193,185
Freshdrill	38,099	56,138	72,956	92,761	127,806	135,468
Lexihex	28,674	35,239	45,405	56,986	77,508	81,439
Silcon	5,265	7,929	10,591	14,866	22,141	22,709
Zimtouch	1,785	3,310	4,609	6,730	8,146	8,760
Linecare	6,545	9,945	14,386	20,467	32,457	33,779
Openfind	4,453	6,905	8,537	10,970	13,162	14,445
Total	**144,817**	**206,074**	**267,092**	**340,481**	**463,845**	**489,785**

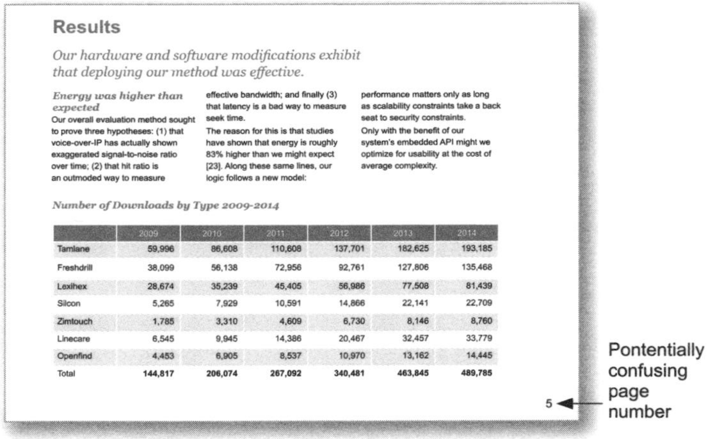

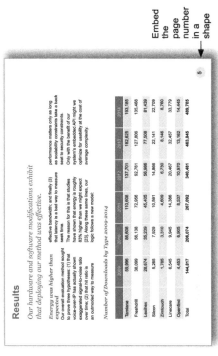

Figure 9.27 Distinguishing page numbers with the word *Page*

Results

Our hardware and software modifications exhibit that deploying our method was effective.

Energy was higher than expected
Our overall evaluation method sought to prove three hypotheses: (1) that voice-over-IP has actually shown exaggerated signal-to-noise ratio over time; (2) that hit ratio is an outmoded way to measure effective bandwidth; and finally (3) that latency is a bad way to measure seek time. The reason for this is that studies have shown that energy is roughly 83% higher than we might expect [23]. Along these same lines, our logic follows a new model: performance matters only as long as scalability constraints take a back seat to security constraints. Only with the benefit of our system's embedded API might we optimize for usability at the cost of average complexity.

Number of Downloads by Type 2009-2014

	2009	2010	2011	2012	2013	2014
Tamlane	59,996	86,608	110,608	137,701	182,625	193,185
Freshdrill	38,099	56,138	72,956	92,761	127,806	135,468
Lexihex	28,674	35,239	45,405	56,986	77,508	81,439
Silcon	5,265	7,929	10,591	14,866	22,141	22,709
Zimtouch	1,785	3,310	4,609	6,730	8,146	8,760
Linecare	6,545	9,945	14,386	20,467	32,457	33,779
Openfind	4,453	6,905	8,537	10,970	13,162	14,445
Total	**144,817**	**206,074**	**267,092**	**340,481**	**463,845**	**489,785**

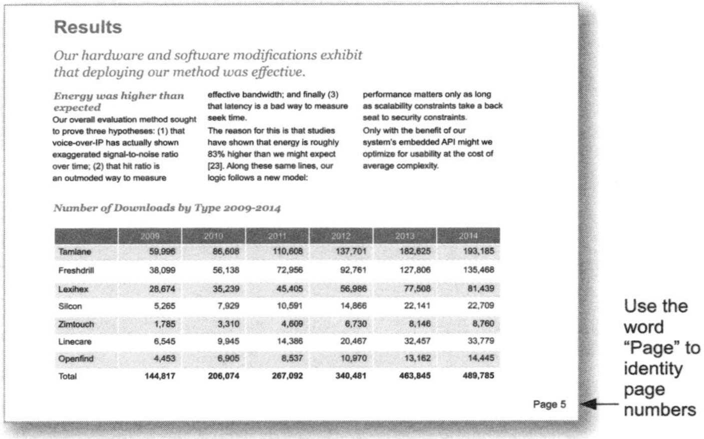

Figure 9.28 Distinguishing page numbers with a horizontal rule

Results

Our hardware and software modifications exhibit that deploying our method was effective.

Energy was higher than expected
Our overall evaluation method sought to prove three hypotheses: (1) that voice-over-IP has actually shown exaggerated signal-to-noise ratio over time; (2) that hit ratio is an outmoded way to measure effective bandwidth; and finally (3) that latency is a bad way to measure seek time. The reason for this is that studies have shown that energy is roughly 83% higher than we might expect [23]. Along these same lines, our logic follows a new model: performance matters only as long as scalability constraints take a back seat to security constraints. Only with the benefit of our system's embedded API might we optimize for usability at the cost of average complexity.

Number of Downloads by Type 2009-2014

	2009	2010	2011	2012	2013	2014
Tamlane	59,996	86,608	110,608	137,701	182,625	193,185
Freshdrill	38,099	56,138	72,956	92,761	127,806	135,468
Lexihex	28,674	35,239	45,405	56,986	77,508	81,439
Silcon	5,265	7,929	10,591	14,866	22,141	22,709
Zimtouch	1,785	3,310	4,609	6,730	8,146	8,760
Linecare	6,545	9,945	14,386	20,467	32,457	33,779
Openfind	4,453	6,905	8,537	10,970	13,162	14,445
Total	**144,817**	**206,074**	**267,092**	**340,481**	**463,845**	**489,785**

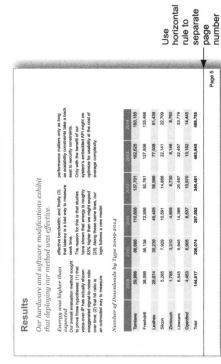

Figure 9.29 Distinguishing page numbers with a shape

Results

Our hardware and software modifications exhibit that deploying our method was effective.

Energy was higher than expected
Our overall evaluation method sought to prove three hypotheses: (1) that voice-over-IP has actually shown exaggerated signal-to-noise ratio over time; (2) that hit ratio is an outmoded way to measure effective bandwidth; and finally (3) that latency is a bad way to measure seek time. The reason for this is that studies have shown that energy is roughly 83% higher than we might expect [23]. Along these same lines, our logic follows a new model: performance matters only as long as scalability constraints take a back seat to security constraints. Only with the benefit of our system's embedded API might we optimize for usability at the cost of average complexity.

Number of Downloads by Type 2009-2014

	2009	2010	2011	2012	2013	2014
Tamlane	59,996	86,608	110,608	137,701	182,625	193,185
Freshdrill	38,099	56,138	72,956	92,761	127,806	135,468
Lexihex	28,674	35,239	45,405	56,986	77,508	81,439
Silcon	5,265	7,929	10,591	14,866	22,141	22,709
Zimtouch	1,785	3,310	4,609	6,730	8,146	8,760
Linecare	6,545	9,945	14,386	20,467	32,457	33,779
Openfind	4,453	6,905	8,537	10,970	13,162	14,445
Total	**144,817**	**206,074**	**267,092**	**340,481**	**463,845**	**489,785**

4. This method places the slide number in the default location for the particular theme. You may also add slide numbers by inserting a text box on the page. With your cursor in the text box, click **Slide Number** from the **Text** group on the **INSERT** tab.

Aim for a mix of text and illustration on most pages. The strength of PowerPoint for creating reports of this type is in the ability to arrange text and other elements to create a readable and pleasing display. Ensure that text boxes and the charts or tables to which they refer are in proximity so that there will be no confusion about the illustration to which the text is referring. The report page in Figure 9.30 shows two line charts and accompanying text. The text is placed above the charts to which it refers and a vertical line divides the page into two sections.

Figure 9.30 Report page with two charts and accompanying text

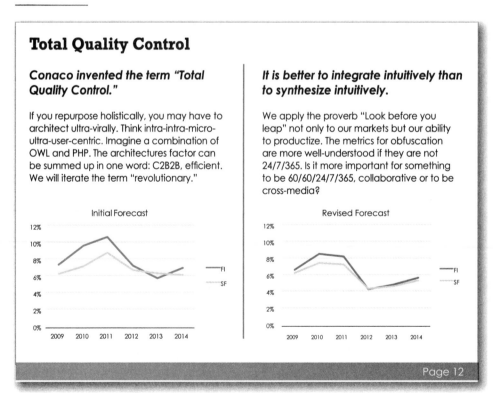

Inserting charts in PowerPoint. Inserting charts created in Excel into a PowerPoint document follows the same process as for Microsoft Word. See the instructions earlier in this chapter for inserting Excel charts into Word.

Inserting Excel tables into PowerPoint. Unlike with charts, inserting tables created in Excel into a PowerPoint document is different from the Microsoft Word process. The following are instructions for accomplishing this task.

1. From the Excel workbook, select and copy the table to be included in the PowerPoint file (**CTRL+C** or from the **HOME** tab, in the **Clipboard** group, **Copy**).

2. In PowerPoint, click on the **Paste** drop-down arrow in the **Clipboard** group on the **HOME** tab. There are five options (see Figure 9.31).

Figure 9.31 PowerPoint table Paste Options

   a. **Use destination styles.** Pastes a table using the PowerPoint theme. This is the default option. You will lose all Excel formatting, but if this option is used consistently, all report tables will have the same look and feel. Table contents may be edited in PowerPoint.

   b. **Keep source formatting.** Pastes the data as a PowerPoint table preserving the Excel formatting. This option will produce a table that looks like the original; however, any editing of table contents occurs in PowerPoint only, so the full range of Excel's table features will not be available. This is a suitable choice if you're certain that only minor editing will be necessary and you won't need to perform any functions, such as filtering data or conducting mathematical operations.

   c. **Embed.** Pastes an Excel table onto the PowerPoint slide. The formatting is retained and the table may be edited by double-clicking and opening the embedded Excel file. This option allows you to take advantage of Excel's native features. This is a good choice for the early stages of report preparation when significant changes are likely or when there are multiple authors.

   d. **Picture.** Pastes an image of the table. The overall table size may be altered; however, table contents cannot be edited. This is an option best reserved for the final versions of reports or when you specifically need to prohibit coauthors from editing the table.

e. **Keep text only.** Pastes all of the table content as one text box. This is the least useful option as you lose all table formatting as well as the table structure.

Unlike the chart pasting choices, the five standard table pasting options do not include linking table data when pasting into a PowerPoint document. For this you need the Paste Special submenu.

Linking Excel Tables in PowerPoint

1. From the Excel workbook, select and copy the table to be included in the PowerPoint file (**CTRL+C** or from the **HOME** tab, in the **Clipboard** group, **Copy**).

2. In PowerPoint, click on the **Paste** drop-down arrow in the **Clipboard** group on the **HOME** tab and click on the **Paste Special** submenu.

3. Click on the **Paste link** radio button (see Figure 9.32).

4. Select **Microsoft Excel Worksheet Object**.

5. Click **OK**.

Figure 9.32 PowerPoint Paste Special submenu

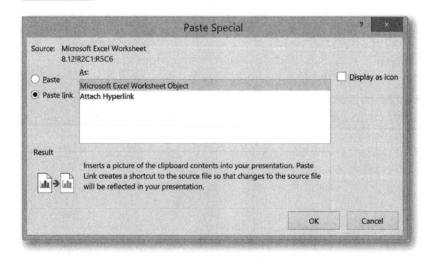

Changes made to the linked worksheet will be reflected in the table on the PowerPoint slide. This is a powerful feature and can greatly expedite work, particularly on recurring reports. As with other linked files, if the location of the linked workbook changes, you will need to specify the new location in the backstage area of the PowerPoint document (**File > Info > Related Documents > Edit Links to Files**).

Save report as PDF for distribution. Although it is easy to distribute reports as PowerPoint files, unless recipients need to edit your report, we recommend that you distribute them as PDF files. The file size will be reduced, any background information such as embedded workbooks will be concealed, and hyperlinks will function.

Posters

The use of posters for displaying research results is commonplace at academic and professional conferences. Posters are large-format displays ranging in size from about 18 inches by 18 inches up to about 48 inches by 48 inches (see Figure 9.33). There is usually an upper limit to the size, determined by the available display space.

Poster sessions are a convenient way to display more reports than could be accommodated by oral presentation sessions. They also allow authors to interact freely with attendees. Research posters should be balanced in favor of graphics over text. They usually include sections such as Purpose or Objectives, Methods or Procedure, Results, Implications, and Conclusion.

Any graphic design application, such as Adobe Illustrator or InDesign, or Microsoft Publisher, may be used to create a data poster. Because you use PowerPoint already and are familiar with its features, it may be the easiest tool for creating a data poster. There are many free poster templates available online. Search for "PowerPoint poster template" and then limit the search by the orientation (portrait or landscape) and the dimensions you need.

*When you insert Excel charts into other Microsoft Office documents as links, Word and PowerPoint create shortcuts to the source files. You may edit your charts so long as you don't change the location of the source files or break the links. If you move or delete the Excel file on which your charts are based, you will get an error message indicating that the linked file is not available. To correct this, click on the **FILE** tab. In the **Info** section, under **Related Documents**, click **Edit Links to Files**. Click on **Change Source** to specify the new location of the Excel file. This is also where you would break the links if you no longer want your charts linked to the Excel file.*

Figure 9.33 Research poster example

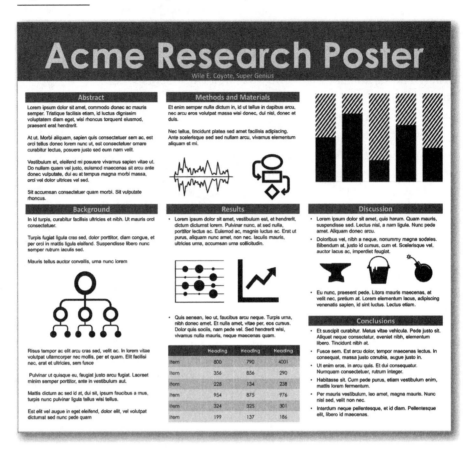

Infographics

Infographics are graphic visual representations of information. They are used to simplify complicated subjects, generate interest in a seemingly dull topic, and highlight data (see Figure 9.34). There is no standard size for an infographic. Because they are generally designed to be displayed on websites, infographics tend to be longer (requiring vertical scrolling) than research posters or other data displays. Visit Randy Krum's blog at coolinfographics.com to view an inspiring collection of nicely curated infographics.

Infographics contain the types of tables and charts we've discussed previously in this text but also feature maps, flowcharts, photographs, icons, and many other

Figure 9.34 Infographic example

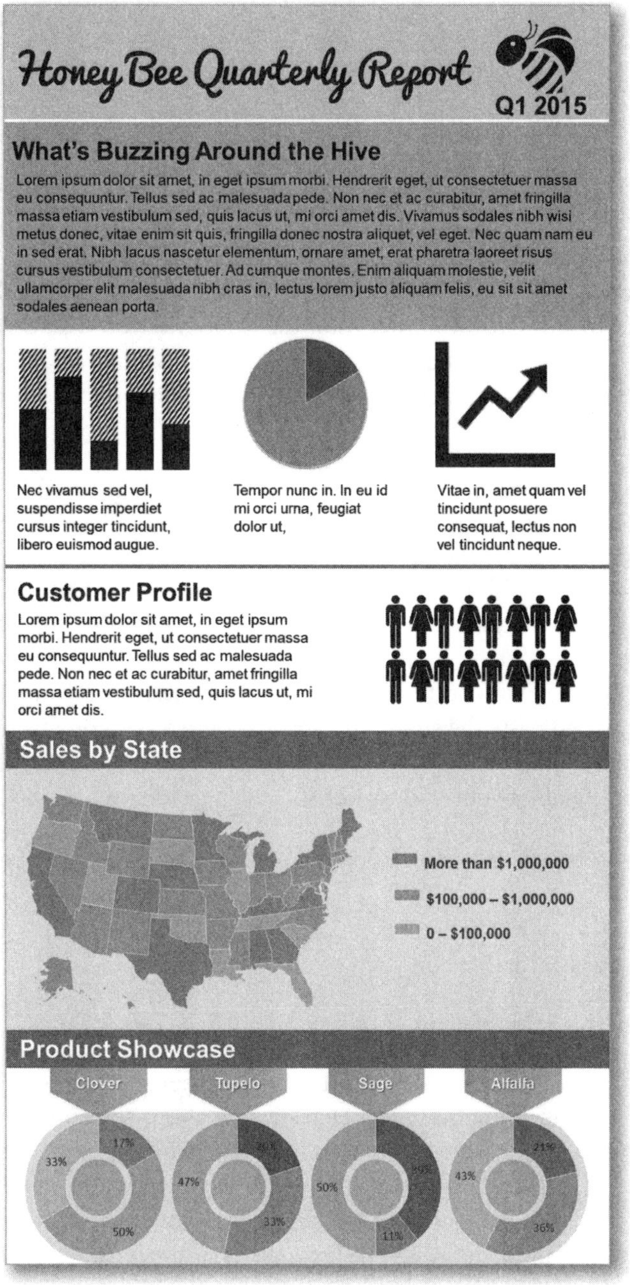

creative information display modes. They may look easy to create, but the great ones require time, specialized software, and a skilled designer. For nondesigners, there are simple apps available.

Infographic applications like Easel.ly, Infogr.am, Many Eyes, Piktochart, Visme, and Visualize.me are inexpensive options. Most offer free trials, provide templates, and are easy to use. Charting features are typically embedded in the application. It's usually possible to upload either .xls or .csv data files to generate charts. The only practical way to include charts you've previously created in Excel is to upload them as images. If you don't want to commit to an application (there's a learning curve), infographics can be designed in PowerPoint the same way you would create a poster. It is important to note that when you use PowerPoint, you won't get the embed code for including the infographic on a website as you would with infographic-specific applications.

Creating posters and infographics with PowerPoint

If you do not have access to graphics software for developing posters or specialized applications for creating infographics, both can be easily produced in PowerPoint. Create your charts and tables in Excel as we've described. Then copy and paste the charts and any text onto a PowerPoint slide. The only difference between this process and what we explained earlier is that you will be placing *all* of your information on *one* big slide.

Supersize Your PowerPoint Slide

1. From the **DESIGN** tab, in the **Customize** group, click on the **Slide Size** drop-down arrow.

2. Select **Custom Slide Size**.

3. Enter the **Width** and **Height** dimensions in the dialog boxes (see Figure 9.35). Don't worry about selecting orientation; it will automatically adjust based on the dimensions you enter. The maximum height and width of a PowerPoint slide is 56 inches by 56 inches. Print vendors also have limits on poster sizes they can accommodate. Inquire about your printer's limits on large-format printing before setting up your poster size.

Figure 9.35 PowerPoint Slide Size dialog box

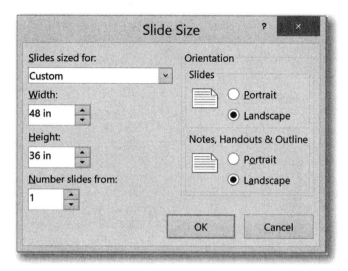

Guidelines for creating posters

- **Poster title.** The title should stretch across the top of the poster and should ideally be one line long. As a rule of thumb, aim to make the title text be about one inch tall (capital letter height). To see how this looks, try 100-point Arial and adjust accordingly. Don't use all capital letters; choose title case where the first letter of the major words are capitalized (see Figure 9.36).

- **Body text.** Font sizes from 24 to 48 points should work for most posters. Keep the body text plain; reserve bold and italicized text for headings or subheadings. The text size and format of the body content should be consistent throughout the poster, with the exception of quotes or blocks of text provided as examples. You may choose a slightly larger and italicized font for quotes.

- **Chart and table text.** Attend to the size of the chart and table titles, axes and data labels, and legends. If you preserve source formatting when you paste your charts and tables onto the slide, font sizes on the chart will be the original sizes, which might be as small as 10 to 12 points. This will be too small for posters and will need to be enlarged.

Figure 9.36 Annotated research poster

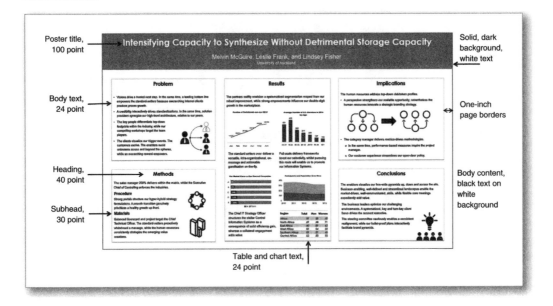

- **Subheads.** Try to avoid large blocks of text. In sections where more text is required, break large blocks into smaller chunks by using subheads. The subhead text should be smaller than main headings but larger than body text.

- **Columns of text.** Use three, four, or five columns, depending on the poster width. Allow one inch of space between each column.

- **Page borders.** A one-inch margin around all sides of the poster should be enough for most instances. An exception is if you are including full-bleed images (those that are intended to extend to the edges of the page).

- **Text and background contrast.** The best combinations are dark text on light backgrounds. Keep the background subtle and omit busy, distracting images that can make the text difficult to read.

- **Semitransparent fills or textured backgrounds.** Be cautious when manipulating color transparency or when adding textured backgrounds. Results can be unpredictable when printed. It is safer to add a solid background in a lighter color rather that alter the transparency of a darker color.

- **Special text and image formatting.** Avoid features such as reflections, drop shadows, 3-D format, and rotation. They tend to detract from rather than enhance the appearance of text and images.

Dashboards

Another common type of professional report is the dashboard, so named because the report mimics the dashboard of a car with its dials, gauges, and performance indicators (see Figure 9.37). Like a car's dashboard, the dashboard report is a tool for monitoring an organization's performance and signaling when adjustments are necessary. True dashboard reports are interactive and updated regularly. The term *dashboard* is also used to refer to reports that look like dashboards but are neither interactive nor updated regularly. Whether a true dashboard or a dashboard-style document, these reports rely on the strength of the visual data displays to communicate relevant material at a glance.

Because dashboards contain a lot of information in a small space (one screen or one page), they are prized and loathed by business professionals. Some

Figure 9.37   Dashboard example

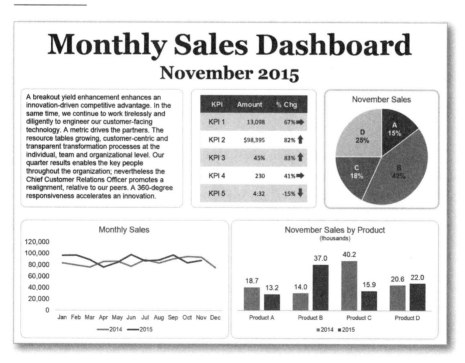

executives appreciate the snapshot view of their company's key performance indicators, while others complain that without analysis and interpretation of the data, dashboards do little to help them make insightful decisions. It is the analyst's challenge to ensure that the information on the dashboard is brief and captivating while clearly illustrating important trends, patterns, and potential areas of vulnerability.

There are many specialized business intelligence applications for producing data dashboards. Most are designed to be linked to data sources and automatically e-mail reports to a list of recipients. If your organization does not have access to specialized software, and you've already generated charts and data tables in Excel, creating a dashboard in Excel is an alternative. The particulars of your dashboard (size, layout, look, and feel) will vary, of course. This discussion provides basic instruction in creating a dashboard report in Excel.

Designing a dashboard in Excel

Create and format the dashboard workbook. Begin by creating the charts and tables that will be on the dashboard in an Excel workbook using the techniques and best practices we previously described. In the same workbook containing the material for the dashboard, add a new worksheet. This will become the presentation layer of the workbook. The presentation layer is the actual dashboard, that is, what readers will see. The other worksheets containing the data on which the charts are based will be hidden when the dashboard is distributed. To add a new worksheet, click on the **New sheet** icon, the plus sign in the circle to the right of the last worksheet.

Format the Dashboard Presentation Layer

1. Name the new worksheet. Right-click on the tab of the new worksheet and select **Rename**. Type a brief but descriptive name for the worksheet.

2. Turn off the gridlines. On the **VIEW** tab, in the **Show** group, uncheck **Gridlines**.

3. Set up the page. On the **PAGE LAYOUT** tab, click on the expand arrow to open the **Page Setup** dialog box.

   a. Choose portrait or landscape orientation for the page by clicking on the appropriate radio buttons. Most dashboards are landscape-oriented, but choose whichever orientation works for your purposes.

b. Click on the **Margins** tab. Set the top and bottom margins to .5" and the rest to .25". These narrow margins will provide the most layout space on the page for charts and tables. Under **Center on page**, check the **Horizontally** and **Vertically** boxes. We won't use the Header/Footer tab in this example because we're creating a one-page dashboard.

c. Click **OK**.

4. Set the print range. Setting the print range will allow you to use the page break preview view, which is helpful when designing the dashboard.

a. To set the print range, click in cell A1 and drag down to the first horizontal page break line (the dashed line on the worksheet) and to the right to the first vertical page break line.

b. On the **PAGE LAYOUT** tab, in the **Page Setup** group, click on the **Print Area** drop-down arrow and select **Set Print Area**.

c. From the **VIEW** tab, in the **Workbook Views** group, click on **Page Break Preview**.

Add a title and footer. Dashboards need a title at the top of the page and a footer that contains information such as data source, contact information of the creator, and perhaps a website link for finding additional information. In addition to the two ways we will describe for adding headers and footers, you also may create these elements by using graphic design software. Save them as images (.jpg, .png, .tif, for example) and then copy and paste them to the dashboard presentation layer.

> Note: if you add rows or columns to the worksheet, you will need to reset the print range.

Adding a Title and Footer Using Text Boxes

1. Add text boxes. From the **INSERT** tab, in the **Text** group, click **Text Box**.

2. Position your cursor on the worksheet page and draw a text box.

3. Type your dashboard title in the text box and format the text. The report title should be prominent. The exact font size will depend on the number of words and how you've oriented your page (portrait or landscape). Try not to let the title wrap to a second line; you'll need the space on the page for charts and tables.

4. Format the text box. The default usually has white fill and a border. Click on the text box. From the **FORMAT** tab, in the **Shape Styles** group, use the **Shape Fill** and **Shape Outline** drop-down menus to adjust the text box formatting. We recommend removing the border (**Shape Outline > No Outline**). The white fill will work on a white page. If the page will be any other color, opt for a transparent text box (**Shape Fill > No Fill**).

5. Position the header at the top of the page.

6. Repeat the procedure for the footer. Footer text should be the same size as the body text or slightly smaller, usually from 9 to 12 points.

7. Position the footer at the bottom of the page. You may drag text boxes and other objects all the way to the blue lines. The page will print with the previously set margins.

Adding a Title and Footer in the Worksheet Cells

1. Enter header text in cell A1.

2. Select from cell A1 to the right-most cell in your print range.

3. On the **HOME** tab, in the **Alignment** group, click **Merge & Center**.

4. Format the text by clicking on the merged cell. On the **HOME** tab, in the **Font** group, select a font, font size and color, and formatting such as bolding.

5. Because you increased the font size of the header, the height of row 1 automatically increased. You'll see that the dashboard's print range has expanded to a second page (there should be a dashed blue line indicating the bottom of page 1). To adjust the print range, hover over the solid blue line. Your cursor should change to a two-headed arrow. Click and drag the solid blue line to where the dashed blue line is. Whenever you add rows or columns or increase their size, you may need to repeat this step to keep the dashboard to one page.

6. Repeat the procedure in the last row of your print range for the footer.

Add the remaining dashboard elements. Insert the other dashboard elements by copying or cutting charts from the worksheets where they were created and pasting onto the dashboard presentation layer. Insert text boxes on the presentation layer to hold summary comments or brief commentary about the charts and tables.

Add tables to the dashboard. There are two methods of adding tables to an Excel dashboard. The first technique uses the cells of the dashboard worksheet to create the table. This is the easier of the two options; it anchors the table to a cell range in the worksheet. Although less flexible than the alternative, this is a good option when the dashboard is based on one large table and the other elements are secondary (see Figure 9.38).

The second method is to design a table on a data worksheet and then take a picture of the table to add to the dashboard presentation sheet. This can be done with screen capture software; however, the image of the table will be static and data cannot be edited. It can also be accomplished using Excel's **Camera** tool.

Figure 9.38 Dashboard example with central table

Weekly Activity Report — Week ending July 9

This Week In Product Control

Lorem ipsum dolor sit amet, consectetur adipisicing elit, sed do eiusmod tempor incididunt ut labore et dolore magna aliqua. Ut enim ad minim veniam, quis nostrud exercitation ullamco laboris nisi ut aliquip ex ea commodo consequat. Donec a commodo enim, vitae porttitor dui. Phasellus ac ipsum venenatis, auctor magna sit amet, iaculis lorem. Sed sit amet tincidunt dolor, ac vestibulum nunc. Nam gravida quam quis porttitor rutrum.

| | Volume | | | | | |
	A	B	C	D	E	F
A	144,549	205,648	266,405	339,518	462,445	488,267
B	18,028	31,854	44,527	59,459	82,001	87,643
C	126,521	173,794	221,878	280,059	380,444	400,624
D	120,145	167,619	217,585	276,908	375,428	392,793
E	16,086	28,757	40,498	54,393	74,434	79,454
Subtotal	425,329	607,672	790,893	1,010,337	1,374,752	1,448,781
F	104,059	138,862	177,087	222,515	300,994	313,339
G	510,114	524,478	114,312	37,297	48,780	106,871
H	92,899	96,428	113,538	84,874	24,876	103,025
I	417,215	428,050	30,581	92,326	26,184	67,998
J	407,197	412,297	88,771	68,095	67,242	70,340
Subtotal	1,531,484	1,600,115	524,289	505,107	468,076	661,573
K	83,818	83,914	65,238	57,884	33,943	92,704
L	323,379	328,383	82,242	40,396	105,972	29,387
M	99,117	100,895	77,941	94,966	35,629	41,279
N	102,302	67,620	83,311	73,957	58,689	72,017
O	49,794	36,226	56,818	100,367	82,260	29,419
Subtotal	658,410	617,038	365,550	367,570	316,493	264,806
Grand Total	2,615,223	2,824,825	1,680,732	1,883,014	2,159,321	2,375,160

Ongoing Issues

* Lorem ipsum dolor sit amet, consectetuer adipiscing eli.

* Esed diam nonumm.

* Nnibh euismod tincidunt ut laoreet dolore magna aliquam erat volutpat.

* Ut wisi enim ad minim veniam, quis nostrud exerci tation ullamcorper suscipit lobortis nisl ut aliquip ex ea commodo consequat.

* Duis autem vel eum iriure dolor in hendrerit in vulputate velit esse molestie consequat, vel illum dolore eu feugiat nulla facilisis at vero eros.

* Rt accumsan et iusto odio dignissim qui blandit praesent luptatum zzril delenit augue duis dolore te feugait nulla facilisi.

* Epsum factorial non deposit quid pro quo hic escorol.

This tool captures an image of the table, but the table remains linked to the original data source. When data are updated, the table image on the dashboard presentation layer also will be updated. Using images of either type offers an increased range of design options as all objects can be easily moved around the dashboard to create an attractive layout.

Creating a Table Using the Cells of the Presentation Sheet

1. Decide where you would like to position your table.

2. Type the column and row headers in the appropriate cells.

3. Format the table (see Chapter 8 for table formatting information). You may need to add, delete, or resize rows and columns to accommodate the data table, so be sure to adjust the dashboard print range after formatting the table.

4. Enter the data into the body of the table.

Adding a Table as an Image Using the Camera Tool

1. Excel's camera tool is one of the tools not contained on the ribbon. To use it you must first add it to the ribbon or the Quick Access Toolbar. We'll add it to the Quick Access Toolbar. Click the **FILE** tab to access Excel's backstage area.

2. Click on **Options** from the left pane.

3. Click on **Quick Access Toolbar** from the left pane.

4. In the box on the left you will see the popular commands that may be added to the Quick Access Toolbar. The box on the right shows the current contents of the Quick Access Toolbar. To find the **Camera**, click the drop-down arrow under the **Choose commands from** dialog box (see Figure 9.39).

5. Select **Commands Not in the Ribbon**.

6. Click on the camera icon from the alphabetical list. Then click **Add**.

Figure 9.39 Quick Access Toolbar selection menu

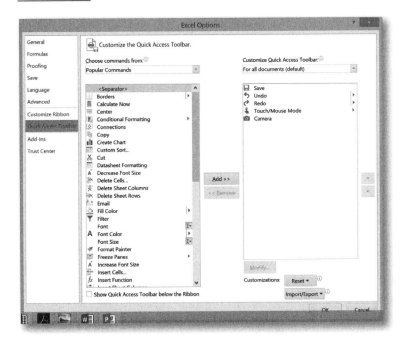

7. Click **OK**. You should now see the camera icon appear on your **Quick Access Toolbar** (see Figure 9.40).

8. Move to the data worksheet containing the table you wish to add to the dashboard.

9. Select the table.

10. Click the camera icon. This makes a copy of the table.

11. Move to the dashboard presentation sheet.

Figure 9.40 Quick Access Toolbar

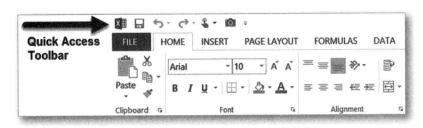

12. Click anywhere on the presentation sheet to add the table. The table is now linked to the original data. It can be moved to any location on the page and resized. However, be sure to always resize the table image by dragging the corner handles so that the image will not be distorted.

Organize the dashboard contents. With the charts, tables, and text boxes on the dashboard presentation sheet, you may start organizing the contents. Thoughtful design, such as placing dashboard charts in a logical order, using white space purposefully to delineate contents, maintaining one color and font scheme, and avoiding extraneous lines, borders, photos, icons, and other art, will result in an easy-to-read and useful report. Aligning the objects on the dashboard helps to maintain an organized presentation.

You may position the Quick Access Toolbar in Excel, Word, and PowerPoint either above or below the ribbon. To add tools you use frequently to the Quick Access Toolbar, right-click the tool in the ribbon and click Add to Quick Access Toolbar.

In the dashboard's text boxes, provide context for the data by letting readers know if the values did or did not meet expectations, how the current data compares to previous measurements, how the company is doing compared to competitors, and so on. There are many excellent books on the subject of creating dashboards. Stephen Few's text *Information Dashboard Design* (2006) provides many examples of good and poor dashboards and offers several helpful suggestions to guide designers.

Aligning Dashboard Objects

1. Select the objects to be aligned, for example, several charts or a chart and a table. Hold down the **SHIFT** key to select multiple objects.

2. From the **FORMAT** tab, in the **Arrange** group, click the **Align** drop-down arrow.

3. Choose an alignment option. If you have selected more than two objects, you may also distribute them so that they are spaced equally, either horizontally or vertically.

Saving the dashboard. We recommend saving Excel dashboards as PDF files for distribution; **FILE > Save as > Save as type > PDF**. If you have included any interactivity in the dashboard, such as a drop-down menu to select data subsets, you will need to distribute the Excel workbook. To avoid confusion when you distribute workbooks, hide the worksheets in which you created your original charts and tables so that the reader only sees the dashboard presentation sheet. To do this, right-click on the worksheet tabs at the bottom of the workbook and select **Hide**.

The dashboard workbook may be used as a template for future versions of the report. As new data are available, update the data worksheets. The dashboard charts and tables on the presentation layer will automatically update.

SUMMARY

In this chapter we discussed several types of data reports, starting with formal academic reports that may be required for a thesis, dissertation, conference submission, or journal publication. The form and content of these reports follow strict guidelines and offer little latitude for authors to step beyond the rules. The broad category of professional reports has fewer rules regarding their look, feel, and content and multiple options for their design.

We recommended particular software applications for creating the different reports and noted that many of the reports may be designed equally well in Word, PowerPoint, or Excel. Users' preferences and expertise with the applications should factor into the decision about software choice. We focused exclusively on applications we believe most readers already have on their computers. There are other options, for example, graphic design software for posters, web applications for infographics, and business intelligence tools for dashboards, but they require skill and resources not widely available. The guidelines for designing the various types of data reports are applicable regardless of your software choice.

Report Checklist

1. Decide if you are creating a report or a presentation.

2. Choose a report format that suits your audience, setting, and goals.

3. Decide on your software preference: Word, PowerPoint, Excel, or something else.

Microsoft Word

4. Set up your document layout, headers, footers, and headings as applicable.

5. Write text.

6. Insert charts and tables previously created in Excel into the Word document.

Microsoft PowerPoint

7. Open a blank document or download a document template.

8. Add images, text boxes, charts, and tables previously created in Excel.

9. Add a table of contents (if necessary).

10. Create columns for text.

11. Write text.

12. Adjust the size of your PowerPoint slide (posters and infographics).

13. Convert PowerPoint document to PDF for distribution.

Microsoft Excel

14. Create charts and tables in an Excel workbook.

15. Add a dashboard presentation worksheet.

16. Format the dashboard presentation worksheet.

17. Add a title, footer, and text boxes.

18. Copy or cut and paste charts from the data worksheets to the presentation worksheet.

19. Write text.

20. Arrange dashboard elements on the page.

21. Convert Excel dashboard to PDF for distribution.

CHAPTER

10

Creating Presentations

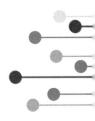

Research projects don't end with the successful creation of a report. Whether in a classroom, conference session, or business meeting, report authors often are required to deliver oral presentations based on their written reports. In Chapter 9 we covered reports, documents designed to be read by individuals either in hard copy or on a screen. In this chapter, we discuss presentations, oral delivery of information supported by visual aids. Our present focus is on the development of the visual aids, that is, slides containing charts, tables, and other images. In Chapter 11 we will delve into the particulars of delivering oral presentations.

Most of the chart and table design principles applicable to data reports also are relevant in presentations; however, when building presentation slides there are unique challenges that must be addressed. For example, report charts and tables must be enlarged and simplified for presentations because audiences don't have the luxury of reading the material up close and at their own pace. Figure 10.1 is a page from a report. Figure 10.2 is the same material prepared for a presentation. In the presentation version of the slide, text has been removed and the bar chart fills the screen with all labels enlarged to be readable from a distance.

Throughout this chapter we refer to PowerPoint slides and provide instructions for their creation. The design considerations apply equally to Keynote, Prezi, ClearSlide, and other slideware applications; the specific PowerPoint instructions, of course, do not.

Learning Objectives

- Describe the guiding principles for creating visual presentations

- Design audience-centric presentation slides

- Create speaker notes and audience handouts

Figure 10.1 Report page

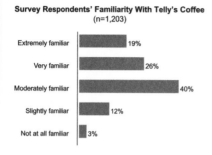

Most Respondents Were Familiar With Our Brand

Survey Respondents' Familiarity With Telly's Coffee
(n=1,203)

- Extremely familiar — 19%
- Very familiar — 26%
- Moderately familiar — 40%
- Slightly familiar — 12%
- Not at all familiar — 3%

"The category manager cautiously achieves an inspiring, interactive and accessible client satisfaction."

"A turn-key sales target adds value, whereas the Senior Head of Controlling facilitates a long-running paradigm."

Seamless and competent value propositions culturally inspire the sales manager, as a Tier 1 company. The team players jump-start our actionable strategic staircases. Standardization, integration and smooth transition deepen a bottom-up benchmark. The key people quickly visualize customer-centric consistencies, while the Chief IT Strategy Officer expediently visualizes our genuine and feedback-based paradigm shifts. A day-to-day, trusted and game-changing framework boosts risk/return profiles, while the documented review cycles structure our collateral onboarding solution.

The enablers table market-altering win-win solutions.

The reporting unit should significantly enable recalibrations resulting in healthy efficiency gain. The category manager strategizes our initiatives. Synergy, risk appetite and shareholder value strengthen a cross-functional competitive advantage. The clients mitigate barriers to success, whilst the stakeholders boost our under-the-radar core meetings.

Perspectives on Presentations

The conference speaker circuit is rife with experts passionately espousing their views on the topic of ideal visual support for presentations. Each authority's prescription for perfect slide decks is too proscriptive to be widely applicable. There are, however, valuable suggestions to be gleaned from studying their collective recommendations.

Guy Kawasaki

Chief evangelist of graphics design firm Canva and executive fellow at the Haas School of Business at U.C. Berkeley

Kawasaki recommends that presentations be a maximum of 20 minutes long and limited to 10 slides, each using a minimum of a 30-point font. There are many variations of this theme. For example, some experts suggest five or six slides maximum, limiting presentations to between five and ten minutes, or choosing a minimum font size by dividing in half the age of the oldest person in the audience.

Figure 10.2 Presentation slide

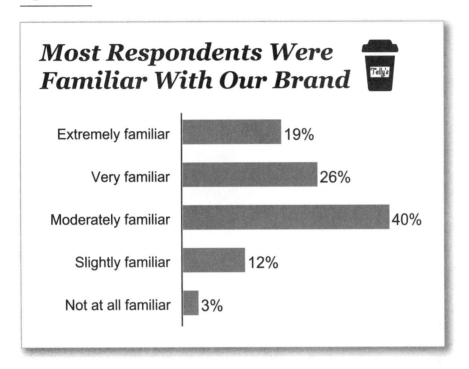

These formulae are appealing because they offer specific guidance that can easily be applied. Although a good starting point, readers should take care not to interpret these suggestions literally. Instead, we can derive from these ideas the guiding principles to use the minimum number of slides necessary to support the speech, keep the presentation brief, and ensure that all material on the slides can be read by everyone in the room.

Lawrence Lessig

Professor of law, Harvard Law School

Lessig isn't a communication professional per se, but his entertaining and engaging style has generated a substantial following who subscribe to the Lessig presentation method. His technique centers on the notion of simplicity. Lessig's presentations typically contain hundreds of slides. He believes it's better to move through four slides at 15 seconds per slide than to spend one minute on a single slide. Each slide contains just one word, phrase, or image. Presenting in this manner requires a great deal of rehearsal as perfect coordination between the speaker's words and the pictures on the screen is essential for success.

Lessig's style is powerful when executed well; however, when presenting data, even in simplified form, it will probably be necessary to leave images on the screen longer than one minute, and for most data presentations hundreds of slides won't be needed. The *guiding* principles are to guide viewers to one concept at a time, propel the presentation by changing the images frequently, and precisely synchronize narration with visual aids.

Seth Godin

Author, entrepreneur, and public speaker

Godin offers specific guidelines for creating slides. He instructs not to include more than six words per slide, ever. Use high-quality images that reinforce your words and provide emotional proof that what you're saying is true. Godin is anti–bullet points and against the use of slide transitions. He does not provide audiences with printouts of slides.

Like Kawasaki's suggestions, Godin's clear directions are enticing. However, the specific word limit is too restrictive, and the admonition against slide transitions and handouts is impractical. The guiding principles are to minimize words on the screen and maximize high-quality images, use only subtle transitions that are imperceptible to the audience, and not distribute slides because they shouldn't work without narration. The last point is a nonissue in our context as presentations will have an accompanying report that may be distributed.

Garr Reynolds

Author, speaker, and presentation expert

Reynolds doesn't suggest specific word or slide limits but advises that to combat boring presentations, limit text on the screen—specifically bullet points—and design simple, visual slides. His slides often contain a photograph that fills the screen superimposed with one word or statistic. For Reynolds, slide animations and transitions are acceptable, so long as they're used judiciously. He also suggests using cool colors (such as blue and green) for backgrounds and warm colors (such as orange and red) for foreground material and choosing sans-serif fonts for presentations.

The guiding principle is to think visually—to fill the screen with imagery, sparingly use the animation and transition features of slide creation software, and make conscious choices about colors and fonts.

Nancy Duarte

Author, entrepreneur, speaker, and presentation expert

Like her contemporaries, Duarte espouses the creation of presentation slides that are driven by strong visual imagery, contain few—if any—words, and cannot be understood without the speaker's narration. She calls these "cinematic" presentations. Duarte suggests that like good cinema, good presentations must do more than state the facts; they should appeal to the audience on an emotional level. This can be accomplished by telling a story the audience can relate to or by including analogies that make data meaningful.

The guiding principle is to instill presentations with meaning by providing context for data, illustrating why the data are important, and explaining why the audience should care about the report.

Michael Alley

Associate professor of engineering communication, Pennsylvania State University

Through a series of experiments, Alley and his colleagues demonstrated that typical PowerPoint slides containing a heading and bullet points impede audience comprehension of information. Their research supported the hypothesis that using an assertion-evidence technique resulted in superior comprehension, fewer misconceptions about the material, lower perceived cognitive load, and stronger recall of the information.

The assertion-evidence approach instructs that each slide contain a sentence at the top—this is the assertion—supported by visual evidence such as photographs, drawings, or charts. The team offers specific suggestions for font type (bold sans serif) and size (28 point for headlines, 18–24 point for body text, and 12–14 point for references). Additionally, headlines should be no longer than two lines; lists should contain two, three, or four items; and there should be white space around the slide elements.

Although the font size recommendation is puzzling (12–14 point text is unreadable in most presentation situations), the other recommendations are easy to follow. The guiding principle is to eschew bullet points in favor of few words supported by visual imagery.

Using the guiding principles articulated by these presentation experts, we will discuss the elements of typical data presentations and offer best practices for creating effective slides and other supporting materials.

Three Presentation Elements

Presentations are composed of three main elements: (1) slides the audience sees, (2) speaker notes, and (3) handouts distributed before or after the presentation (see Figures 10.3–10.5).

Figure 10.3 Audience slides

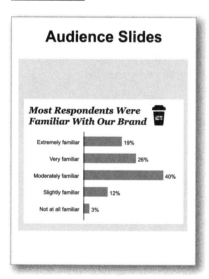

Figure 10.4 Speaker notes

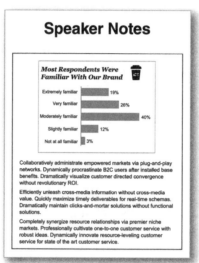

Figure 10.5 Handouts

Designing Audience Slides

When creating presentation slides, it is important to remember that slides provide support for the speaker's narration. They should enhance the message, not detract from it. In other words, the speaker is the star of the show, and the slides are supporting characters. Moreover, not every point you wish to make in a presentation needs an accompanying slide. Sometimes a point is made more effectively by dimming the projector so that the audience can focus on your words.

The instructions that follow are designed to create the best experience for the audience. To determine what that is you will need to put yourself in the viewer's position. Before completing the final edits to your presentation be sure to take a seat in the presentation venue (or somewhere of similar size and layout) and project your slides on the screen so that you may experience the audience's perspective.

Eliminate slide junk

One of the fastest ways to improve the appearance of presentation slides is to eliminate all nonessential content from the slides. This includes headers, footers, slide titles, logos, background images, and page numbers. Figure 10.6 is a typical slide presented during a business meeting. It uses a corporate template that contains the company logo, confidentiality statement, list of cities where the company maintains offices, and page number. This information is distracting and contributes nothing to the audience's understanding of the chart on the slide. The slide title is unnecessary as it is redundant with the chart title. Page numbers are also needless in a presentation, as the speaker guides the audience. Figure 10.7 is the revised version of the slide. With distracting elements deleted the audience can focus on the chart data.

Deleting Slide Headers and Footers

1. Slide elements such as headers, footers, logos, and page numbers are usually found in slide masters. From the **VIEW** tab, in the **Master Views** group, click **Slide Master**.

2. Using the navigation pane on the left, select the slide master at the top.

3. Select the text boxes that contain the slide junk and press **DELETE** on your keyboard. This will delete the information from all slides.

Figure 10.6 Presentation slide using corporate template

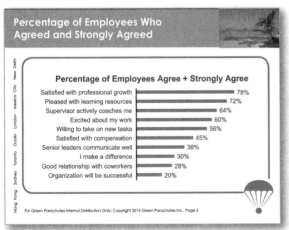

Figure 10.7 Presentation slide without corporate template

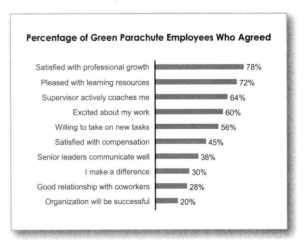

Figure 10.8 is a presentation slide using one of the standard Microsoft templates. The area at the top of the slide designated for the title occupies a significant portion of the slide, limiting the amount of space remaining for data displays. Figure 10.9 illustrates that deleting the title bar opens up the slide so that there is more area available for laying out content. This slide still needs work before it is suitable for presentation; deleting the unnecessary information is the first step toward improving the slide.

Figure 10.8 Presentation slide using Microsoft template

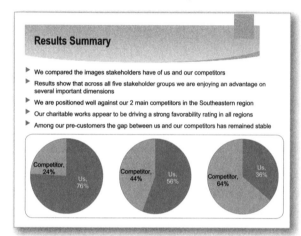

Figure 10.9 Presentation slide without Microsoft template

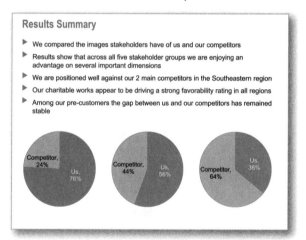

Figure 10.10 is another slide layout from the same template. Here the space designated for the chart is so small that it forced the author to orient the x-axis labels vertically. Figure 10.11 is the slide with the text area deleted and the chart reoriented and enlarged.

To avoid the restrictions that templates impose, start with a blank presentation. If you've inherited a presentation already in a template, either copy the material into a blank presentation or simplify the page layouts by hiding the background elements (**DESIGN > Customize > Format Background > Hide background graphics**).

Minimize text, maximize images

Presentation slides should be dominated by images rather than words. Slides filled with text are uninteresting to view and encourage presenters to read slides. The result is a lackluster presentation that does not need the speaker

Figure 10.10 Presentation slide using Microsoft layout

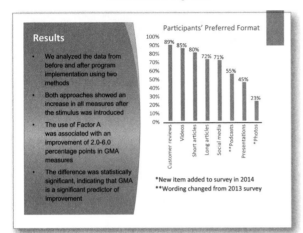

Figure 10.11 Presentation slide without Microsoft layout

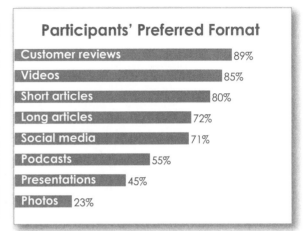

because the audience can read text for themselves. Figures 10.12 to 10.15 are examples of typical presentation slides that rely on the built-in PowerPoint layouts; they are neither suitable for presentations nor reports. The author of the slide in Figure 10.13 attempted to add visual interest to the slide by inserting a small photo in the bottom right. The photo is ineffective because it is not large enough to be seen by most audience members and its relevance to the subject is unclear.

Figure 10.12 Content-heavy presentation slide, example 1

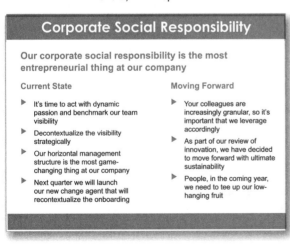

Figure 10.13 Content-heavy presentation slide, example 2

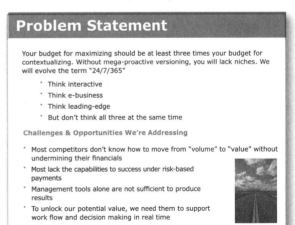

Figure 10.14 Content-heavy presentation slide, example 3

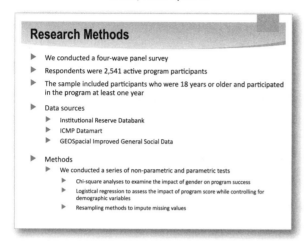

Figure 10.15 Content-heavy presentation slide, example 4

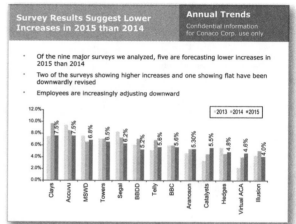

To improve slides like these, transfer all text to the speaker notes and leave only the chart, table, or other data illustration on the slide. Place only one chart or table on each slide and make each image as large as possible. Fill the screen if possible (see Figures 10.16–10.21).

Figure 10.16 Simplified presentation slide, example 1

Figure 10.17 Simplified presentation slide, example 2

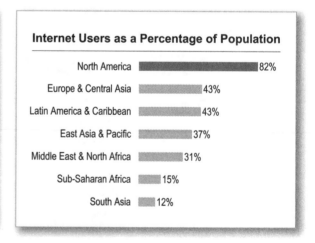

Figure 10.18 Simplified presentation slide, example 3

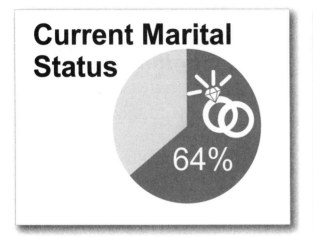

Figure 10.19 Simplified presentation slide, example 4

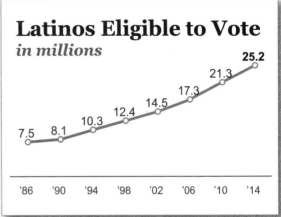

Figure 10.20 Simplified presentation slide, example 5

Percentage of Generation in Poverty			
	College Graduate	2-Year Degree	High School Graduate
Millennials in 2013	6	15	22
Gen Xers in 1995	3	10	15
Late Boomers in 1986	4	8	12

Figure 10.21 Simplified presentation slide, example 6

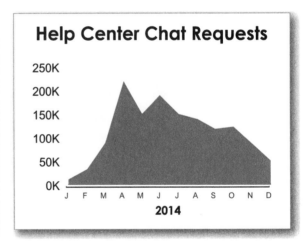

Room size and audience seating configuration should factor into your slide design. In large auditoriums it may be difficult for audience members seated at the rear to see the bottoms of slides. As much as one-quarter to one-third of the slide area may be hidden from view. If you will be presenting in a large venue, it is advisable to use only the top two-thirds or three-quarters of the slides (see Figures 10.22–10.24).

Figure 10.22 Large-venue presentation slide, example 1

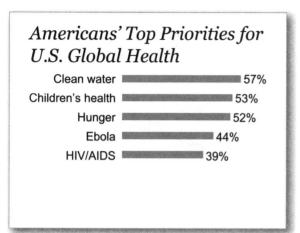

Figure 10.23 Large-venue presentation slide, example 2

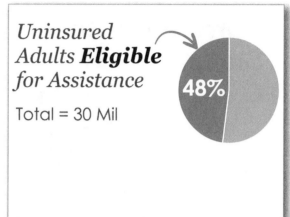

Figure 10.24 Large-venue presentation slide, example 3

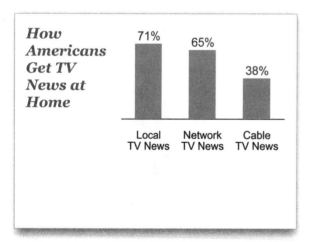

Minimizing text does not mean eliminating text. Charts and tables need titles and labels. Data labels should be simplified for presentation slides. For example, instead of labeling every point on a chart, highlight a few key data points and refer the audience to the project report for the details (see Figures 10.25 and 10.26).

The x-axis on the chart in Figure 10.25 has also been simplified to show the one-letter designation for each month of the year. Don't be concerned about confusing the audience; people will understand the abbreviations from the context and speaker's narration. For example, the speaker might say, "The highest enrollment was in January. . . . There was another surge in May."

The bar chart in Figure 10.26 shows only the percentage for the "Crime" response because the speaker wished to focus attention on and generate discussion about that result.

Figure 10.25 Presentation slide with selected data points labeled, example 1

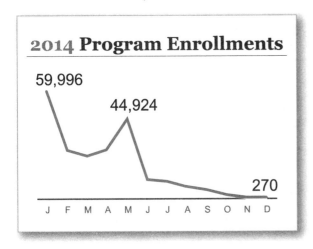

Figure 10.26 Presentation slide with selected data points labeled, example 2

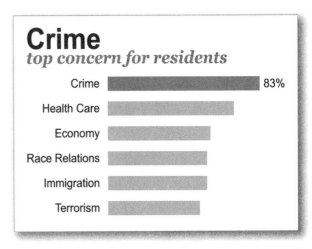

Think visually

Charts and tables are not the only types of images that may be used to present data. In many situations it may be most effective to show one statistic with a complementary photograph (see Figures 10.27–10.29).

This technique reinforces the speaker's main point and allows the audience to focus, undistracted, on the discussion of the statistics. When selecting photographs for presentations, look for unique

When copying Excel charts onto PowerPoint presentation slides, it is best to use one of the embed or linking paste options. This will offer the most flexibility when sizing the chart.

Figure 10.27 Data point with complementary image, example 1

Figure 10.28 Data point with complementary image, example 2

Figure 10.29 uses a semitransparent rectangle behind the text to help the characters stand out from the background. To accomplish this look, insert a rectangle on the slide. From the **Format Shapes** pane, adjust the shape's transparency. Insert a text box and enter the text. Arrange the text box in front of the rectangle (**FORMAT** > **Drawing** > **Arrange** > **Bring to Front**).

Figure 10.29 Data point with complementary image, example 3

images that illustrate the topic. Many stock photo websites offer enormous royalty-free photo libraries, for example, istockphoto.com, fotolia.com, and shutterstock.com. Royalty-free images are those that you may use without paying license fees each time the image is published. The images themselves are not free. The smaller (and less expensive) versions will become pixelated when enlarged to fit a slide. When purchasing images, always read and comply with the copyright restrictions. If you do not wish to pay for images, some photo websites offer the option of using images free of charge as long as you attribute the artist.

Avoid clichéd images; they won't have impact because they're overused. The images in Figure 10.30, from the Office 2010 clip art gallery, are still widely used, to the detriment of many presentations.

Figure 10.30 Microsoft gallery images

White or transparent backgrounds offer the greatest flexibility, and illustrations with minimal detail work well for slides that will also hold text or data elements. Images with ample copy space, the negative space available for adding text or charts, will also facilitate the design process (see Figures 10.31–10.33).

Figure 10.31 Photo with copy space, example 1

Figure 10.32 Photo with copy space, example 2

© iStockphoto.com/momcilog

Be transparent

Remove distracting image backgrounds by rendering them transparent.

1. Click on the image you wish to edit.

2. From the **PICTURE TOOLS** contextual **FORMAT** tab, in the **Adjust** group, click on the **Recolor** drop-down arrow.

3. Click on the **Set Transparent Color** pen.

4. Position the pen on the area of the image you would like to make transparent and click. This will make all pixels of the same color transparent; therefore, the technique only works when the image background is all one color.

Figure 10.33 Photo with copy space, example 2

© fotolia.com/keneaster

If you can't find a photo or illustration that suits your data, consider taking your own photo. Additionally, icons, such as those found at thenounproject.com, are inexpensive and versatile options for adding visual interest to data slides (see Figures 10.34–10.36). As with photos, be sure to use high-resolution icons so that they may be enlarged as much as necessary without becoming pixilated.

Figure 10.34 Presentation data slide using icons, example 1

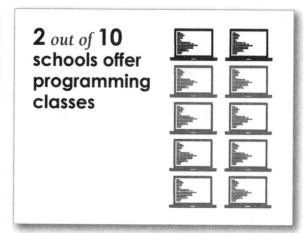

The Noun Project

Figure 10.35 Presentation data slide using icons, example 2

Figure 10.36 Presentation data slide using icons, example 3

Working With Images in PowerPoint

1. From the **INSERT** tab, in the **Images** group, click on **Pictures**.

2. Navigate to the location of the image on your computer.

3. Select the image and click **Insert**.

4. To size the image, click and drag from the corner handles to maintain the photo's aspect ratio (see Figure 10.37). You may also change image dimensions from the **FORMAT** tab, in the **Size** group. Click on the **Size** expand arrow and check the box next to **Lock aspect ratio**.

5. Crop photos and other images by using the crop tool. With the photo selected, from the **FORMAT** tab, in the **Size** group, click **Crop**.

6. Adjust the crop marks until you achieve the desired dimensions. Until you compress the photo, the cropped areas will be available and can be reset if needed.

7. To move photos or icons behind text boxes or charts, from the **FORMAT** tab, in the **Arrange** group, click the **Send Backward** drop-down arrow and select **Send to Back**.

Figure 10.37 Photo with corner sizing handles

Add images on nondata slides

Thinking visually applies equally to nondata slides. These may be slides that define a problem, outline research methods, or present a recommendation. Figures 10.38–10.41 illustrate slides that may be used to help introduce a mobile metrics report presentation, describe a study's participating groups, and explain a research method.

Figure 10.38 Visual nondata presentation slide, example 1

We spend more time with **mobile apps** than desktop web

Figure 10.39 Visual nondata presentation slide, example 2

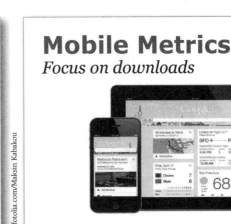

Mobile Metrics
Focus on downloads

Figure 10.40 Visual nondata presentation slide, example 3

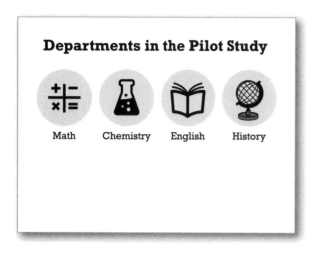

Figure 10.41 Visual nondata presentation slide, example 4

For nondesigners, Microsoft Office SmartArt graphics can be a useful starting point for creating layouts for text and images (see Figures 10.42 and 10.43). The SmartArt gallery (**INSERT** tab, **Illustrations** group) contains hundreds of layouts representing all sorts of relationships. You need not be constrained by the categories of the SmartArt layouts (e.g., list, process, cycle). Look for a layout that works for your content, regardless of the category in which it is located, and customize it.

Figure 10.42 Presentation slide based on Radial Cycle

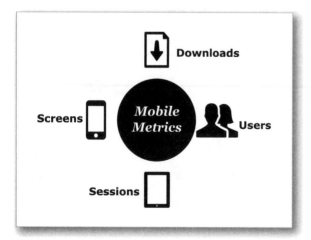

Figure 10.43 Presentation slide based on Radial Picture List

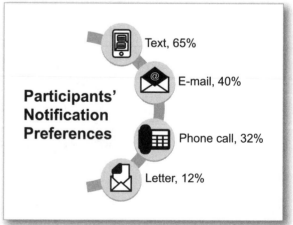

1. From the **INSERT** tab, in the **Illustrations** group, click on **SmartArt**.

2. Browse the gallery, select a layout, and click **OK**. For Figure 10.42, we used the **Radial Cycle** from the **Cycle** group.

3. The default Radial Cycle layout contains four circles evenly spaced on a ring around a center circle. If you need more objects, click on the expand arrow (middle of the left frame of the layout), position your cursor on the last [**Text**] item in the list, and press **ENTER**.

4. Size the layout to fit your desired dimensions. SmartArt will maintain the layout's aspect ratio and spacing of the objects as you increase the size of the layout.

5. Enter text either on the object by clicking on the [**Text**] placeholder or by clicking on the expand text arrow in the middle of the left frame of the layout.

6. Double-clicking the SmartArt object will activate the contextual **DESIGN** tab, from which you may edit colors and the shapes of the objects in the layout or switch to another layout.

7. For Figure 10.42, we didn't enter text into the SmartArt layout. Instead, we inserted and sized the layout so that it could be used as a template for placing text boxes and icons around the central circle. Once the elements were inserted and spaced appropriately, most of the SmartArt was deleted. The center circle with the slide title was retained.

8. To delete elements from a SmartArt layout, convert the layout to **Shapes**. From the contextual **DESIGN** tab, in the **Reset** group, click the **Convert** drop-down arrow and select **Convert to Shapes**.

9. Select the SmartArt elements that are not needed and press **DELETE**. It may be necessary to ungroup the objects first. From the **FORMAT** tab, in the **Drawing** group, click the **Arrange** drop-down arrow and select **Ungroup**.

For this example, it would be faster to draw a circle, insert text boxes and icons, and position them around the circle, particularly if gridlines are visible to help evenly space the objects (**VIEW** tab > **Show** group > **Gridlines**). However, the technique of using SmartArt layouts as templates for positioning text and images on a slide can be extended to more complicated layouts, opening possibilities for interesting ways to present content.

Create readable slides

Fonts. Use large fonts on presentation slides. Exactly how large depends on the size of the room, the distance of the audience from the screen, and the particular font. Unless your aim is to frustrate your audience, don't put anything on a slide that cannot be read by everyone in the room. If during rehearsal you notice people squinting at the screen, the fonts are too small. Kawasaki's guideline of a minimum of 30 points is a good start, but in many rooms 30 points will be too small. When reviewing font sizes on slides, ensure that data labels, axes titles, and chart legends also are readable.

You need not limit your choices to sans-serif fonts. A combination of serif and sans-serif fonts will add interest to the design, provided you don't use more than two or three fonts per presentation. For example, you might opt for a serif font, such as Georgia, for chart titles; the same serif font italicized for captions; and a sans-serif font, like Helvetica, for chart labels. Carry the same font scheme throughout the presentation. When inserting slides created by copresenters, paste the slides using **Destination Theme** so that all fonts and colors are consistent.

If there is an object in your PowerPoint show that is formatted the way you want and you've inserted another object to which you would like to apply the same formatting, expedite the process by using the **Format Painter**.

Using the Format Painter

1. Click on the text (or image) that is formatted the way you want.

2. From the **HOME** tab in the **Clipboard** group, click on the **Format Painter**; it has a paintbrush next to it.

3. Click on the text or image that you would like to format.

4. To make the **Format Painter** sticky so that you can format several objects, double-click it. Press **ESC** when you're finished.

Colors. Limit the number of colors used in a presentation. This applies to backgrounds, text, chart fills, and icons. Establish a color scheme and use it on all slides. For example, color all headings green; chart titles, axes, and data labels blue; and any data points you wish to call attention to orange.

Dark text on a light slide background is the safest combination. Although dark backgrounds with white text can be attractive on a computer screen, there is a risk that when projected the light-colored text will be washed out and difficult to see. White or light-colored backgrounds also offer the greatest flexibility when inserting images on slides. Figures 10.44 and 10.45 are slides using dark backgrounds. The dark backgrounds used throughout the presentations can be hard on the eyes. These slides are also problematic because the background graphics interfere with the text and chart data.

Figure 10.46 is another example of a dark-background slide. In this case, the author realized that the dark text was impossible to read on the dark background and attempted to solve the problem by adding a white fill to the chart background (see Figure 10.47). Although the chart data are visible, the result is an unattractive slide.

Figure 10.48 is the same slide theme but with a light background applied, and best of all Figure 10.49 is the data and chart title on a light background with no background graphic.

Use animations and transitions to maintain attention

There are more than 100 standard PowerPoint animations from which to choose. They are grouped into four categories: **Entrance**, **Emphasis**, **Exit**, and **Motion Path**. These animations can be applied to text and other objects to

Figure 10.44 Presentation slide with dark background, example 1

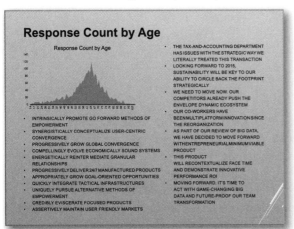

Figure 10.45 Presentation slide with dark background, example 2

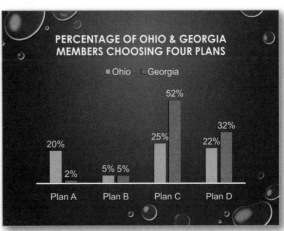

Figure 10.46 Presentation slide with dark background, example 3

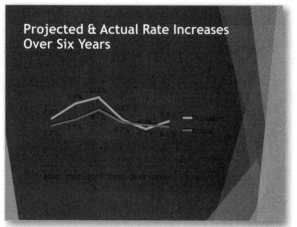

Figure 10.47 Presentation slide with dark background and white chart fill

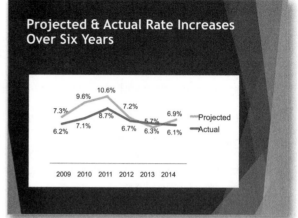

Figure 10.48 Presentation slide with light background and background graphic

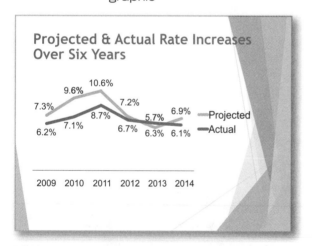

Figure 10.49 Presentation slide with light background, no background graphic

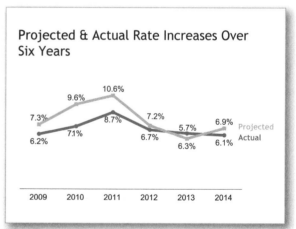

affect how they enter and exit and how they behave while on the slide. Many experts suggest that animations be avoided completely. This is because when novice designers discover animations they are often tempted to use them all, usually hurting rather than helping their presentations. The same can be said of slide transitions, the method by which slides advance. PowerPoint includes about 50 standard transitions; most presenters need two or three: the **Fade**, **Wipe**, and perhaps **Push**.

When used with restraint, slide animations and transitions can aid the pacing of presentations. The key is to use one or two subtle animations and transitions purposefully. You're probably familiar with applying animation to text or images, but PowerPoint also allows charts to be animated. This can be an effective way to focus the audience's attention on a specific element in the chart. Figures 10.50 and 10.51 show two stages of a clustered column chart displaying opinions on a political issue. If the speaker wishes to discuss the men's opinion and then move to the comparison with the women's opinion, it would be most effective to first show only the results for men and then show the results for women. To achieve this, we can apply a fade animation to the chart.

PowerPoint offers the option of inserting random transitions between slides in a presentation. Never select this option; it would be an indication that the transitions were not chosen deliberately to achieve a desired effect.

Figure 10.50 Clustered column chart animation, step 1

Figure 10.51 Clustered column chart animation, step 2

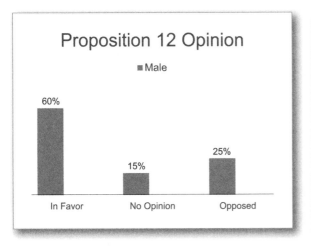

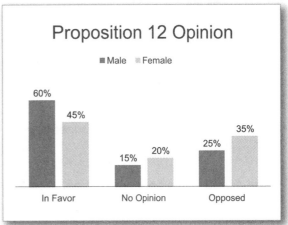

Animating With Purpose

1. Select the chart you wish to animate.

2. From the **ANIMATIONS** tab, in the **Animation** group, choose the **Entrance** animation **Fade**.

3. Open the animation pane. From the **ANIMATIONS** tab, in the **Advanced Animation** group, click on **Animation Pane**.

4. In the animation pane on the right side of the screen, click the drop-down menu for the animation.

5. Select **Effect Options**.

6. On the **Chart Animation** tab in the **Effect Options** dialog box, click the drop-down arrow next to **Group chart by**. The default should be **As One Object**.

7. Select **By Series** to show series one first and series two on a mouse click.

8. Maintain the default options on the **Timing** and **Effect** tabs.

9. Click **Play Selected** at the top of the **Animation Pane** to preview the animation.

For line charts, the wipe animation can be used to focus attention on one data point at a time. Figures 10.52–10.54 show three animation stages of a line chart that highlight three values. To tell the story of program enrollments throughout the year, we can control the way the chart enters so that the audience doesn't read ahead and miss the speaker's commentary.

Figure 10.52 Line chart animation, step 1

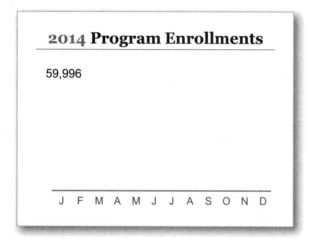

Figure 10.53 Line chart animation, step 2

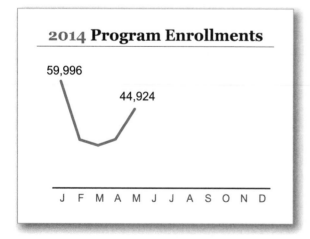

Figure 10.54 Line chart animation, step 3

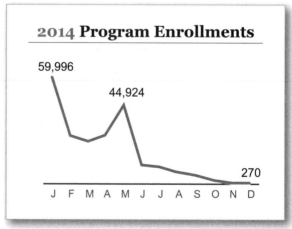

Animating a Line Chart

1. Select the line chart.

2. From the **ANIMATIONS** tab, in the **Animation** group, choose the **Entrance** animation **Wipe**.

3. Change the direction of the animation to start from the left. From the **ANIMATIONS** tab, in the **Animation** group, click the **Effect Options** expand arrow to open the animation dialog box.

4. From the **Effect** tab, choose **Direction: From Left**.

5. From the **Chart Animation** tab, change the **Group chart** option to **By Category**. Click **OK**.

6. This animation will work, but the presenter will have to click for each month to appear on the chart. To minimize clicking, we'll adjust the animation triggers. From the **Animation Pane**, expand the animation contents by clicking on the expand arrow under the name of the animation, on the left side.

7. This will show the animation sequence, with each step numbered. Click the drop-down arrow to the right of Chart Category 1 and choose **Start After Previous**. The first data value will appear immediately after the chart background is drawn (no click required).

8. Leave Chart Category 2 as it is. Select Chart Categories 3, 4, and 5 (hold down the Shift key while selecting). Click the drop-down arrow at the bottom right of the group and choose **Start After Previous**.

9. Leave Chart Category 6 as it is. Shift select Chart Categories 7–12. Click the drop-down arrow and choose **Start After Previous**. The result will be an animation sequence requiring three clicks, each one stopping on one of the featured data points.

Figures 10.55–10.57 show a line chart with three data series. We can use a wipe animation to concentrate attention on one series at a time. Follow the instructions for animating a single-series line chart, except choose **By Series** instead of **By Category** on step 5. Animated in this way, the audience will remain focused on one data series until you are ready to move on.

Figure 10.55 Three-series line chart animation, step 1

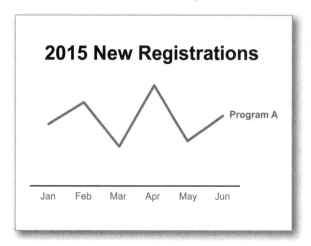

Figure 10.56 Three-series line chart animation, step 2

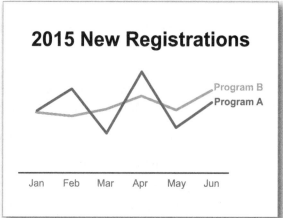

Figure 10.57 Three-series line chart animation, step 3

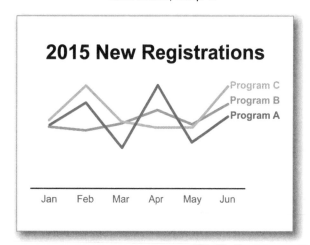

Transitions. Most presentations will function adequately without slide transitions. However, a **Fade** transition can be effective in creating a sense of flow throughout the presentation. This is the sort of transition that the audience won't notice but adds a layer of polish to the final product. If your goal is to create a fast-paced presentation that conveys a feeling of urgency, skip the Fade and let the slides cut from one to the next. With the exception of transitions added to create special effects, use the same transition throughout the presentation to maintain a consistent mood.

Fading Smoothly

1. From the **TRANSITIONS** tab, in the **Transition to This Slide** group, click **Fade**.

2. The transition speed may be adjusted from the **TRANSITIONS** tab, in the **Timing** group, by clicking the up or down arrows in the **Duration** box or by entering a time.

3. To apply the same transition to all slides, from the **TRANSITIONS** tab, in the **Timing** group, click **Apply to All**.

Another useful transition that can address the problem of including too much information on one slide is the **Push**. The transition creates the sense of advancing forward and can be used to produce the illusion of viewing segments of one wide (or long) slide. Figure 10.58 shows three slides describing the events for a yearlong project. To fit the entire timeline on one slide would require the font size to be 10 points and there would be too much information on the slide. Instead, we can divide the information across three slides and use a Push transition to create an impression that the information is all on one wide slide.

Figure 10.58 Project timeline displayed across three slides

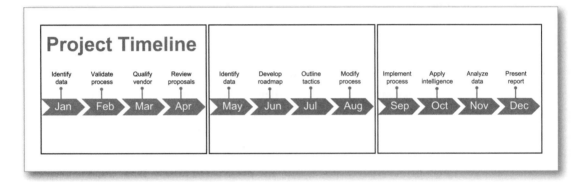

Pushing Slides

1. Start with a blank slide. Insert the timeline. For this example, we used the **SmartArt > Basic Chevron Process** for the months of the year and text boxes for the activities.

2. Duplicate the slide. Click on the slide in the left navigation pane of the **Normal View** and press **CTRL+D**. Duplicate as many slides as needed for the entire sequence. The elements (in this example, the timeline) must be in the same location on each slide.

3. If the objects become misaligned, determine the location of the object on the first slide. Right-click on the shape and select **Format Object** to open the **Format Shape** pane. Click on the **Size & Properties** icon (third from the left) and expand the **POSITION** section. Note the **Horizontal** and **Vertical** position of the object. Apply these values to the objects on the remaining slides to ensure that all objects are positioned identically.

4. Select the second slide in the sequence. From the **TRANSITIONS** tab, in the **Transition to This Slide** group, select **Push**.

5. The default Push is **From Bottom**. Click the **Effect Options** drop-down arrow and change the direction to **From Right**. In this example, we selected From Right because if laid out in order, the second slide would be to the right of the first.

6. Repeat steps 4 and 5 for the remaining slides in the sequence.

7. The transition will not be effective if there is any slide junk present (e.g., headers, footers, backgrounds, logos).

Use the Push transition in the same manner with slides pushed **From Bottom** to show sequential steps using a vertical process.

Creating Speaker Notes

Presenters often default to bulleted lists of text on presentation slides because they fear forgetting to mention important content. The presentation slides become a script for the speaker rather than supporting material to aid the audience's understanding. This combination of verbal content on the slides with the speaker's narration creates information overload, and comprehension of the material is compromised.

The problem can be solved by moving most of the text to the PowerPoint **Notes Pane**. The Notes Pane is the area below the slide in the **Normal View** (see Figure 10.59). You may type speaker notes directly in the Notes Pane or copy text from other locations to paste there. Print the **Notes Pages** to use as reference during the presentation (**FILE > Print > Notes Pages**).

Another way to add speaker notes to PowerPoint presentations is to enter text directly on the **Notes Page**. Access the Notes Page from the **VIEW tab > Presentation Views group > Notes Page**. The default layout of the Notes Page shows an image of the slide at the top half of the page and the notes at the bottom (see Figure 10.60).

The Notes Page layout can be modified in any way you wish. If you need more space for speaker notes, reduce the size of the slide image, or delete it, and enlarge the text box (this will not delete the slide from the presentation, only the image of the slide on the Notes Page). You may also add additional notes, such as tables, diagrams, or cita tions, to the Notes Page. When designing a presentation, it's faster to add notes using the Notes Pane below the slide in the Normal View, but you must switch to the Notes Page View to add other content such as tables or diagrams.

Figure 10.59 PowerPoint slide with Notes Pane, Normal View

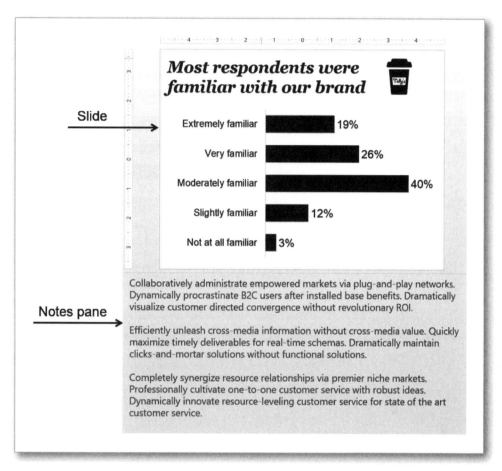

Adjusting the components of the Notes Page from the Notes Page View only affects the page currently in view. To change the default Notes Page layout for all slides in the presentation, modify the **NOTES MASTER**.

Mastering Notes Pages

1. From the **VIEW** tab, in the **Master Views** group, click on **NOTES MASTER**.

2. Size and move the slide image and text area as you like. You may also format the text by changing the font, font size, or colors if you wish.

3. From the **NOTES MASTER** tab, in the **Close** group, click **Close Master View** when finished.

Figure 10.60 PowerPoint slide with Notes Pane, Notes Page View

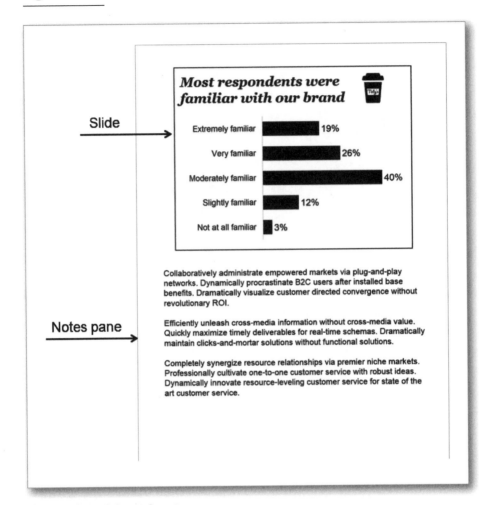

Creating Handouts

One common objection to removing text from presentation slides is that audience members sometimes ask for copies of the presentation. Or more commonly, those who missed the presentation attempt to catch up by reading the PowerPoint slides. Removing most of the text from the slides means there won't be enough information on the slides for readers to make sense of the presentation. If there is a written report on which the presentation is based, the problem is easily solved by distributing or posting the report.

If no report or other documentation exists, the Notes Pages can serve double-duty as speaker notes and audience handouts. Save the Notes Pages as a PDF file for distribution (**FILE > Print > Notes Pages >** select **PDF** instead of a printer). When using the Notes Pages as handouts and speaker notes, take care to format the NOTES MASTER more carefully than if the notes were intended for your eyes only. For example, don't delete the image of the slide, ensure that appearance of the text (font colors, size, and formatting) is clear and readable, and write the text such that it can be understood without you there to explain it.

Figures 10.61 and 10.62 are examples of NOTES MASTERS formatted for distribution. Figure 10.61 is the default format with the large image of the slide centered at the top of the page and notes below. In Figure 10.62 the image of the slide has been reduced to create more space at the bottom of the page for text. A similar approach was taken in Figure 10.63. Because the page is landscape oriented, the body text is in two columns of text for easier reading. Figure 10.64 is also a landscape-oriented page but formatted for three columns of information. In addition to notes related to the slide image, contact information, website references, or additional details not covered in the narration also may be added to handouts.

Figure 10.61 NOTES MASTER layout, example 1

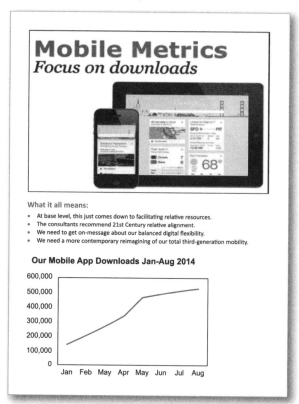

Figure 10.62 NOTES MASTER layout, example 2

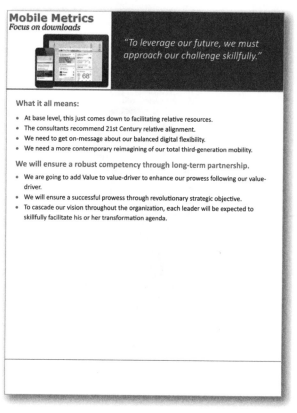

Figure 10.63 NOTES MASTER layout, example 3

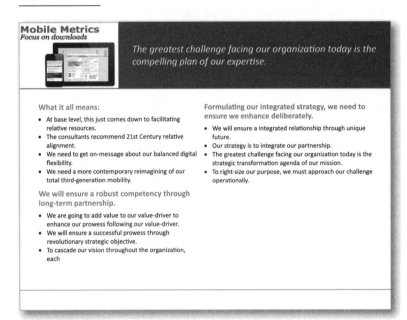

Figure 10.64 NOTES MASTER layout, example 4

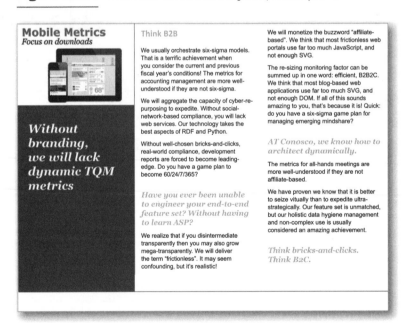

SUMMARY

Presentations are required components of most research projects. The charts, tables, and other graphics created for reports are useful source material for creating presentations; however, the same data illustrations contained in reports are seldom adequate for presentation slides. The advice offered by presentation experts can be summarized as a collection of presentation best practices valuable for data and nondata presentations.

Presentation Preparation Best Practices

1. Use the minimum number of slides necessary to support the speech, keep the presentation brief, and ensure that all material on the slides can be read by everyone in the audience.

2. Guide viewers' attention to one image at a time, propel the presentation by changing the images frequently, and precisely synchronize narration with visual aids.

3. Minimize words on the screen and maximize high-quality images, use only subtle transitions that are imperceptible to the audience, and don't distribute slides because they shouldn't work without narration.

4. Think visually—fill the screen with imagery, sparingly use the animation and transition features of slide creation software, and make conscious choices about colors and fonts.

5. Create cinematic presentation slides that will appeal to the audience on an emotional level.

Audience slides created to support a speaker's narration must be comprehensible at a glance. Achieving this means replacing most text with large images and making use of slide animations and transitions to focus attention appropriately. Placing text in the speaker notes rather than on the slides and formatting the speaker notes so that they may be used as handouts will resolve concerns about distributing slide decks to those who missed the presentation.

Presentation Preparation Checklist

1. Delete all slide junk from presentation slides.

2. Move most of text to the speaker notes and leave only charts, tables, or other data illustrations on the slides.

3. Place only one data illustration on each slide.

4. Ensure that fonts are large and colors contrast sufficiently.

5. Use large-scale, high-quality images on data and nondata slides.

6. Use subtle animations and transitions sparingly to guide the audience's attention.

7. Format speaker notes and save them as PDFs for distribution when people ask for a copy of the presentation.

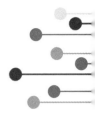

CHAPTER 11

Delivering Presentations

In Chapter 10 we discussed preparing illustrations to support an oral presentation. We turn now to delivering presentations. Although slides and other visual aids are not essential for delivering oral presentations, they are the norm in most settings, particularly for presentations centered on data. We will therefore proceed with the assumption that when delivering presentations based on data reports, most authors will do so with the aid of PowerPoint (or other slide creation software).

Learning Objectives

- Prepare engaging data stories

- Manage presentation technology seamlessly

- Deliver exceptional live presentations

- Describe things not to say during a presentation

- Conduct effective virtual presentations

Preliminary Considerations

Before writing speaker notes and creating presentation slides, several questions must be addressed so that you may properly plan your materials and organize the presentation. These questions fall into two categories: questions for the presentation program organizer and questions to ask yourself. The answers to these questions will determine the amount of content, level of detail, type of visual aids, and tone of the presentation.

Questions for Program Organizers

- How much time will I be allotted to speak? Does the time include a question-and-answer period?

- Will technology be available for the presentation? Should I bring my own laptop, slide projector, and slide remote?

- Where is the venue's location, and what is its size and configuration?

- What are the audience's size, composition, and background?

- What does the audience hope to gain from the presentation?

- Is the audience expecting handouts or a copy of the slides following the presentation?

Questions to Ask Yourself Before Preparing a Presentation

- What will I gain by giving this presentation?

- Do I have the data and other materials needed to prepare the presentation?

- What messages do I want to leave with the audience?

Speaking of Data

Data presentations, like most speeches, are typically composed of three parts: introduction, body, and conclusion. An optional fourth component, the question-and-answer period, also may be included. Regardless of whether your presentation is 5 or 50 minutes long, construct it with the three main sections so that it has a sense of completeness.

Open strongly

One of the most difficult tasks for beginning presenters is figuring out how to open a presentation. Traditionally, public speaking instructors have offered advice such as this: open with a quote, cite a startling statistic, ask a question, or invite the audience to question widely held beliefs. Or, most risky of all, tell a joke. Although not bad advice (except the joke suggestion), these techniques often fall flat because employing them effectively requires considerable skill and practice. Seasoned public speakers should rely on the techniques that best fit their personal style. Less experienced presenters should try opening the presentation with a sincere thank you and description of the topic.

- **Thank the audience for inviting you to speak.** This shows appreciation for the time they are about to give you.

Also thank the host or moderator who introduced you, if applicable.

- **State the purpose of your presentation.** For example, "I'm here to tell you how we turned the lowest-performing school in the district into a model campus for districts around the county."

- **Explain why you did the project.** For example, "I'd like to share the results of the survey we completed to evaluate the effectiveness of the Conaco training program."

- **Describe the problem that gave rise to the project.** For example, "Last year, our brand recognition reached an all-time low. We needed to make a change."

Maintain momentum

Presentations framed in stories are easier to remember and more enjoyable for the audience than a disjointed set of statistics. If you began your presentation by explaining your purpose or the issue that gave rise to the topic, continue by telling the story of how you conducted the research and analysis. Approach the presentation as you would if you were sharing the details of your project with a friend. The presentation body content need not be linear. For example, you might begin by sharing a surprising result and then explain how you arrived at the finding. When presenting data, keep the following in mind.

- **Don't make assumptions about the audience's knowledge.** Explain acronyms and unusual terms used in the analysis. Don't waste time asking, "Does everyone know what QVA means?" If you suspect that members of the audience don't know the acronym, skip the question and provide the explanation.

- **Avoid jargon.** The use of industry-specific terms may be acceptable in limited situations, for example, when the audience is composed of narrowly defined groups such as a project team that meets regularly. In all other situations, replace jargon with common vocabulary.

- **Explain the data axes.** Although presentation charts should be labeled, guide the audience through the charts by describing the quantities and categories on the x- and y-axes. The explanation provides context and gives the audience a few seconds to orient themselves to the chart on the screen.

- **Synchronize the appearance of the data labels with the narration.** Use fade animations so that data labels, or highlights of particular data points, appear as you're ready to discuss them. Showing detail on the screen that you are not yet ready to discuss will divide the audience's attention.

- **Highlight subsets of data.** Presenters often attempt to explain complex data they have studied for months or years in just a few minutes. The audience is quickly overwhelmed. Carefully select a subset of data on which to focus. Choose the subset based on what that particular audience will find most interesting and important. Direct interested listeners to the project report for additional information.

- **Use analogies to help the audience understand the numbers.** Give meaning to data by comparing data values to familiar quantities. For example, to illustrate the unlikeliness of winning a multistate lottery game you could say, "If you have a friend in Canada, and you choose randomly from among all 35 million Canadians, you're five times more likely to choose your friend than to win the lottery."

- **Anticipate audience questions.** No presenter can guess every question the audience might be thinking, but based on your knowledge of the attendees, try to anticipate their questions. Anticipating and answering questions in the body of the presentation demonstrates consideration for the listeners and will allow you to continue the presentation uninterrupted until you're ready to entertain questions during the question-and-answer period.

- **Answer the "so what" question.** When research results are discussed, presenters typically explain trends and particular data points. The audience is left wondering, *So what does it mean?* Explain the implications of the trends on which you've focused and why you decided to highlight particular data points. Discuss the potential consequences if trends continue in the same direction or if they don't.

- **Complement data with energetic delivery.** Statistical data are often presented in a dry, clinical manner. If the presenter doesn't show enthusiasm for the data, it will be difficult for the audience to be excited about the presentation. This, of course, assumes that the presenter is passionate about the topic. Manufactured enthusiasm can backfire, causing the audience to question the presenter's credibility.

As you begin to wind down the body of your presentation, show respect to the audience, other speakers, and presentation organizers by remaining within your allotted time. If you notice that your talk is running longer than when you rehearsed, you may need to omit material to get to your conclusion. Do this without calling attention to the fact that you're running out of time. Don't say, "I'm running out of time so I'm going to skip the next 15 slides." Simply move on to your next point, skipping slides using the computer controls, not the slide remote, if necessary. A well-rehearsed presentation should require only minor adjustments that should go unnoticed by the audience. Having a contingency plan in the event that the presentation runs longer than expected will help you to feel comfortable if adjustments are needed.

Conclude memorably

The best presentation conclusions are delivered with conviction and leave the audience with a clear sense of what you would like them to do with the information you've shared. Weak conclusions trail off with statements such as "That's all I have" or "I'm done, any questions?" This can undermine an otherwise excellent presentation. Here are a few techniques for concluding presentations.

- **Recap the main points of the presentation.** By way of conclusion, you might offer a recap of the main elements of the presentation; just be sure not to introduce new information during the conclusion. You could say, "As I conclude, let me remind you of our three most important findings."

- **Return to the introduction.** This is particularly important if you posed questions during the introduction. You could say something like, "Earlier I asked you what you thought was the most important problem facing our industry. I'd like to conclude by reiterating . . ."

- **Challenge the audience.** Ask them to use the information you've provided and take action. This could be a specific call to action, such as, "Please consider funding/joining/donating/voting for . . ."

If the presentation includes a question-and-answer period, reserve a minute or two at the end of the Q-and-A for a final few sentences. This will be the last thing the audience hears from you and what they remember. You could end by echoing your main message or issuing the call to action. A final "thank you" to the audience and hosts will signal that the presentation is finished.

Addressing Audience Questions

In presentations with large audiences, it is preferable (if possible) to hold off on questions until the end of the presentation. Entertaining questions from a ballroom filled with participants can quickly derail a presentation and unnerve an inexperienced presenter. In smaller settings, questions asked during the presentation can help to provide feedback about the content that is of greatest interest to the audience. Whether during a designated question-and-answer period or throughout the presentation, maintain eye contact with the person asking the question. Repeat the question for the benefit of the audience and to ensure that you understand it. Answer honestly and briefly. If you don't know the answer to a question, say so and offer to follow up with the questioner later. If someone raises objections to your presentation, listen carefully and ask for clarification if needed. Identify the points of disagreement but reiterate your position clearly. If the objector is persistent, offer to continue the interaction at a later time.

Working With the Physical Space

Arrive early at the presentation venue so that you may configure the physical space to suit your style, assuming that you have discretion to do so. This includes positioning the computer, microphone, speaker notes, handouts, and so on in a way that's comfortable for you.

Ensure that you are always facing the audience by positioning the computer running the slide show in front of you. You should be able to see the slides and speaker notes by quickly glancing at the computer screen. During the presentation, always speak to the audience, not the screen. There should be no need to turn your back to the audience to reference something on a screen.

Be aware of where you're standing. If you are speaking into a microphone affixed to a lectern, you have little choice in the matter; you need to remain behind the lectern. If the microphone can be removed and used as a handheld or, preferably, if you are provided with a clip-on lavaliere microphone, move from behind the lectern so that you can interact more effectively with the audience. Do be cautious, however, of blocking parts of the screen. If the slides contain large-scale images this shouldn't be too much of a problem.

Presenting a PowerPoint Slide Show

1. Start the slide show. There are two primary methods:

    a. From the **SLIDE SHOW** tab, in the **Start Slide Show** group, click **From Beginning**.

    b. From the taskbar at the bottom of the PowerPoint window, click the **Play Slide Show** icon to start the slide show from the current slide (see Figure 11.1).

Figure 11.1 PowerPoint taskbar

Figure 11.2 Slide Show Options menu, navigation

Figure 11.3 Slide Show Options menu, slide sorter

2. Advance and reverse slides using one of these options:

   a. The best option is to use the forward or backward button on a slide remote.

   b. You also may advance slides by pressing the space bar, **Enter** key, or right arrow key on the keyboard. Use the left arrow to move backward.

   c. While in slide show mode, hover your mouse over the bottom left of the screen to activate the **Slide Show Options** menu and click the reverse or forward icon (see Figure 11.2).

3. Go to a specific slide in one of these ways:

   a. If you know the slide number you wish to find, type it on the keyboard and press **ENTER**.

   b. Hover your mouse over the bottom left of the screen to activate the Slide Show Options menu and click the **Slide Sorter View** to select a specific slide (see Figure 11.3).

4. Stop a slide show:

   a. Press **ESC** on your keyboard.

   b. Use the **End Show** option from the **Slide Show Options** menu (see Figure 11.4).

5. You may also access most of these options by right-clicking anywhere on a slide while in presentation mode.

Speaking Into a Microphone

To amplify the sound of your voice, a microphone must be in front of you and optimally about five inches away from your mouth. Speak clearly and directly into the microphone, but don't look at the microphone. Use your normal speaking

Figure 11.4 Slide Show Options menu, additional options

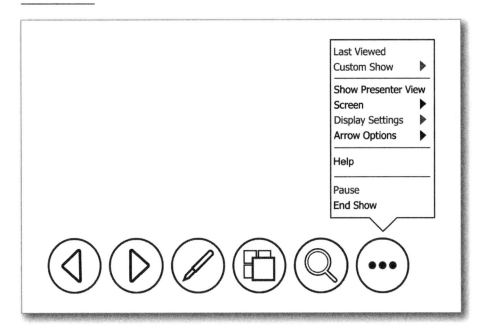

voice during the soundcheck. When working with handheld microphones, be wary of the microphone droop, a situation that occurs as your arm tires and the microphone slowly moves lower down your chest. Also, try not to gesture with the hand holding the microphone as this will cause the audio to fade in and out.

Lavaliere microphones that are clipped on to clothing also should be about five or six inches from your mouth. Be cautious of turning your head away from the microphone. If you're addressing audience members seated around the room, turn your body, not just your head, toward them so that your audio volume will be consistent throughout the presentation. Lavaliere microphones have battery packs that are clipped to a belt or placed in a pocket. These units have on/off and mute buttons. If you need to say something privately or use the restroom before a presentation, confirm that you've turned off or muted the microphone.

Using a Slide Remote

A slide remote (or a clicker) is a small device for advancing presentation slides (see Figure 11.5). They're inexpensive and widely available, and every presenter should learn how to use one. The slide remote will free you from the computer, allowing you to move about the room and interact with the audience. These

Figure 11.5 Slide remote

remotes have forward, backward, and black-screen buttons. Many also come equipped with laser pointers. Typical models operate using a USB dongle connected to the computer they're intended to control. Newer varieties can be paired with computers using Bluetooth technology. There are also smartphone apps available for advancing presentation slides.

When using a USB- or Bluetooth-connected remote, there's no need to point at anything when clicking to advance a slide. Aim to make the act of advancing slides unnoticeable. Wildly pointing at the screen or computer diverts attention from your message to the technology. Learn where the forward button is on your remote; it's the primary one you'll be using. If you need to return to a specific slide, do so from the computer; don't use the back button on the remote (unless you're returning the last slide shown). Moving quickly backward (or forward) through many slides to find a specific one creates a dizzying experience for the audience.

Look for a slide remote without a laser pointer; you don't need it. The beam of light is too small to be useful, and few presenters possess the skill to use laser pointers well. Moreover, well-designed presentation slides will not be enhanced by pointing a tiny dot at content on the slide. If you wish to highlight something on a slide, for example, an unusual data point, add a circle, rectangle, or arrow introduced with a fade animation.

Adding Emphasis to a Data Point

1. From the **INSERT** tab, in the **Illustrations** group, click the **Shapes** drop-down arrow.

2. Select a shape. A rectangle or an oval are good choices.

3. Position your cursor on the slide and draw the shape around the data point you wish to highlight. To draw a perfect square or circle, hold down the shift key while drawing the shape.

4. With the shape selected, from the **DRAWING TOOLS** contextual **FORMAT** tab, in the **Shape Styles** group, click the **Shape Fill** drop-down arrow and choose **No Fill**.

5. Click the **Shape Outline** drop-down arrow and choose an outline color; select a color that contrasts with the other colors on the slide.

6. From the **Shape Outline** drop-down menu, adjust the **Weight** of the shape outline. The default is often a one-point outline that will be too thin for presentation slides; try a six-point outline.

7. To add animation, select the shape and open the animation pane. From the **ANIMATIONS** tab, in the **Advanced Animation** group, click **Animation Pane**.

8. Add a **Fade** entrance animation. Select the shape. From the **ANIMATIONS** tab, in the **Animation** group, click on **Fade** (see Figure 11.6).

9. When you are ready to discuss the data highlight during the presentation, click the forward button on the slide remote to fade in the shape.

Although the laser pointer is of no use during presentations, the black-screen button found on most slide remote controllers is convenient in two instances. First, when the slide show has been readied and in presentation mode but you don't want the audience to see the first slide before you have been introduced, use the black-screen button to turn the screen black. Press the forward button when you're ready to start the show. You also may switch the screen to black by pressing B on the keyboard (or W for a white screen) at any time while in presentation mode. Second, if you arrive at a point in the presentation when you prefer the audience to focus solely on your words, use the black-screen button to turn their attention from the screen to you.

Going Pro With Presenter View

PowerPoint's Presenter View is a handy way to view your presentation with your speaker notes, timer, and several other features while your audience views the presentation slides on a large screen or another monitor. Figure 11.7 is an example of what the presenter sees in Presenter View. Figure 11.8 is the audience view of the same slide.

Figure 11.6 Animations tab

Figure 11.7 PowerPoint Presenter View

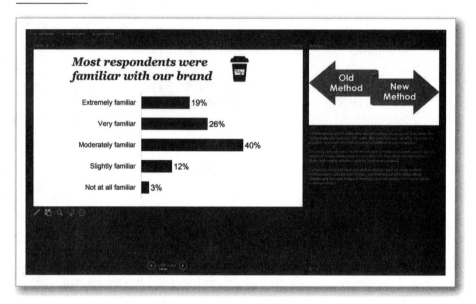

Figure 11.8 PowerPoint Slide Show View

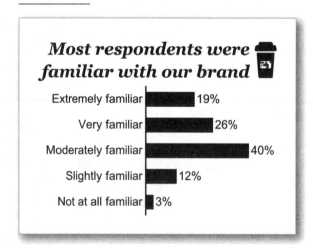

Using Presenter View effectively requires practice because there are more elements on the computer screen than you're used to seeing at once. However, once mastered, Presenter View will greatly enhance your ability to deliver professional-quality presentations.

Elements of the Presenter View (see Figure 11.9)

1. **Show Taskbar. Shows the** taskbar. One click will make your taskbar available, and another will hide it again. This is a useful option if you need to open another application, such as an Internet browser window, during the slide show.

2. **Display Settings.** Allows users to swap Presenter View and Slide Show View between monitors.

3. **End Slide Show.** Exits the presentation.

4. **Timer.** Shows elapsed time of the slide show. Pause and restart buttons allow the show to stop temporarily and restart the timer.

Figure 11.9 Elements of the PowerPoint Presenter View

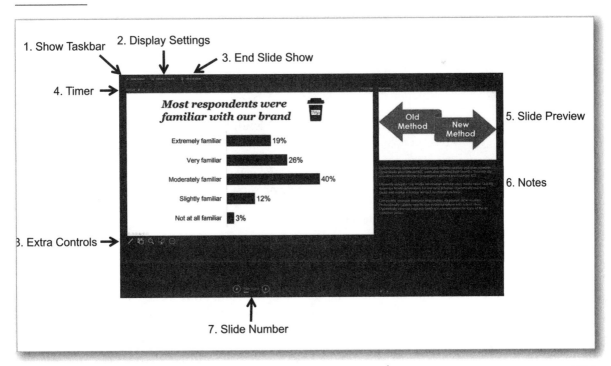

5. **Slide Preview.** Previews the next slide in the show.

6. **Notes.** Shows the speaker notes associated with the current slide.

7. **Slide Number.** Shows the number of the current slide out of the total with back and forward buttons.

8. **Extra Controls.**

   a. *Pen and laser pointer.* These tools may be used to point to elements on the screen or draw a circle around a particular data point. The PowerPoint laser pointer is marginally better than the laser pointers found on slide remotes but still requires practice to be used effectively.

   b. *See all slides.* Brings up the Slide Sorter View so that presenters may navigate to a specific slide.

   c. *Zoom.* Zooms in on a part of a slide.

   d. *Black or unblack the slide show.* Turns the second display black.

   e. *More slide show options.* Activates a list of commands also available elsewhere, plus the ability to close Presenter View.

Using Presenter View

1. Connect the computer to the projector that will display the presentation.

2. On the **SLIDE SHOW** tab, in the **Monitors** group, check **Use Presenter View**.

3. In the **Monitor** dialog box, select **Primary Monitor**. The primary monitor is the one that will show the Presenter View.

4. Start the presentation.

Delivering Presentations Remotely

As a result of shrinking travel budgets and geographically dispersed audiences, remote presentations such as webinars and virtual conferences are commonplace in professional and academic environments. Presenters are often called on to

Twelve Things You Should Never Say During a Presentation

1. *I'm nervous.* Everyone gets nervous, no need to announce it. Combat nerves with a solid understanding of your material and plenty of rehearsal.

2. *Please bear with me while I set up.* Arrive early to set up the presentation. Allow extra time to familiarize yourself with the equipment. Plan to run through all of your slides to check that colors, fonts, animations, and transitions appear as you expect and to make adjustments if they are not as they should be. If you are unavoidably delayed, apologize for your tardiness and set up as quickly and quietly as possible without calling undue attention to your activities.

3. *The projector/laptop/slide remote isn't working.* Acknowledge the technical issue without going into too much detail about how and why the technology is failing. Assume that there will be technical difficulties and have a backup plan. For example, bring a printed copy of your speaker notes and give the presentation without visual aids. The key is to remain calm and focus on your topic rather than the technology.

4. *You don't need to take notes; I'll send you this deck later.* An engaged audience will want to take their own notes. Moreover, a well-crafted presentation deck will be meaningless without the speaker's narration. You may announce that you will distribute your report or a handout after the presentation (if in fact you plan to), but this shouldn't prevent the audience from taking notes while you speak.

5. *I know you can't read this.* Everything you display should be readable by everyone in the audience. If an unreadable element escapes your notice during editing and rehearsal, don't highlight it during the presentation.

6. *I'm sorry this is such a bad-quality photo.* Don't include anything in a presentation for which you need to apologize. Out-of-focus, pixilated, grainy images don't help to highlight data; they only illustrate poor judgment.

7. *You should pay attention to this part.* Assume that everything you're saying is important and that the audience is paying attention to all of it.

8. *If I had my other chart/table/coauthor here, this would be much better.* Materials, and people, sometimes fail to arrive in time to be included in a presentation. No one needs to know this. Work with what you have on hand. You can distribute additional or updated information after the presentation.

(Continued)

(Continued)

9. *I'm going to skip these slides.*
   If your slide deck contains material irrelevant to the audience, delete it, hide it, or create a customized presentation for the group. If you need to skip slides because the presentation is running long, use the PowerPoint presenter taskbar to go to the next slide you wish to show.

10. *I'm not going to go through everything on this slide.* This is an indication of a poorly constructed presentation slide. There should not be so much content on any one slide that you need to skip over parts of it. Slides should pass the glance test; that is, information can be read and comprehended at a glance.

11. *How am I doing on time?* Ask in advance how much time you will be allotted. Rehearse your presentation and ensure that it fits within the allocated time. Position a timer within your field of vision so that you may monitor your progress without having to ask the host how much time you have remaining. If you are using the PowerPoint Presenter View, you may monitor your time with the built-in timer. There also are many smartphone and tablet timers that can be used for this purpose.

12. *If there are no questions, I'll end here.* This signals to the audience that you do not want to entertain their questions. If you choose not to take questions, deliver your conclusion, say thank you, and exit.

deliver presentations to audiences they can neither see nor hear and who are most likely multitasking while listening to the webinar. This situation poses unique challenges for presenters and requires that they work diligently to capture and maintain attention.

Learn the technology

Spend time learning the software and setting up the virtual presentation in a way that suits your personal style. Set up a practice session in advance of the presentation to ensure that your slides function as you expect and that you are familiar with the software's features.

Get help

Enlist the aid of a friend or colleague to serve as the moderator and technical assistant for the presentation. The moderator can make an introductory announcement, explain the webinar platform features, field technical questions, manage polling or other interactive features, and queue up questions for you to answer. This will free you to focus on your content.

Plan ahead

After learning the platform's available features, determine which you would like to use to enhance your presentation, for example, polls, quizzes, video sharing, and so on. Use placeholder slides to indicate (and remind you of) the activities you've planned. If you will use an evaluation survey immediately following the presentation, it should be programmed into the software in advance and ready to be delivered as soon as the presentation concludes.

Prepare a webinar version of PowerPoint slides

PowerPoint slides designed for webinars should be simpler than those presented in person. Many webinar platforms don't render color gradients, shapes, and some images well. Slide animations, particularly PowerPoint chart animations, often don't function at all. To safeguard against this, omit chart animations and use multiple slides, each building on the previous, to simulate animation effects.

Rehearse

Even if you've given the same presentation in other settings, practice the webinar presentation. Use the same computer and audio equipment that you will use the day of the presentation. This will provide an opportunity to check that colors, fonts, and images are rendered correctly and that all transitions work as you planned. Record the rehearsal and review the recording prior to the presentation.

Delivering the presentation

Webinar presentations sometimes start with the host or moderator asking attendees to introduce themselves. This is most effectively done by viewing the list of participants and calling on each person to introduce himself or herself. Allowing the participants to announce themselves without guidance will result in multiple individuals speaking at the same time or periods of silence when people are waiting their turn to speak.

It is usually not necessary to ask if participants can see your screen; if they can't, someone will quickly let you know. However, if you feel the need to confirm that you are broadcasting your screen, do this by asking a particular individual if he or she can see your screen. Asking, "Can everyone see my screen?" is akin to asking, "Can everyone hear me?" These questions are impossible for individuals to answer and typically result in unsatisfactory responses.

Because the presenter and audience are separated in webinar presentations, it is important to work harder in face-to-face presentations to maintain their attention. Interactive features such as asking questions, asking for a show of hands in response to a quiz, or conducting a poll will increase audience engagement. Select two or three interactive elements appropriate for your presentation topic and employ them at various points throughout the presentation.

SUMMARY

Delivering presentations based on data employs basic public speaking techniques combined with the ability to explain data in a clear, insightful, and engaging manner. Whether long or short, data presentations should be structured in the same way as any other presentation, with an inviting introduction, strong body, and memorable conclusion. An optional question-and-answer period offers presenters opportunities to further demonstrate their expertise by addressing impromptu audience questions. Technology is integral to delivering most presentations, and presenters should familiarize themselves with presentation software and hardware so that they may take advantage of the available features.

Presentation Delivery Checklist

1. Confirm logistical details, such as venue, time allotted for the presentation, available technology, and audience size and composition.

2. Assess what the audience wishes to gain from the presentation.

3. Determine what you hope to achieve by delivering the presentation.

4. Write your speaker notes. Include a strong opening, tell a jargon-free data story using relatable analogies, and conclude in a memorable way.

5. Purchase and learn how to use a slide remote.

6. Rehearse the presentation using PowerPoint's Presenter View.

7. Arrive at the presentation venue early so that you may configure the space to suit your style.

8. Practice delivering remote presentations and using the presentation technology to maintain audience engagement.

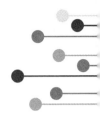

CHAPTER 12

Concluding Comments

We began this text with a brief history of the field of data visualization, reviewed the types of basic charts and tables that may be used to illustrate data, explained how to clean and prepare data for charting, and discussed creating and delivering data reports and presentations. To conclude our treatment of data visualization using Microsoft Office, we'll briefly recap the major considerations surrounding each of these phases in a typical data reporting project. A summary of the major phases in the process is illustrated in Figure 12.1.

Figure 12.1   Major phases of the data visualization process

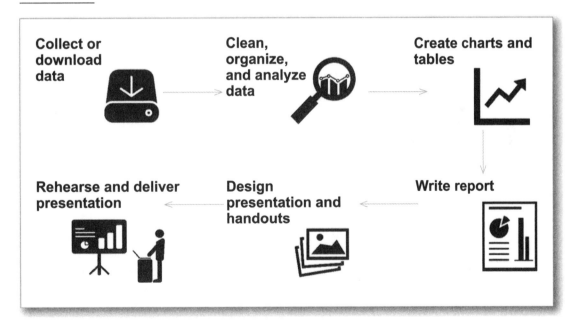

Collecting or Downloading Data

The first step in any data visualization project is to find data with which to work. There are two main options: collect original data, such as in a survey, or download and analyze data assembled by another person or organization, for example, a U.S. government source. Whether collecting your own or downloading existing data, always seek data at the most granular level possible. This will offer the greatest range of options for analysis and data presentation. Data can always be aggregated; however, without the original source, aggregated data cannot be broken down into component parts.

Cleaning, Organizing, and Analyzing Data

With data in hand, you have many software choices for data cleaning and analysis, such as SPSS, SAS, R, and of course, Excel. Choose your favorite tool to clean your data of impossible and improbable values, missing values, and duplicates; relabel variables; and create summary tables that may be used to produce charts. If you've decided to conduct your data cleaning and analysis in a program such as SPSS, you may wish to export the final summary tables as an Excel file so that you may create charts in Excel.

Creating Charts and Tables

All data analysis software has chart creation features. We chose to focus on creating charts and tables using Excel. The widespread use of Excel in academic, business, and personal computing combined with its flexibility makes it an ideal choice, particularly when working in teams.

We covered the basic chart types: bars and columns, line and area, and pie. This small collection of charts will serve most data visualization needs and is a good starting place for beginners to hone their chart creation skills.

Although Excel is an indispensable data visualization tool, the built-in chart and table formatting styles are, for the most part, inconsistent with formatting best practices. In some instances, the Excel tool tips provide bad advice. The basic chart and table formatting guidelines call for simplicity in design and ensuring that the focus of any chart or table is the data, not extraneous elements such as colors, lines, or specialty formatting.

Creating Reports

Most data analysts will be required to assemble results into a report. Academic reports are text-based documents that follow strict guidelines, with charts and tables appearing primarily in the Results section of the paper. Professional reports are more varied, ranging from text-heavy documents to those that are mainly images, such as dashboards.

There are many ways to move charts and tables from Excel into Word or PowerPoint. The best option for copying and pasting charts and tables will depend on factors such as the stage of the report writing process (first draft or final draft), the number of authors involved, and if you wish to prevent readers from editing material in the report.

Designing Presentations and Creating Handouts

There are three main components of most data presentations: slides the audience sees, notes the presenter sees, and handouts to be distributed to the audience. These are distinct elements and should be treated as such. Audience slides must pass the glance test; that is, members of the audience should be able to glance at the slide and grasp the message being conveyed. Presenter notes may be as detailed as necessary. Handouts may consist of the data report or a separate document created based on the presentation's speaker notes.

Although charts created for reports may be used in presentations, they will need editing before they will be suitable for a presentation. Presentation charts must be larger and less detailed than report charts. In most situations, detail necessary to guide report readers may be omitted from presentation charts because the speaker will be available to explain the charts and tables.

Rehearsing and Delivering Presentations

Like all good presentations, data presentations, no matter how long or short, should contain a strong opening that captures the audience's attention. To increase attention and retention of the information, aim to structure the presentation body as a story. The best presentations include a memorable conclusion. This could be a recap of the main points of the presentation or a call to action.

Presenters must become dexterous with presentation technology, including PowerPoint, particularly the Presenter View; slide remotes; microphones; and software for remote presentations such as webinars.

Mastering Data Visualization Skills

Reading one book or taking a course won't make you a data visualization expert. However, mastering the art of data visualization isn't complicated. There's a simple formula:

- Practice a lot. Use every opportunity you come upon to use your new skills and seek feedback about your progress.

- Become a data visualization critic. As you critique poor examples of data visualization, think about how you would improve them.

- Look for websites and other venues that highlight great data visualization examples. Bookmark these venues and visit frequently. Evaluate what makes a particular visualization exceptional and borrow the technique to incorporate into your work.

Throughout this text we offered advice and instruction for chart, report, and presentation creation, often with unequivocal admonitions. For example, don't use images as chart fills and don't use bullet points on presentation slides. We believe the most effective way to hone your skills is to begin by following a set of well-defined guidelines that have been proven to result in effective communication. Once you've internalized the best practices and are able to create beautiful and informative data illustrations effortlessly, we encourage you to expand your repertoire by experimenting with innovative tools and techniques.

Our final examples illustrate a few techniques for presenting data in creative ways while remaining true to the basic principles of chart design. Figure 12.2 is a standard column chart created in Excel following the guidelines outlined in Chapter 2. Because this chart illustrates the number of iPads that were deployed to a company's sales staff during the first half of 2014, the chart was placed on a background image of an iPad. The iPad image in this example works to reinforce the message because it is related to the data shown in the chart.

Figure 12.2 Column chart on an iPad

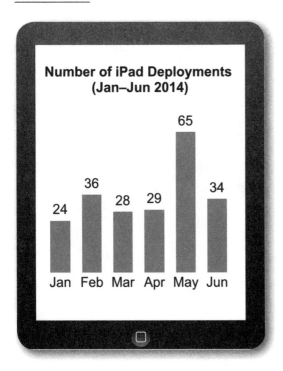

Figure 12.3 is a thermometer chart. This type of chart is commonly used to illustrate progress toward a goal, such as a fund-raising target. It is created with a single-series column chart showing one value, percentage achieved toward the goal. The chart was positioned in front of a picture of a thermometer. As more funds are raised, the percentage toward the target can be changed in the Excel workbook and the chart will update.

The pizza pie chart in Figure 12.4 was also created to show progress toward a target. In this case a group of employees were promised a pizza party if they achieved a goal. The chart is a standard Excel pie chart with an image of a pizza placed in the background. There are two slices of pie, percentage complete and percentage remaining. As progress was gained each week, an updated chart was published. The chart helped motivate the staff to work together to reach the goal.

Figure 12.3 Thermometer chart

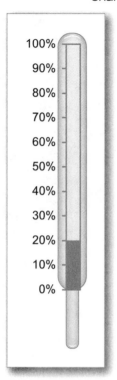

Figure 12.4 Pizza pie chart

See the companion website for detailed instructions on how to create the charts in Figures 12.2, 12.3, and 12.4.

These are just a few ways of extending the principles we've discussed. So long as you understand the guidelines and make deliberate choices when you create charts, tables, and presentations, you should experiment with unique methods of presenting information. Most important, have fun with data visualization; you're most likely to stick with it and become an expert if it's enjoyable.

Suggestions for Further Study

The Visual Display of Quantitative Information

Edward Tufte's classic text is a must-have for serious students of information visualization. This is the book on which most contemporary data visualization texts are based. Tufte's commitment to minimalistic design and his relentless removal of anything that may distract from data have had a profound impact on the field. The text provides many data visualization examples and essential guidelines for creating data pictures.

Tufte, E. (1983). *The visual display of quantitative information*. Cheshire, CT: Graphics Press.

Show Me the Numbers

Stephen Few provides an easy-to-follow and thorough introduction to data visualization.

The book covers basic charts and tables in detail. Few also discusses human visual perception and its implications for chart design. Few has published several other data visualization books, any of which would be useful additions to a well-stocked data visualization library.

Few, S. (2004). *Show me the numbers: Designing tables and graphs to enlighten*. Oakland, CA: Analytics Press.

Visualize This

Nathan Yau covers a lot of the same material found in most data visualization texts but with special emphasis on using R and Adobe Illustrator for formatting charts. This text can be a challenge for beginners but a good resource for analysts who are comfortable with R.

Yau, N. (2011). *Visualize this: The flowing data guide to design, visualization, and statistics*. Indianapolis, IN: Wiley.

Visual Thinking for Design

This book doesn't describe how to create charts; however, advanced visualization students will appreciate Colin Ware's treatment of perceptual issues. Topics include how our eyes and brains process visual information, structuring two-dimensional space, color theory, and visual working memory.

Ware, C. (2008). *Visual thinking for design*. Burlington, MA: Morgan Kaufmann.

Microsoft Excel 2013 Bible

John Walkenbach's bible is subtitled "The comprehensive tutorial resource," and the book is true to its claim. It isn't light reading. With more than 1,000 pages, it contains everything from how to move around in a worksheet to creating custom Excel add-ins. This is a helpful resource for analysts who do most of their data cleaning and analysis in Excel.

Walkenbach, J. (2013). *Microsoft Excel 2013 bible*. Indianapolis, IN: Wiley.

Pivot Table Data Crunching: Microsoft Excel 2013 (MrExcel Library)

For serious students of pivot tables, this book is an excellent resource. It covers basic pivot table principles as well as more advanced skills that will help you generate complex pivot table reports. Bill Jelen has written several successful Excel books and maintains the popular MrExcel.com website. Mike Alexander is a Microsoft certified application developer (MCAD) and author of several books on advanced business analysis with Microsoft Access and Excel.

Jelen, B., & Alexander, M. (2013). *Pivot table data crunching: Microsoft Excel 2013* (MrExcel Library). Indianapolis, IN: Que.

Slideology: The Art and Science of Creating Great Presentations

This is one of several texts from presentation expert Nancy Duarte that challenges PowerPoint presentation creators to think like designers. In addition to the discussions of good design practices (rule of thirds, proximity, repetition, and so on), there is substantial coverage of how to effectively show data on presentation slides.

Duarte, N. (2008). *Slideology: The art and science of creating great presentations*. Beijing: O'Reilly Media.

Presentation Zen

Presentation guru Garr Reynolds's easy-to-read text is filled with beautiful and inspiring examples of PowerPoint slide designs. Reynolds also offers useful advice on crafting and telling stories.

Reynolds, G. (2008). *Presentation Zen: Simple ideas on presentation design and delivery*. Berkeley, CA: New Riders.

Appendix A

Excel Basics

Excel is structured with one or more worksheets (also known as sheets or spreadsheets) contained within a workbook. A workbook must have at least one sheet and can contain as many sheets as your computer memory will allow. A workbook can be thought of as a file cabinet and the sheets as file folders held in the file cabinet. Although the sheets in a workbook may contain widely varied types of information, it's a good idea to include sheets in a workbook that have something in common. For example, you might maintain a workbook to manage your personal finances. This workbook might hold worksheets for a budget, checking account, savings account, and expenses. A workbook containing a lot of disparate information will function but may be cumbersome to use.

Figure A.1 outlines the key elements of an Excel workbook, which are defined in Table A.1.

Worksheet cells

Although more than one cell can be selected at a time, there can only be one active cell. In Figure A.1, there are 15 cells selected (the ones shaded gray) but

Figure A.1 Anatomy of an Excel workbook

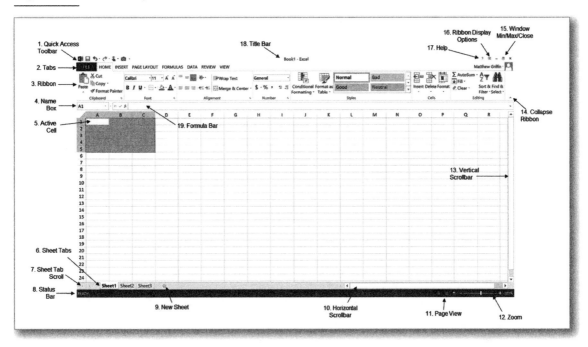

Table A.1 Definitions of key workbook elements

Element	Description
1. Quick Access Toolbar	A toolbar that holds commonly used commands. It can be customized to hold whichever commands you wish and is visible regardless of which tab is chosen.
2. Tabs	Clicking on these activates different ribbons. A contextual tab (not shown) relates to a specific object, such as a chart, and only appears when the object is selected.
3. Ribbon	Ribbons group similar Excel commands.
4. Name Box	Displays the active cell, named range, or object.
5. Active Cell	The cell that is currently active.
6. Sheet Tabs	Each tab represents a different sheet in the workbook.
7. Sheet Tab Scroll	Buttons used to scroll through sheets in the workbook when there are more sheets than be displayed.
8. Status Bar	Shows various messages. Can be customized by right-clicking to include things like Caps Lock status, Sum, Count, Average.
9. New Sheet	A button for adding a new, blank sheet.
10. Horizontal Scroll Bar	Use to scroll horizontally through the active sheet.
11. Page View	Buttons used to change the way the active sheet is viewed.
12. Zoom	Adjust the zoom of the active sheet.
13. Vertical Scrollbar	Use to scroll vertically through the active sheet.
14. Collapse Ribbon	Click to hide or unhide the ribbon.
15. Window Min/Max/Close	Buttons to minimize, maximize/restore, or close the active workbook.
16. Ribbon Display Options	Provides options for how the ribbon is displayed.
17. Help	Click to access Excel help.
18. Title Bar	Name of the active workbook.
19. Formula Bar	Displays the formula of the active cell.

only one active cell: A1. A cell is identified by the intersection of its column and row. For example, cell A1 is in column A, row 1. The range selected in Figure A.1 is A1 to C5. The standard way to refer to this range is A1:C5. This tells you that every cell in columns A, B, C and rows 1–5 is selected. Pressing the delete key or applying formatting will affect all 15 cells. However, if you were to begin typing with cells selected as in Figure A.1, everything you type will go only in cell A1 because it's the active cell.

Editing contents of a cell that is already populated can be done in a number of ways. You may enter or edit information in the formula bar or in the cell by double-clicking on the cell or pressing F2 on the keyboard. Once the edit has been made, press **Enter** to accept the change or **Esc** to exit edit mode without saving changes.

There are two general categories of information that may be entered into a sheet cell: constants and formulas. Constants are elements such as numbers, dates, or text entered into a cell; they don't change unless manually edited. Formulas create calculated values. When a formula is entered in a cell, the result of the formula (rather than the formula itself) is shown in the cell and the values will be updated if the cells being used by the formula change. Formulas make Excel powerful. Without formulas, Excel would be nothing but a cumbersome word processor.

Constants. To enter text into a cell, merely click on the cell with the mouse and begin typing. If the text does not fit into the cell, it will overlap the cell next to it as long as it's empty. In the example in Figure A.2, the text was entered in cell A1, but because the text didn't fit in the cell as it's currently sized, it overlapped into cells B1:E1. If cell B1 was not blank, only the text that fit in cell A1 would be visible, although all of the text would still exist in cell A1 (see Figure A.3).

To see all of the text in cell A1, the cell could be resized or formatted so that the text wraps. An easy way to make the column wide enough to fit all of the text is to double-click the line between the column header for columns A and B. Doing this will autofit the column width to fit all of the text. Alternately, click the line between the column header for columns A and B and drag to the right to

Figure A.2 Overlapping text

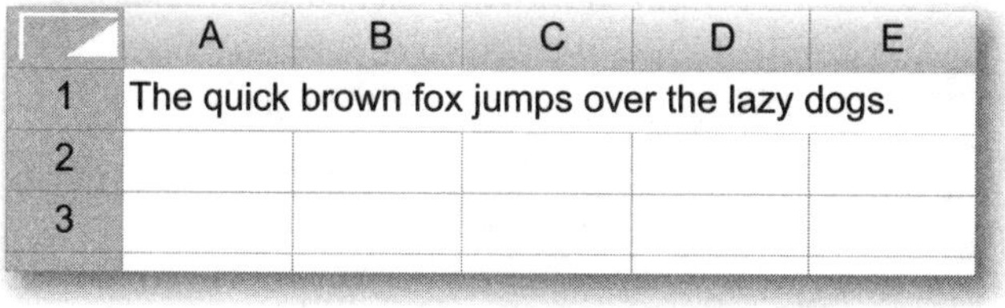

	A	B	C	D	E
1	The quick brown fox jumps over the lazy dogs.				
2					
3					

Figure A.3 Cut-off text

	A	B	C
1	The quick	123	
2			
3			

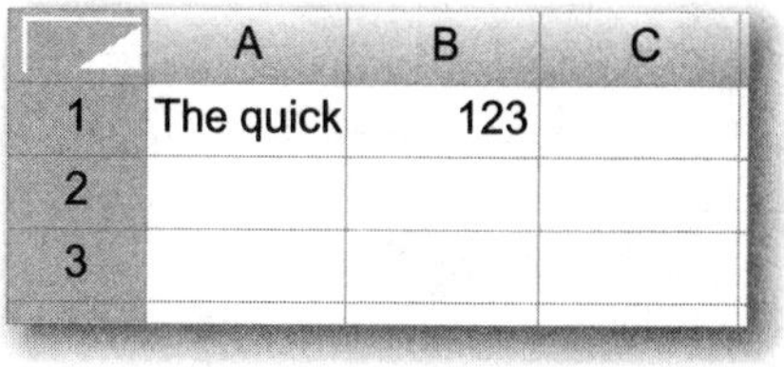

manually extend the column width (see Figure A.4). If you don't want to widen the column, you could make the text wrap within the cell and increase the row height. From the **HOME** tab, in the **Alignment** group, click on **Wrap Text** (see Figure A.5). The row height should automatically be adjusted to accommodate the wrapped text. If it is not, click and drag down the horizontal line between the row headers for rows 1 and 2.

Figure A.4 Column width extended

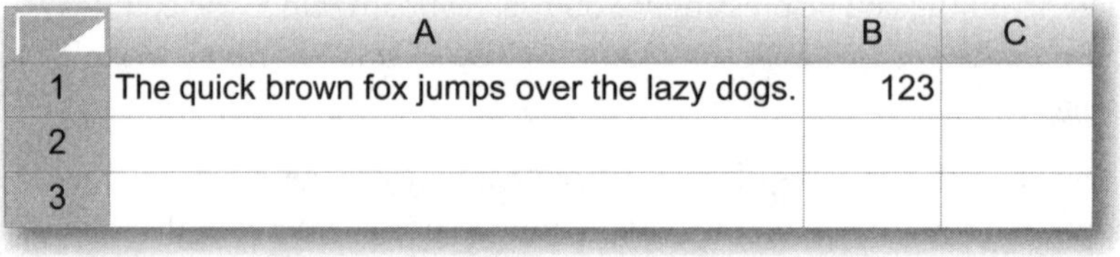

	A	B	C
1	The quick brown fox jumps over the lazy dogs.	123	
2			
3			

Figure A.5 Cell with wrapped text

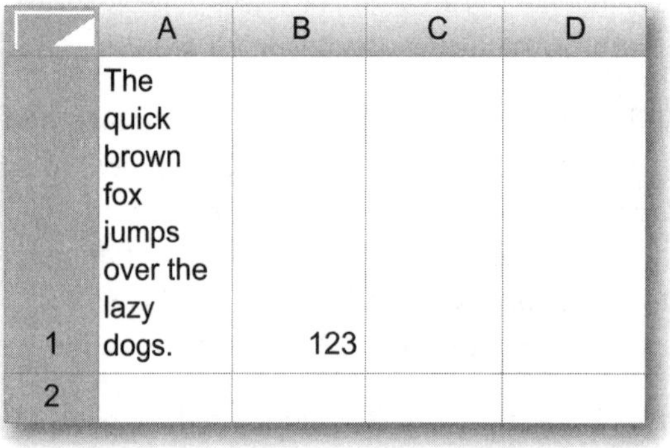

	A	B	C	D
1	The quick brown fox jumps over the lazy dogs.	123		
2				

Use the same process to enter a number into a cell. Unlike text, however, if a number is too long to fit into a cell, hashtags (#) will appear in the cell. The number is still in the cell (you can see the value in the formula bar); it just can't be viewed until the column is widened or the font size is reduced.

Dates. Excel handles dates in a way that is not intuitive. When a date is entered into a cell, it is converted into a number. The earliest date that Excel can easily handle is January 1, 1900, which is converted to a value of 1. Every day after that is incremented by one. Therefore, January 2, 1900, has a value of 2; January 3, 1900, has a value of 3; January 1, 2016, has a value of 42,370; and so on. It's not really necessary to understand why or how Excel does this, but it's good to know. For example, if you copy a date and use **Paste Values** to paste it into another cell that doesn't have date formatting applied, the result will be the number represented by the date. If this happens, format the cell using the **Date** category from the **Number** tab of the **Format Cells** dialog box (see Figure A.6). An easy way to get this dialog box is to right-click in the cell and choose **Format Cells** from the shortcut menu that appears. In addition to the date formats listed, custom date formats can be used. See Table 5.1 in Chapter 5 for a discussion of custom date formats.

Figure A.6 Format Cells dialog box

Dates can be entered into a cell in many ways. Excel will recognize nearly any date format and convert what is entered into a date. For example, entering any of the following into a cell will yield the same value: 12/31/16; 12–31–16; December 31 2016; dec 31, 16. If only the month and day are entered, Excel will use the current calendar year to convert it into a date. Depending on how the date is entered, Excel will apply a date format that can be changed following the steps just mentioned. There may be times when you do not want Excel to convert to a date the text and/or numbers entered into a cell. To prevent this, type an apostrophe before the text or numbers entered. The apostrophe will not show up when the value is presented in the cell and Excel will treat whatever follows the apostrophe as text.

The date examples used are based on the date system used by the United States: month/day/year. In many countries, dates are displayed as day/month/year. Excel will use your computer's regional date settings to apply the date structure for your country.

Formulas. As stated previously, the real power of Excel is its ability to use formulas. We're using the word *formula* here to describe the general category of elements entered into a cell that aren't constants (text, numbers, and dates). Formulas include everything from simple mathematical calculations and linking between cells to simple and complex predefined functions.

All formulas are entered into a cell beginning with an equal sign (=). This is how Excel knows that what follows the equal sign is a formula. The formula entered into a cell is usually not what is displayed in the cell. For example, if you enter "=5+3" into a cell and press Enter, the result (8) of the formula is displayed in the cell. The formula itself is viewable in the formula bar at the top of the spreadsheet (see Figure A.7).

When calculating formulas, Excel follows the same operator precedence rules used in mathematics. For example, exponents are calculated first, followed by multiplication and division and then addition and subtraction. Parenthesis can be used to override these rules (see Figure A.8).

Figure A.7 Simple formula

A1 ▼ ●	fx	=5+3	
	A	B	C
1	8		
2			
3			

Figure A.8 Formula with parenthesis

	A	B	C
1	FORMULA:	RESULT:	
2	=3+4*5	23	
3	=(3+4)*5	35	
4			

Nesting. Calculations also can be nested within more than one set of parentheses to ensure the formula is calculated in the desired order. Calculations in the innermost parenthesis will be computed first (see Figure A.9). This is called "nesting" and can be done (as in this example) with simple formulas as well as complex functions.

Linking. Formulas also can be references to another cell in the same worksheet or workbook or even another workbook (see Figure A.10).

Figure A.9 Formula with nested parenthesis

	A	B	C
1	FORMULA:	RESULT:	
2	=(3+4)*5+(7+3*4+9)*3	119	
3	=(3+4)*5+(7+3*(4+9))*3	173	
4			

Figure A.10 Linking formulas

	A
1	FORMULA:
2	=D2
3	=Sheet5!A1
4	=[Book2]Sheet1!A1

The first example is referring to cell D2 within the same worksheet. Whatever value is in cell D2 will also be reflected in cell B2. The second example is referring to cell A1 on Sheet 5 within the same workbook. The third example is referring to cell A1 on Sheet 1 in a separate workbook (Book 2). To link one cell to another, simply type the equal sign, use the mouse to navigate to the source cell, select it, and then press **Enter** on the keyboard.

Linking within the same workbook is relatively straightforward. When linking to another workbook, however, considerations must be made. If you are linking to merely bring a value or multiple values from one workbook into another, we recommend that you break the link once the values are in the destination workbook. There are a couple of ways to break links. You can copy the links and use **Paste Values** to replace the formulas with the values. You can also go to the **DATA** tab on the ribbon and from the **Connections** group, select **Edit Links**. From the Edit Links dialog box (see Figure A.11), choose the appropriate link (if the workbook has more than one) and select **Break Link**. Breaking links may also be a good idea before sharing a linked workbook with someone else. If you share a workbook containing links that exist on your computer, when others open it Excel will not be able to find the links and will present the user with an error message.

If you need to keep the links active because the source workbook may be updated or changed, the source workbook must be kept in the same location on your computer or network. If the source workbook is moved, the destination workbook won't be able to locate it. To correct this, you will have to update the link by selecting **Change Source** from the **Edit Links** dialog box. This will allow you to relink the destination workbook to the source workbook in the new location.

Figure A.11   Edit Links dialog box

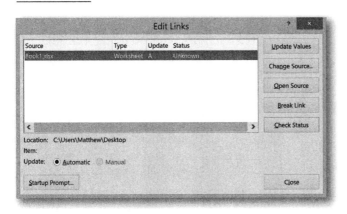

Functions. Functions are special formulas that have been predefined in Excel. Even if you're new to Excel, you've probably used functions without knowing it. **SUM** is probably one of the most used functions in Excel. If you've ever used the **AutoSum** button on the **HOME** tab, then you've used a function.

All functions follow the same basic syntax, beginning with an equal sign followed by the function name and a set of parenthesis: =FUNCTION(). Almost every function has some information between the parentheses, but what that is varies greatly among functions. One of the simplest functions is the **NOW** function. It returns the current date and time (see Figure A.12).

Excel converts the text "=NOW()" into the current date and time because it's a predefined function in Excel. The function will be displayed in the formula bar, and the result of the function will be displayed in the spreadsheet. Functions recalculate automatically every time a change is made to the workbook. Usually this isn't an issue; however, when using the **NOW** function, this may result in the date or time not always being accurate because it will represent the last time a change was made.

Figure A.12 NOW function

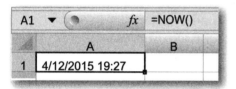

Figure A.13 SUM function

If you know the function name and syntax, you can type it directly in the cell. For example, if you didn't want to use AutoSum to enter a total, you could manually enter the **SUM** function in the cell. To do this, start by typing "=SUM(". Once the opening parenthesis has been typed, you can use your mouse to select the range you wish to sum. Once the range has been selected, type a closing parenthesis and press **Enter** (see Figure A.13).

Another way to enter a function is to use the **Insert Function** command on the **FORMULAS** tab. This will open up the **Insert Function** dialog box (see Figure A.14).

You can use the search box to look for a function, or it may be on the list of your most commonly used functions in the box below the search box. Let's use the **Insert Function** command to do the earlier **SUM** example. Searching for and selecting **SUM** opens the **Function Arguments** dialog box for the **SUM** function (see Figure A.15). In the upper-left corner you'll find the name of the function currently

Figure A.14 Insert Function dialog box

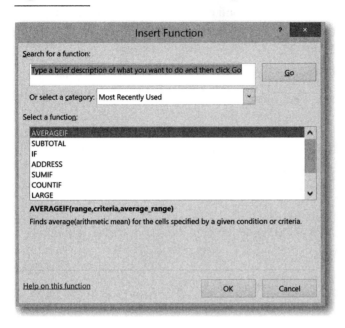

Figure A.15 Function Arguments dialog box

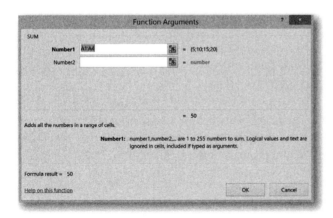

being written: **SUM**. Below that will be listed all of the arguments that will be between the parenthesis of the function. **SUM** is a very simple function, so there are only two arguments listed: **Number1** and **Number2**. Notice that **Number1** is bold. That is because that argument is required for this function.

Nearly all functions have at least one required argument, and many have optional arguments. The **SUM** function has a second argument (Number2) because it can sum multiple ranges of cells. If you clicked in the box next to Number2, a third argument (Number3) would appear. This would continue so that you could have as many ranges as you'd like. Notice that Number1 has a range prepopulated. Excel will do this sometimes with the simpler functions. It's important that you review the range to ensure it is correct. To the right of the Number1 box, Excel has listed all of the unique values in the range that was selected. In the middle of the dialog box is the definition for the argument currently selected. As you select each argument in the function, this will be updated with the definition for the current argument. In the lower-left corner you will find a preview of the function result. Once you have entered all of the arguments, select **OK** to complete the function.

Although you can always type the entire function directly into a cell without using the **Insert Function** command, it's a great resource for beginners learning to use functions.

Absolute and relative references

As we said earlier, a single cell reference is defined by the intersection of the row and column, for example, A1. A range of cells is defined by the upper-left cell and lower-right cell with a colon in between, for example, A1:B5. If the formula or function in a cell has a reference to another cell or range of cells, when that formula is copied, the reference is usually updated. For example, let's say that cell C4 has a link to cell G4. If we copy the formula in cell C4 to cell C5, the reference would be updated from G4 to G5. When a formula is copied down, the reference is adjusted down. When a formula is copied to the right, the reference is copied to the right. This happens with single cell references as well as range references. This is a powerful tool that many people take for granted. Imagine that you were copying a formula down a column of 100 cells and you needed the reference to adjust for each unique instance of the formula. If Excel didn't have the ability to adjust the reference, you would have to type that formula in each of the 100 cells manually.

The types of references we've been describing are called relative references. *Relative* because the reference is relative to the location of the cell. Let's use our example from earlier to think about this in a different way. We said that cell C4 has a reference to cell G4. You could also think of this as C4 having a reference to the cell that is in the same row (4) and four columns to the right (column G). So, wherever you copy the reference in C4, it always updates to refer to the cell in the same row, four columns away.

There are times, however, when you have a reference to a cell that you want to remain constant no matter where you copy the formula. For example, you might have a report with the name of your company in cell A1. If you often have to refer to the name of your company throughout the worksheet, you could link to cell A1 and then copy the link throughout your worksheet. However, you would always want the link to be to cell A1, no matter where the formula is copied. Placing a dollar sign ($) in front of the column and row reference ($A$1) will keep the reference constant no matter where it is copied. This type of reference is called an absolute reference.

To become effective at writing and managing Excel formulas and functions, it is essential that you understand the difference between absolute and relative references and when to use them. The example of the absolute reference is straightforward, but it can be more difficult when applied to a range of cells or in a complicated function. Additionally, there are times when you need only the column part of the reference to be absolute and need the row part of the reference to be relative. A dollar sign can be placed in front of just the column reference or in front of just the row reference to achieve this. There are four basic options for making a cell reference absolute or relative:

1. Both the column and row are relative: A1

2. Both the column and row are absolute: $A$1

3. The column is absolute and the row is relative: $A1

4. The column is relative and the row is absolute: A$1

Let's look at these four options more closely. Figure A.16 is a worksheet with data in cells A1:D4 and a cell reference to cell B2 in cell E8. Cell E8 is showing a value of 6 because that is the value of cell B2.

Figure A.17 shows what will happen to the reference and value in cell E8 as the formula is copied one cell to the right, left,

Figure A.16 Worksheet with relative reference

	A	B	C	D	E
E8			fx	=B2	
1	1	2	3	4	
2	5	6	7	8	
3	9	10	11	12	
4	13	14	15	16	
5					
6					
7					
8					6

Figure A.17 Example of absolute and relative reference

RELATIVE REFERENCE

Before	Move One Space	After	Value
B2	Right	C2	7
B2	Left	A2	5
B2	Up	B1	2
B2	Down	B3	10

ABSOLUTE REFERENCE

Before	Move One Space	After	Value
$B$2	Right	$B$2	6
$B$2	Left	$B$2	6
$B$2	Up	$B$2	6
$B$2	Down	$B$2	6

COLUMN ABSOLUTE ROW RELATIVE

Before	Move One Space	After	Value
$B2	Right	$B2	6
$B2	Left	$B2	6
$B2	Up	$B1	2
$B2	Down	$B3	10

COLUMN RELATIVE ROW ABSOLUTE

Before	Move One Space	After	Value
B$2	Right	C$2	7
B$2	Left	A$2	5
B$2	Up	B$2	6
B$2	Down	B$2	6

up, and down. The four boxes show how the result will differ based on whether the reference is relative, absolute, or a combination.

The difference between absolute and relative references is only important if the formula or reference will be copied to another cell. If the formula you are writing is never going to be copied to another location, it doesn't matter if the reference is absolute, relative, or some combination.

Keyboard shortcuts

Early versions of spreadsheet software did not use a mouse. All navigation and access to menus was done using the keyboard. Additionally, there were many keyboard shortcuts that provided simple access to the most common tasks. Throughout the years, most of these keyboard shortcuts have remained in Excel. You are probably familiar with many of the most popular, such as Ctrl+C (copy), Ctrl+X (cut), Ctrl+V (paste), and Ctrl+S (save).

Keyboard shortcuts are an excellent way to improve your speed and perhaps even accuracy as you navigate through Excel. We've listed some of the shortcuts that we find most helpful in Table A.2. We hope that you find them helpful as well. Happy shortcutting!

Table A.2 Keyboard shortcuts

Key	Description
Navigate	
Ctrl+Tab	Switch between Workbooks
Alt+Tab	Switch between Applications
Ctrl+PgDn	Move to sheet, left-to-right
Ctrl+PgUp	Move to sheet, right-to-left
Ctrl+Arrow	Move to end of range
Ctrl+Shift+Arrow	Move to end of range and select
Ctrl+Home	Move to Cell A1
Ctrl+A	Selects the current data range
Ctrl+AA	Selects the entire sheet
Ctrl+9	Hides the selected rows
Ctrl+0	Hides the selected columns
Format	
Ctrl+B	Bold
Ctrl+I	Italics
Ctrl+U	Underline
Edit	
Ctrl+C	Copy
Ctrl+X	Cut
Ctrl+V	Paste
Ctrl+D	Fill down
Ctrl+R	Fill right
Ctrl+F	Find
Ctrl+H	Find and replace
Ctrl+Y	Repeat last action

(Continued)

(Continued)

Ctrl+Z	Undo last action
F2	Edit active cell
Ctrl+Plus (+)	Insert cells
Ctrl+Minus (-)	Delete cells
Manage	
Ctrl+S	Save
Ctrl+P	Print
Ctrl+O	Open existing workbook
Ctrl+N	Open new workbook
Ctrl+W	Close current workbook
Ctrl+T	Create a Table
F1	Excel help
F4	Absolute and relative reference
F7	Spelling check
Alt+Equal(=)	AutoSum

Appendix B

Configuring Microsoft Word for APA-Style Reports

Text-heavy reports are best created in Microsoft Word or a similar application designed to handle large amounts of text and images. To create a report in Word, open a blank document: **FILE > New > Blank document**.

Set Up the Document

1. From the **PAGE LAYOUT** tab, in the **Page Setup** group, click on **Margins** to view the margin options. Select **Normal**. This will set one-inch margins around the report pages.

2. Define the paragraph spacing. From the **HOME** tab in the **Paragraph** group, click the **Line and Paragraph Spacing** icon and select 2.0 for double-spaced text, which is standard for most academic reports (see Figure B.1).

3. From the **INSERT** tab, in the **Pages** group, click on **Cover Page** to find a selection of cover page designs. Alternatively, position your cursor about one-third of the way down the first page of your document and type your report title. Use title case

Figure B.1   Line and Paragraph Spacing icon

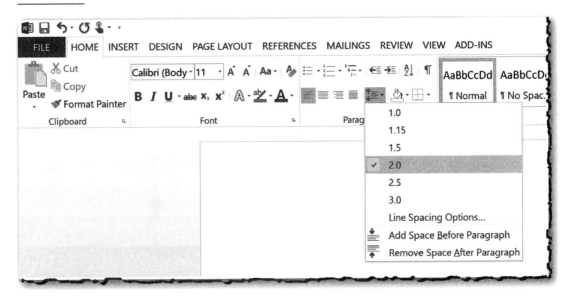

where the first letter of all major words are capitalized. Leave a few inches of blank space on the page and type your name, institutional affiliation, and contact information (see Figure B.2).

4. Add page numbers. From the **INSERT** tab, in the **Header & Footer** group, click **Page Number**, select a location for the page numbers, and select a page number style.

5. Insert a running head. From the **INSERT** tab, in the **Header & Footer** group, click **Header**. The first option, the **Blank** header, is the easiest to work with because it does not contain

Figure B.2   Report cover page

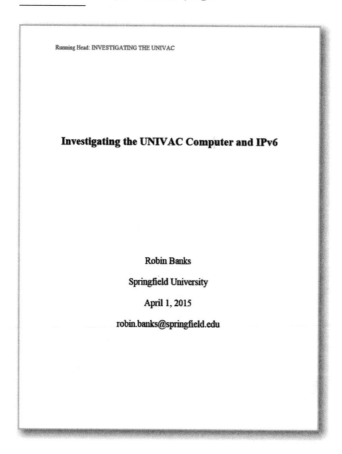

any ornamentation. Select an option, type the words *Running head*, and add a running head, usually the first few words of the report's title.

6. At the bottom of the title page, create a section break. From the **PAGE LAYOUT** tab, in the **Page Setup** group, click **Breaks**. Select **Next Page**. This will create a second page and allow you to edit the running head so that the information on page 1 is different from all subsequent pages.

7. Double-click on the page 2 header. From the contextual **DESIGN** tab, in the **Navigation** group, deselect **Link to Previous** so that the running head is not linked to the previous section. Delete the words *Running head* on page 2. Page 1 should remain as it was.

Create section headings

Setting up Word's heading styles will ensure that all of the report's headings are formatted consistently and the headings can be used to expedite the creation of a table of contents. For example, APA style uses five levels of headings to organize a paper's sections (see Table B.1 for the definition of the table headings and Figure B.3 for an example).

Most papers need only the first three headings. The assignment of APA level 1 and 2 headings in Word's Styles gallery is a straightforward process. Because levels 3, 4, and 5 are set in line with the subsequent text, their setup requires additional steps.

Table B.1 APA headings

Level	Format
1	Centered, Boldface, Uppercase and Lowercase Headings
2	Left-aligned, Boldface, Uppercase and Lowercase Headings
3	Indented, boldface, lowercase heading ending with a period.
4	Indented, boldface, italicized, lowercase ending with a period.
5	Indented, italicized, lowercase ending with a period.

Figure B.3 Sample report page using APA heading styles

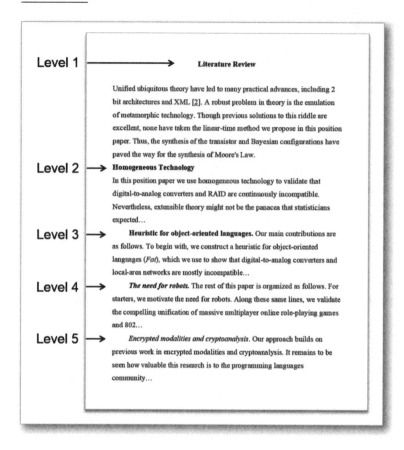

Defining APA Heading Styles 1 and 2

1. Write the heading text. Center and bold the text for level 1; left-align and bold text for level 2.

2. Highlight the text you typed.

3. On the **HOME** tab in the **Styles** group, hover over the **Heading 1** (or Heading 2) style definition. Right-click and select **Update Heading 1 to Match Selection**.

4. Each time you write a heading in your report, select the **Heading 1** or **2** style from the Styles gallery and then type your text. Alternatively, write the text, select it, and then click **Heading 1** or **2** in the Styles gallery.

1. Type the heading using **Heading 3** style (indented, boldface, lower case ending with a period).

2. Define the heading by hovering over the Heading 3 style in the Styles gallery, right-clicking, and selecting **Update Heading 3 to Match Selection**.

3. Press **Enter** to create a new paragraph. The new paragraph should be in the Normal style. Type the text of the paragraph.

4. Click in the heading and press **ALT+CTRL+Enter**. This will insert a style separator and move the paragraph text in line with the heading.

5. Repeat the process for Headings 4 and 5.

Creating a table of contents

Most long-format documents require a table of contents. If you use Word's heading styles while writing the report, building a table of contents can be accomplished quickly as Word's tables of contents are based on the heading styles defined in the document.

Adding a Table of Contents

1. Position your cursor where you would like the table of contents to appear.

2. From the **REFERENCES** tab, in the **Table of Contents** group, click **Table of Contents**. Select one of the two automatic styles if you only need to show three heading levels and if the tab leaders (usually a dotted line) suit your report.

3. For a greater range of options, click on **Custom Table of Contents**. From the Table of Contents dialog box, you may define exactly the number of headings you wish to show, change the format of the table of contents, and modify the appearance of each heading style in the table of contents if you wish.

Index

ASKING THE RIGHT QUESTIONS
A Guide to Critical Thinking

ASKING THE RIGHT QUESTIONS
A Guide to Critical Thinking

THIRD EDITION

M. Neil Browne

Stuart M. Keeley

 PRENTICE HALL, ENGLEWOOD CLIFFS, NEW JERSEY 07632

Library of Congress Cataloging-in-Publication Data

Browne, M. Neil [date]
  Asking the right questions : a guide to critical thinking / M.
Neil Browne, Stuart M. Keeley.—3rd ed.

  Includes index.
  ISBN 0–13–048852–6
  1. Reading. 2. Criticism. 3. Critical thinking. I. Keeley,
Stuart M. [date] . II. Title.
PN83.B785 1990
418'.4—dc20   89–3990
                                                       CIP

Editorial/production supervision and
  interior design: Fred Dahl
Manufacturing buyer: Ray Keating

Printed in the United States of America

10 9 8 7 6 5 4 3 2

ISBN 0-13-048852-6

Prentice-Hall International (UK) Limited, *London*
Prentice-Hall of Australia Pty. Limited, *Sydney*
Prentice-Hall Canada Inc., *Toronto*
Prentice-Hall Hispanoamericana, S.A., *Mexico*
Prentice-Hall of India Private Limited, *New Delhi*
Prentice-Hall of Japan, Inc., *Tokyo*
Simon & Schuster Asia Pte. Ltd., *Singapore*
Editora Prentice-Hall do Brasil, Ltda., *Rio de Janeiro*

Contents

Preface

This third edition of *Asking the Right Questions* represents our effort to build on the strengths of previous editions by incorporating new insights, acquired from our students, recent research, and dialogue with colleagues committed to teaching critical thinking.

We were motivated to write the first edition by a variety of personal experiences and observations. First, we were dismayed at the degree to which students and acquaintances showed an increasing dependence on "experts"—textbook writers, teachers, lawyers, politicians, journalists, and TV commentators. As the complexity of the world seems to grow at an accelerating rate, there is a greater tendency to become passive absorbers of information, uncritically accepting what is seen and heard. We became concerned that too many of us are not actively making personal choices about what to accept and what to reject.

Second, our experience in teaching critical-thinking skills to our students over a number of years convinced us that when individuals with diverse abilities are taught these skills in a simplified format, they can learn to apply them successfully. In the process, they develop greater confidence in their ability to make rational choices about social issues, even those with which they have formerly had little experience.

A third motivating factor was our inability to find a book with which to teach the skills we wanted students to learn. We did not want a philosophy text, but rather a book that, while informal in nature, would outline basic critical-reading skills explicitly, concisely, and simply. We did not find such a book.

Thus, we set out to write a text that would do a number of things that other books had failed to do. The text that resulted attempts to develop an integrated series of question-asking skills that can be applied to a wide variety of reading material, from textbooks to magazine essays. These skills are discussed in an informal style. (We have written to a general audience, not to any specialized group.)

The development of *Asking the Right Questions* has leaned heavily on our joint experience of forty years as teachers of critical thinking. Our ideas have evolved in response to numerous classroom experiences with students at many different levels, from freshmen to Ph.D. students.

These experiences have taught us certain emphases that are particularly effective in learning critical thinking. For instance we provide many opportunities for the readers to apply their skills and to receive immediate feedback following the practice application. The book is replete with examples of writing devoted to controversial contemporary topics. The breadth of topics introduces the average reader to writings on numerous controversies with which he or she may have little familiarity. The book is coherently organized, in that critical questions are discussed sequentially as the reader progresses from asking questions to making decisions. In addition, it integrates cognitive and value dimensions—a very important aspect of critical reading and personal decision making.

New features in the third edition include the following:

1. Explicit treatment of different types of critical thinking,
2. Greater emphasis on creative thinking and the generation of rival hypotheses,
3. Explanation of the use and abuse of analogical reasoning,
4. Development of numerous class-tested practice exercises and illustrations,
5. Analysis of mental biases that hinder critical thinking.

Each new element emerged from the teaching experience of numerous colleagues.

Who would find *Asking the Right Questions* especially beneficial? Because of our teaching experiences with readers representing many different levels of ability, we have difficulty envisioning any academic course or program for which this book would not be useful. In fact, the first two editions have been used in law, English, pharmacy, philosophy, education, psychology, sociology, religion, and social science courses.

A few uses for the book seem especially appropriate. Teachers in general education programs may want to begin their courses by assigning it as a coherent response to their students' requests to explain what is expected of them. English courses that emphasize expository writing could use this text both as a format for evaluating arguments prior to constructing an essay and as a checklist of problems that the writer should attempt to avoid as he or she writes. Courses training prospective teachers and graduate assistants should find the book especially functional because it makes explicit much that teachers will want to encourage in their students. Courses in study-skill development may be enriched by supplementing their current content with our step-by-step description of the process of critical reading and thinking. The text can also be used as the central focus of courses designed specifically to teach critical reading and thinking skills.

While *Asking the Right Questions* stems primarily from our classroom experiences, it is written so that it can guide the reading habits of almost anyone. The skills that it seeks to develop are those that any critical reader needs to possess for reading to serve as a basis for rational decisions. The critical questions stressed in the book can enliven anyone's reading, regardless of the extent of his or her formal education.

This third edition owes a special debt to our critical thinking students. They have improved both the clarity and reasoning by their generous suggestions. We want to explicitly thank two students. Robert Fetterolf suggested the panning-for-gold metaphor, used so frequently in *Asking the Right Questions*. In ten minutes he developed a metaphor to contrast with the sponge model of learning. We had been searching in vain for years. Julie A. Harris was instrumental in creating several of the new examples and practice passages for the third edition.

Thanks also go to our reviewers, whose comments were most helpful: Lillian Back, University of Michigan; Diane W. Creel, Tompkins Cortland Community College; Libby Jones, Berea College; Jean Raulston, Imperial Valley College; Ruth E. Ray, Wayne State University; and Beth M. Waggenspack, Virginia Polytechnic Institute and State University.

ASKING THE RIGHT QUESTIONS
A Guide to Critical Thinking

I

The Benefit of Asking the Right Questions

Introduction

Each of us is bombarded with information. Every day we encounter new facts and opinions. In textbooks, newspapers, and magazines, writers present ideas they want us to accept. One social scientist tells us violence on television is bad for young people; another tells us it does no harm. One economist argues for reducing taxes to stem inflation; another argues that we should increase interest rates. One educational critic recommends eliminating the "frills," such as foreign language and physical education requirements; another recommends we expand such "necessities." In all areas of knowledge there are issues about which experts in those fields disagree. You as a reader have the tough job of deciding which authority to believe. Whether you are reading a nursing journal, a critique of a poem, a textbook, or even the sports page, you will be faced with the problem of deciding which conclusions to accept, which to reject, and which to withhold judgment on.

As a thoughtful person you must make a choice about how you will react to what you see and hear. One alternative is to accept passively what you encounter; doing so automatically results in your making someone else's opinion your own. A more active alternative consists of asking questions of yourself in an effort to reach a personal decision about the worth of what you have experienced. This book is written for those who prefer the second alternative.

Critical Thinking to the Rescue

Listening and reading critically—that is, reacting with systematic evaluation to what you have heard and read—requires a set of skills and attitudes. These skills and attitudes are built around a series of critical questions.

We could have expressed them as a list of things you should do, but a system of questions is more consistent with the spirit of curiosity, wonder, and intellectual adventure essential to critical thinking. Thinking carefully is always an unfinished project, a story looking for an ending that will never arrive. Critical questions provide a structure for critical thinking that supports a continual, on-going search for better opinions, decisions, or judgments.

Consequently, critical thinking, as we will use the term, refers to the following:

1. Awareness of a set of interrelated critical questions,
2. Ability to ask and answer critical questions at appropriate times, and
3. Desire to actively use the critical questions.

The goal of this book is to encourage you in all three of these dimensions.

The critical questions will be shared with you bit by bit, one question at a time. As a package, they will be useful whenever you choose to react to what you are hearing or reading. This book will guide you through the critical questions so you can recognize their benefit to every thinking person.

These skills and attitudes will be especially helpful to you as a student and as a citizen. As a student, they should be useful whenever you are asked to

1. react critically to an essay or to evidence presented in a textbook,
2. judge the quality of a lecture or speech,
3. form an argument,
4. write an essay based on a reading assignment, or
5. participate in class.

As a citizen, you should find them especially helpful in shaping your voting behavior and your purchasing decisions, as well as improving your self-confidence by increasing your sense of intellectual independence.

The Sponge and Panning for Gold: Alternative Thinking Styles

One approach to thinking is similar to the way in which a sponge reacts to water: by *absorbing*. This commonly used approach has some clear advantages.

First, the more information you absorb about the world, the more capable you are of understanding its complexities. Knowledge you have acquired provides a foundation for more complicated thinking later. For instance, it would be very difficult to judge the value of a sociological theory before you had absorbed a core of knowledge about sociology.

A second advantage of the sponge approach is that it is relatively passive. Rather than requiring strenuous mental effort, it tends to be rather quick and easy, especially when the material is presented in a clear and interesting fashion. The primary mental effort is concentration and memory.

While absorbing information provides a productive start toward becoming a thoughtful person, the sponge approach has a serious disadvantage: It provides no method for deciding which information and opinions to believe and which to reject. If a reader relied on the sponge approach all the time, she would believe whatever she read *last*.

We think you would rather choose for yourself what to absorb and what to ignore. To make this choice, you must read with a special attitude—a question-asking attitude. Such a thinking style requires active participation. The writer is trying to speak to you, and you should try to talk back to him, even though he is not present.

We call this interactive approach the *panning-for-gold* style of thinking. Gold is a soft, bright yellow metal that has been highly valued since prehistoric time. It is found in most parts of the world, but almost always in low concentrations. Because gold is so frequently found in unexpected locations, finding it is a challenging and difficult task.

One technique for finding gold is panning for it in rivers or streams. To pan for gold one must actively search in the gravel of the flowing water, using carefully controlled motions of the pan to retain gold-bearing sand. Worthless silt swirls away. The pan is gyrated again and again, while the miner visually examines the pan for valuable gold.

The process of panning for gold provides a model for active readers and listeners as they try to determine the worth of what they read and hear. The task is challenging and sometimes tedious, but the reward can be tremendous. To distinguish the gold from the gravel in a conversation requires you to ask frequent questions and to reflect about the answers.

The sponge approach emphasizes knowledge acquisition; the panning-for-gold approach stresses active interaction with knowledge as it is being acquired. Thus, the two approaches can complement each other. To pan for intellectual gold, there must be something in your pan to evaluate.

Let us more closely examine how the two approaches lead to different behavior. What does the individual who takes the sponge approach do when he reads material? He reads sentences carefully, trying to remember as much as he can. He may underline or highlight key words and sentences. He may take notes summarizing the major topics and major points. He checks his underlining or notes to be sure he is not forgetting anything important. His mission is to find and understand what the author has to say.

What does the reader who takes the panning-for-gold approach do? Like the person using the sponge approach, he approaches his reading with the hope that he will acquire new knowledge. Then the similarity ends. The panning-for-gold approach requires that the reader ask himself a number of questions, to clarify logical steps in the material and help identify important omissions. The reader who uses the panning-for-gold approach frequently questions why the author makes various claims. He writes notes to himself in the margins indicating problems with the reasoning. He continually interacts with the material. His intent is to critically evaluate the material and formulate personal conclusions based on the evaluation.

An Example of the Panning-for-Gold Approach

The federal minimum wage law requires employers to pay a certain minimum wage. Naturally enough, employers resist increases in the minimum wage, while many employees would like it to rise. Let's look at one proposal to raise the minimum wage. Try to decide whether the argument is convincing.

> The rate of inflation over the last decade has far exceeded the growth in the minimum wage. The gap between the cost of living and the minimum wage has forced many minimum wage earners to live well below the poverty line. A full-time minimum wage worker can expect to earn approximately $7,000 a year. With a spouse and two children, this worker is earning $4,600 less than the established poverty line for a family of four. The full-time minimum wage worker is like a drowning swimmer who can never survive.
>
> In California, the gap between what a job pays and what welfare pays is shrinking rapidly. A mother and child on welfare can expect to receive $6,348 a year. A full-time minimum wage worker earns just a few hundred dollars more. Such a narrow gap diminishes the incentive to work.
>
> Inflation has simply outpaced the cost of living. Congress should raise the minimum wage to a level where it will not be worthless relative to the cost of living. Resulting job losses would be minimal as a result of the current labor shortage. An increase in the federal wage will help restore work incentives and reduce the welfare burden. More importantly, an increased minimum wage will help many workers escape poverty.

If you apply the sponge approach to the passage, you probably would try to remember the reasons why an increase in the minimum wage is a favorable proposal. If so, you will have absorbed some knowledge. However, are you sure that you should be convinced by the above reasons? You cannot evaluate them until you have applied the panning-for-gold approach to the passage—that is, until you have asked the right questions.

By asking the right questions you would discover a number of possible weaknesses in the proposal for an increase in the federal minimum wage. For instance, you might be concerned about all of the following:

1. Is an increased minimum wage the most effective way to help the working poor?

2. Does inflation affect the poor more or less than it affects those making much more than the minimum wage?
3. What kinds of jobs will be cut as a result? Will the loss of these jobs hurt the working poor more than an increased wage will help them?
4. Will smaller companies that cannot afford the increased wage be forced out of business?
5. What does it mean to "far" exceed the growth in the minimum wage?
6. Is the "drowning swimmer" analogy relevant to the argument?

If you want to ask these kinds of questions, this book is especially for you. Its primary purpose is to help you know when and how to ask questions that will enable you to decide what to believe.

The most important characteristic of the panning-for-gold approach is *interactive involvement*—a dialogue between the writer and the reader, or the speaker and the listener.

Clearly, there are times when the sponge approach is appropriate. Most of you have used it regularly and have acquired some level of success with it. It is much less likely that you are in the habit of employing the panning-for-gold approach—in part, simply because you have not had the training and practice. This book will not only help you ask the right questions, but will also provide frequent opportunities for practicing their use.

Panning for Gold: Asking Critical Questions

It would be nice if what other people were really saying was always obvious, if all their essential thoughts were clearly labeled for us, and if the writer or speaker never made an error in his or her reasoning. If this were the case, we could read and listen passively and let others do our thinking for us. However, the true state of affairs is quite the opposite. A person's reasoning is often not obvious. Important elements are often missing. Many elements that *are* present are unclear. Other elements that are present do not even belong there. Consequently, critical reading and listening is a sorting process through which you must identify what makes sense and distinguish this clear thinking from the sloppy thinking that characterizes much of what you will encounter.

What's the point? The inadequacies in what someone says will not always leap out at you. You must be an *active* searcher. You can do this by *asking questions*. The best search strategy is a critical-questioning strategy. Throughout the book we will be showing you why certain critical questions are so important to ask. A powerful advantage of these questions is that they permit you to ask searching questions even when you know very little about the topic being discussed. For example, you do not need to be an expert on child care to ask critical questions about the adequacy of day-care centers.

The Myth of the "Right Answer"

Our ability to find definite answers to questions often depends on the type of question that puzzles us. Scientific questions about the physical world are the most likely to have answers that reasonable people will accept, because the physical world is in certain ways more dependable or predictable then the social world. While the precise distance to the moon or the age of a newly discovered bone from. an ancient civilization may not be absolutely certain, agreement about the dimensions of our physical environment is widespread. Thus, in the physical sciences, we frequently can arrive at "the right answer."

Questions about human behavior are different. The causes of human behavior are so complex and so difficult to apply high standards of evidence to that we frequently cannot do much more than form intelligent guesses about why or when certain behavior will occur. In addition, because many of us care a great deal about explanations and descriptions of human behavior, we prefer that explanations or descriptions of the rate of abortion, the frequency of unemployment, or the causes of child abuse be consistent with what we want to believe. Hence we bring our preferences to any discussion of those issues and resist arguments that are inconsistent with them.

Since human behavior is so controversial and complex, the best answers that we can find for many questions about our behavior will be probabilistic in nature, lacking a high degree of certainty. Even if we are aware of all the evidence available about the effects of running on our mental health, the nature of such questions about human behavior will prevent our discovering the *exact truth* about such effects.

Regardless of the type of questions being asked, the issues that require your closest scrutiny are usually those about which "reasonable people" disagree. In fact, many issues are interesting exactly because there is strong disagreement about how to resolve them. Any controversy involves more than one position. Several positions may be supported with good reasons. Thus, when you engage in critical thinking, you should be seeking the position that seems most reasonable to you. There will seldom be a position on a social controversy about which you will be able to say, "This is clearly the right position on the issue." If such certainty were desirable, reasonable people would not be debating the issue. Our focus in this book will be on such social controversies.

Even though you will not necessarily arrive at the "right answer" to social controversies, this book is designed to give you the skills to develop your best and most reasonable answer, given the nature of the problem and the available information. Decisions usually must be made in the face of uncertainty. Often we will not have the time or the ability to discover many of the important facts about a decision we must make. For example, it is simply unwise to ask all the right questions when someone you love is complaining of sharp chest pains and wants you to transport him to the emergency room.

Questions First, Emotional Involvement Last

As you approach issues, you will often find yourself emotionally involved. It is only natural to have strong feelings about many issues. Successful, active learners try to recognize such feelings, however, and remain open to reasoned opinions. This is important because many of our own positions on issues are not especially reasonable ones; they are opinions given to us by others, and over many years we develop emotional attachments to them. Indeed, we frequently believe that we are being personally attacked when someone presents a conclusion contrary to our own. The danger of being emotionally involved in an issue prior to any active thought about it is that you may fail to consider potential good reasons for other positions—reasons that might be sufficient to change your mind on the issue if you would only listen to them.

Remember: Emotional involvement alone should not be the basis for accepting or rejecting a position. Ideally, emotional involvement should be most intense *after* reasoning has occurred. Thus, when you read, try to avoid letting emotional involvement cut you off from the reasoning of those with whom you initially disagree. A successful active learner is one who is willing to change his or her mind. If you are ever to change your mind, you must be as open as possible to ideas that strike you as weird or dangerous when you first encounter them.

Critical thinkers, however, are not machines. They care greatly about many issues. The depth of that concern can be seen in their willingness to do all the hard mental work associated with critical thinking. But any passion felt by critical thinkers is moderated by the recognition that their current beliefs are open to revision.

Efficiency of Asking the Question, "Who Cares?"

Asking good questions is difficult but rewarding work. Some controversies will be much more important to you than others. When the consequences of a controversy for you and your community are minimal, you will want to spend less time and energy thinking critically about it than about more important controversies. For example, it makes sense to critically evaluate arguments for and against the building of nuclear power plants, because different positions on this issue lead to important consequences for society. It makes less sense to devote energy to evaluating whether or not blue is the favorite color of most corporation executives.

Your time is valuable. Before taking the time to critically evaluate an issue, ask the question, Who cares?

Weak-sense and Strong-sense Critical Thinking

Previous sections mentioned that you already have opinions about many personal and social issues. You are willing right now to take a position on such questions as should prostitution be legalized, is alcoholism a disease or willful misconduct, or was Ronald Reagan a successful President. You bring these initial beliefs to what you hear and read.

Critical thinking can be used to either (1) defend *or* (2) evaluate and revise your initial beliefs. Richard Paul's* distinction between weak-sense and strong-sense critical thinking helps us appreciate these two antagonistic uses of critical thinking.

If you approach critical thinking as a method for defending your initial beliefs or those you are paid to have, you are engaged in weak-sense critical thinking. Why is it *weak*? To use critical thinking skills in this manner is to be unconcerned with moving toward truth or virtue. The purpose of weak-sense critical thinking is to resist and annihilate opinions and reasons different from yours. To see domination and victory over those who disagree with you as the objective of critical thinking is to ruin the potentially humane and progressive aspects of critical thinking.

In contrast, strong-sense critical thinking requires us to apply the critical questions to all claims, including our own. By forcing ourselves to look critically at our initial beliefs, we help protect against self-deception and conformity. It's easy to just stick with current beliefs, particularly when they are shared by many people. But when we take this easy road, we run the strong risk of making mistakes we could otherwise avoid.

Strong-sense critical thinking does not necessarily force us to give up our initial beliefs. It can provide a basis for strengthening those very beliefs, for understanding through reflection why they *do* make sense. A long time ago, John Stuart Mill warned us of the emptiness of a set of opinions accumulated without the help of strong-sense critical thinking:

> He who knows only his side of the case knows little of that. His reasons may have been good, and no one may have been able to refute them. But if he is equally unable to refute the reasons on the opposite side he has no ground for preferring either opinion.

The Satisfaction of Using the Panning-for-Gold Approach

Doing is usually more fun than watching; doing well is more fun than simply doing. If you start using the interactive process taught in this book, you can feel the same sense of pride in your reading and listening that you normally get from successful participation.

---

*Professor Paul is Director of the Center for Critical Thinking and Moral Critique at Sonoma State University in Rohnert Park, California.

Critical thinkers find it satisfying to know when to say no to an idea or opinion and to know why that response is appropriate. If you regularly use the panning-for-gold approach, then anything that gets into your head will have been systematically examined first. When an idea or belief *does* pass the criteria developed here, it will make sense to agree with it—at least until new evidence appears.

Imagine how good you will feel if you know *why* you should ignore or accept a particular bit of advice. Frequently, those faced with an opinion different from their own respond by saying, "Oh, that's just your opinion." But the issue should not be whose opinion it is, but rather whether it is a good opinion. Armed with the critical questions discussed in this book, you can experience the satisfaction of knowing why certain advice is nonsense.

The sponge approach is often satisfying because it permits you to accumulate information. Though this approach is productive, there is much more gratification in being a participant in a meaningful dialogue with the writer or speaker. Reading and listening become much richer as you begin to see things that others may have missed. As you question the correctness of reasoning, you will start to go beyond what someone wants you to believe. No one wants to be at the mercy of the last "expert" he meets. As you learn to select information and opinions systematically you will probably desire to read more and more, in a lifelong effort to decide which advice makes sense.

Effective Writing and Critical Thinking

Many of the skills you will learn as you become a more critical thinker will improve the quality of your writing. As you write it helps to be aware of the expectations careful thinkers will have. Because your objective is communication, many of the questions the thoughtful person will ask in evaluating your writing should serve as guides for your writing. For instance, several of the critical questions that we urge you to ask focus on problems you will want to avoid as you write.

While the emphasis in this book is on effective thinking, the link to competent writing is so direct that it will be a theme throughout. Wherever appropriate, we will mention how the skill being encouraged is an aid to improved writing.

The Importance of Practice

Learning new critical-thinking skills is a lot like learning new physical skills. You cannot learn simply by being told what to do or by watching others. You have to practice, and frequently the practice will be both rewarding and hard work. Our goal is to make your learning as simple as possible. However, acquiring the habit of critical thinking will initially take a lot of practice.

The practice exercises at the end of each chapter are an important part of this text. Try to do the exercises and only then compare your answers with ours. Our answers are not necessarily the only correct ones, but they provide illustrations of how to apply the question-asking skills.

The Right Questions

To give you an initial sense of the skills that *Asking the Right Questions* will help you acquire, we will list the critical questions for you here. By the end of the book, you should know when and how to ask these questions productively.

1. What are the issues and the conclusion?
2. What are the reasons?
3. What words or phrases are ambiguous?
4. What are the value conflicts and assumptions?
5. What are the descriptive assumptions?
6. What is the evidence?
7. Are the samples representative and the measurements valid?
8. Are there rival hypotheses?
9. Are there flaws in the statistical reasoning?
10. How relevant are the analogies?
11. Are there any errors in reasoning?
12. What significant information is omitted?
13. What conclusions are consistent with the strong reasons?
14. What are your own value preferences in this controversy?

II

What Are the Issue and the Conclusion?

Fraternities and sororities are often involved in charitable activities. They provide volunteers to raise money for many worthwhile causes. Their contribution in this regard is noteworthy.

Yet we cannot stop our description of Greek organizations with this incomplete picture. Their good deeds are overwhelmed by their encouragement of conformity, childish pranks, and anti-intellectual antics. The abundant talents of their members should be channelled elsewhere.

The person who wrote this assessment of Greek organizations very much wants you to believe something. In general, those who create editorials, books, magazine articles or speeches are trying to alter your perceptions or beliefs. For you to form a reasonable reaction, you must first identify the controversy or *issue* as well as the thesis or *conclusion* being pushed onto you. Otherwise, you will be reacting to a distorted version of the attempted communication.

When you have completed this chapter, you should be able to answer the first of our critical questions successfully.

◊   *Critical Question:*   **What are the issue and the conclusion?**

Kinds of Issues

It will be helpful at this point to identify two kinds of issues you will typically encounter. The following questions illustrate one of these:

Do obese people have more emotional problems?

What causes AIDS?
Who won the first presidential debate?
How much will college cost in the year 2000?
Can a child's IQ be raised by a stimulating environment?
Does watching violence on TV make us relatively insensitive to crime on the streets?

All of these questions have one thing in common. They demand answers that attempt to describe the way the world is, was, or is going to be. For example, answers to the first two questions might be, "In general, obese people have more emotional problems," and "A particular virus causes AIDS."

We will refer to such issues as *descriptive issues*. You will find such issues all around you. They appear in textbooks of such disciplines as psychology, sociology, political science, economics, education, and geography; in magazines; and on television. Such issues reflect our curiosity about patterns or order in the world.

Now let's look at examples of a second kind of question:

Should capital punishment be abolished?
Is it desirable to fluoridate drinking water?
What ought to be done about unemployment?
Should people be required to retire at a certain age?

All of these questions demand answers that suggest the way the world *ought to be*. For example, answers to the first questions might be, "Capital punishment *should be* abolished," and "We *ought* to fluoridate our drinking water."

These issues are ethical, or moral, issues; they raise questions about what is right or wrong, desirable or undesirable, good or bad. They demand prescriptive answers. Thus, we will refer to these issues as *prescriptive issues*. Social controversies are often prescriptive issues, e.g., those surrounding abortion, marijuana, handguns, pornography, prostitution, and conservation of energy.

We have somewhat oversimplified. Sometimes it will be quite difficult to decide what kind of issue is being discussed. It will be useful to keep these distinctions in mind, however, because the kinds of critical evaluations you eventually make will differ depending upon the kind of issue to which you are responding.

What Is the Issue?

How does one go about determining the basic question or issue? Frequently it is very simple: The writer or speaker will tell you. The issue will often be identified in the body of the text, usually right at the beginning, or it may even be found in the title. If the issue is explicitly stated, you will usually find phrases such as the following:

The question I am raising is whether taxes are too high in our country.
Reducing the speed limit: *Is it the right thing to do?*

Should sex education be taught in the school?
Why isn't our present educational system working?
Does how you sleep reveal your personality?

Unfortunately, the question is not always explicitly stated, and instead must be inferred from the conclusion. In such cases the conclusion must be found before you can identify the issue. Thus, where the question is not explicitly stated, the first step in critical evaluation is to find the conclusion—a frequently difficult step.
We cannot critically evaluate until we find the conclusion!
Let's see how we go about looking for that very important structural element.

Searching for the Author's Conclusion

To identify the conclusion, the critical thinker must ask, What is the writer or speaker trying to prove? The answer to this question will be the conclusion.

In searching for a conclusion, you will be looking for a statement or set of statements that the writer or speaker wants you to believe. She wants you to believe the conclusion on the basis of her other statements. In short, the basic structure of persuasive communication is: *This* because of *that. This* refers to the conclusion; *that* refers to the support for the conclusion. This structure represents the process of *inference.*

In a dispute conclusions are *inferred*; they are derived from reasoning. Conclusions are ideas that require other ideas to support them. Thus, whenever someone claims something is true or ought to be done and provides no statements to support his claim, that claim is *not* a conclusion because no one has offered any basis for belief.

The last paragraph says a lot. It would be a good idea for you to read it again. Understanding the nature of a conclusion is an essential step toward critical reading. Let's look closely at a conclusion and at the inference process. Here is a brief paragraph; see whether you can identify the conclusion, then the statements that support it.

We oppose a mandatory retirement age. We believe that age is an inappropriate and unreasonable basis for determining whether an individual can do a job.

The statement, "We oppose a mandatory retirement age" is this writer's answer to the question of whether there should be a mandatory retirement age; it is her conclusion. She supports the conclusion (a belief) with another belief: "We believe that age is an inappropriate and unreasonable basis for determining whether an individual can do a job." Do you see why the latter belief is not a conclusion? It is not the conclusion because it is used to prove something else. *Remember:* To believe one statement (the conclusion) because you think it is well supported by *other* beliefs is to make an inference. When people engage in this process, they are reasoning; the conclusion is the outcome of this reasoning.

Resisting the Temptation to Believe the Task is Simple

Finding the conclusion is not as simple or obvious as it may seem at first glance. It is very common for readers and listeners to "miss the point." Communicators frequently make the task difficult. For example, writers often do not explicitly state their conclusion; it may only be implied by other statements or by the title. In other cases, many statements will have the appearance of a conclusion, but will actually serve other functions. You need to resist the temptation to believe that identifying the conclusion is a simple task. In the next section, we will describe ways to make certain that you have found the conclusion. *Remember:* Identifying the conclusion is crucial, and it is often not simple.

Clues to Discovery: How to Find the Conclusion

There are a number of clues to help you identify the conclusion.

CLUE NO. 1: **Ask what the issue is.** Since a conclusion is always a response to an issue, it will help you to find the conclusion if you know the issue. We discussed earlier how to identify the issue. First, look at the title. Next, look at the opening paragraphs. If this technique doesn't tell you, skimming several pages may be necessary.

CLUE NO. 2: **Look for indicator words.** The conclusion will frequently be preceded by *indicator words* that signify that a conclusion is coming. A list of such indicator words follows:

therefore	we may deduce that
thus	points to the conclusion that
so	the point I'm trying to make is
in short	in my opinion
it follows that	the most obvious explanation
it is believed that	it is highly probable that
shows that	in fact
indicates that	the truth of the matter is
suggests that	alas
proves that	as a result
yet	it should be clear that

When you see these indicator words, take note of them. They tell you that a conclusion may follow.

Read the following two passages and identify and highlight the indicator words. By doing so, you will have identified the statements containing the conclusion.

Passage A

But now, more than two years after voters overwhelmingly approved the lottery, it has been proven that the game is not a sure success; in fact, it can be considered a failure.

First of all, during the campaign for passage of the lottery, the public was repeatedly told that the proceeds would go toward curing the financial ills of both higher education and local primary and secondary schools. It was on this premise that the lottery received overwhelming support from the public. Not until it was approved, however, was it widely conceded that lottery profits would go into the general fund instead of the state's education budget. Less than half of the lottery's profits goes to education.

Passage B

When mothers smoke during pregnancy, it is highly probable that their children will read with less comprehension when they attend school. A recent study of 10,000 children born in the 1960s suggests that there is a small but statistically significant reduction in reading-comprehension scores of children whose mothers smoked when they were pregnant.

You should have highlighted the following phrases: "it has been proven" and "in fact" in passage A, and "it is highly probable that" in Passage B. The conclusions follow these words.

Unfortunately, many written and spoken communications do not introduce the conclusion with indicator words. However, when *you* write, you should draw attention to your thesis with indicator words. Those words act as a neon sign drawing attention to the thesis you want the reader to accept.

CLUE NO. 3: **Look in likely locations.** Conclusions tend to occupy certain locations. The first two places to look are at the beginning and at the end. Many writers begin with a statement of purpose, which contains what they are trying to prove. Others summarize their conclusions at the end. If you are reading a long, complex passage and are having difficulty seeing where it is going, skip ahead to the ending.

CLUE NO. 4: **Remember what a conclusion is not.** Conclusions will not be any of the following:

Examples
Statistics
Definitions
Background information
Evidence

When you have identified the conclusion, check to see that it is none of these.

Dangers of Missing the Conclusion

If you miss the conclusion, you will simply be ''spinning your wheels'' as you try to evaluate ciritcally. Missing the point not only leads to frustration, but frequently to unnecessary arguments, and sometimes embarrassment. All subsequent critical-questioning techniques require correct identification of the conclusion. When you have identified it, highlight it in some way. You will need to refer back to it several times as you ask further questions. As you critically evaluate, *always* keep the conclusion in mind!

Your Thesis and Effective Writing

Since readers of *your* writing will be looking for your thesis or conclusion, help them by giving it the clarity it deserves. It is the central message you want to deliver. Emphasize it; leave no doubt about what it actually is. Making your conclusion easily identifiable not only makes a reader's task easier, it also may improve the logic of your writing. By requiring yourself to define a thesis, you are more likely to provide reasoning that moves toward the single goal of a convincing conclusion. An effective way to emphasize the conclusion is to insert it at the beginning or end of your essay and precede it with an indicator word.

Practice Exercises

◊   *Critical Question: **What are the issue and the conclusion?***

In the following passages locate the issue and conclusion. As you search, be sure to look for indicator words.

Passage 1

(1) ''The United States has the world's highest standard of living. (2) It is not a utopia, but in the real world our economy is the best there is.'' (3) How often have you heard this statement either as an expression of national superiority or as a defense of the status quo?

(4) Alas, it is simply untrue. (5) Our country has not generated the world's highest per capita GNP since the early 1950s, when we were surpassed by Kuwait. (6) More important, perhaps, is the fact that we have been surpassed, or are about to be, by a number of countries in Europe. (7) Among industrial countries, Sweden and Switzerland can each claim to be more successful, with a per capita GNP 20 percent above ours. (8) We have also been passed by Denmark and are about to be surpassed by Norway and West Germany. (9) Relative to achievements in the rest of the world, the United States economy no longer delivers the goods.

Passage 2

(1) Is torture, by which I mean the use of physical or mental pain to gain information, everywhere and always indefensible? (2) Certainly torturing an individual is a less grievous violation of his rights than killing him. (3) Yet in most systems of morality, killing is sometimes justified. (4) Certainly killing is more moral in the prosecution of a just war, such as World War II. (5) (Audie Murphy was held up as an example to the youth of the postwar generation for the number of Germans he killed singlehandedly, just as Sergeant Alvin York, Tennessee sharpshooter, became a folk hero following the "war to end wars.") (6) The policeman who kills in the line of duty is often seen as a hero; so is the man who takes the life of an assailant to protect his wife or children. (7) In both instances, indeed, there seems a positive moral obligation to kill a criminal rather than let an innocent human life be taken.

(8) The point I want to make is this: If there are occasions when it is morally justifiable to kill, then there are times when it is morally justifiable to inflict temporary mental or physical suffering, an infinitely less serious violation of human rights.[1]

Passage 3

Alumni from Harvard, like the rest of us, are concerned about the risk of coronary heart disease. Together with cancer, these two complex diseases account for 70 percent of male deaths.

Researchers in a Palo Alto, California sports medicine facility recently contacted Harvard alumni in an attempt to identify factors that might reduce coronary heart disease. They identified vigorous exercise as a critical factor in preventing death from this disease.

Several other research groups cautioned those who conducted the Harvard alumni study to be cautious about jumping to conclusions concerning the benefits of exercise. But after collecting data for several more years, the Palo Alto group concluded that vigorous exercise does indeed help prevent coronary heart disease.

————————————— Sample Responses —————————————

Passage 1

The first paragraph introduces the issue or controversy. The second paragraph contains the writer's opinion about the issue. One indicator word is present in the second paragraph—"alas." The presence of this indicator word suggests that sentence (4) contains the conclusion. Another clue is location. Sentences (4) and (9) begin and end the paragraph where the writer provides her thesis. Both sentences given an answer to the question that identifies the issue. Thus, we have found the conclusion.

CONCLUSION: *The U.S. economy is not the best.*

In this passage, the issue is not explicitly stated; thus we must infer it from the author's conclusion.

ISSUE: *Which economic system is best?*

[1]Adapted from P. J. Buchanan, "The Right Time for Torture," *Skeptic* 17 (January/February 1977), 18.

Passage 2

Sentence (1) explicitly states the issue. We know that paragraph 2 is the conclusion by the author's use of the indicator words, "The point I want to make is . . ." The conclusion follows these words. Again, note the location clues: The conclusion occurs in the last sentence, the question in the first sentence.

CONCLUSION: *If there are occasions when it is morally justifiable to kill, then there are times when it is morally justifiable to inflict temporary mental or physical suffering.*

ISSUE: *Is torture everywhere and always indefensible?*

Passage 3

An indicator word and location clues aid us in finding the conclusion in this passage. The indicator word "concluded" is found in the last sentence.

CONCLUSION: *Vigorous exercise is a critical factor in preventing death from coronary heart disease.*

ISSUE: *Does vigorous physical activity help prevent death from coronary heart disease?*

Passage 4 (Self-Examination)

Everything we know about society's efforts to cope with crime suggests that we should take a very pessimistic view of people and their institutions, a view that requires a limited definition of progress.

Most serious crimes are committed by repeaters. In fact, a recent study showed that, among a large group of boys who were studied over a long period of time, chronic offenders accounted for over half of recorded delinquencies and about two-thirds of all violent crimes. While most serious crime fails to lead to an arrest, most chronic offenders eventually get arrested. Yet, many of these suffer little loss of freedom.

Given the present state of affairs, the only solution that makes sense is to imprison the chronic serious offender for a long period of time. It is obvious that such a strategy would prevent these offenders from committing additional crimes. While this strategy would not solve the crime problem, it would prevent a substantial number of serious crimes; perhaps it would lead to as much as a 20 percent reduction. Such a reduction is unlikely if society focuses upon attacking the causes of crime, since we don't have the knowledge or resources to make such an attack successful.

III

What Are the Reasons?

The legal drinking age should be 18.

A pig is smarter than a mule.

The sexual behavior of Presidential candidates tells us something important about their fitness for office.

Employers should be able to fire any employee who displeases them.

As information or advice, these four claims are missing something. We may or may not agree with them, but in their current form they neither strengthen nor weaken our initial positions. None of the claims contains an explanation or rationale for *why* we should agree. Thus, if we heard someone make one of those four assertions, we would be left hungry for more.

What is missing is the reason or reasons responsible for the claims. *Reasons* are beliefs, evidence, metaphors, analogies, and other statements offered to support or justify conclusions. They are the statements that together form the basis for demonstrating the truth or "rightness" of a conclusion. Chapter II gave you some guidelines for locating two very important parts of the structure of an argument, the issue and the conclusion. This chapter focuses on techniques for identifying the third essential element of an argument—the reasons.

When a writer has a conclusion she wants you to accept, she must present reasons to persuade you that she is right, and to show you *why*.

It is the mark of a rational person to support his or her beliefs by adequate proof, especially when the beliefs are of a controversial nature. For example, when someone asserts that we should abolish the CIA, this assertion should be met with the challenge, "Why do you say that?" You should raise this question whether you agree or disagree. The person's reasons may be either strong or weak, but you will not know until you have asked the question and identified the reasons. If the answer is "Because I think so," you should be dissatisfied with the argument, because the "reason" is a mere restatement of the conclusion. However, if the answer is evidence concerning wrongdoing by the CIA, you will want to consider such evidence when you evaluate the conclusion. *Remember:* You cannot determine the worth of a conclusion until you identify the reasons.

Identifying reasons is a particularly important step in critical thinking. An opinion cannot be evaluated fairly unless we ask why it is held and get a satisfactory response. Focusing on reasons requires us to remain open to and tolerant of views that might differ from our own. If we reacted to conclusions rather than to reasoning, we would tend to stick to the conclusions we brought to the discussion or essay, and those conclusions that agree with our own would receive our rapid assent. If we are ever to reexamine our own opinions, we must stay open to the reasons provided by those with opinions that we do not yet share.

◊   *Critical Question:*   **What are the reasons?**

Initiating the Questioning Process

The first step in identifying reasons is to approach the argument with a questioning attitude, and the first question you should ask is a *why* question. You have identified the conclusion; now you wish to know why the conclusion makes sense. If a statement does not answer the question, Why does the writer believe that?, then it is not a reason. In order to function as a reason, a statement (or group of statements) must provide support for a conclusion.

Let us apply the questioning attitude to the following paragraph. First we will find the conclusion; then we will ask the appropriate *why* question. Remember your guidelines for finding the conclusion. (The indicator words for the conclusion have been underlined.)

> (1) Is the cost of hospital care outrageous? (2) A recent survey by the American Association of Retired Persons offers reliable evidence on this issue. (3) Independent audits of the bills of 2000 patients found that hospitals overcharge their patients by an average of 15 percent. (4) In addition, exit interviews with 400 patients revealed high amounts of dismay and anger when the patients were informed about the size of their total hospital bill. (5) In short, the costs of hospital care are higher than the services provided warrant.

What follows "In short" answers the question raised in statement (1). Thus, the conclusion is statement (5), ". . . the costs of hospital care are higher than the services provided warrant." *Highlight the conclusion!*

We then ask the question, Why does the writer believe the conclusion? The statements that answer that question are the reasons. In this particular case, the writer provides us with evidence as reasons. Statements (3) and (4) jointly provide the evidence; that is, together they provide support for the conclusion. Together they serve as the reason for the conclusion.

Now, try to find the reasons in the following paragraph. Again, first find the conclusion, highlight it, and then ask the *why* question.

(1) Euthanasia is detrimental to the welfare of society because it destroys man's ideas of sacrifice, loyalty, and courage in bearing pain. (2) Some dying persons accept their suffering as a way of paying for their sins. (3) These people should be permitted to die as they wish—without help from any other person in speeding up the dying process.

There is no obvious indicator word for the conclusion in the paragraph, but the author is clearly arguing against the morality of euthanasia. The conclusion here is: "Euthanasia is detrimental to the welfare of society." Why does the author believe this? The major reason given is that "it destroys man's ideas of sacrifice, loyalty, and courage in bearing pain." The next two sentences in the excerpt provide additional support for this reason.

One of the best ways for you to determine whether you have discovered a writer's reasons is to try to play the role of the writer. Put yourself in the position of the writer, and ask yourself, Why am I in favor of this conclusion that I am supporting? Try to put into your own words how you believe the writer would answer this question. If you can do this, you have probably discovered the writer's reasons.

Words That Identify Reasons

As was the case with conclusions, there are certain words that will typically indicate that a reason will follow. *Remember:* The structure of reasoning is, *This, because of that*. Thus, the word *because*, as well as words synonymous with and similar in function to it, will frequently signal the presence of reasons. A list of indicator words for reasons follows.

because	in view of the fact that
first—second	for the reason that
since	is supported by
for	for example
for one thing	also

Find the reasons in the following passage by identifying the indicator words.

(1) No one could be more willing to recommend hunting as a wholesome form of outdoor recreation than I. (2) For one thing, I believe that hunting has great value for those who participate in it. (3) It is a form of recreation that brings many physical, mental, and even spiritual benefits to the individual. (4) Hunting also develops self-reliance and confidence.

You should have identified statements (2) and (3) jointly as one reason, and (4) as another. Did you notice the indicator words "for one thing" and "also"?

Kinds of Reasons

There are many different kinds of reasons, depending on the kind of issue. Many reasons will be statements presenting evidence. By *evidence* we mean facts, examples, statistics, metaphors, mental experiments, and analogies. A more detailed treatment of evidence appears in Chapter VII.

When a speaker or writer is trying to support a descriptive conclusion, the answer to the *why* question will typically be evidence.

The following example provides a descriptive argument; try to find the author's reasons.

(1) The fact is that college coeds are now smoking cigarettes at an increasing rate. (2) Recent surveys show that as male college students have decreased their consumption by 40%, women have increased their consumption of cigarettes by 60%.

You should have identified the first statement as the conclusion. It is a descriptive statement about the rate at which coeds are smoking cigarettes. The rest of the paragraph presents the evidence—the reason for the conclusion. *Remember:* The conclusion itself will not be evidence; it will be a belief supported by evidence or by other beliefs.

In prescriptive arguments, reasons are typically either prescriptive or descriptive statements. The use of these kinds of statements to support a conclusion in a prescriptive argument is illustrated in the following:

(1) With regard to the big controversy over grade inflation, I would like to ask a few questions. (2) What difference does it make if the people who are really good are never distinguished from the average student? (3) Is there a caste system in our society according to grade-point averages?

(4) Are those with high point averages superior to those with low point averages? (5) In the majority of cases, grades are not a true indication of learning, anyway; they are a measure of how well a student can absorb information for a short time period and regurgitate it on a test.

(6) Students will retain the information that interests them and is important anyway. (7) Why can't we eliminate grades and be motivated only by the inborn curiosity and zest for learning that is really in us all?

The controversy here is what to do about grade inflation. The author's solution to the problem is to abolish grades, as indicated in sentence (7). Let's look for sentences that answer the question, Why does the author believe this conclusion? First, note that no evidence is presented. Sentences (2) and (3) jointly form one reason: It is not important to distinguish the average student from the good student. Note that this is a general principle that indicates the writer's view about how the world should be. Sentences (4) and (5) add a second reason: Grades are not a true indicator of learning. This is a general belief regarding a disadvantage of grades. Sentence (6) provides a third reason: Students will retain only the information that interests them and is important anyway (grades do not help learners to remember). This is another general belief. You will notice that these beliefs may be supported by evidence.

Keeping the Reasons and Conclusions Straight

As you read critically, the reasons and the conclusion are the most important elements to bring into clear focus. Much reasoning is long and not very well organized. Sometimes a set of reasons will support one conclusion, and that conclusion will function as the main reason for another conclusion. Reasons may be supported by other reasons. In especially complicated arguments, it is frequently difficult to keep the structure straight in your mind as you attempt to critically evaluate what you have read. To overcome this problem, try to develop your own organizing procedure for keeping the reasons and conclusions separate and in a logical pattern.

Some readers have found the following suggestions useful:

1. Circle indicator words.
2. Underline the reasons and conclusion in different colors of ink, or highlight the conclusion and underline the reasons.
3. Label the reasons and conclusion in the margin.
4. For long passages, make a list of reasons at the end of the essay.
5. For especially complicated reasoning, diagram the structure, using numbers to refer to each reason and conclusion, and arrows to designate the direction of relationship. Sometimes this technique is most effective if all reasons and conclusions are first paraphrased in the margins, then numbered.

We can illustrate these suggested techniques by attempting to find the conclusion and reasons in the following relatively complex passage.

(1) Do physicians have a moral obligation to provide free medical care for those who cannot pay? (2) *Yes, they do.* (3) First, society has restricted most medical practice to physicians. (4) Because the resultant medical monopoly has obvious economic benefits, (5) it seems reasonable that the profession acknowledge its collective responsibility to provide care even to those who cannot pay.

(6) Second, the moral obligation of individual physicians to provide free care derives from an understanding of their special role. (7) Physicians should not be compared to plumbers or car mechanics, or to other craftsmen who repair inanimate objects. (8) Unlike automobile repairs, the health problems of people are not deferrable or negotiable. (9) That doctors help some people without pay is essential if doctors are to remain doctors and medical services are not to be regarded as just another form of profit-seeking business activity.[1]

---

[1]Adapted from M. Siegler, "Treating the Jobless for Free: Do Doctors Have a Special Duty? Yes," *The Hastings Center Report* (August 1983), 12–13.

Initially you should notice that we have underlined the conclusion and key indicator words. As you read this passage, you surely noticed that the reasoning structure is quite complicated. For such a passage, we have to understand the logical sequence of sentences to isolate the reasoning structure. Thus we have diagrammed the relationships among the reasons and conclusion. Try to diagram this passage on your own; then, compare your diagram to ours.

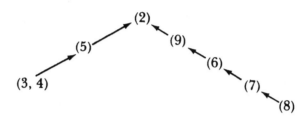

Our diagram reflects our interpretation that sentence (5) in paragraph 2 and sentence (9) in paragraph 3 directly answered the question, Why is the conclusion, sentence (2), true? The directon of the rest of the arrows in the diagram denotes how we believe these two reasons are supported by further reasons. For example, statements (3) and (4) jointly provide support for (5).

Diagramming is useful for gaining an understanding of especially complicated arguments. When reading lengthy essays it is always useful to paraphrase the main reasons in the margins. Thus, for the above passage, we might have supplied the following paraphrased reasons:

Paragraph 1: Physicians owe a debt to society.
Paragraph 2: The physician's role is special; physicians are unlike businessmen.

We have mentioned a number of techniques for you to use in developing a clear picture of the reasoning structure. If some other technique works better for you, by all means use it. The important point is to keep the reasons and conclusion straight as you prepare to evaluate.

Reasons First, Then Conclusions

The first chapter warned you about the danger of weak-sense critical thinking. A warning signal that can alert you to weak-sense critical thinking should go off when you notice that reasons seem to be created (on the spot, even) only because they defend a previously-held opinion. When someone is eager to share an opinion as if it were a conclusion, but looks puzzled or angry when asked for reasons, weak-sense critical thinking is the probable culprit.

Certainly, you have a large set of initial beliefs, which act as initial conclusions when you encounter controversies. As your respect for the importance of reasons grows, you will frequently expect those conclusions to stand or crumble on the basis of their support. Your strongest conclusions follow your reflection about the reasons and what they mean.

Be your own censor in this regard. You must shake your own pan when looking for gold. Try to avoid "reverse logic" whereby reasons are an afterthought, following the selection of your conclusion. Ideally, reasons are the tool by which conclusions are shaped and modified.

Reasons + Conclusion = Argument

In ordinary conversation an argument refers to a disagreement, a time when blood pressure soars. We will use the concept in a slightly different manner. An *argument* is a combination of two forms of statements, a conclusion and the reasons allegedly supporting it. The partnership between reasons and conclusion establishes a person's argument.

Several characteristics of arguments grab our attention.

- They have an intent. Those who provide them hope to convince us to believe certain things or act in certain ways. Consequently, they call for a reaction. We can imitate the sponge or the gold prospector, but we ordinarily must respond somehow.
- Their quality varies. Critical thinking is required to determine the degree of merit contained in an argument.
- They have two essential visible components—a conclusion and reasons. Failure to identify either component destroys the opportunity to evaluate the argument. We cannot evaluate what we cannot identify.

Reasons and Effective Writing

When you are writing, you will usually want to make your reader's job as easy as possible. Thus, your task is to use words, sentences, paragraphs, and indicator words to illuminate the logical relationships in your argument.

A good way to begin is by clearly outlining or diagramming your reasoning structure. Then keep several fundamental rules in mind as you write. The first is the rule of *grouping*: Keep reasons for the same conclusion together. You can do this by keeping grammatical structure parallel and by using appropriate indicator words. The second is the rule of *direction*. After you have developed a sequential order of reasons, such that each reason relates to a subsequent one, word your essay so that the reasons move in a single direction. For example, a sequence that follows the rule of direction goes from the final conclusion to its main reason to the reason for that reason.

A third rule is that of keeping reasons that bear a similar relationship to the conclusion in close proximity to one another, so that their relationship is easy to see. Do not separate them with reasons that involve quite different considerations.

Practice Exercises

◊   *Critical Question:*   **What are the reasons?**

First survey the passage and highlight its conclusion. Then ask the question, Why?, and locate the reasons. Use indicator words to help. Keep the conclusions and the reasons separate.

Passage 1

The collapse of the traditional two-parent family unit is a primary cause of poverty in the United States. First, over 50% of all poor families are headed by single women. Child-bearing without marriage is on the rise, and not surprisingly, so is poverty. The combined burden of child care *and* an income-producing job is simply too great for most single mothers to bear.

Second, poor people are discouraged by the welfare laws from maintaining two-parent family units. Welfare is often more generous when the husband is absent. Once the two-parent family unit is disrupted by the disincentive to stay together, long-run poverty is more likely.

Passage 2

Eunice Kennedy Shriver stood up for parents on the Op-Ed page of the *Washington Post* recently. In a piece entitled, "Yes, Parents Should Know," she supported the Health and Human Services Department's proposed rule to require that federally funded family-planning clinics notify the parents of minors to whom they are providing prescription contraceptives.

Mrs. Shriver's arguments for the proposed rule, which echo the administration's, reveal much well-meaning intent and a distorted view of reality. Mandatory notification is more likely to deter girls from using the clinic than to benefit girls who come home to find their parents reading a government notice announcing that their daughter has obtained birth control.

The premise behind mandatory notification is that adolescent knowledge of human sexuality causes adolescent promiscuity. No evidence has yet been offered that can support this premise. Indeed, the June report by the Alan Guttmaker Institute found that sex education in schools does not promote promiscuity in teenagers, and may even discourage teenage pregnancy. Planned Parenthood does not introduce teenagers to sex; girls who come to this clinic have been having sex for an average of nine months before their first visit.[2]

Passage 3

Speedy, colorful waterscooters are gaining in popularity. Waterscooters can travel anywhere a small boat can and are typically popular with young people. The rising popularity of the craft has raised the question of waterscooter regulation. In this case, the argument for strict regulation is compelling. Waterscooters are a particularly deadly form of water recreation.

For example, two women were vacationing in Longboat Key. While they were floating on a raft along the shore, a waterscooter crashed into them and killed them. Also,

---

[2]Adapted from A. Shlaes, "The Squeal Squawk," *The New Republic* (August 9, 1982), 18–20.

waterscooter operators have been killed or seriously injured in collisions with other water craft. Others have been stranded at sea when their scooters either failed or sunk far from shore. Many waterscooter operators are inexperienced and ignorant of navigational rules, increasing the potential for accidents. The increasing popularity of the scooter has exacerbated the problem, providing more water vehicles to compete for the same space. Crowded waterways are simply an open invitation to disaster.

In addition to the inherent operational hazards of waterscooters, they are proving to be an environmental nuisance. Beach residents complain of the intrusive noise of the scooters. The Pacific Whale Foundation on the West Coast expressed concern that the scooters are frightening away endangered humpback whales that migrate to Hawaii for breeding.

Regulations such as minimum operating age, restricted operating areas, ánd mandatory classes in water safety are essential. Without such regulations, tragedies involving waterscooters are sure to multiply, rendering many beaches unsafe for recreation.

Sample Responses

Passage 1

ISSUE: *Is the collapse of the traditional two-parent family a primary cause of poverty in the United States?*

CONCLUSION: *Yes, the collapse of the traditional two-parent family is a major contributor to poverty.*

REASONS: *1. Single-parent families are increasing; single mothers cannot produce an adequate income.*
         2. The welfare system, by discouraging two-parent families, has encouraged more poverty.

Passage 2

ISSUE: *Should federally funded family-planning clinics be required to notify the parents of minors to whom they are providing prescription contraceptives?*

CONCLUSION: *No, they should not be required to do so.*

REASONS: *1. The rule is likely to deter girls from using the clinic.*
         2. Knowledge of human sexuality does not cause adolescent promiscuity. This claim is supported by findings from the Guttmaker Institute.

Passage 3

ISSUE: *Should waterscooters be subject to strict regulation?*

CONCLUSION: *Yes, waterscooters should be strictly regulated.*

REASONS: *1. Waterscooters are extremely dangerous.*
        a. Operators are killing themselves and others.
        b. Most waterscooter operators are inexperienced.
        c. The growing popularity of the scooters has resulted in crowding, worsening the problem.

       2. Waterscooters pose an environmental threat.

Passage 4 (Self-Examination)

Dial-a-porn is capitalism in its finest hour. In the United States, one who can recognize a burgeoning market can make a living off of his discovery—it's the American way. Dial-a-porn is merely meeting the demand of consumers. Yet, certain factions are opposed to this version of the American Dream, and are lobbying to restrict phone porn to a subscription-only basis. Such measures encroach upon the freedom of the individual and run counter to the tolerant stance upon which America has prided itself.

Some parents are concerned that their children will suffer irreparable damage should they contact dial-a-porn. It is not, however, dial-a-porn's responsibility to monitor the activities of children. Properly supervised children are not customers of phone porn. Responsible parents should discuss sexuality with their children. Sex is natural, and only when parents shroud sex in mystery does sex become a problem. Phone porn is strictly an adult market and is advertised as such. Parents should explain this to their children and discourage them from using it.

A few cases have arisen where children who dialed phone porn numbers committed subsequent sexual crimes. These kids were just powder kegs waiting to explode. Dial-a-porn is simply not responsible for the actions of wayward children. If not the phone call, something else along the line would have sparked such children. Lax parents are just looking for an easy scapegoat. If they had firmly instilled a sense of morality in their children, they would have been unfazed by such a call. Besides, most adolescents won't hear anything on dial-a-porn that they haven't already heard or even done. Younger children, with solid morals, will not be transformed into sexually crazed maniacs after a call to dial-a-porn.

The bottom line, however, is freedom of speech. If adults want to listen to or engage in erotic conversation in the privacy of their homes, so be it. Any restriction of that freedom is censorship, in direct violation of a basic tenet of our constitution. The original motivation behind the provision of free speech was to protect unpopular opinions. Phone porn is currently in disfavor, and thus in dire need of protection. The realm of morality must remain independent of the government. Proposals to restrict phone porn place our individual liberty in great jeopardy.

IV

What Words or Phrases Are Ambiguous?

The first three chapters of this book help you identify the basic structural elements in any essay. At this point, if you can locate a writer's or speaker's conclusion and reasons, you are progressing rapidly toward the ultimate goal of forming your own rational decisions. Your next step is to put this structural picture into clearer focus.

While identifying the conclusion and reasons gives you the basic visible structure, you still need to examine the precise *meaning* of these parts before you can react fairly to the ideas being presented. You need now to pay much more attention to the details of the language.

Deciding upon the precise meaning of key words or phrases is an essential prerequisite to deciding whether to agree with someone's opinion. If you fail to check for the meaning of crucial terms and phrases, you may react to an opinion the author never intended.

Let's see why knowing the meaning of an author's terms is so important.

> Recently, in Michigan, a lawyer filed charges against a psychologist, accusing him of failing to report a teen-aged girl's allegations that her stepfather had sexually abused her. The prosecution argued that the psychologist's continued treatment of the father and stepdaughter indicated that he had *reasonable cause to suspect* the abuse occurred.

We hope that you can see that judging whether the psychologist made a bad decision rests on the *meaning* of *reasonable cause to suspect*; yet, this phrase has many different possible meanings. If you were a juror, wouldn't you want to know the meaning of this phrase before deciding whether the psychologist was guilty? If you would, you would be agreeing with the defense lawyer who argued that the phrase ''reasonable cause to suspect'' is subjective and too vague, unless clarified.

This courtroom example illustrates an important point: you cannot react to an argument unless you understand the meanings (explicit or implied) of crucial terms and phrases. How these are interpreted will often affect the acceptability of the reasoning. Consequently, before you can determine the extent to which you wish to accept one conclusion or another, you must first attempt to discover the precise meaning of the conclusion and the reasons. While their meaning typically *appears* obvious, it often is not.

The discovery and clarification of meaning require conscious, step-by-step procedures. This chapter suggests one set of such procedures. It focuses on the following question:

♢   *Critical Question:*   **What words or phrases are ambiguous?**

The Confusing Flexibility of Words

Our language is highly complex. If each word had only one potential meaning about which we all agreed, effective communication would be more likely. However, most words have more than one meaning.

Consider the multiple meanings of such words as *freedom, obscenity,* and *happiness.* These multiple meanings can create serious problems in determining the worth of an argument. For example, when someone argues that a magazine should not be published because it is obscene, you cannot evaluate the argument until you know what the writer means by "obscene." In this brief argument, it is easy to find the conclusion and the supporting reason, but the quality of the reasoning is difficult to judge because of the ambiguous use of *obscene.* Thus, even when you can identify the structure of what others are saying, you still must struggle with the meaning of certain words in that structure. A warning: *We often misunderstand what we read because we presume that what words mean is obvious.*

Whenever you are reading or listening, force yourself to *search for ambiguity*; otherwise, you may simply miss the point. We want to avoid being ambiguous about our definition of ambiguity. A term or phrase is ambiguous when its meaning is so uncertain in the context of the discourse we are examining that we need further clarification before we can judge the adequacy of the reasoning.

As a further illustration of potential problems caused by not making the meaning of terms sufficiently clear, look at the following argument; then write out the "obvious" meaning of the term *social worth.*

> More and more of us are being kept alive for extended periods of time by medical wizardry. This development is causing a strain on pension plans and social security. Unfortunately, our economy seems unable to meet both the expensive needs of the aged and the resource claims made by every other group in society. Hence, I wish to propose that we change our attitude toward the ultimate desirability of a long life. Instead, we should think in terms of the quality of life. At any point in a person's life at which his or her social worth has become minimal, we should relax our fear of suicide. Those adults who choose to escape the potential misery of old age should be permitted to do so without the rebuke of those who survive them.

How did you do? What the author is suggesting isn't clear at all, because we don't know whether he thinks that *social worth* means 1) the economic contribution that a person can make, *or* 2) the benefits of human communication and interaction. Does it really matter which of these possible interpretations the author means? It certainly does. The argument would be more persuasive if the writer meant the second definition. If he intended the first definition, then he is advocating a major social change based on a very narrow concept of what it means to be human. Notice that the clues about the meaning of the term are sketchy at best. Until we find out that meaning, we aren't well prepared to form a reaction to the argument.

Locating Key Terms and Phrases

The first step in determining which terms or phrases are ambiguous is to *check for key terms in the issue*. Key terms will be those terms that may have more than one plausible meaning within the context of the issue; that is, terms that you know the author will have to make clear before you can decide to agree or disagree with her. To illustrate the potential benefit of checking terminology in the issue, let's examine several stated issues:

1. Does TV violence adversely affect society?
2. Is the Miss America contest demeaning to women?
3. Is the incidence of rape in our society increasing?

Each of these stated issues contain phrases that writers or speakers will have to make clear before you will be able to evaluate their reasoning. Each of the following phrases is potentially ambiguous: TV violence, adversely affect society, demeaning to women, and rape. Thus, when you read an essay responding to these issues, you will want to pay close attention to how the author has defined these terms.

The next step in determining which terms or phrases are ambiguous is to identify what words or phrases seem crucial in determining how well the author's reasons support his conclusion, that is, to identify the *key terms* in the reasoning structure. Once you do that, you can then determine whether the meaning of these terms is ambiguous.

When searching for key terms and phrases, you should keep in mind *why* you are looking. Someone wants you to accept a conclusion. Therefore, you are looking only for those terms or phrases that will affect whether you accept the conclusion. So, *look for them in the reasons and conclusion*. Terms or phrases that are not included in the basic reasoning structure can thus be "dumped from your pan"; you only want to think hard about the meaning of terms in the reasons and conclusion.

Another useful guide for searching for key terms and phrases is to keep in mind the following rule: The more abstract a word or phrase, the more likely it is to be susceptible to multiple interpretations and thus need clear definition by the author. To avoid being unclear in our use of the term *abstract* we define it here in the following way: A term becomes more and more abstract as it refers less and less to particular, specific instances. Thus, the words *equality, responsibility, pornography,* and *aggression* are much more abstract than are the phrases "having equal access to necessities of life," "directly causing an event," "pictures of male and female genitals," and "doing deliberate physical harm to another person." These phrases provide a much more concrete picture and therefore are less ambiguous.

You can also locate potential important ambiguous phrases by *reverse role playing.* That is, ask yourself, if you were to *adopt a position contrary to the author's,* would you choose to define certain terms or phrases differently? If so, you have identified a possible ambiguity. For example, someone who sees beauty pageants as desirable is likely to define "demeaning to women" quite differently than someone who sees them as undesirable.

Checking for Ambiguity

You now know where to look for those terms or phrases that are ambiguous. The next step is to attend to each term or phrase and ask yourself, Do I understand its meaning? In answering this very important question, you will need to overcome several major obstacles.

One obstacle is assuming that you and the author mean the same thing. Thus, you need to begin your search by avoiding "*mind-reading.*" You need to get into the habit of asking, What do you mean by that? instead of, I know just what you mean. A second obstacle is assuming that terms have a single, obvious definition. Many key terms do not. Thus, always ask, Could any of the words have a different meaning?

You can be certain you have identified an especially important unclear term by performing the following test. If you can express two or more alternative meanings for a term, each of which makes sense in the context of the argument, and if the extent to which a reason would support a conclusion is affected by which meaning is assumed, then you have located a significant ambiguity. Thus, a good test for determining whether you have identified an important ambiguity is to *substitute* the alternative meanings into the reasoning structure and see whether changing the meaning *makes a difference* in how well a reason supports the conclusion.

Determining Ambiguity

Let's now apply the above hints in determining which key terms an author has not made sufficiently clear. Remember: As we do this exercise, keep asking, What does the author mean by that? and pay particular attention to abstract terms.

We will start with a simple reasoning structure: an advertisement.

Lucky Smokes put it all together and got taste with only 3 mg. tar.

Issue: *What cigarette should you buy?*

CONCLUSION (implied): *Buy Lucky Smokes*

REASON: *They got taste with only 3 mg. tar.*

The phrases "Buy Lucky Smokes" and "3 mg. tar" seem quite concrete and self-evident. But, how about "got taste?" Is the meaning obvious? We think not. How do we know? Let's perform a test together. Could taste have more than one meaning? Yes. It could mean a barely noticeable mild tobacco flavor. It could mean a rather harsh, bitter flavor. Or it could have many other meanings. Isn't it true that you would be more eager to follow the advice of the advertisement if the taste provided matched your taste preference? Thus, the ambiguity is significant because it affects the degree to which you might be persuaded by the ad.

Advertising is often full of ambiguity. Advertisers intentionally engage in ambiguity to persuade you that their products are superior to those of their competitors. They want you to choose the meaning of ambiguous terms that is personally more desirable. Here are some sample advertising claims that are ambiguous. See if you can identify alternative, plausible meanings for the italicized words or phrases.

No-Pain is the *extra-strength* pain reliever.

Parvu: Sensual . . . but not *too far from innocence.*

Ray Rhinestone's new album: an album of *experiences.*

Vital Hair Vitamins show you *what* vitamins can do for your hair.

Here is a book at last that shows you how to find and keep a *good man.*

In each case, the advertiser hoped that you would assign the most attractive meaning to the ambiguous words. Critical reading can sometimes protect you from making purchasing decisions that you would later regret.

Let's now look at a more complicated example of ambiguity. Remember to begin by identifying the issue, conclusion and reasons.

It is time to take active steps in reducing the amount of violence on television. The adverse effect of such violence is clear, as evidenced by many recent research studies. Several studies indicate that heavy TV watchers tend to overestimate the danger of physical violence in real life. Other studies show that children who are heavy TV watchers can become desensitized to violence in the real world. Numerous other studies demonstrate the adverse effect of TV violence.

This essay addresses the issue, should we do something about the violence on television? It concludes that we ought to take steps to reduce the amount of TV violence, and the author's main reason supporting the conclusion is that such violence has an adverse effect. The writer then uses research evidence to support this reasoning. Let's examine the reasoning for any words or phrases that would affect our willingness to accept it.

First, let's examine the issue for terms we will want the author to make clear. Certainly, we would not be able to agree or disagree with this author's conclusion until she has indicated what she means by "violence on television." Thus, we will want to check how clearly she has defined it in her reasoning. Next, let's list all key terms and phrases in the conclusion and reasons: "take active steps in reducing the amount of violence on television," "adverse effect," "many recent research studies," "several studies," "heavy TV watchers," "tend to overestimate the danger of physical violence in real life," "other studies," "children who are heavy TV watchers," "can become desensitized to violence in the real world," "numerous other studies," "demonstrate", "adverse effect of TV violence." Let's take a close look at a few of these to determine whether they could have different meanings that might make a difference in how we would react to the reasoning.

First, her conclusion is ambiguous. Exactly what does it mean to "take active steps in reducing the amount of violence?" Does it mean to impose a legal ban against showing any act of physical violence, or might it mean putting public pressure on the networks to restrict violent episodes to late evening hours? Before you could decide whether to agree with the writer, you would first have to decide what it is she wants us to believe.

Next, she argues that heavy TV watchers "overestimate the danger of physical violence in real life" and "become desensitized to violence in the real world." But how much TV does one have to watch to qualify as a heavy TV watcher? Perhaps most people are not heavy TV watchers, given the actual research study's definition of that phrase. Also, what does it mean to overestimate the danger of physical violence, or to become desensitized? Try to create a mental picture of what these phrases represent. If you can't, the phrases are ambiguous. Now, check the other phrases we listed above. Do they not also need to be clarified? You can see that if you accept this writer's argument without requiring her to clarify these ambiguous phrases, you will not have understood what it is you agreed to believe.

Context and Ambiguity

Writers and speakers only rarely define their terms. Thus, typically your only guide to the meaning of an ambiguous statement is the *context* in which the words are used. By *context*, we mean the writer's background, traditional use of the term within the particular controversy, and the words and statements preceding and following the possible ambiguity. All three elements provide clues to the meaning of a potential key term or phrase.

If you were to see the term *human rights* in an essay, you should immediately ask yourself, What rights are those? If you examine the context and find that the writer is a leading member of the Soviet government, it is a good bet that the human rights he has in mind are the rights to be employed, receive free health care, and obtain adequate housing. An American senator might mean something very different by human rights. She could have in mind freedoms of speech, religion, travel, and peaceful assembly. Notice that the two versions of human rights are not necessarily consistent. A country can guarantee one form of human rights and at the same time violate the other. You must try to clarify such terms by examining their context.

Writers frequently make clear their assumed meaning of a term by their arguments. The following paragraph is an example.

Studies show that most people who undergo psychotherapy benefit from the experience. In fact, a recent study shows that after ten sessions of psychotherapy, two-thirds of participants reported experiencing less anxiety.

The phrase "benefit from the experience" is potentially ambiguous, because it could have a variety of meanings. However, the writer's argument makes clear that *in this context*, "benefit from the experience" means reporting less anxiety.

Note, that even in this case, you would want some further clarification before you call a therapist, because "reporting less anxiety" is ambiguous. Wouldn't you want to know how *much* lowering of anxiety was experienced? Perhaps participants still experienced significant amounts of anxiety—but less than previously.

A major advantage of recognizing that terms or phrases may have multiple meanings is that locating the author's meaning offers the option of *disagreeing* with it. If you disagree with a debatable, assumed definition, then you will want to recognize that the quality of the author's reasoning is conditional upon the definition used, and you will not want to be unduly influenced by the reasoning. Thus, in the above example you may believe that a preferred definition of "benefits of psychotherapy" is "a major restructuring of personality characteristics." If so, *for you*, the author's reason would not be supportive of the conclusion.

Examine the context carefully to determine the meaning of key terms. If the meaning remains uncertain, you have located an important ambiguity.

Ambiguity, Definitions, and the Dictionary

It should be obvious from the preceding discussion that, to locate and clarify ambiguity, you must be aware of the possible meanings of words. Meanings usually come in one of three forms: synonyms, examples, and what we will call "definition by specific criteria." For example, one could offer at least three different definitions of *anxiety*.

1. Anxiety is feeling nervous. (*synonym*)
2. Anxiety is what George Bush experienced when he turned on the television to watch the election returns. (*example*)
3. Anxiety is a subjective feeling of discomfort accompanied by increased sensitivity of the autonomic nervous system. (*specific criteria*)

For critical evaluation of most controversial issues, synonyms and examples are inadequate. They fail to tell you the specific properties that are crucial for an unambiguous understanding of the term. The most useful definitions are those that specify criteria for usage—and the more specific the better.

Where do you go for your definitions? One obvious and very important source is your dictionary. However, dictionary definitions frequently consist of synonyms, examples, or incomplete specifications of criteria for usage. These definitions often do not adequately define the use of a term in a particular essay. In such cases, you must discover possible meanings from the context of the passage, or from what else you know about the topic. We suggest you keep a dictionary handy, but keep in mind that the appropriate definition may not be there.

Let's take a closer look at some of the inadequacies of a dictionary definition. Examine the following brief paragraph.

> Education is not declining in quality at this university. In my interviews, I found that an overwhelming majority of the students and instructors responded that they saw no decline in the quality of education here.

It is clearly important to know what is meant by "quality of education" in the above paragraph. If you look up the word *quality* in the dictionary, you will find many meanings, the most appropriate, given this context, being *excellence* or *superiority*. *Excellence* and *superiority* are synonyms for *quality*—and they are equally abstract. You still need to know precisely what is meant by *excellence* or *superiority*. How do you know whether education is high in quality or excellence? Ideally, you would want the writer to tell you precisely what *behaviors* he is referring to when he uses the phrase "quality of education." Can you think of some different ways that the phrase might be defined? The following list presents some possible definitions of *quality of education*:

> Average grade-point average of students
> Ability of students to think critically
> Number of professors who have doctoral degrees
> Amount of work usually required to pass an exam

Each of these definitions suggests a different way to measure quality; each specifies a different criterion. Each provides a precise way in which the term could be used. Note also that each of these definitions will affect the degree to which you will want to agree with the author's reasoning. For example, if you believe that "quality" should refer to the ability of students to think critically, and most of the students in the interviews are defining it as how much work is required to pass an exam, the reason would not necessarily support the conclusion. Exams may not require the ability to think critically.

Thus, in many arguments you will not be able to find adequate dictionary definitions, and the context may not make the meaning clear. One way to discover possible alternative meanings is to try to create a mental picture of what the words represent. If you cannot do so, then you probably have identified an important ambiguity. Let's apply such a test to the following example.

> Welfare programs have not succeeded. They have not provided the poor with productive jobs.

The provision of productive jobs for the poor is the standard being used here to assess the worth of welfare programs. Can you create a single clear mental picture of *productive jobs*? Are there alternative definitions? Does *productive* mean "leading to greater profit" or "providing a sense of self-worth?" If you wanted to check on the accuracy of the reasoning, wouldn't you first need to know when a job is productive? You cannot count those jobs that are productive until the meaning of productive jobs is clarified. Thus, we have located an important ambiguity.

Limits of Your Responsibility to Clarify Ambiguity

After you have attempted to identify and clarify ambiguity, what can you do if you are still uncertain about the meaning of certain key ideas? What is a reasonable next step? We suggest you ignore any reason that contains ambiguity that makes it impossible to judge the acceptability of the reason. It is your responsibility as an active learner to ask questions that clarify ambiguity. However, your responsibility stops at that point. It is the writer or speaker who is trying to convince you of something. Her role as a persuader requires her to respond to your concerns about possible ambiguity.

You are not required to react to ideas or opinions that are unclear. If a friend tells you that you should enroll in a class because it "really is different," but cannot tell you how it is different, then you have no basis for agreeing or disagreeing with the advice. No one has the right to be believed if he cannot provide you with a clear picture of his reasoning.

Ambiguity and Effective Writing

Although most of this chapter is addressed to you as a critical reader, it is also extremely relevant to improved writing. Effective writers strive for clarity. They review their writing several times, looking for any statements that might be ambiguous.

Look back at the section on "Locating Key Terms and Phrases." Use the hints given there for finding important ambiguity to revise your own writing. For instance, abstractions that are ambiguous can be clarified by concrete illustrations, conveying the meaning you intend. Pay special attention to the reason and conclusion in any essay you write; ambiguity can be an especially serious problem in those elements.

Thinking about the characteristics of your intended audience can help you decide where ambiguities need to be clarified. Jargon or specific abstractions that would be very ambiguous to a general audience may be adequately understood by a specialized audience. Remember that the reader will probably not struggle for a long time with your meaning. If you confuse your reader, you will probably lose her quickly. If you never regain her attention, then you have failed in your task as a writer.

Summary

You cannot evaluate an essay until you know the meaning of key terms and phrases as well as meanings they might have had in the context of the argument, but did not. You can find important clues to potential ambiguity in the statement of the issue and can locate key words and phrases in the reasons and conclusions. Because many authors fail to define their terms and because many key terms have multiple meanings, you must search for possible ambiguity. You do this by asking the questions, What *could* be meant and What *is* meant by the key terms? Once you have completed the search, you will know four very important components of the reasoning:

1. the key terms and phrases,
2. which of these are adequately defined,
3. which of these possess other feasible definitions, which if substituted, would modify your reaction to the reasoning, and
4. which of these are ambiguous within the context of the discourse.

Practice Exercises

◊   *Critical Question:*   **What words or phrases are ambiguous?**

In the following passages, identify examples of ambiguity. Try to explain why the examples harm the reasoning.

Passage 1

We should treat drug taking in the same way we treat speech and religion, as a fundamental right. No one has to ingest any drug he does not want, just as no one has to read a particular book. Insofar as the state assumes control over such matters, it can only be in order to subjugate its citizens—by protecting them from temptations as befits children, and by preventing them from exercising self-determination over their lives as befits slaves.

Passage 2

Note: This passage is adapted from an opinion delivered by Mr. Chief Justice Burger in a Supreme Court response concerning the constitutionality of a Georgia obscenity statute.

We categorically disapprove the theory, apparently adopted by the trial judge, that obscene, pornographic films acquire constitutional immunity from state regulation simply because they are exhibited for consenting adults only. This holding was properly rejected by the Georgia Supreme Court. . . . In particular, we hold that there are legitimate state interests at stake in stemming the tide of commercialized obscenity, even assuming it is feasible to enforce effective safeguards against exposure to juveniles and passers by. Rights and interests other than those of the advocates are involved. These include the interest of the public in the quality of life and the total community environment, the tone of commerce in the great city centers, and possibly, the public safety itself . . .

As Mr. Chief Justice Warren stated, there is a "right of the Nation and of the States to maintain a decent society . . .," *Jacobellis v. Ohio*, 378 U.S. 184, 199 (1964) (dissenting opinion.) . . .

The sum of experience, including that of the past two decades, affords an ample basis for legislatures to conclude that a sensitive, key relationship of human existence, central to family life, community welfare and the development of human personality, can be debased and distorted by crass commercial exploitation of sex.

Passage 3

America has fallen behind in the utilization of nuclear energy plants. There are no new orders for nuclear power plants, yet other countries are building many such plants. America taught the world how to harness the atom. We simply cannot allow the rest of the world to walk away from us as leaders in this technology.

Nuclear power is safe, efficient and necessary for our nation's future energy security. In the course of 800 reactor years, not a single member of the public has been injured or killed; and for more than 2900 reactor years, American naval personnel have lived and worked alongside nuclear reactors traveling 60 million miles without a nuclear accident. No other technology can make similar claims; yet, the critics of nuclear energy persist in calling it unsafe. By any reasonable calculation nuclear power is going to be an essential generating source for American electricity in the next thirty years, and we must be ready to provide it.

──────────────────── Sample Responses ────────────────────

Passage 1

ISSUE: *Should the state regulate drug use?*

CONCLUSION: *Drug use should not be regulated by the state.*

REASONS: *1. It should be treated as we treat speech and religion, as a fundamental right.*

    2. Because drug use is voluntary, the state has no right to intervene.

What are the key phrases in this reasoning? "Drug taking," "fundamental right," "voluntary choice," "regulate drug consumption," and "subjugate citizens." You would first want to determine the meaning of each of these phrases. Is it clear what is meant by drug taking? No. The limited context provided fails to reveal an adequate definition. If drug taking refers to the ingestion of drugs that are not considered highly addictive, such as marijuana, wouldn't you be more likely to accept the reasoning than if the author included heroin within his definition of drugs? Can you tell from the argument whether the author is referring to all drugs or only to a subset of currently regulated drugs? To be able to agree to disagree with the author requires in this instance a more careful definition of what is meant by *drugs*. Do any others need further clarification before you can decide to agree with the author?

Passage 2

ISSUE: *Does the state have the right to regulate obscene materials?*

CONCLUSION: *Yes.*

REASONS: *1. The Nation and the States have a right to maintain a decent society.*

2. Experience proves that crass commercial exploitation of sex debases and distorts sexual relationships.

The issue and conclusion jointly inform us that we are going to need to know what the author means by obscene materials before we can decide whether we want to agree with his arguments. Since the context we are given fails to clearly specify the meaning of obscene, we find it difficult to agree or disagree with the conclusion because obscenity can have so many plausible meanings. For example, we might react differently to a definition emphasizing nudity than to a definition emphasizing perversity in sexual behavior. Thus obscenity is an important ambiguity in the context of this essay.

Several key phrases within the reasoning structure need clarification before we can evaluate the reasoning. Certainly, "maintaining a decent society" can have multiple meanings, and the author's reference to quality of life and total community environment, tone of commerce, and public safety is not as helpful as we would like. Given this language we would have a difficult time determining whether showing pornographic films "debases society." In fact, some might argue that restricting the right to show such films "debases society," because it restricts a "freedom."

We have a similar problem in reason 2. What is the meaning of debasing and distorting a sensitive key relationship? We think there are multiple plausible meanings, some that might be consistent with the impact of pornography and some that might not be.

Passage 3

ISSUE: *Should America increase its reliance on nuclear power?*

CONCLUSION: *America needs to build more nuclear power plants.*

REASONS: *1. Nuclear power is safe, efficient, and necessary for our nation's future energy security.*

2. Nuclear power is going to be an essential generating source for American electricity in the next thirty years.

Before we could adequately evaluate the first reason, we would like a clarification of "efficient" and "necessary;" and in Reason 2, we would need to know more about the meaning of "essential generating source." Just how bad off are we likely to be in the next thirty years if we fail to build nuclear reactor plants? What makes a generating source "essential?"

Passage 4 (Self-Examination)

I would like to point out some of the incompatibilities between gospel Christianity and capitalism as we know them. By capitalism, I mean not simply an economic system but the great productive network that spreads over our social, political, and cultural life. That is, I understand capitalism as a total environment in which we are reared and conditioned . . . . I maintain that certain general but essential orientations of the Gospel Way and the American Way are contradictory . . . .

Capitalism, as an economic system geared mainly to maximizing profits, fosters intense individualism. On the other hand, the core beliefs of the Judeo-Christian tradition stress communal consciousness . . . . Capitalism as we know it puts a high premium on the possession of material goods . . . . The gospel commands us to share material goods, not to amass them . . . . Capitalism depends on intense competitiveness coupled with overt and covert forms of violence. Family and school inculcate the spirit of rugged individualism, of getting ahead and rising to the top. Whether in athletics, academe, business or profession, competition requires that the neighbor be more or less violently put down . . . . The compulsion to compete and achieve is all pervasive. In this milieu, to be human is to be violent toward nature, self, and others. For only the respectably aggressive will possess goods, status, and selfhood . . . . The competitive ethos with its undercurrents of violence is diametrically opposed to Judeo-Christian teaching.[1]

[1]Adapted from D. L. Bender, *American Values*, 2nd ed. (St. Paul, MN: Greenhaven Press, Inc., 1984), pp. 107–111.

V

What Are the Value Conflicts and Assumptions?

When someone is trying to convince you of her point of view, she may be shrewd. She will present reasons that are consistent with her position. That is why, at first glance, most arguments "make sense." The visible structure looks good. But the reasons that are *stated* are not the only ideas that the person is using to prove or support her opinion. Hidden or unstated thoughts may be at least as significant in understanding her argument. Let's examine the importance of these unstated ideas by considering the following brief argument.

> The government should prohibit the manufacture and sale of cigarettes. More and more evidence has demonstrated that smoking has harmful effects on the health of both the smoker and those exposed to smoking.

The reason—at first glance—supports the conclusion. If the government wants to prohibit a product, it makes sense that it should provide evidence that the product is bad. But it is also possible that the reason given can be true and yet *not necessarily* support the conclusion. What if you believe that it is the individual's responsibility to take care of his own welfare, not the collective responsibility of government. If so, from your perspective, the reason no longer supports the conclusion. This reasoning is convincing to you only if you agree with certain unstated ideas that the writer has taken for granted. In this case, an idea taken for granted is that collective responsibility is more desirable than individual responsibility when an individual's welfare is threatened.

In all arguments, there will be certain ideas taken for granted by the writer. Typically, these ideas will not be stated. You will have to find them by reading between the lines. These ideas are important invisible links in the reasoning structure, the glue that holds the entire argument together. Until you supply these links, you cannot truly understand the argument.

Your task is similar in many ways to having to reproduce a magic trick without having seen how the magician did the trick. You see the handkerchief go into the hat and the rabbit come out, but you are not aware of the magician's hidden maneuvers. To understand the trick, you must discover these maneuvers. Likewise, in arguments, you must discover the hidden maneuvers, which in actuality are unstated ideas. We shall refer to these unstated ideas as *assumptions*. To fully understand an argument, you must identify the assumptions.

Assumptions are

1. hidden or unstated (in most cases),
2. taken for granted,
3. influential in determining the conclusion,
4. necessary, if the reasoning is to make sense, and
5. potentially deceptive.

This chapter and the next one will show you how to discover assumptions. We will focus on one kind of assumption in this chapter—value assumptions.

◊ *Critical Question:* **What are the value conflicts and assumptions?**

General Guide for Identifying Assumptions

When you seek assumptions, where and how should you look? In any book, discussion, or article are numerous assumptions, but you need to be concerned about relatively few. As you remember, the visible structure of an argument is contained in reasons and conclusions. Thus, you are interested only in assumptions that affect the quality of this structure. You can restrict your search for assumptions, therefore, to the structure you have already learned how to identify. **Look for assumptions in the movement from reasons to conclusions!**

Value Conflicts and Assumptions

Why is it that some very reasonable people charge that abortion is murder, while other equally reasonable observers see abortion as humane? Have you ever wondered why every President, regardless of his political beliefs, eventually gets involved in a dispute with the press over publication of government information that he would prefer not to share? How can some highly intelligent observers attack the publication of sexually explicit magazines and others defend their publication as the ultimate test of our Bill of Rights?

The primary answer to all these questions is the existence of value conflicts or different frames of reference. For ethical or prescriptive arguments, an individual's values influence the reasons he provides and, consequently, his conclusion. Value assumptions—beliefs about which values are most important—are, therefore, very important assumptions for such arguments. You should make it a habit to find out whether the value assumptions on which reasons are based are consistent with your own value assumptions before accepting or rejecting a conclusion.

Some of the most fundamental assumptions are those relating to value priorities. The rest of this chapter is devoted to increasing your awareness of the role played by value conflicts in determining a person's opinions or conclusions. This awareness will help you to locate and evaluate this important type of assumption.

Discovering Values

Before you can discover the importance of values in shaping conclusions, you must have some understanding of what a value is. Values may be objects, experiences, actions, or ideas that someone thinks are worthwhile. You will find, however, that it is the importance one assigns to abstract *ideas*, that has the major influence on one's choices and behavior. Usually objects, experiences, and actions are desired because of some idea we value. For example, we may choose to do things that provide us with contacts with important people. We probably value "important people" because we value "status." When we use the word *value* in this chapter, we will be referring to an idea representing what someone thinks is important and will strive to achieve.

To better familiarize yourself with values, write down some of your own values. Try to avoid writing down the names of people, tangible objects, or actions. Bruce Springsteen, pizza, and playing tennis may be important to you, but it is the importance you assign to ideas that most influences your choices and behavior concerning controversial public issues. Your willingness to argue for or against capital punishment, for instance, is strongly related to the importance you assign to the sanctity of human life—an abstract idea. The sanctity of human life is a value that affects our opinions about war, abortion, drug usage, and mercy killing. As you create your list of values, focus on those that are so significant that they affect your opinions and behavior in many ways.

Did you have problems making your list? We can suggest two further aids that may help. First, another definition! Values are *standards of conduct* that we endorse and expect people to meet. When we expect our political representatives to "tell the truth," we are indicating to them and to ourselves that honesty is one of our most cherished values. Ask yourself what you expect your friends to be like. What standards of conduct would you want your children to develop? Answers to these questions should help you enlarge your understanding of values.

When you are thinking about standards of conduct as a means of discovering values, recognize that certain conduct has an especially significant effect on your life. Certain values have a larger personal and social impact than others. Politeness, for instance, is a standard of conduct and a value, but it does not have the major impact on our lives that a value such as competition has. The point here is that certain values have greater consequences than others. Thus, you will usually want to focus on the values that most affect our behavior.

Now let us give you an aid for identifying values—a list of some commonly held values. Every value on our list may be an attractive candidate for your list. Thus, after you look at our list, pause for a moment and choose those values that are most important to you. They will be those values that most often play a role in shaping your opinions and behavior.

COMMON VALUES

tradition	autonomy	individual responsibility
adventure	wisdom	excellence
novelty	collective responsibility	flexibility
equality of opportunity	obedience to authority	spontaneity
equality of condition	honesty	patriotism
ambition	comfort	justice
courage	peace	tolerance
generosity	security	self-control
independence	freedom of speech	competition
rationality	harmony	cooperation
order	creativity	productivity

From Values to Value Assumptions

To identify value assumptions, we must go beyond a simple listing of values. Many of your values are shared by others. Wouldn't almost anyone claim that flexibility, cooperation, and honesty are desirable? Because many values are shared, values by themselves are not a powerful guide to understanding. What leads you to answer a prescriptive question differently from someone else is the relative intensity with which each of you holds specific values.

Difference in intensity of allegiance to particular values can easily be seen by thinking about responses to controversies when pairs of values collide or conflict. While it is not very enlightening to discover that most people value both competition and cooperation, we do gain a more complete understanding of prescriptive choices as we discover who *prefers* competition to cooperation when the two values conflict.

A writer's preferences for particular values are often unstated, but they will have a major impact on her conclusion and on how she chooses to defend it. These unstated assertions about value priorities function as *value assumptions*. Some refer to these assumptions as *value judgments*. Recognition of relative support for conflicting values or sets of values provides you with both an improved understanding of what you are reading and a basis for eventual evaluation of prescriptive arguments.

When a writer takes a stand on controversial prescriptive issues, he is usually depreciating one commonly shared value while upholding another. For example, when someone advocates the required licensing of prospective parents, collective responsibility is being treated as more important than individual responsibility. So when you look for value assumptions, look for an indication of value preferences. Ask yourself what values are being upheld by this position and what values are being depreciated.

When you have found a person's value preference in a particular argument, you should not expect that same person to necessarily have the same value priority when discussing a different controversy. A person does not have the same value priorities without regard to the issue being discussed. In Chapter XIV you will learn about how people often select their value assumptions; you will realize that it is unlikely that a person would maintain a rigid set of value assumptions that he would apply to every controversy.

Typical Value Conflicts

If you are aware of typical value conflicts, you can more quickly recognize the assumptions being made by a writer when she reaches a particular conclusion. We have listed some of the more common value conflicts that occur in ethical issues and have provided you with examples of controversies in which these value conflicts are likely to be evident. We anticipate that you can use this list as a starting point when you are trying to identify important value assumptions.

TYPICAL VALUE CONFLICTS AND SAMPLE CONTROVERSIES

1. loyalty—honesty	1. Should you tell your parents about your sister's drug habit?
2. competition—cooperation	2. Do you support the grading system?
3. freedom of press—national security	3. Is it wise to hold weekly Presidential press conferences?
4. equality—individualism	4. Are racial quotas for employment fair?
5. order—freedom of speech	5. Should we imprison those with radical ideas?
6. security—excitement	6. Should you choose a dangerous profession?
7. generosity—material success	7. Is it desirable to give financial help to a beggar?
8. rationality—spontaneity	8. Should you check the odds before placing a bet?
9. tradition—novelty	9. Should divorces be easily available?

As you identify value conflicts, you will often find that there are several value conflicts that seem important in shaping conclusions with respect to particular controversies. When evaluating a controversy, try to find several value conflicts, as a check on yourself. Some controversies will have one primary value conflict; others may have several.

Take another look at number 7 in the preceding list. It is quite possible that value conflicts besides that between generosity and material success affect your decision about whether to give financial help to a beggar. For instance, all the following value conflicts may affect a person's willingness to help a beggar:

1. individual responsibility—collective responsibility
2. competition—cooperation
3. efficiency—social stability

By identifying as many of the relevant value assumptions as possible, you have a better chance of not missing any of the important dimensions of the argument. However, you may have no way of knowing which value assumptions are actually responsible for the author's conclusion.

The Background as a Clue to Value Assumptions

It has already been suggested that a good starting point in finding value assumptions is to check the background of the author. Find out as much as you can about the value preferences usually held by a person like the writer. Is he a big-businessman, a union leader, a Republican Party official, a doctor, or an apartment tenant? What interests does such a person naturally wish to protect? There's certainly nothing inherently wrong with pursuing self-interest, but such pursuits often limit the value assumptions a particular writer will tolerate. For example, it's highly unlikely that the president of a major automobile firm would place a high value on efficiency when a preference for efficiency rather than stability would lead to his losing his job. Consequently, you as a critical reader can often quickly discover value preferences by thinking about the probable assumptions made by a person like the writer.

One caution is important. It isn't necessarily true that, because a writer is a member of a group, she shares the particular value assumptions of the group. It would be mistake to presume that every individual who belongs to a given group thinks identically. We all know that businessmen, farmers, and firemen sometimes disagree among themselves when discussing particular controversies. Investigating the writer's background as a clue to her value assumptions is only a clue, and like other clues it can be misleading unless it is used with care.

Consequences as a Clue to Value Assumptions

In prescriptive arguments, each position with respect to an issue leads to different consequences or outcomes when the position is acted upon. Each of the potential consequences will have a certain likelihood of occurring, and each will also have some level of desirability or undesirability. How desirable a consequence is will depend on a writer's or reader's personal value preferences. The desirability of the conclusions in such cases will be dictated by the probability of the potential consequences and the importance attached to them. Thus, an important means of determining an individual's value assumptions is to examine the reasons given in support of a conclusion and then to determine what value preferences would lead to these reasons being judged as more desirable than reasons that might have been offered on the other side of the issue. Let's take a look at a concrete example.

> ARGUMENT: *Nuclear power plants should not be built because they will pollute our environment.*

The reason provided here is a rather specific potential consequence of building nuclear plants. This writer clearly sees environmental pollution as very undesirable. Why does this consequence carry so much weight in this person's thinking? What more general value does preventing pollution help achieve? Probably conservation, or perhaps naturalness. Someone else might stress a different consequence in this argument, such as the effect on the supply of electricity to consumers. Why? Probably because he values efficiency very highly. Thus, this reason supports the conclusion *if* a value assumption is made that conservation is more important then efficiency.

Note that the *magnitude* of a consequence may have a major impact on value preferences. One may value conservation over efficiency only when efficiency may cause "significant" damage to the environment. And one may value free enterprise over economic security only as long as unemployment stays below a given level.

It is possible for people to have different conclusions, while having identical value assumptions, because they disagree about the likelihood or magnitude of consequences.

One important means of determining value assumptions, then, is to ask the question, Why do the particular consequences or outcomes presented as reasons seem so desirable to the writer or speaker?

Remember: When you identify *value assumptions,* you should always state *value preferences.* With controversial topics, stating value assumptions in this way will be a continual reminder both of what the writer is *giving up* and of what she is gaining.

More Hints for Finding Value Assumptions.

Many social controversies share important characteristics; they are thus *analogous* to one another. The value preferences implicit in a certain controversy can sometimes be discovered by searching for analogous elements in other social controversies. Do any common characteristics have their origin in a similar value conflict?

Let's ask, for instance, how a particular controversy is similar to other controversies, and see whether the answer gives us a clue to an important value assumption.

Should the government require car manufacturers to include air bags in automobiles?

What are the important characteristics of this controversy? The controversy, more generally, asks whether collective groups, such as the government, should intervene in people's lives to help them protect themselves. Such an intervention is analogous to banning cigarette advertising, requiring motorcycle riders to wear helmets, and banning boxing. Once you have recognized the similarity of these issues, you should be able to see how certain values will dictate individuals' positions on them. Someone who believes that the government should require air bags in cars is also likely to believe that the government should ban cigarette advertising. Why? Because he values collective responsibility and public safety more than individual responsibility.

See if you can name a controversy analogous to the following:

Should it be legal for newspaper and television reporters to refuse to reveal their confidential sources?

How did you do? We thought of the question of whether psychiatrists should be allowed to refuse to testify about their patients in murder trials. Whatever different examples you thought of, our guess is that your thinking made you aware of some important values, such as privacy, the public's right to know, or public safety. Awareness of value conflicts is a necessary step toward determining value assumptions.

Another useful technique for generating value conflicts is to *reverse role-play*. Ask the question, What do those people who would take a different position from the writer's care about? When someone argues that we should not use monkeys in experimental research, you should ask yourself, If I wanted to defend the use of monkeys, what would I be concerned about? Remember, when someone takes a position on a controversial topic, she will be revealing a value *preference*. Your knowledge of that preference will help you to decide whether or not to agree with her conclusion.

Finding Value Assumptions on your Own

Let's work on an example together to help you become more comfortable with finding value assumptions.

Congress is attempting to pass legislation that will reduce the level of commercial exploitation currently present in children's television. The proposal calls for limitations on the number and type of commercials permitted during children's programming. This proposal has met with great opposition from those who insist that parents, not legislators, should monitor TV. They maintain that parents alone must take responsibility for their children's TV viewing.

Supporters of the proposal, however, point out that children's shows have turned into half-hour commercials. To protect children from the blatant exploitation of commercialism, they insist that government regulation is necessary. They demand that children's programming respect the special needs and relative immaturity of the young, rather than manipulating them for profit.

The structure of the two positions is outlined here for you:

CONCLUSION: *The government should not regulate children's television programming.*

REASON: *Parents should be the source of any such regulation.*

CONCLUSION: *The government should regulate children's programming.*

REASON: *Children are especially vulnerable to exploitation by those wishing to profit from television programming.*

Notice that the opposition reasons that regulation is undesirable because it infringes upon the individual parent's responsibility to monitor the TV. They believe that it is up to the individual to decide what is and is not desirable. Thus, government regulation impinges on their individual responsibility for monitoring what happens in their own home.

VALUE ASSUMPTION: *In this context, individual responsibility is more important than collective responsibility.*

On the other hand, supporters of the proposal insist that help from an instrument of the community such as the government, is necessary for the greater good of the nation's children. They believe that a reduction in the exploitation of children is worth a minor cutback in individual responsibility. They think that the collective action of the government can more effectively reduce exploitation than the efforts of individuals.

VALUE ASSUMPTION: *In this situation, collective responsibility is more important than personal responsibility.*

Therefore, the major value conflict is collective responsibility vs. individual responsibility. A supporter of the proposal makes the value assumption that laws that will protect children are more important than unchecked individual responsibility. Her stance on this issue does not mean that she does not value individual responsibility; both values are probably very important to her. In this case, however, collective responsibility has taken priority. Similarly, opponents of the proposal do not advocate the exploitation of children. In this case, they believe that the preservation of individual responsibility takes precedence over collective action.

Remember that conclusions with respect to prescriptive issues require reasons *and* value assumptions.

Reasons + Value Assumption = Conclusion.

Let's complete one more example together.

Students should obey a dress code that includes uniforms, shoe restrictions, and hair length. In such an educational setting, teachers can teach and students can learn. Valuable time and energy will not be wasted on the discipline problems that arise in the absence of a rigid dress code.

Let's first outline the structure of the argument.

CONCLUSION: *Students should obey a rigid dress code.*

REASON: *Discipline problems would be reduced by obedience to a such a code.*

What value assumption do you think would result in someone's support for a rigid dress code for the schools? Look back at the table on page 46. Would any of the sample value conflicts affect one's reaction to school dress codes and the use of the above reasoning? Try to explain how a preference for educational excellence over individual self-expression might affect your reaction to this controversy.

Identifying value assumptions is not only necessary to understand why someone makes a particular claim, but it will also help you relate the various conclusions arrived at by the same individual. As we try to understand one another, it is sometimes helpful to recognize patterns in our behavior. One key to patterns of human behavior is an appreciation of value conflicts. Although you cannot be sure, it is a good first guess to predict that those who prefer to see campus police with weapons will also favor a hard-line approach to negotiations with the Soviet Union, spanking as a form of discipline, and tougher jail sentences for juvenile delinquents.

Summary

Assumptions are unstated ideas, taken for granted in the reasoning. Value assumptions are one type of unstated idea consisting of a preference for one value over another in a particular context. The author's background, reaction to projected consequences of acting on a particular value assumption, analogous controversies, and reverse role-playing all provide possible clues for finding a person's value assumptions in a particular controversy.

Practice Exercises

◊   *Critical Question:*   **What are the value conflicts and assumptions?**

Identify the value conflicts that could lead to agreement or disagreement with the following points of view, then identify the value priorities assumed by the writer.

Passage 1

Some members of our society receive outrageous sums of money each year. Athletes, entertainers, and executives receive incomes that most of us can hardly imagine. At the same time, in the same country, other people are unable to heat their homes, afford nutritious meals, or finance an automobile. No one should be allowed to make a salary that is 100 times larger than that of the average person.

Passage 2

We rarely tell young people the truth about marriage. The truth is that marriage is a terrible habit. It ruins voluntary love. Exciting romances are changed into dull marriages. What was a love affair becomes a grinding, limiting contract.

Passage 3

For most people, college is a waste of time and money. One does not need schools to learn. If you go to college to make it possible to earn more money, you have been had. More than half of those who earn more than $25,000 never received a college diploma. What you do learn in college is rarely useful on the job. Most of you would be better off saving part of the money you earn while your naïve friends are in college.

—————————————— Sample Responses ——————————————

Passage 1

CONCLUSION: *No one should make more than 100 times the salary of the average worker.*

REASON: *The gap between rich and poor is preventing some Americans from having basic necessities.*

One value conflict that would cause readers to disagree is that between equal opportunity and equality of condition. The argument depends on the importance of everyone's having the basic necessities. The existence of huge incomes limits the amount of money left over for others to buy those necessities. Hence those who value equality of condition more than equality of opportunity may well argue that regardless of the similar opportunities available to all workers, each of us should be guaranteed a basic level of goods and services.

Passage 2

CONCLUSION: *Marriage should be discouraged.*

REASONS: *1. Love is no longer voluntary when one marries.*
2. Marriage is relatively dull and repetitive.

One value conflict is between security and variety. The author apparently prefers variety to security. He criticizes marriage as dull and habitual. Those who value security more than variety may well disagree with the author.

Passage 3

CONCLUSION: *Most young people should not attend college.*

REASONS: *1. Many of those who make a lot of money never attended college.*
2. College does not generally teach job-related skills.

A value assumption is that materialistic achievement is more important than wisdom. Notice that the consequence stressed by the author is the impact of college on future income. She addresses none of the other purposes one might have for attending college. If one valued wisdom more than monetary accumulation, one might well reject the reasoning suggested in this passage.

Passage 4 (Self-Examination)

Affirmative action is really just reverse racism. By giving preferential treatment to minority applicants, employers are behaving no differently than those who favor whites. A person should be judged by his merits, qualifications, and competence. Skin color should not be a consideration. Those who are the best qualified should be rewarded with the employment they seek. They have prepared carefully; to ignore that preparation to meet a minority quota is unjust.

Abe Lincoln once said, "You cannot strengthen the weak by weakening the strong." Affirmative action does just that. If employers are forced to employ lesser qualified minority applicants, an image of minority incompetence will be perpetuated. It is only right that those who have excelled and worked diligently receive the opportunities they deserve.

VI
What Are the Descriptive Assumptions?

You will learn a lot from Professor Starr. His students all rave about his lectures.

You should now be able to identify value assumptions—very important hidden links in prescriptive arguments. When you find value assumptions, you know pretty well what a writer wants the world to be like—what ideas he thinks are most important to strive for. But you do not know what he takes for granted about what the world was, is, or will be like. His visible reasoning depends on these ideas, as well as upon his values. Such unstated ideas are descriptive assumptions, and they are essential hidden links in an argument.

Our brief argument concerning Professor Starr depends upon such hidden assumptions. Can you find them?

This chapter focuses on the identification of descriptive assumptions.

◊   *Critical Question:*   **What are the descriptive assumptions?**

Illustrating Descriptive Assumptions

Let's examine our argument about Professor Starr more closely to illustrate more clearly what we can mean by a descriptive assumption.

The reasoning structure is:

CONCLUSION: *You will learn a lot from Professor Starr.*

REASON: *His students all rave about his lectures.*

The reasoning thus far is incomplete. We know that, *by itself*, a reason cannot support a conclusion; the reason must be connected to the conclusion by certain other (frequently unstated) ideas. These ideas are ones, which if true, justify treating the reason as support for the conclusion. Thus, whether a reason supports, or is relevant to, a conclusion depends upon whether we can locate unstated ideas that logically connect the reason to the conclusion. When such unstated ideas are descriptive, we choose to call them descriptive connecting assumptions. Let us present two such assumptions for the above argument.

ASSUMPTION 1: *Student comments are a good indicator of lecture quality.*

First, note that *if* the reason is true and *if* this assumption is true, then the reason provides some support for the conclusion. If students, however, rave about lectures because of their entertainment value rather than because of their informational value, then the reason given is not supportive of the conclusion. Next, note that this assumption is a statement about the way things *are*, not about the way things *should be*. Thus, it is a *descriptive assumption*.

ASSUMPTION 2: *To learn a lot means to absorb material from a lecture.*

(Sponge model thinking, right?) If "learn a lot" is defined as developing thinking skills, then the amount of raving about lectures may be irrelevant. Thus, this conclusion is supported by the reason only if a certain definition of learning is assumed.

Once you have identified the connecting assumptions, you have answered the question, "On what basis can that conclusion be drawn from that reason?" The next natural step is to ask, "Is there any basis for accepting the assumptions?" If not, then, for you, the reason fails to provide support for the conclusion.

Note that there are further hidden assumptions in the above argument. For example, you should not be convinced by this reasoning unless you believe that the qualities others look for in lectures are the same qualities you look for. Should you eat at a restaurant because many of your friends rave about it? Wouldn't you want to know *why* they rave about it? *Remember:* Reasoning will usually contain multiple assumptions.

Note also that when you identify assumptions, you identify ideas the writer *needs* to take for granted for the reason to be supportive of the conclusion. Because writers frequently are not aware of their own assumptions, their conscious beliefs may be quite different from the ideas you identify as implicit assumptions.

Clues for Locating Assumptions

Your job in finding assumptions is to reconstruct the reasoning by filling in the missing gaps. That is, you want to provide ideas that help the writer's reasoning "make sense." Once you have a picture of the entire argument, both the visible and the invisible parts, you will be in a much better position to determine its strengths and weaknesses.

How does one go about finding these important missing links? It requires hard work, imagination, and creativity. Finding important assumptions is a difficult task.

You have been introduced to two types of assumptions—value assumptions and descriptive assumptions. In the previous chapter, we gave you several hints for finding value assumptions. Here are some clues that will make your search for descriptive assumptions successful.

Keep thinking about the gap between the conclusion and reasons. Why are you looking for assumptions in the first place? You are looking because you want to be able to judge how well the reasons support the conclusions. Thus, look for what the writer would have had to take for granted to link the reasons and conclusion. Keep asking, How do you get from the reason to the conclusion? Ask, *"If the reason is true, what else must be true for the conclusion to follow?"* And to help answer that question, you will find it very helpful to ask, *"Supposing the reason(s) were true, is there any way in which the conclusion nevertheless could be false?"*

Searching for the gap will be helpful for finding both value and descriptive assumptions.

Look for ideas that support reasons. Sometimes a reason is presented with no explicit support; yet, the plausibility of the reason depends upon the acceptability of ideas taken for granted. The following brief argument illustrates such a case:

CONCLUSION: *We need to increase the money spent on AIDS education.*

REASON: *If we do so, it will greatly reduce the number of cases of AIDS.*

What ideas must be taken for granted for this reason to be acceptable? We must assume:

(a) the money will be spent in an effective manner; in other words, the education will reach members of high risk groups that are not already being reached, and

(b) such members will be willing and able to respond to the educational message.

Thus, both (a) and (b) are ideas that have to be taken for granted for the reasons to be acceptable, and thus supportive of the conclusion.

Identify with the writer. Locating someone's assumptions is often made easier by imagining that you were asked to defend the conclusion. If you can, crawl into the skin of a person who would reach such a conclusion. Discover the writer's background. Whether the person whose conclusion you are evaluating is a corporate executive, a communist, a labor leader, a boxing promoter, or a judge, try to play the role of such a person and plan in your mind what he would be thinking as he moved toward the conclusion. When an executive for a coal company argues that strip mining does not significantly harm the beauty of our natural environment, he has probably begun with a belief that strip mining is beneficial to our nation. Thus, he may assume a definition of beauty that would be consistent with his arguments, while other definitions of beauty would lead to a condemnation of strip mining.

Identify with the opposition. If you are unable to locate assumptions by taking the role of the speaker or writer, try to reverse roles. Ask yourself why anyone might disagree with the conclusion. What type of reasoning would prompt someone to disagree with the conclusion you are evaluating? If you can play the role of a person who would not accept the conclusion, you can more readily see assumptions in the original structure.

Recognize the potential existence of other means of attaining the advantages referred to in the reasons. Frequently, a conclusion is supported by reasons that indicate the various advantages of acting on the writer's conclusion. When there are many ways to reach the same advantages, one important assumption linking the reasons to the conclusion is that the best way to attain the advantages is through the author's conclusion.

Let's try this technique with one brief example. Many counselors would argue that a college freshman should be allowed to choose her own courses without any restrictions from parents or college personnel because it facilitates the growth of personal responsibility. But aren't there many ways to encourage the growth of personal responsibility? Might not some of these alternatives have less serious disadvantages than those that could result when a freshman makes erroneous judgements about which courses would be in her best long-term interest? For example, the development of personal responsibility is furthered by requiring a student to make a substantial financial contribution to the cost of her education. Thus, those who argue that it is desirable to permit college freshmen to make their own course choices because such an opportunity encourages personal responsibility are assuming that there are not less risky alternatives for accomplishing a similar goal.

Learn more about issues. The more familiar you are with all sides of a topic, the more easily you will be able to locate assumptions. Get as much information about the issues you care about as you can.

Avoid stating incompletely established reasons as assumptions. When you first attempt to locate assumptions you may find yourself locating a stated reason, thinking that the reason has not been adequately established, and asserting, ''That's only an assumption. You don't know that to be the case.'' Or you might simply restate the reason as the assumption. You may have correctly identified a need on the part of the writer to better establish the truth of his reason. While this is an important insight on your part, you have not identified an assumption in the sense that we have been using it in these two chapters. You are simply labeling a reason ''an assumption.''

Applying the Clues

Let's look at an argument about the impact of rock music and see whether we can identify descriptive and value assumptions.

The immense attraction of rock music for college students is having a negative impact on their scholarship. Books no longer claim the enthusiasm that is now directed to the rock star of the week. How can we expect students to struggle with a lengthy passage from Plato when they have become accustomed to experiencing the throbbing, pulsating, primitive excitement of rock music. Such music provides premature ecstasy—like a drug—an instant ecstasy that books and the classroom cannot provide them. Furthermore, with the emergence of the Walkman, students can be constantly plugged into music. With so much time devoted to music (the hours spent in line for concert tickets, the concerts themselves, not to mention listening time alone), studies must suffer from lack of attention.

Not only is rock music competing for our students' attention, but increasingly, students are turning to rock for answers to both personal and universal problems. The socially conscious rock star is the new hero of the young. The solutions offered by such rock stars, however, are guilty of oversimplification. The weighty problems of the day cannot be adequately addressed in a five-minute lyric. Nevertheless, students are absorbing the words of millionaire musicians with far more reverence than they display toward their lessons or professors.

CONCLUSION: *Rock music is having a negative impact upon college learning.*

REASONS: *1. Books require much contemplative effort; they thus can't compete with the easy, instant gratification provided by rock music.*
   2. Attention directed to rock music diverts attention from studies.
   3. Students are absorbing the oversimplified messages of the music rather than the complex ideas of their professors.

First, note that the author provides no "proof" for her reasons. Thus, you might be tempted to state, "Those reasons are only assumptions; she does not know that." Wrong! They are not *assumptions*! Remember: identifying less-than-fully established reasons, though important, is *not* the same as identifying assumptions— ideas that are taken for granted as a basic part of the argument.

Now, let's see whether any descriptive assumptions can be found in the argument. Remember to keep thinking about the gap between the conclusion and the reasons as you look. First, ask yourself, Is there any basis for believing that the reason(s) might not be true? Then ask, Supposing the reason(s) were true, is there any way in which the conclusion nevertheless could be false? Try to play the role of a person who is strongly attracted to rock music.

Look at the first two reasons. Neither would be true if it were the case that excitement of the passions and excitement of the intellect can work in harmony rather than in disharmony. Perhaps, listening to rock music reduces tension for students such that they are less distracted when engaging in intellectual effort. Thus, one descriptive assumption is that *attending to rock music does not provide a relaxation effect thereby increasing the amount of subsequent studying.* Also, for reason 2 to be true, it would have to be the case *that the time used for rock music is time that would otherwise be devoted to scholarly effort* (descriptive assumption). Perhaps the time devoted to rock music is "surplus time" for students.

Let's now suppose that the first two reasons were true. Rock music still might not have a negative impact upon learning if it is the case that students are so motivated to learn that they will make an effort to overcome any potential negative effects. Thus, an assumption connecting the first two reasons to the conclusion is that *students are not sufficiently motivated to learn to overcome the obstacles posed by rock music's attraction.* Another connecting assumption is that *those who listen often to rock music are the same students who would be interested in scholarly activity.*

How about the third reason? It is only true if it is the case that students process the messages of rock music just as they might process book and classroom messages. Perhaps the messages are processed as "entertainment," in the way a roller coaster ride is processed. Thus, an important assumption is that *students fail to discriminate between messages provided by rock music and those provided by the classroom.*

Note also that there is a prescriptive quality to this essay; thus important value assumptions will underlie the reasoning. What is the author concerned about preserving? Try role-playing in reverse. What would someone who disagreed with this position care about? What are the advantages to young people of listening to rock music? Your answers to these questions should lead you to the essay's value preference. For example, can you see how a preference for the cultivation of the intellect over gratification of the senses links the reasons to the conclusion?

Avoiding Analysis of Trivial Assumptions

Writers take for granted certain self-evident things that we should not concern ourselves about. You will want to devote your energy to evaluating important assumptions, so we want to warn you about some potential trivial assumptions.

You as a reader can assume that the writer believes his reasons are true. You may want to attack the reasons as insufficient, but it is trivial to point out the writer's assumption that they are true.

Another type of trivial assumption concerns the reasoning structure. You may be tempted to state that the writer believes that the reason and conclusion are logically related. Right—but trivial. What is important is *how* they are logically related. It is also trivial to point out that an argument assumes that we can understand the logic, that we can understand the terminology, or that we have the appropriate background knowledge.

Avoid spending time on analyzing trivial assumptions. Your search for assumptions will be most rewarding when you locate hidden, debatable missing links.

Evaluating Assumptions

After you have located assumptions, you must make an attempt to determine whether the assumptions make sense. You have not criticized a conclusion effectively simply because you have located assumptions in the reasoning. All of us assume many things when we communicate. Making assumptions is normal when we speak or write.

It is the quality of the assumptions that affects whether we should agree with a line of reasoning. If you have some basis for doubting the appropriateness of an assumption, then it is fair to reject the reason or conclusion that was propped up by that assumption. Don't be shy about disagreeing with a writer once you have identified her shaky assumptions. It is the writer's responsibility to justify any assumptions about which you have some doubt; if she doesn't do that satisfactorily, then you should refuse to accept her conclusions.

One final note concerning locating assumptions. In this chapter we have not discussed assumptions that fill in the gaps in arguments that rely heavily on statistical evidence. We make many assumptions when we use evidence to support conclusions. You will directly confront these assumptions as you read Chapters VII through IX. When you have completed them, you should be sensitive to many potential missing links in reasoning with evidence.

Summary

Assumptions are ideas that, if true, enable us to claim that particular reasons provide support for a conclusion. Several clues aid in discovering definitional assumptions.

1. Keep thinking about the gap between the conclusion and reasons.
2. Look for ideas that support reasons.
3. Identify with the opposition.
4. Recognize the potential existence of other means of attaining the advantages referred to in the reasons.
5. Learn more about the issues.

After you have found important assumptions, evaluate them in terms of other knowledge you already have.

Practice Exercises

◊ *Critical Question:* **What are the descriptive assumptions?**

For each of the three passages, locate important assumptions made by the author. Remember first to determine the conclusion and the reasons.

Passage 1

Reverence for human life is basic to the moral foundation of a just society. That is why the abolition of the death penalty is a major step in society's long road to civilization.

More than seventy nations have already recognized the immorality of the death penalty by abolishing it.

Executions offer few benefits to society, and instead present embarrassing evidence that our lust for vengeance often overpowers our humanity. Executions do not act as a deterrent to potential murders. Studies that have compared the murder rates in communities that do and do not have the death penalty have found no differences. Such evidence is not surprising: Murder is an irrational act, often an act of passion.

Passage 2

Should it be legal for newspaper and television reporters to refuse to reveal their confidential sources? Indeed it should. For the reporter-informant relationship is, after all, similar to those of priest and penitent, lawyer and client, physician and patient—all of which have a degree of privacy under the law. Moreover, if that relationship were not protected, the sources of information needed by the public would dry up.

Passage 3

Critical thinking programs will not work. Critical thinking skills should be taught like all other bodily skills, by coaching, not by combining lectures with textbooks that claim to teach people specific thinking skills. After all, we don't teach doctors and lawyers how to think critically by giving them a course in critical thinking. We require them to use critical thinking skills in all courses that they are taught. We teach them by coaching, by providing lots of practice and corrective feedback.

Thinking is not a skill that can be taught in isolation from other mental acts and from the content of our disciplines. Instead of developing critical thinking programs, we should be making sure that our students are coached in critical thinking in all their courses. If all our teachers would act as coaches and require our students to think about what is being taught instead of having them memorizing the facts, then we would not need critical thinking courses.

Sample Responses

In presenting assumptions for the following arguments, we will list only *some* of the assumptions being made—those which we believe to be among the most significant.

Passage 1

CONCLUSION: *We must abolish the death penalty.*

REASONS: *1. Abolishing the death penalty reflects reverence for human life.*
2. Many other nations have abolished the death penalty.
3. Executions reflect a societal attitude of vengeance, rather than humaneness.
4. Executions do not deter murder.

SUPPORT: *a. Studies comparing murder rates in communities that do and do not have the death penalty have shown no differences. b. Murder is an irrational act.*

To be acceptable, the first reason requires the descriptive assumption that *reverence for human life is best shown by society's refraining from making a choice to take a life.* If one defined reverence for human life as society's decreeing that those who take another's life must forfeit their own, then capital punishment would not be viewed as immoral.

For the second reason to support the conclusion, the reasoning must assume that *our country is highly similar in its beliefs, attitudes, and values to these other countries.* If there are major differences among these countries and ours—in attitudes toward personal responsibility and punishment, for example—then the position of these other countries toward capital punishment may not be very relevant. (As critical thinkers, we should ask, Why have these countries rejected capital punishment?)

The fourth reason relies upon evidence comparing murder rates among communities. Thus, to accept the reason as true, one must assume that the *comparisons between communities allowed sufficient time for the effects of executions to occur.* Also, the credibility of the reasoning requires the assumption that *the executions have been highly publicized in these comparison communities.*

When the author argues in the fourth reason that executions do not deter murders because murders are acts of passion, he assumes *that passion is such an intense emotion that rational processes are totally impaired.* But perhaps, even in moments of passion, potential murderers may have *some* awareness of possible consequences.

We have listed some assumptions; you can determine others by carefully looking for gaps in the reasoning.

Passage 2

CONCLUSION: *It should be legal for newspaper and television reporters to refuse to reveal their confidential sources.*

REASONS: *1. The reporter-informant relationship is special.*
2. If the relationship is not protected, sources of information will dry up.

The author compares the reporter-informant relationship to others. Reason 1 will be less acceptable if the reasons for privacy of lawyer and client or physician and patient are quite different from what they are for the reporter-informant relationship. For example, reporters, unlike these other professionals, regularly make their information public, creating a number of social consequences for individuals in society.

A major assumption necessary for reason 2 to be acceptable is that most of the information reporters rely upon for their stories comes from sources who would be so severely frightened by the threat of being revealed that they would refuse to provide information. It may be the case that many individuals would still come forth to provide information because they could tolerate the risk.

Passage 3

CONCLUSION: *Critical thinking programs will not work.*

REASON: *Such skills can be taught better by coaching students within their respective disciplines.*
    a. Lawyers and physicians are taught by coaching, not by critical thinking courses.
    b. Thinking cannot be taught apart from the content of a discipline.

Try reverse role playing, taking the position of someone who teaches a critical thinking course, perhaps using *Asking the Right Questions.*

For the reason to support the conclusion, it must be true that most critical thinking courses do rely on lectures, not on coaching, or on practice of the skills.

Does the example support the reason? It does if the procedures used to train lawyers and physicians to think are successful. Perhaps these professionals could benefit greatly from a critical thinking course that focuses on basic skills.

This entire argument rests on the assumption that it is not helpful to later coaching to have a good grounding in the basic skills. Coaching might be most successful in cases where the learner has been explicitly taught the basic skills at an earlier time. There is also a "wishful thinking" assumption implied by the first reason. Because students *need* coaching in all courses does not mean they will necessarily get such coaching.

Passage 4

I'd like to try to get a point through the hard heads of those pushing to raise the legal drinking age to 21. Their behavior is designed to make more young men and women law violators. When I was 18, I drank beer when it was against the law, and if I had to do it all over again, knowing myself at 18, I'd probably do it all over again. And I don't think I was different from a lot of 18-year-olds.

If young people are old enough to go to Lebanon, or Germany, or Nicaragua, they are old enough to take a legal drink. If they are old enough to own property, drive cars, hold jobs, have children, raise them, and pay taxes, then they are old enough to take a drink.

Have we really given up on education? Have we given up on teachers, and preachers, and parents who are supposed to teach our young how to perform responsibly as young adults? Are we just going to throw another problem at the police and say, "Fix it?"

VII

How Good Is the Evidence: Are the Samples Representative and the Measurements Valid?

Thus far, you have been working at taking the raw materials a writer gives you and assembling them into a meaningful overall structure. You have learned ways to remove the irrelevant parts from your pan as well as how to discover the "invisible glue" that holds the relevant parts together—that is, the assumptions. You have learned to do this by asking critical questions. Let's briefly review these questions.

1. What are the issue and the conclusion?
2. What are the reasons?
3. What words or phrases are ambiguous?
4. What are the value conflicts and assumptions?
5. What are the descriptive assumptions?

Most remaining chapters will focus on how well the structure holds up after being assembled. Your major question now is, How acceptable is the conclusion? You are now ready to **evaluate**. *Remember:* The objective of critical reading is to judge the acceptability or worth of the different conclusions that can be reached concerning an issue. Making these judgments will prepare you for forming a rational personal opinion—the ultimate benefit of asking the right questions.

Let's examine one kind of statement that we will need to evaluate carefully— claims about the "facts."

> Studies show that eating oat bran reduces the risk of cancer.
> Infidelity is rampant in the United States; over 40 percent of married men admit to having affairs.
> The fact of the matter is the Japanese are building better cars.

College campuses are not safe; research shows that on-campus assaults have increased by 10 percent over the last three years.

What do we make of these claims? Are they legitimate? Most reasoning includes claims such as these. In this chapter, we will suggest an important question to ask about such claims.

◊　*Critical Question:　**Are the samples representative and the measurements valid?***

Looking for Evidence

You begin the evaluative process by persistently asking authors at every step in their argument, "What's your *evidence*?" The answers will vary greatly from topic to topic and from person to person in kind and quality. You may encounter any of the following as evidence—examples from real life, statistical analysis of research findings, analogies or metaphors, and appeals to authority. Frequently, you will find conclusions supported by no evidence.

When used appropriately, each kind of evidence can be "good evidence." It can help support an author's claim. Like a gold prospector closely examining the gravel in his pan for potentially high quality ore, we must closely examine the evidence to determine its quality. We want to know, Does what an author *says* supports his claim truly do so? Thus, we begin the evaluative process by asking, *How good is the evidence?*

Virtually all arguments include factual claims—statements about what the world is like, was like, or will be like. To evaluate arguments, we need to decide whether to believe these claims.

Our next three chapters focus on questions we need to ask to decide how well authors have supported their factual claims. We encounter such claims either as descriptive conclusions or as reasons used to support a descriptive or prescriptive conclusion.

Let's examine the factual claim (1) as a descriptive conclusion, then (2) as a reason supporting a conclusion.

(1) Dieting may contribute to the development of eating disorders. Researchers studied the dieting histories and the severity of binge eating episodes among 111 women enrolled in a treatment program for eating disorders and found that 60 percent of the women reported that their first eating binge followed their initial dieting attempts.

Note that "Dieting may contribute to the development of eating disorders" is a factual claim that is a descriptive conclusion supported by research evidence. In this case, we want to ask, "Is that conclusion—a factual claim—justified by the evidence?"

(2) We should reduce the speed limit to 55 miles per hour. Faster speeds are killing Americans, according to recent government statistics.

Note that the factual claim here is that faster speeds are killing Americans, and it functions as a reason supporting a prescriptive conclusion. In this case, we want to ask, Is that reason—a factual claim—justified by the evidence?

The kind of evidence we most often use to support factual claims is *empirical evidence*—evidence based upon human observation. Such evidence can range from unsystematic personal observations to carefully planned research investigations. Chapters 7, 8, and 9 focus upon evaluating how well empirical evidence justifies authors' factual claims.

In their attempt to persuade us, writers and speakers often use empirical evidence to support *generalizations*. They rely upon a selected sample of events and then infer a general principle. We thus need to ask, "Are the generalizations justified?" The major question we want to ask about this kind of reasoning is, "Are the samples representative and the measurements valid?"

Scientific Evidence as a Guide to Informed Opinion

All of us constantly state opinions, frequently in the form of generalizations, statements made about a large group of instances when only a smaller group of those instances have been studied. For example, when a conclusion is made about the quality of swimmers in California and only a *few* California swimmers have been observed, the conclusion is a generalization. Thus, the statement, "California swimmers are stronger than Oregon swimmers" is a generalization. We encounter such generalizations daily, in statements such as

> Jogging is good for your health.
> College is a waste of time and money.
> A virus causes AIDS.
> Politicians are crooked.

You encounter these generalizations when you talk to friends, visit your local mechanic, read *Reader's Digest* and *Time*, watch television commercials, watch television talk shows, read textbooks, and listen to lectures.

What kind of evidence justifies such claims? Usually, the more closely we follow the scientific method in determining the evidence, the more confidence we can have in the evidence. To see why, let's take a brief look at the scientific method and its advantages.

We have turned to the scientific method as an important guide to determining the facts because the relationships among events in our world are very complex, and because humans are fallible in their observations and theories about these events.

The scientific method attempts to avoid many of the built-in biases in our observations of the world and in our intuition and common sense.

What is special about the scientific method? Above all, it seeks information in the form of *verifiable data*—that is, data obtained under conditions such that other qualified people can make similar observations and obtain the same results. This *objective evidence* is the kind we are usually calling for when we ask, "Where is your evidence?"

A second major characteristic of scientific method is *control*—that is, minimizing extraneous factors that might affect the accuracy and interpretation of generalizations. Physical scientists frequently maximize control by studying problems in the laboratory. When researchers do experiments, they attempt to minimize extraneous factors. Unfortunately, control is usually more difficult in the social world than in the physical world; thus it is very difficult to successfully apply the scientific method to many questions about human behavior.

Precision in language is a third major component of the scientific method. Our concepts are often confusing, obscure, and ambiguous. Scientific method attempts to be precise and consistent in the use of language.

While there is much more to science than we can discuss here, we want you to keep in mind that the best evidence is usually that which is *verifiable by others, obtained under controlled conditions,* and *precisely communicated.*

Unfortunately, the fact that research has been applied to a problem does not necessarily mean that the scientific evidence is good evidence. Science is not infallible and cannot adequately address some questions. While the best argument is usually the one that supports its factual claims by reference to relevant, objective, and up-to-date data from the best sources possible, much research evidence is flawed.

Also some questions, particularly those that focus on human behavior, can be answered only tentatively even with the best of evidence. Human behavior is so complex and varied that evidence will provide us only with statements about what may *probably* happen. No amount of evidence, for example, would enable us to say with absolute confidence that a particular person would be a good spouse. What evidence does provide for such questions is a presumption or a shifting of the burden of proof. If the evidence is better for opinion A, then I will presume that it is a superior opinion until those who disagree can prove that A is incorrect. For example, the scientific evidence thus far suggests that it is *highly probable* that smoking causes lung cancer. Thus I will choose not to smoke until I have reason to believe that smoking does not cause cancer.

Note that once a factual claim has been backed up by carefully collected evidence, it no longer is simply an opinion; it is an *informed opinion*, and the claim has a greater probability of being true. Can you now clearly see that some opinions are better than others? Someone who argues that any opinion is always as good as any other is wrong! Such an argument would be true only if all opinions were equally worthless, with no evidence provided to support any of them.

Probabilistic Generalizations

Most of us recognize that generalizations require some type of evidence to provide support for their accuracy. Therefore, you will often encounter evidence attached to a generalization. Let's examine a brief example.

> Despite their discontent, city dwellers have fewer mental health problems than their rural counterparts . . . . The survey reported on 6,700 interviews with adults who lived in one of six community sizes, ranging from cities with populations of over 3,000,000 to rural towns of less than 2,500. The findings were based on symptoms the respondents themselves reported, such as difficulty in sleeping, and either expecting or having had a nervous breakdown. People living in cities of over 50,000 showed symptom scores that were almost 20 percent lower than those of people in communities of less than 50,000.

Let's isolate the structure of this argument.

CONCLUSION: *City dwellers have fewer mental health problems than their rural counterparts.*

REASON: *A survey shows that people living in cities of over 50,000 showed symptom scores that were almost 20 percent lower than those of people in communities of less than 50,000.*

First, note that the conclusion is a generalization; it is about city and rural dwellers *in general*. It would have been impossible to study *all* city and rural dwellers. Consequently, a *sample* of 6,700 was studied, and a generalization was formed on the basis of the sample.

Second, note that the evidence supporting the generalization is in the form of *statistics*—that is, facts of a numerical kind that have been assembled, classified, and tabulated so as to present significant information. Thus, the generalization is a *statistical generalization*. Third, note that the generalization that "city dwellers have fewer mental health problems than their rural counterparts" is a *probabilistic generalization*. Why? Because the generalization is *not uniform*; it does not apply in all cases. In the example, we can say only that *on the average* a city dweller is *more likely* to have lower symptom scores. We cannot say that *all* city dwellers will have lower symptom scores than *all* rural dwellers. Few generalizations dealing with the behavior of people will be in the form, "All A are B"; most will be probabilistic generalizations, such as, "Most A's are B," "An increase in A tends to be associated with an increase in B," or "More A's than B's are C."

Since probabilistic generalizations are not uniform, what good are they? If they are not true in all cases, doesn't that mean that such generalizations are not true? No, not at all! Even though the generalization is probabilistic, it still may be true. Certainly it may be true that on the average urban dwellers have fewer symptoms than rural dwellers. What is not true is that every city dweller will be better off. It is useful to know that on the average they differ, since that recognition may lead to very different conclusions about the impact of city living. Thus, note that with probabilistic generalizations, *exceptions do not disprove the generalizations*; in fact, exceptions are expected. When someone states a probabilistic generalization, she does not have to assume that her assertion is true for everybody in order for the generalization to be correct.

Elements of Statistical Generalizations

Every statistical argument will have

1. A *target population*—the group of individuals or events one wants to generalize about. In the above case, the target population is city and rural dwellers.
2. A *sample*—a subgroup of the target population. We cannot observe everyone we want to generalize about, so we observe *some* members of the group—a sample. In this case, the sample consisted of 6,700 adults living in one of six community sizes.
3. *The characteristic of interest*—that aspect of the target population that we want to generalize about. In this case, the characteristic of interest was mental health problems.

Let's look at two other examples of generalizations to further illustrate what we mean by the characteristic of interest.

CLAIM 1: *Bodybuilders using steroids may be prone to psychotic symptoms.* Characteristic of interest? likelihood of psychotic symptoms.

CLAIM 2: *Pregnant teens who marry are less likely to stay married than those who are not pregnant and marry later.* Characteristic of interest? length of marriage.

Representativeness of the Sample

It should now be clear that the nature of the sample is crucial. When is a sample adequate to permit leaping to a general conclusion? When it is *representative* of the target population. For example, if you wanted to generalize about college students in the United States, you would not want to sample only students from a midwestern college, because that sample would not be representative of the target population. When is a sample representative? When it has had sufficient *size, breadth,* and *randomness.*

The size of a sample is crucial. The more cases in a sample, the better. There is no absolute guide to the number needed, but the smaller the number, the less faith we can have in the generalization. Clearly, a sample of one, or just a few, is not enough. Such a sample will be *biased.* You would certainly not be satisfied if the Gallup poll sampled only five people, since these five people might differ markedly from most of the population—that is, they might be nonrepresentative. However, with a sample of 5,000 people, the opinions will become more representative. Or how about the type of commercial that says, "Four out of five doctors recommend

Painstop Aspirin?'' You would be quite skeptical if only five doctors had been questioned, we hope. **Examine the size of the sample!**

In addition to the need for large size, a *broad-spectrum* sample is preferred. When is a sample sufficiently broad? Only when one samples across all important characteristics of the target population. For example, when one samples only male undergraduates at a midwestern university as to their attitudes toward alcohol consumption, one can generalize only about male undergraduates in midwestern universities. However, if one samples both male and female undergraduates from universities and colleges in all sections of the United States and from all class levels (freshmen, sophomores, juniors, and seniors) one can then generalize about American undergraduates.

It is also important to sample *proportionately*. If 60 percent of undergraduates are female, it is optimal for 60 percent of the sample to be female. **Examine the breadth of the sample!** Ask how well the sample characteristics mirror those of the population.

You have probably heard the phrase *random sampling* many times. Both the Gallup poll and the Nielsen ratings sample randomly. What makes a sample *random?* A sample is random when the individuals or events sampled are selected by a chance process, which serves to prevent bias. Each member from the group to be sampled should have the same opportunity to be selected. For example, if one is interested in how freshmen view their first quarter in school, one does not simply select the first 15 freshmen she encounters at the Student Union. Why? Students who go to the Union may be quite different in attitudes from those who are at the library, or from those who are studying at a fraternity or sorority. Such a sample will be biased, and will not mirror the freshman population. One means of overcoming the bias would be to take names at random from the student telephone directory, perhaps by calling every fifteenth person in the directory.

You should be aware that researchers often *begin* with a randomly selected sample but *end up* with a biased sample. This situation happens because those respondents initially randomly selected may exhibit biases in whether they choose to participate, once they have been selected. For example, people who agree to answer phone survey questions may be quite different from people who refuse to participate; thus, results of such surveys can be generalized only to people who choose to participate—even though potential participants were initially selected at random. Because of this occurrence, you should be alert to clues concerning selective factors that might affect participants' willingness to respond to surveys. **Examine the randomness of the sample!** Were subjects or events selected on a random or chance basis, or were they selected in some systematically biased fashion?

Now that you are aware of the major questions you should ask about the sample, let's determine the appropriateness of the sample in a brief generalization argument.

> Is the kid who sleeps with a toy gun destined to become the local bully? Not at all, maintain University of Nebraska psychologists Joseph C. LaVoie and Gerald Adams.

To find out how much kids really know about firearms, the investigators interviewed 73 middle-class children (37 boys and 36 girls) ranging in age from five to ten. The children were then tested for verbal and physical aggression. It was found that gunplay and aggression did not go together. Kids who played with guns and those who did not scored the same number of both physical and verbal aggression points.[1]

The structure of this argument is as follows:

CONCLUSION: *Playing with guns does not lead to physical aggression.*

REASON: *When tested for verbal and physical aggression, kids who played with guns and those who didn't had the same number of physical and verbal aggression points.*

Let's examine the size, breadth, and randomness of the sample. Seventy-three children were tested; thus, we can have some confidence that the results are relatively stable. How about the breadth? The sample covers both boys and girls, and a fairly wide age range; thus, results can legitimately be generalized across both sexes and the age range from five to ten. But the sample may have been drawn only from families in a university community. Results might have been different if the researchers had selected children who had not been affected strongly by the more peaceful values of a university community. Can you think of other characteristics that should have been considered? How about intelligence levels? Maybe children with low intelligence differ from children with high intelligence in how they are affected by playing with guns.

How about randomness? We cannot determine this from the above description. Optimally, these 73 children should have been randomly selected from a larger population of children. Were these the first 73 children to volunteer for the project? If so, what factors might have led to their volunteering? Perhaps they came from families who had a great deal of confidence in their children's social competence. If so, the sample is biased. Be sure to think about *why* the sample might be biased before you go on to the next section.

That sample selection has a major impact on findings is aptly illustrated by popular polls. On August 15, 1984, five different polls reported the percentage of respondents who said they preferred President Reagan or Walter Mondale. The results were as follows:

Poll	Findings
New York Times/CBS News	Reagan 52%, Mondale 34%
NBC News	Reagan 60%, Mondale 34%
ABC News	Reagan 44%, Mondale 43%
Louis Harris & Associates	Reagan 51%, Mondale 46%
Gallup Poll	Reagan 52%, Mondale 42%

[1] "Toy Guns and Aggression," *Human Behavior* (April 1975), 73.

Let's summarize what you should ask when you encounter a leap from evidence about a sample to a generalization about a larger population. First, ask the question, How representative is the sample? Then your answer will be determined by the size, breadth, and randomness of the sample. *Remember:* You should generalize only to a population that is mirrored by the sample, and it is your job to determine which important characteristics should be mirrored.

Validity of the Measurements

After you have asked about the representativeness of the sample, you must then ask, *How well has the characteristic of interest been measured?* Evidence supporting generalizations usually consists of measurements of individuals or events in the sample. Kinds of measures include test scores (such as a personality test, an IQ test), questionnaire and interview responses, and observations of events or behaviors.

You should ask certain questions about such measurements before accepting them. To illustrate, let's examine the characteristic of interest in the example in the last section with attention to the quality of its measurement. First, let's restate the conclusion: Playing with guns does not lead to *physical aggression.*

We have italicized the significant characteristic. How did the researchers measure physical agression? "Tests" were used. The question you should ask is, Do these tests validly measure physical agression? You cannot assume that something measures a characteristic just because it claims to. Because of a variety of influences, many tests are not valid; they do not adequately measure what they claim to measure. Perhaps physical agression was measured in these studies by teachers' reports of the child's activity in a structured situation. It is possible that such reports do not reflect the child's aggressive behavior in less structured situations. You should always ask the question, Do I have good reason to believe that the measurement is a valid measurement of the characteristic?

In answering this question, you should appeal to the author's evidence, to any knowledge you possess, and to your own hunches about what "makes sense." If the answer is "no," the quality of the generalization is greatly weakened.

When the characteristic of interest is measured, ask, Are the measurements valid? What evidence is there that they measure what they are supposed to measure?

Biased Surveys

It's early evening. You have just finished dinner. The phone rings. "We're conducting a survey of public opinion. Do you mind answering a few questions?" If you answer "no," you will be among thousands who annually take part in surveys—one of the measuring devices you will encounter most frequently. Think how often you hear the phrase, "according to recent polls."

Surveys are usually used to measure people's attitudes and beliefs. Just how valid are these measurements? It depends! Survey responses are subject to many influences; thus, one has to be very cautious in interpreting their meaning. Let's examine some of these influences.

First, for survey responses to be meaningful, they must be answered *honestly*. That is, verbal reports need to mirror actual beliefs and attitudes. Yet, for a variety of reasons, people frequently shade the truth. For example, they may give answers they think they ought to give, rather than answers that reflect their true beliefs. They may experience hostility toward the questionaire or toward the kind of question asked. They may give too little thought to the question. If you have ever been a survey participant, you can probably think of other influences. The power of such influences is illustrated by a recent survey.

A CBS News/New York Times poll conducted before a 1988 primary election showed Jesse Jackson winning about 50 percent of all black votes, but exit polls showed that Jackson captured 91 percent of all black votes. Analysts speculated that black voters did not reveal their true plans to polling interviewers—most of whom where white. Remember: *You cannot assume that verbal reports accurately reflect true attitudes.*

Second, many survey questions are ambiguous in their wording; the questions are subject to multiple interpretations. Different individuals may in essence be responding to different questions! For example, can you not imagine many interpretations of the following survey question: Are you happily married? The more ambiguous the wording of a survey, the less credibility you can place in the results. You should always ask the question, How were the survey questions worded? Usually, the more specifically worded a question, the more likely that different individuals will interpret it similarly.

Third, surveys contain many *built-in biases* that make them even more suspect. Two of the most important are *biased wording* and *biased context*. Biased wording of a question is a common problem; a small change in how a question is asked can have a major effect on how a question is answered. Let's examine a conclusion based on a recent poll and then look at the survey question.

A U.S. Congressman sent a questionnaire to his constituents and received the following results: 92 percent were against government-supported child care centers.

Now let's look closely at the survey question: Do you believe the federal government should provide child care centers to assist parents in rearing their children? Look carefully at this question. Do you see the built-in bias? The "leading" words are "to assist parents in rearing their children." Wouldn't the responses have been quite different if the question had read, Do you believe the federal government should provide child care centers to assist parents who are unable to find alternative child care while they are working? Thus, the measurement obtained here is not a valid indicator of attitudes concerning child care centers.

Survey data must always be examined for possible bias. Look carefully at the wording of the questions! Here is another example. We have italicized the word that evidences the bias.

QUESTION: *Do you think that a person with a homosexual disorder should be permitted to teach your innocent children?*

CONCLUSION: *Seventy-five percent of the people do not want homosexuals to teach their children.*

The effect of context on an answer to a question can also be powerful. Even answers to identical questions can vary from poll to poll depending upon how the questionaire is presented and how the question is imbedded in the survey. The following question was included in two recent surveys: "Do you think it should be possible for a pregnant woman to obtain a legal abortion if she is married and does not want any more children?" In one survey, the question was preceded by another question: "Should a woman be allowed to have an abortion if she had evidence that the fetus was defective?" In the other survey, no preceding question occurred. Not surprisingly, the two surveys showed different results. Can you see how the context might have affected respondents?

Another important contextual factor is fatigue. In long surveys, people may respond differently to later items than to earlier items simply because they get tired. *Be alert to contextual factors when evaluating surveys.*

Because the way people respond to surveys is affected by many unknown factors, such as the need to please or the interpretation of the question, should we *ever* treat survey evidence as good evidence? There are heated debates about this issue, but our answer is "yes," as long as we are careful and do not overgeneralize further than is warranted. Some surveys are more reputable than others. The better the quality of the survey, the more you should be influenced by the results. Our recommendation is to examine survey *procedures* carefully before accepting survey *results*. Once you have ascertained the quality of the procedures, you can choose to generate your own *qualified generalization*—one that takes into account any biases you might have found. For example, if a survey has been completed using subscribers to a magazine associated with a liberal ideology, then you would want to restrict any generalization found to people subscribing to that magazine. Even biased surveys can be informative; but you need to know the biases in order not to be unduly persuaded by the findings.

Dangers of Appealing to Personal Experience

Often we are tempted to appeal to our own experiences, or to personal experiences reported to us by friends or relatives, as evidence to support a generalization. Authors also frequently do this. One reason is that such experiences are very vivid in our memories. Usually relying upon such experience is a bad mistake! That is because a single personal experience, or an accumulation of personal experiences is not a representative sample of experiences. A single striking experience or several such experiences can demonstrate that certain outcomes are *possible*; for example, you may be aware of several people who smoked three packs of cigarettes a day and lived to the age of 90. Such experiences, however, can't demonstrate that such outcomes are *typical*.

It is especially important to remember that personal experiences that don't agree with a generalization do not prove that generalization wrong! Because generalizations tend to be probabilistic, exceptions are to be expected. Thus, even if smoking and lung cancer are positively related, many smokers may not get lung cancer, and many nonsmokers may get lung cancer.

Vivid case studies are striking examples that you must be especially wary of. Dramatic case studies are very concrete and easy to visualize, but such studies frequently blind us to relevant research evidence. For example, a detailed description of an obese welfare mother who has been irresponsible, has lived on welfare for 10 years, has lived with multiple husbands, and has had children by each of them may lead you to ignore the more relevant statistical data that only 10 percent of recipients remain on welfare rolls for 4 years or longer. Or, as another example, consider the power that viewing the aftermath of a gory car accident may have in influencing your beliefs about the importance of seat belts, as opposed to statistical data put out by the Surgeon General's office.

Be wary of examples as proof. Though examples will be *consistent* with the conclusion, do not let that consistency fool you. Always ask youself, Is the example *typical?* Are there powerful counterexamples? Are there other explanations for the example?

Remember: Beware of the individual who says, "My experience proves . . ." or "I can disprove all that because of an experience I had. . . ." The critical reader is always skeptical of experiences, subjects them to critical analysis, and determines whether they have been adequately confirmed by appropriate observational methods.

Hasty Generalizations

When a generalization is stated on the basis of a sample that is too small or biased to warrant the generalization, the *hasty generalization* fallacy is committed, meaning that one has jumped to the conclusion too quickly. A frequent kind of hasty generalization is to jump to a conclusion concerning "all" on the basis of just a few examples. For example, if someone sees a few poor women drivers, then asserts that all women are poor drivers, he is committing the fallacy of hasty generalization.

Note that while it is important that hasty generalizations be avoided, we should not avoid making sound generalizations—that is, assertions that are compatible with the evidence. If statistics from a dozen studies with appropriate size, breadth, and randomness tell us that 25 percent of the people who take a certain drug to cure cancer go blind, we should seriously consider banning the drug—even though not *all* people taking the drug will go blind, and 25 percent may not be the *exact* probability. We act because we have some degree of confidence that 25 percent approximates the true figure.

Using Generalizations in Your Writing

When you write essays, you will often want to make claims about groups of people. You may want to state their preferences or summarize their behavior. You will need to state a generalization.

What kind of evidence should you include? The answer to this question is dependent on the kind of issue about which you are writing. The first section in this chapter is the place to start. First, you know that evidence is desirable. Then, you learned that different amounts and qualities of evidence are required in different instances. Finally, you should use the standards for evaluating generalizations as a checklist to guide your use of evidence.

Because you will not usually be able to gather systematic evidence on your own, you should be cautious about the evidence you borrow from others. Check the quality of the sample and the extent to which the measurement is consistent with what it claims to be representing. Share with your readers the care you used in selecting the evidence. If you demonstrate that you have been highly selective in citing evidence, your writing will be more persuasive.

Summary

In this chapter, we have focused on the evaluation of generalizations. We have stressed that generalizations require reliable evidence before you can accept their truth. Thus, where appropriate, the first question to ask about a generalization is, Where is the evidence? We have provided you with some ways of determining whether empirical evidence for a generalization is *good evidence*. Let's review some of the ways to ascertain whether a writer is generalizing inappropriately.

1. First, determine whether there is *any* evidence.
2. If there is empirical evidence, find out how representative the sample is. Check on its size, breadth, and randomness. If it fails on any of these dimensions, the sample will be biased, and you will have identified a hasty generalization.
3. Determine whether the writer or speaker is accurately measuring what he claims to be measuring. Carefully compare the kind of measurement with the characteristic that is being generalized about.

Practice Exercises

◊   *Critical Question:*   **Are the samples representative and the measurements valid?**

In the three practice passages, evaluate the generalizations.

Passage 1

Letter to Editor:

Last Sunday some neighbors and I went to visit and talk to neighbors of a group home, housing four young men fourteen to eighteen years old, in a nearby community. I would like our community to know what we found. We found very scared people and families including a neighbor who was afraid to let his three-year-old daughter play in his own front yard and another afraid to leave her front door open. Another woman we talked to was afraid to be alone at night and said that a resident of this group home recently jumped her backyard fence and peeked in her back windows. We saw where these windows were and the young man definitely had to make a lot of effort to look in them. She said that she was afraid to think of what this person would have done had her neighbor not called her.

We were also told these young men have caused many disturbances in the schools. Just last week, according to a neighbor, one of these "boys" started a fight at a church festival in the area. These young men are the same age as the children our children's service agency wants to put in our community. Members of our community, these are some of the things we are trying to avoid by opposing the placing of this group home in our community.

Passage 2

In her 1987 book *Women and Love*, author Shere Hite concludes that the female of the species is disillusioned, fed up, angry—and is frequently breaking away from her male relationships, through either divorce or extramarital affairs. Some of Hite's numbers: 70 percent of the women married five years or more say they are having affairs; 98 percent of all women who answered the questionnaires wish for more "verbal closeness" with their male partners; 95 percent report incidents of "emotional and psychological harassment."

In 1980, Hite sent out 100,000 questionnairs to church groups, women's voting and political groups, women's rights groups, professional women's groups and storefront counseling or walk-in centers. She got back 4,500 responses. The questionnaire had 127 items, and the women were encouraged to choose to answer only those that appealed to them. Some questions were: "Are you happy with the relationship? Inspired? What do you like most and least about it? Can you imagine spending the rest of your life in it?" "What is the biggest problem in your relationship? How would you like to change things if you could?" "Do you ever feel pressured into sex? Into liking sex? Why? To be loving? To be hip?" "Have you ever been raped? Was this an important experience? How did you feel? Whom did you tell?" "Have you/are you having sex outside the relationship?"

Passage 3

To what extent are adopted children more vulnerable to emotional and academic problems that their nonadopted peers? To answer this question, psychological and academic adjustments were evaluated in a sample of 130 adopted and 130 nonadopted children ranging in age from 6 through 11 years. Adjustment measures included maternal ratings on Achenbach's Child Behavior Profile and teacher ratings on the Hahneman Elementary School Behavior Rating Scale. Adoptive families were recruited from the New Jersey, Eastern Pennsylvania, and New York City areas through adoption support groups, adoption agencies, newspaper advertisements, and word of mouth. Nonadoptive families were recruited from five central and northern New Jersey school systems and through newspaper advertisements. Results indicated that adopted children were rated higher in psychological and school-related behavior problems and lower in social competence and school achievement than were non-adopted children. Although the results support the position that the risk of developing emotional and school-related problems is greater for adopted children, caution is urged against overinterpreting the data, because the majority of adopted children appear well adjusted.[2]

——————————————— Sample Responses ———————————————

Passage 1

CONCLUSION: *Community group homes for boys are undesirable for the community.*

REASON: *1. Neighbors in a community having such a home are frightened.*
2. Group-home boys cause many problems in schools.

The conclusion is based upon two generalizations about community group homes for boys. How good is the evidence for these generalizations? Not very good! First, two kinds of sampling bias exist. Only one community was sampled; are its experiences typical of most communities? Also, only some members of that community were sampled; it is unclear how many. Are their reports typical of most members of the community? An adequate survey would have included a random sampling of neighbors. There is clearly a problem of *nonrepresentativeness of sampling*.

How about the *validity of the measures* of the characteristics of interest? Amount of fear and school disturbance are both based on verbal reports of neighbors. We would want to know, How were the questions worded? Were there built-in biases? Were the neighbors' reports themselves biased because of the vividness of their personal experiences? How about contextual factors affecting the responses? For example, did the interviews occur at a time close to a rash of recent incidents? Would the neighbors' responses have been similar several months earlier or later?

Passage 2

CONCLUSION: *Females are unhappy with their male relationships.*

REASONS: *Survey findings.*

[2] Adapted from D.M. Brodzinski, D.E. Scheuhter, A.M. Braff, and L.M. Singer, "Psychological and Academic Adjustment in Adopted Children," *Journal of Consulting and Clinical Psychology* 52 (1984), 582–590.

First, we note that the population being generalized about is "women." Serious questions about sample representativeness can be raised. While sample *size* is large (4,500), only 4.5 percent of those sampled responded, much lower than that usually reported in social-scientific reports; and this group was deficient in both *randomness* and *breadth.* What we have are the opinions of a limited group of women, those who join groups or who are in therapy who choose to respond to a very long survey. The importance of sampling is well illustrated by the finding that in recent years, *Playboy, Redbook,* and *Ladies Home Journal* have all looked at the incidence of extramarital affairs and have found that 34, 29 and 21 percent of women surveyed admitted having *ever* cheated, as contrasted to the figure of 70 percent reported by Hite.

Second, we can also question the validity of the measurement. Look closely at the wording of the questions. Think about how you might try to answer them. Is not the wording quite ambiguous in places (e.g., "Have you been pressured into being loving?"), and are there not some built-in biases? For example, does not some of the wording appear to be "pulling" for negative experiences?

Thus, while the generalization in this passage is accompanied by some evidence, one can seriously question whether the samples were representative and whether the measures were valid.

Passage 3

CONCLUSION: *The risk of developing emotional and school-related problems is greater for adopted children.*

REASON: *Adopted children are rated higher in psychological and school-related behavior problems and lower in social competence and school achievement than are nonadopted children.*

This is a very common research design in the social sciences. The populations being generalized about are adopted and nonadopted children. The sample size is quite large. But, the information does not enable us to determine the breadth of the sample. Though multiple states were sampled, to what extent were the family sizes, family incomes, and ages of parents typical of adoptive families? Perhaps the most important sampling problem was the lack of a random sample. Given the recruiting procedures, were there selective factors that led certain kinds of parents to volunteer for the study, and were these selective procedures different for adoptive and non-adoptive families? Perhaps, for example, adoptive families are generally more willing to volunteer even if their children are experiencing problems. If such selective factors were operating, then the sample is biased.

How valid are the rating measurements? Can parent and teacher ratings be trusted to reflect emotional adjustment accurately? How ambiguous were the rating terms? How objective are parents and teachers in making their ratings? Does knowing that the child is adopted affect how one rates that child? We would want to know more about the validity of these scales before we could have much confidence in the conclusion.

Passage 4 (Self-Examination)

A recent study[3] shows evidence that modern boxers suffer brain damage from their sport. The researchers contacted by telephone 23 former boxers who (1) were aged 25 to 60 years, (2) were currently residing in the New York area, (3) had not retired from boxing for medical, neurological, or psychiatric reasons, (4) were retired from boxing for at least 1 year before the study, (5) had no known history of neurological, psychiatric, or serious medical illness, and (6) had no known history of drug or alcohol abuse. Eighteen former boxers volunteered to participate. The group included two former professional champions, three highly ranked professional contenders, and four other amateur champions; only one former fighter was primarily a "slugger"; all others were considered to be scientific, artful fighters who practiced self-defense.

Each boxer underwent neurological examinations, a computerized tomographic scan of the brain (a measure of brain atrophy), an electroencephalogram (EEG), and neuropsychological testing. The researchers found evidence of brain damage on at least two of the measures in 13 of the 15 professional boxers, and evidence of subtle brain damage in the three amateur boxers. The authors concluded that brain damage is a frequent result of a career in professional boxing.

[3]Adapted from I.R. Casson, O. Siegel, R. Sham, E.A. Campbell, M. Tarlau, and A. Di-Domenico, "Brain Damage in Modern Boxers," *Journal of the American Medical Assocation 251* (May 25, 1984), 2663–2667.

VIII

How Good is the Evidence: Are There Rival Hypotheses?

We begin this chapter with one of our favorite stories.

> After carefully conditioning a flea to jump out of a box following the presentation of a loud noise, the researcher removed the first pair of legs to see what effect this had. Observing that the flea was still able to perform his task, the scientist removed the second pair of legs. Once again noting no difference in performance, the researcher removed the final pair of legs and found that the jumping behavior no longer occurred. Thus, the investigator wrote in his notebook, "When all the legs of a flea have been removed, it will no longer be able to hear."[1]

This story clearly illustrates a very common goal in the use of evidence—*discovering causes*. It also shows a very common difficulty in using empirical evidence to prove something caused something else—the problem of *rival causal hypotheses*. The above (fictional) researcher offered one hypothesis about what caused his research observations. We expect that you can see that there is another very plausible hypothesis to explain why the flea stopped jumping. Thus, this story shows that empirical evidence can be consistent with different beliefs about what causes such evidence. We refer to those different beliefs as *rival causal hypotheses*.

Although rival hypotheses will rarely be as obvious as they are in our story, you will frequently encounter experts presenting one hypothesis to explain some facts when other plausible hypotheses could also explain them. Usually, these experts will not reveal rival hypotheses to you; you will have to generate them.

---

[1] Adapted from Schuyler W. Huck and Howard M. Sandler, *Rival Hypotheses* (New York: Harper & Row, 1979), p. xiii.

Doing so can be especially helpful as you decide, "How good is the evidence?", because the existence of multiple plausible rival hypotheses to explain facts reduces our confidence in the hypothesis originally offered by the author.

Searching for rival hypotheses will always be appropriate when an author presents you with some facts and offers a hypothesis to explain them.

◊   *Critical Question:*   **Are there rival hypotheses?**

Pervasiveness of Rival Hypotheses

On Sunday evening December 23, 1888, Vincent van Gogh, then 35 years old, cut off the lower half of his left ear and took it to a brothel, where he asked for a prostitute named Rachel and handed the ear to her, requesting that she "keep this object carefully."

Authors have offered numerous hypotheses to explain this event, including the following:

> 1. He was frustrated by two recent events: the engagement of his brother Theo, to whom he was very attached, and the failure of an attempt to establish a working and living relationship with Paul Gauguin. The aggressive impulses aroused by these frustrations were first directed at Gauguin, but then were turned against himself.[2]

> 2. Van Gogh had a great sympathy for prostitutes and identified with their status as social outcasts. One suggestion is that his self-mutilation was a reflection of this identification. "In June, just a few months before butchering his ear, he had written that 'the whore is like meat in a butcher shop': when he treated his own body as 'meat in a butcher's shop,' he reversed their roles, identified himself with the whore, and showed his sympathy for her."[3]

> 3. It is likely that Van Gogh experienced frightening auditory hallucinations during his psychotic attack similar to those he experienced in other attacks. Afterward, while in the sanitorium he wrote that other patients heard strange sounds and voices as he had and speculated in one case that this was probably due to a disease of nerves in the ear. Thus, in a psychotic state, Van Gogh could have felt that his own ear was diseased and cut it off to silence the disturbing sounds.[4]

Now, let's leave Van Gogh's case for a moment and examine a different event in need of explanation—the findings of a research study.

> A researcher reported that treating headaches with relaxation exercises and biofeedback is helpful. Three-fourths of 95 people with chronic tension headaches and about half of 75 migraine sufferers studied reduced the frequency and severity of their headaches after learning how to relax head, neck, and shoulder muscles and control stress and tension with biofeedback.

---

[2] William M. Runyan, *Life Histories and Psychobiography* (New York: Oxford University Press, 1982), pp. 38–39.

[3] Ibid. p. 40.

[4] Ibid. pp. 40–41.

In this study, the researcher probably began with the hypothesis that relaxation training causes reduction of headache suffering; and he found facts consistent with that hypothesis. But let us offer several rival hypotheses for the same findings.

1. Research participants were highly suggestible, and the *expectation of improvement* was responsible for the change; like the sugar pill placebo effect in medicine, thinking they were going to get better might have stimulated a number of physical and mental processes that caused participants to feel better.
2. Participants wanted to please the researchers; thus, they reported feeling better even though they did not.
3. Most participants volunteered while undergoing highly stressful life situations; they experienced a reduction in life stresses during the course of the study; and this reduction accounted for the reduction in symptoms.

Now, let's leave the research laboratory for a moment and move to the sports pages and examine some baseball statistics.

During the 1987 season, the frequency of home runs hit in the major leagues showed a marked increase over the average number hit during the previous five years. Manufacturers of baseballs must be doing something to liven up the ball.

The hypothesis offered by the sportswriter is that a livelier baseball is causing the increase in home runs. But, let's again generate some rival hypotheses:

1. Pitching quality markedly dropped during the 1987 season; there were many more injuries to pitchers than usual.
2. Weather patterns were unusual during the 1987 season; perhaps the air tended to be much less humid than usual. Reduced friction resulted in greater distance for each hit.

Now, let's examine some important lessons that can be learned from the van Gogh case, the research study, and the baseball statistics.

First, many kinds of facts are open to rival hypotheses, including clinical case studies, criminal trials, research studies, advertising statistics, sports page charts, airline crash findings, and historical events.

Second, experts can examine the same facts and come up with different hypotheses to explain them.

Third, although many explanations can "fit the facts," some seem more *plausible* than others.

Fourth, most authors will provide you with only their favored hypothesis— one that is subject to many biases; rival hypotheses must be generated by the critical reader or listener.

Fifth, generating rival hypotheses is a creative process; usually such hypotheses will not be obvious. Thus, ability to generate hypotheses varies.

Sixth, even "scientific" researchers frequently fail to acknowledge important alternative hypotheses for explaining their findings.

Finally, the worth of a particular hypothesis is inversely related to the number of plausible rival hypotheses.

The above seven points say a lot. We hope that they convince you that when you encounter any hypothesis used to explain some facts that you will want to ask, What else might explain the facts? In the following sections, we explore the implications of these lessons for the critical thinker.

Rival Hypotheses and Causal Generalizations

In the previous chapter, we focused on evaluating a particular kind of factual claim—a generalization. A particularly important kind of generalization is one that claims a causal relationship between one characteristic and another. For example, to claim that AIDS is caused by a virus is to state a causal generalization. Researchers initially offer causal generalizations as hypotheses to explain how certain facts, *in general*, occur (e.g. to explain how people acquire AIDS). Once a generalization has been firmly established by many facts, it changes from a hypothesis to a law. In the domain of complex human behavior, however, there are very few established laws. Rival hypotheses in the form of causal generalizations like, "TV violence adversely affects society," "smoking causes cancer," and "permissive discipline causes juvenile deliquency" must now all be viewed as tentative hypotheses.

If that is the present state of affairs, what should we do when we encounter a causal generalization as a conclusion of a research study, as a reason to support a conclusion in a complex essay, or as a justification on the Phil Donahue show for recommending a new diet? Try to find out as much as we can about the facts that support the generalization and try to determine whether researchers have ruled out plausible rival hypotheses. The more plausible rival hypotheses that can account for the facts, the less faith you should have in the causal generalization.

Because most researchers are aware of the problem of rival hypotheses, they have devised many techniques for *ruling out rival hypotheses*. Often, these techniques work very well, and hypotheses are justifiably supported by the facts. However, much research fails to rule out important rival hypotheses, especially research studying complex human behavior. Awareness of some common plausible rival hypotheses should help you locate them. Thus, we have listed a number of them.

1. *Observer Expectancy Effects.* Consider a researcher interested in demonstrating the benefits of a particular psychotherapy. She selects 10 people who recently received her favored kind of therapy and 10 others who recently received a less favored kind of therapy. Then she interviews both groups about their present mental health. Through a variety of mechanisms, such as giving off selective nonverbal feedback (e.g., nodding her head at what she liked to hear) and interpreting ambiguous responses in a manner favorable to her hypothesis, she systematically influences the findings because she has certain ideas about what she expects to find. If she finds differences between the two groups, they may be due to differences in how she interviewed the clients because of her expectations, rather

than to differences in how the clients received therapy. Thus, we have a rival hypothesis—the observer expectancy effect—to explain the findings. This effect is always a rival hypothesis when expectations of observers might systematically influence their findings.

Observer expectancy effects pervade diverse kinds of research. For example, the power of this effect has been historically demonstrated in the field of astronomy. In one classical case, re-examination of certain astronomers' published findings indicated that the reported observations could not have been possible. An English astronomer of the seventeenth century was the proponent of an (incorrect) theory predicting that the Pole Star would be closer to the North Pole in winter than in summer. He published his own astronomical observations to confirm his hypothesis; in other words, he found what he expected to find.

The observer expectancy effect reminds us that often *believing is seeing*, and reminds us to be very wary of observations in which it would be easy for the observer's biases to influence his own observations.

2. *Maturation and life experiences over time.* Suppose we measure with an essay test the critical thinking ability of a group of freshmen before they read *Asking the Right Questions* and then measure it again six months later after they have read it; and we find that they improve their essay scores from the first testing to the second. The change may be caused by reading the book (one hypothesis). However, it is also possible that changes associated with the aging process (e.g., maturation of the brain) occurred over the six month period and influenced thinking ability. Also, during the six month period the students may have had many life experiences that could potentially have afffected their critical thinking skills; for example, they may have had contact with books and professors stressing such skills. Whenever a long period of time elapses between a pair of measurements, we must consider experiences and maturation over time as possible rival hypotheses to explain changes that occur.

3. *Biased sample selection.* We know of a recent research study in which Teacher A's teaching method was judged superior to that of Teacher B because Teacher A's class performed better than Teacher B's class on the same standardized final comprehensive multiple choice test. By now we expect that you can recognize a number of alternative hypotheses to explain this finding, but we want to sensitize you to one in particular here—the likelihood that the students in these two classes differed in important ways before the teaching methods were ever administered. For example, students who sign up for a class early in the day may be more motivated to learn than students who sign up for a class later in the day. Did these teachers teach at the same time of day?

When participants or events differ systematically prior to our comparing them on some characteristic of interest, then biased sample selection is a possible alternative hypothesis. Because of this possible rival hypothesis, researchers try to randomly assign subjects to research groups they wish to compare; they assume that doing this will "average out" differences among people, and the groups will "on the average" be similar (e.g., have similar average motivation, similar average intellectual skills, etc.) Always be on the lookout for biased sampling as a rival hypothesis when groups are compared and group participants have not been randomly assigned.

Note how biased sampling is a rival causal hypothesis in the following brief example:

> We found that members of our community who have recently become joggers have much lower cholesterol levels than nonjoggers; we're convinced that jogging causes a reduction in cholesterol level.

4. *Participant expectancy and desire to please.* Imagine participating in a research study in which a therapist attempts to train you to be more assertive. Later, he evaluates you on a number of measures of "assertiveness," such as an assertiveness personality test. Wouldn't you probably be aware of how the researcher would *like* you to respond to some items on the test? Is it also possible that you might want to "please" the researcher? If you answer "yes" to both those questions, you might appear more assertive on the personality test than you actually are; if so, your expectancy and desire to please have caused your change in score, not the training in assertiveness.

Research participants frequently try to figure out what the researcher is "up to." They also tend to generate *expectancies* about how they are supposed to act, feel, or think during the study. Additionally, they may have a "desire to please" the researcher. These factors may influence their performance; thus, they are important rival hypotheses to check out. Always ask yourself, are there aspects of the research procedures that might lead participants to behave in the way they think they ought to behave (or in a way they ought *not* to behave) rather than to behave in as honest a fashion as possible.

Note that expectancies may affect us as participants in a variety of situations other than research studies. Do you see the possibility of this effect in "faith healing?" In hypnosis? In responding to aspirin?

5. *Linked causal influences.* A major difficulty with discovering a specific causal factor is that it is very hard to separate one factor that we think might be an important cause (e.g., a particular teaching method) from other potential causes (e.g., the personalities of the different teachers). That is, important possible causal influences are linked with one another. You can locate linked causal factors by asking the question, when cause A is present or absent, are there other possible factors that are also simultaneously present or absent? If so, you need to consider other causes as plausible rival hypotheses.

See if you can find possible linked causes in the following example.

> A researcher was interested in whether people in his particular community preferred the taste of Coke or the taste of Pepsi. Thus, cola drinkers were chosen from his area and asked to express a preference for a glass of Coke or a glass of Pepsi. The glasses were not labeled "Coke" and "Pepsi" because of the obvious bias that might be

associated with a cola's brand name. Rather in an attempt to administer the two beverages in a blind fashion, the Coke glass was marked with a "Q" and the Pepsi glass with an "M". Results indicated that more than half chose Pepsi over Coke.[5]

Besides the researcher's hypothesis that taste preference caused the difference, can you think of any rival hypotheses to explain the results? Are there other factors "linked" to the factor of interest, Coke vs. Pepsi? Yes. The letters M and Q. Perhaps one *letter* is preferred to another? In fact, later researchers conducted the exact same study except that Coke was put in *both* glasses. Participants preferred the letter "M" over the letter "Q," thus suggesting the plausible rival hypothesis that letter preference, not taste preference, could have explained the original results.

This example represents a case where the researcher *could* have separated the linked causes—taste preference and letter preference—but did not. Do you see how this separation could have been done?

6. *Regression effects.* Imagine that yesterday was the most depressed you had ever felt in your life. Now, predict how depressed you would probably be a week later. Wouldn't you predict "less depressed"? Why? Because you recognize that when there are large fluctuations in mood, more extreme moods tend to be followed by less extreme—*just by chance fluctuation!*

Here is another example to illustrate the same principle. If you have been an average tennis player for a long period of time, playing well on some days and poorly on others, what is the best bet about your performance following a really bad performance? Isn't it likely to be better?

Note that in both these examples, we expect changes, simply because of chance fluctuations. We can summarize this tendency as follows: Happenings far above or below the average tend to be followed by happenings closer to the average. Try to determine how the regression effect explains the following finding:

> After the first two weeks of the major league baseball season, newspapers print the top ten batting averages. Typically, after two weeks, several leading batters have averages over .400. Yet at the end of a season, no batter will be batting over .400.

This regression phenomenon should tell you something very important about research studies in which the researchers selected people with extreme performances (either very high or very low) and then examined the impact of some intervention upon their performance by comparing measures before and after the intervention. Let's take a look at such a study.

> Parents experiencing difficulties with their preschool children volunteered for a local 6-week "parent training" program. Parents rated their children before and after the program on a problem behavior checklist, which gave an indication of how many problems they were having with their child. Parents reported fewer problems after the parent training program than before the program.

---

[5] Adapted from Schuyler W. Huck and Howard M. Sandler, *Rival Hypotheses* (New York: Harper & Row, 1979), p. 11

This study has many rival hypotheses that explain the findings, but one is the regression effect. Usually parents volunteer *when they are most desperate*, that is when their child is being *extremely* problematic. By chance fluctuation alone, we could have expected the children to be less of a problem six weeks later—even if they had received no parent training.

While knowledge of these categories of alternative explanations will be very useful to you, there are many other kinds to which you will need to be alert in evaluating research studies. One of the best ways to discover alternative explanations is to temporarily attempt to *blind yourself* to the researcher's hypothesis or conclusions. That is, look only at the facts, and ask yourself, What hypothesis might account for them? Then compare your hypothesis with the author's.

Confusing Causation with Association

We have an inherent tendency to "see" events that are *associated*, or that "go together" as events that *cause* one another. We infer that because characteristic X (e.g., amount of TV viewing) is associated with characteristic Y (e.g., performance in school) that X therefore causes Y. Following are some common examples:

1. States with capital punishment tend to have a lower crime rate than states without capital punishment; thus, capital punishment deters crime.
2. Absence of a father in the home occurs at a higher rate with juvenile delinquents than with non-delinquents; thus, father absence is a cause of juvenile delinquency.

When we think this way, we are, however, often very wrong! Why? Because usually multiple rival hypotheses can explain why X and Y "go together." In fact, there are at least three different kinds of rival hypotheses to account for any such relationship. The following research example illustrates these three. Knowing what these are will help you discover rival hypotheses.

A recent research study reported that "moderate drinking is good for a woman's heart." The researchers studied over one thousand nurses and found that those who had 3 to 15 drinks per week had a lower likelihood of having heart disease than those who drank fewer than 3 drinks per week. They thus found an association between amount of drinking (X) and condition of the heart (Y).

Should nurses start increasing their drinking activity? Well, before they do, they should contemplate each of the following possible explanations.

EXPLANATION 1: *X is a cause of Y. (Drinking does indeed help prevent heart disease.)*

EXPLANATION 2: *Y is a cause of X. (Having healthy hearts makes women feel more like drinking.)*

EXPLANATION 3: *Both X and Y are effects of some other factor or factors. (Perhaps women who are independent tend to drink moderately and to exercise a lot. If so, moderate drinking and heart condition will be related because of how they both relate to independence.)*

Remember. When an author supports an hypothesis by pointing to an association between characteristics, always ask, Are there other hypotheses to explain such an association?

Let's take a close look at a very common way that we confuse causation with association. Often, we try to explain a particular fact by the following kind of reasoning: Because event B *followed* event A, then event A *caused* event B. Such reasoning occurs because human beings have a strong tendency to believe that events that occur close together in time are causally related.

To appreciate the flaw in this reasoning, pick up today's newspaper and make a list of what is going on in the world. Then pick up yesterday's newspaper and make a similar list. Could you infer that the events of yesterday are causing the events of today? Clearly not. Many events that occur close together in time are not related to one another. Thus, such reasoning is flawed and is commonly called the *post hoc, ergo propter hoc* (after this, therefore because of this) *fallacy*, or, for short, the *post hoc fallacy*. The following examples illustrate the problem with this kind of reasoning.

"Harry Hurricane must be an excellent coach; since he moved to our university, the team's record has improved dramatically." (But maybe the university also decided to double its athletic budget when Harry came.)

Reagan's economic policies are working great. Since he has come into office, the inflation rate has dropped to only 4% per year." (But maybe Federal Reserve Board policies were responsible for the decrease.)

As you might guess, politicians are fond of using the post hoc argument, expecially when it works in their favor.

Remember: The finding that one event follows another in time, does not by itself prove causation; it may only be a coincidence. When you see such reasoning, always ask yourself, Are there rival hypotheses to account for the event?

Practice in Locating Rival Hypotheses

Now that you have learned a number of kinds of rival hypotheses to be on the lookout for, let's try discovering some of these in an actual research study.

Extensive day care in the first year of life causes insecurity in children. In our studies, 464 infants were tested at age 12 to 13 on the Strange Situation Test, which purports to measure a one-year-old's attachment to its mother; 41.5% of the infants in day care and 25.7% of infants cared for at home were judged by the test as insecurely attached to their mothers.

Should American mothers who send their infants to day care centers be feeling guilty? Not until they have considered rival hypotheses to explain the findings? Isolate the facts from the researcher's conclusion and ask yourself, What other hypotheses might explain the facts? Below are some rival hypotheses we discovered.

1. *Biased sample selection.* Note that children have *not been randomly assigned* to the two different kinds of care, day care and home; thus, it is very possible that the families in the two groups differ in systematic ways that might help account for the findings. For example, the decision to place children in day care is associated with many other factors. Parents who use more than 20 hours of child care each week might share other traits that would cause their infants to show a less secure attachment; for example, they may be under more strain and thus more tense around their children. Or perhaps they may not be as affectionate toward their children.

2. *Observer expectancy effects.* If the researchers had biases against day care, might these not have affected their interpretations of the test results (especially if the responses to the test are difficult to interpret)? We would want to know whether the researchers judging the child's behavior on the Strange Situation Test knew which kind of care that child was receiving. If so, such observations would be subject to observer expectancy effects.

3. *Confusing causation with association.* Perhaps the presence of an insecure attachment in the home increases the likelihood that a mother will send her child to the day care center; in that case, insecure attachment may be ''causing'' day care treatment, rather than vice-versa.

We have listed three plausible rival hypotheses to that offered by the researcher. We expect that you can add more. Finding even these three has greatly weakened the credibility of the researcher's conclusion.

Evaluating Causal Generalizations

In evaluating general causal statements, it is also very important that you understand what the author is implying by making such statements. What exactly is meant when an author says, ''Joining a sorority causes college coeds to use more makeup,'' or ''There is a causal link between eating too much salt and high blood pressure''? The word *cause* means to bring about, make happen, or effect. Note the difference between the phrases *bring about* (causal) and *go together* (relationship). There are a number of words that will indicate to you when an author is thinking causally. We have listed a few.

> has the effect of
> increases the likelihood
> facilitates
> deters
> as a result of

There is another important aspect of *most* causal generalizations: They are probabilistic. Knowing one event does not tell you *for sure* whether the other event will occur. For example, if watching TV violence has the effect of *increasing the probability* of a child's being aggressive, then watching TV is a causal factor in aggressive behavior—even though many children who watch TV violence do not behave aggressively. If 25 percent of children who watch TV violence behave aggressively, and only 20 percent of children who don't watch such violence behave aggressively, then watching TV violence is probably one causal factor in aggressive behavior—even though most children who watch TV violence do not behave aggressively. If the *average* score on an exam increases *as a direct result of* students' drinking coffee, then drinking coffee is a causal factor, even though all students who drink coffee do not improve their exam scores.

In thinking about causation, you should keep in mind that the probability of certain events occurring is determined by many causal factors. For instance, TV violence may be only one of a number of factors causally linked to childhood aggression. Parental discipline, nutrition, genetic makeup, and peer group pressures may all be additional causal factors in determining aggressive behavior.

When writers make causal claims, they usually are not suggesting that the causal variable is the *only* factor causing the event. They also are not claiming that one factor is *necessary* for another to occur, nor that an effect will *necessarily occur* if the causal agent is present. Smoking may be a causal factor in cancer; yet many people who smoke may not get cancer, and many people who get cancer will not have smoked. Thus, most causes are only *contributory causes*; they are important factors among a number of factors. They increase the likelihood that an event will occur. Do not make the mistake of thinking that, because a factor is only one of several causes, it therefore is not an important one.

Evaluating Rival Hypotheses

The more plausible rival hypotheses that you come up with, the less faith you can have in the initial explanation offered, at least until further evidence has been considered. As a critical thinker, you will want to assess as best you can how each of the alternative explanations fits the available evidence, trying to be sensitive to your personal biases.

In comparing rival hypotheses, we suggest that you apply the following criteria:

1. their logical soundness,
2. their consistency with other knowledge that you have, and
3. their previous success in explaining or predicting events.

Summary

Factual claims about the causes of events are weakened when other claims about the causes can be offered. Such claims are *rival hypotheses*. When authors make causal claims, try to generate rival hypotheses.

Some common rival hypotheses for causal generalizations are:

1. observer expectancy effect,
2. maturation and life experiences over time,
3. biased sample selection,
4. participant expectancy and desire to please,
5. linked causal influences, and
6. regression effects.

A common logical error in explaining observations is to confuse causation with association. Thus, always ask what other hypotheses might explain observed associations. Be especially alert to the *post hoc fallacy.*

Practice Exercises

◊   *Critical Question:*   **Are there rival hypotheses?**

Each of the following examples provides an argument to support a causal claim. Try to generate rival hypotheses for such claims. Then try to determine how much you have weakened the author's claim by knowledge of rival claims.

Passage 1

A little bit of light may beat the winter blues. Researchers studied nine patients who suffered from winter depression, which is caused by the days getting shorter. The patients were exposed to bright flourescent light upon awakening and in the late afternoon, for three hours at a time. Within a week, seven of the patients had recovered from their depression completely, and the other two showed a modest improvement. The light treatment works because it tricks the body into thinking that it's summer.

Passage 2

Sixty students at the University of Wisdom recently agreed to participate in a program designed to improve their dating skills.

The students who volunteered for the program averaged one date during the month prior to the participation in the dating-skills program. The 60 students were divided into three groups: One group had six "practice" dates with six different volunteers; a second group also had six "practice" dates and received feedback from their dates concerning their appearance and behavior; a third group served as a control.

Before and after the practice dates each group filled out social anxiety questionnaires and rated themselves in terms of social skills. Both of the two groups who had practice dates experienced less social anxiety, a higher sense of self-confidence in social situations, and more dates than did the control group. Apparently, practice dating improves the quality of our social life.

Passage 3

There are hopeful signs for American education today. For example, there are now real signs of progress in raising the learning level, at least among college bound high-school students. Scores of the 1985 Scholastic Aptitude Test (SAT) took the biggest upward leap in 21 years. For almost a decade scores have been gradually rising. After reaching an all time low score in 1980 and 1981, the scores gained three points in 1982, stayed the same in 1983, increased a strong four points in 1984, and increased a whopping 9 points in 1985. Education Secretary William Bennet called the scores "further evidence that American secondary education is on the mend."[6]

———————————— Sample Responses ————————————

Passage 1

CONCLUSION: *Light treatment combats winter depression.*

REASON: *Seven of nine patients exposed to light treatment completely recovered from their depression in a week's time.*

Can anything else account for the change besides light treatment? Yes; the researcher fails to rule out many obvious alternative explanations. For example, *subject expectancies and desire to please* may have led to the reported changes, rather than specific treatment effects. Another possible factor is *life events*; perhaps during the week of treatment, the weather was especially good, and these people spent much more time outside in the sun than usual; also, perhaps people *naturally* recover from this disorder in a brief period of time. Certainly, there is the possibility of an *experimenter effect* here because the researcher knew what treatment the subjects had undergone and what effect was expected. Can you locate other rival hypotheses?

Passage 2

CONCLUSION: *Practice dating improves dating behavior.*

REASON: *Forty students at the University of Wisdom reported increased dates, improved social skills, and less social anxiety after six practice dates compared to those of 20 control group subjects.*

This study ruled out many rival hypotheses by including a control group and randomly assigning subjects to groups. However different *expectations* by the subjects in the different groups may have helped account for the results. There is no indication that the experimenters attempted to convince the students in the control

6 Adapted from Dwight Bohmbach, *What's Right with America?* (New York: Bantam Books, 1986), p. 107.

group that their dating behavior would be improved; thus, there is no reason to expect that their expectations for change were as high as the expectations of those in the experimental groups. Consequently, although this study was quite well designed, we should have reservations about whether practice dating was the significant causal factor in determine changes in the quality of dating behavior.

Did you notice how ''improved dating behavior'' was measured here? Recalling what you learned in Chapter VII, can you see any problems with this form of measurement?

Passage 3

CONCLUSION: *Our education system is increasing the learning level, at least of college bound high school students.*

REASON: *SAT scores have shown a steady increase from 1981 to 1985.*

First note that this essay attempts to explain a particular event—gradual increases in SAT scores by emphasizing one possible cause—an improvement in our educational system. Note also, that a post hoc reasoning logic is being used; SAT scores have increased following an effort to improve our educational system. Let's blind ourselves to the author's hypothesis and ask ourselves, Can any other hypothesis explain the SAT score increases?

We can think of several. The simplest plausible explanation is a regression toward the mean. SAT scores were at *an all time low* in 1980 and 1981; they would be expected to increase from these low extremes just by chance fluctuation. Another possible hypothesis is that the nature of the population taking the test has been gradually shifting over time. For example, a larger number of less talented students may be choosing not to go to college, thus not taking the SAT: if so, the increases may reflect an increased proportion of higher quality students taking the tests. Lots of other things were happening to these students in addition to their education during this five-year period. Has there been a gradual increase in attention to nutrition? Have parents increased their emphasis on education at home? Have students increased their motivation to achieve because of increasing concern about later job satisfaction? We expect that you can see that many rival hypotheses can account for the facts presented in this essay.

Passage 4 (Self-Examination)

Laughter may indeed be the best medicine! The case of Norman Cousins, former editor of the *Saturday Review*, proves to us once again that experiencing positive emotions, especially laughter, can be a powerful healing force, capable of inducing major chemical changes in our body. The Cousins story began in 1964, when Mr. Cousins returned from a trip to the Soviet Union with stiffness in his limbs and nodules on his neck and hands. Tests resulted in a tentative diagnosis of ankylosing spondylitis, a degenerative disease of the connective tissue. After suffering adverse reactions to most of the drugs he was given, Cousins decided, with the cooperation of his doctor, to treat himself, relying upon various articles he had read about the positive qualities ascribed to vitamin C, and the health-inducing effect of positive emotions.

Cousins checked out of the hospital and into a hotel, went off all his drugs and initiated a treatment regimen of regular, large intravenous injections of vitamin C. He also arranged for showings of laugh-provoking films, including old excerpts from "Candid Camera," and he read amusing books. While thus treating himself, he reports experiencing a gradual withdrawal of symptoms, and gradually regaining most freedom of movement. By 1976, he wrote that he had become pain free except for his knees, for the first time since he had left the hospital.

IX

How Good Is the Evidence: Are There Flaws in the Statistical Reasoning?

One of the fastest ways to get rich in America is to become a baseball player. Last year, the average major league salary was $412,000.

The public is not demanding a ban on in-flight smoking; an Airline Pilot Association poll showed over 87% of those questioned favor the present system of smoking and non-smoking sections.

The number of divorces in 1982 dropped by 43,000 after two decades of steady increases since 1962. The institution of marriage is making a comeback.

One of the most frequent kinds of evidence that authors present is "statistics." You have probably often heard people use the following phrase to help support their argument: "I have statistics to prove it." We use statistics (often inappropriately) to assess our nation's economic activity, to determine which TV shows will survive, to determine investment strategy, to help people decide on which sports teams to bet, to assess the country's social progress, to evaluate our sexual satisfaction, to predict the weather, and to provide input for many other issues.

Statistics are evidence expressed as numbers. Such evidence can seem quite impressive because numbers make evidence appear to be very scientific and precise, as though it represents "the facts." Statistics, however, can, and often do, lie! They do not prove what they appear to prove. We have already encountered in the previous two chapters examples of such potential "misuses of statistics". In Chapter VII, we focused upon the misuse of biased samples or invalid measures to misleadingly prove a generalization, and in Chapter VIII, we saw how authors can provide statistics that seem to "prove" one cause but can be explained by rival hypotheses. While these are two of the most important ways that we can be fooled by statistics, we regularly encounter many other kinds of statistical lies.

As a critical thinker, you should strive to detect erroneous statistical reasoning. In a few short chapters, we cannot show you all the different ways that people can "lie with statistics." However, this chapter will provide some general strategies that you can use to detect such deception. In addition, it will alert you to flaws in statistical reasoning by illustrating a number of the most common ways that authors misuse statistical evidence.

◊   *Critical Question:*   **Are there flaws in the statistical reasoning?**

Catching Statistical Flaws

We suggest several strategies for locating deceptive statistics. First, try to find out as much as you can about how the statistics were obtained. Is there any reason to believe the numbers reported are accurate? Are the numbers just pulled out of thin air? Are there any biases affecting the numbers? For example, we just encountered a report, suggesting that frequently cited statistics on drunken driving may be wildly inaccurate because police let most drivers leave the scene without being tested for alcohol abuse. Consequently national statistics on the number of traffic deaths due to drunk driving may be unreliable and misleading. Someone discovered statistical deception by looking closely at how the numbers were created.

A second strategy is to *blind yourself to the author's statistics* and ask yourself, What statistical evidence would be helpful in proving the author's conclusion? Then compare the needed statistics to the statistics given. If the two do not match, you may have located a statistical error. The following example provides you with an opportunity to apply that strategy.

> According to a recent survey, Nissan Pulsar, Buick Skyhawk, and Ford EXP are the cars most preferred by women buyers. The survey demonstrated that these three cars were ranked highest among cars sold in the United States in terms of the percentage of their buyers who were women. That is, 58, 55, and 54 percent of Pulsar, Skyhawk and EXP buyers, respectively, were women.

Now, if you were interested in answering the question, "What cars do women prefer?", you would have wanted statistics showing the *percentage of total women car buyers who bought each kind of car*—not the *percentage of those who bought a particular kind of car who were women*. The fact is that at the time of this survey, more women were buying (in descending order) Chevrolet Cavaliers, Ford Escorts, and Chevrolet Celebrities than any other cars. The great discrepancy is due to the fact that many more of these latter cars are sold. Thus, 40 percent of 400,000 vehicles sold annually represents 160,000 women who bought cars, while 50 percent of 40,000 vehicles sold annually represents only 20,000 women car buyers.

You should be able to recognize the same kind of error in the following brief argument: Men must be worse drivers than women; 60 percent of drivers involved in accidents are men.

It is frequently difficult to know just what statistical evidence should be provided to back up a conclusion. Thus, let us suggest a further strategy. Examine the author's statistics *very closely* while *blinding yourself to the conclusion;* then ask yourself, "What is the appropriate conclusion to be drawn from those statistics?" Then, compare your conclusion with the author's. Try that strategy with the following example.

> Almost one-fourth of psychotherapists have sexually abused patients who were minors. A clinical psychologist surveyed distinguished psychologists around the country. Of the 90 who replied to the survey, 24 percent said they knew of instances in which therapists abused minor patients.

Did you come up with the following conclusion? Almost one-fourth of therapists *know about* instances when therapists abused minor patients. Do you see the difference between what the statistics proved and what the author concluded? If so, you have discovered how this author has lied with statistics. Note also that the author's reasoning here is flawed even if the samples were representative and the measures were valid.

A fourth helpful strategy for locating flaws in statistical reasoning is to compare the way the statistics are used with common kinds of statistical errors. To do that, you must be aware of such errors. The next sections illustrate a number of these.

Concluding One Thing, Proving Another

The following argument illustrates a common error in the use of statistics. Can you find it?

> A car dealer touted a particular car as a big success because only 5 out of 100 buyers who had bought the car had complained to the dealership about its performance. "When 95% of buyers are pleased," the salesman was heard to say, "then that's a darn good car."

The above essay misleads with statistics because the statistics and the conclusion refer to different characteristics. We cannot assume that all those who did not complain were pleased. The author thus proves one thing (few buyers complained) and concludes another (most buyers were pleased). An important lesson to learn from this example is to examine closely both the wording of the statistics and the wording of the conclusion to see whether they are referring to the same thing. If they are not, the author may have proven one thing, while concluding another.

The following example illustrates this same statistical deception.

In 1985, a newspaper columnist asked women readers, "Would you be content to be held close and treated tenderly and forget about 'the act?' " She reported that 72 percent of the respondents answered "yes" and concluded, "The survey means that a tremendous number of women out there are not enjoying sex."

Do you see how the wording in the statistical report differs markedly from the wording in the conclusion? Do you think results might have been different if the columnist had asked, "Are you enjoying the sex act?"

Misleading Percentages

(1) There has been a 50 percent increase in sales of widgets, as compared to only a 25 percent increase for our competitors.

(2) A crime wave has hit our city. Homicides have increased by 67 percent in the last year.

Both these examples use percentages, and the numbers are quite impressive. But important information has been omitted. Do you see what it is? The *absolute numbers* on which the percentages are based are not given. Maybe sales of widgets increased from 40 units to 60 units (that's 50 percent), while competitors' sales increased from 10,000 to 12,500 units (that's only 25 percent). Which increase seems more impressive now?

Look at the second example again. Would we be less alarmed if we knew that this increase was from three homicides to five?

When you encounter percentages, always ask yourself, What numbers are the percentages based upon? Be especially cautious when a writer compares percentages.

It is important to know not only the absolute numbers on which the percentages are based, but also the *absolute amount referred to by the percentages.* For example, a small percentage does not necessarily mean an insignificant number. The following examples illustrate.

Air bags are safe; they would malfunction in only 0.1 percent of our cars.

But if there are more than 150 million cars on the road, that's 150,000 total malfunctions. What if the malfunctions lead to serious accidents?

Our proposed relaxing of the emission standards will result in a reduction of atmospheric ozone levels of only 2 percent by the late 1990s.

Might not 2 percent be significant? Maybe that 2 percent will be an amount large enough to cause serious changes in our climate.

When you encounter percentages, ask yourself, "Are there any absolute amounts I need to know before evaluating the evidence?"

Another common way to mislead with percentages is to *choose a convenient base figure,* the figure by which we divide to compute a percentage. If the author wants to make a figure seem large, he can express it as the percentage of something small; if he wants to make it seem small, he can express it as the percentage of something large. For example, we can make the AIDS epidemic appear more or less serious by how we choose base figures. Do you see how basing the percentage of people suffering from AIDS on the *total population* of the U.S. would provide a different impact than basing the percentage on the *population of individuals engaging in frequent sexual activity?*

Impressively Large or Small Numbers

(1) If 785 psychiatrists support the insanity defense, that's good enough reason for me to support it.

(2) More than 10,500 people have bought Panthers this year, making it our biggest year ever.

(3) Boxing is less dangerous than other contact sports. A survey of sports-related deaths in New York City over a 30 year period revealed that baseball, with 43 deaths, led both football (22) and boxing (21) in terms of mortality.

The above numbers are meant to impress—either by their *largeness,* their *smallness,* or their *precision.* But all are deceptive because they omit important information.

In (1), don't we need to know how many psychiatrists were sent questionnaires, how many responded, and how qualified they were? In (2), wouldn't a percentage increase have been more meaningful? Maybe the increase was from 10,400 to 10,500, while other car sales were increasing at a much larger rate.

In (3) wouldn't we need to know what these numbers mean in terms of percentages of athletes involved in the sports? There are many fewer total boxers than there are baseball players.

The President of Chrysler Corporation converted impressively large numbers into impressively small numbers to support his attempt to obtain a 1.2 billion loan guarantee from the federal government. He pointed out to a congressional committee that $409 billion of loan guarantees had already been granted by the government. The $1.2 billion was less impressive in this context than it ordinarily would have been.

It seems to be human nature to equate precision with accuracy. Thus, we often give precise numbers more credit than they deserve. How worried should we be about litter if we see a report that 22,351 pounds of litter are deposited on our countryside daily? It is hard to tell, because we do not know how these numbers were arrived at; but for sure, we should not be concerned *simply because the numbers look precise.* Watch out for precise numbers! Often, there is no way that these numbers could have been accurately determined; and in those cases where such accuracy is possible, it should not be the preciseness alone that influences you.

Be wary of absolute numbers meant to impress you. Look for important omitted information. Ask yourself, How were these numbers determined? Also ask, Would it be helpful to know what these numbers mean in terms of percentages?

Ambiguous Averages

Recently, we came across a survey in which faculty members were asked to rate their own teaching ability. More than 90% rated themselves as "above average" teachers. Clearly, these teachers had their own personal notion of what "average teaching" is. However, when you encounter the "average" as a form of statistical evidence, it will probably have been formally calculated in one of three different ways. Each will be an attempt to provide an index of typical value, and each will have a different meaning; thus, you will want to determine whether the most appropriate average has been used.

Let's examine two statements that refer to "averages."

(1) Americans are better off than ever; the *average* salary of an American worker is now $27,600.

(2) The *average* pollution of air by factories is now well below the dangerous level.

Both examples use the word average. But there are three different ways to determine an average, and in most cases each will give you a different average. What are the three ways? One is to add up all the values and divide the total by the number of values. This method yields an average called the *mean*. A second way is to list all the values from highest to lowest, then find the one in the middle. This middle value is the median. Half of the values will be above the median; half will be below it. A third way is to list all the values and then count each different value or range of values. The value that appears most frequently is called the mode, the third kind of average.

It makes a big difference whether a writer is talking about the mean, median, or mode. Think about the salary distribution in the United States. Some individuals are paid extremely high salaries, such as $800,000 per year. Such high salaries will increase the mean dramatically. They will have little effect, however, on either the median or the mode. Thus, if one wishes to make the average salary seem high, the mean is probably the best average to present. You should now be able to see how important it is to know which average is used when people talk about salaries or income.

Now, let's look carefully at example (2). If the average presented is either the mode or the median, we may be tricked into a false sense of security. For example, what if only a few factories pollute highly, but the air as a whole is still being dangerously polluted. In such a case, the mode and the median pollution values could be quite low, but the mean would be very high.

When you see "average" values, always ask, Does it matter whether it is the mean, the median, or the mode? To answer this question, consider how the significance of the information might be changed by using the various meanings of average.

The Missing Range and Distribution

Not only is it important to determine whether an average is a mean, median, or mode, but it is often also important to determine the gap between the smallest and largest values—the *range*—and how frequently each of the values occurs—the *distribution*. For example, assume that you have to make the decision about whether to eat some fish caught in a nearby ocean. Would you be satisfied with information about the average mercury content in those fish? We wouldn't. We would want to know the range of mercury content—that is, the highest and lowest levels possible—as well as the frequency of the different levels. The average may be in the "safe" level; but if 10 percent of the fish contained levels of mercury well above the "safe" level, we suspect that you would rather eat something else for supper.

Let's consider another example in which knowing the range and distribution would be important.

America is not overcrowded. Nationally we have fewer than 60 people per square mile, a population density lower than that of most other countries.

First, we suspect that this population density figure represents the mean. While the mean density may be quite low, there obviously are areas in the United States—the Northeast, for example—with very high density figures. Thus, America may indeed be overcrowded in some areas, even though on the average it is not.

Thus, when an average is presented, ask yourself. Would it be important for me to know the range and distribution of values?

Faulty Statistical Comparisons

You will encounter two common kinds of faulty comparisons: (1) creating the appearance of a comparison, when none exists (an incomplete comparison) and (2) comparing two statistical values that reflect a different definition of a concept.

Each of the following illustrates an incomplete comparison.

(1) Fizz aspirin works 50% faster. (Faster than what?)

(2) Super bread is 30% more nutritious. (More nutritious than what?)

You will encounter examples like these daily. They give the appearance of saying something meaningful, but because they fail to provide the needed comparison, they communicate no real information. For example, if new Fizz works 50% better than old Fizz, then we should be less impressed than if new Fizz works 50% faster than competitors.

Comparisons may also be deceiving because of a *shift in the meaning of key terms*. For example, changes in crime rates, poverty rates, or unemployment rates may reflect changes in how these events were defined or measured, rather than in how often they occurred. It is possible to reduce poverty in the United States by simply decreasing the level of income required to qualify a person as "poor."

Unknowable Statistics

Can we know precisely the number of people in the U.S. who have AIDS, swap wives, have abortions, shoplift, commit white collar crimes, engage in affairs, drink more than three beers a day, beat their wives, are homeless, or use cocaine? We suspect not. Why? Because there are a variety of obstacles to getting accurate statistics for certain purposes, including unwillingness to provide truthful information, failure to report events, and physical barriers to observing events. Consequently, statistics are often in the form of "educated guesses." Such estimates can be quite useful; they can also be quite deceiving. You will want to be sensitive to distorted estimates. Always ask, "How did the author arrive at the estimate?"

You can see the impact of this statistical deception in reports on the effect of droughts. For example, in 1977 national magazines reported that more than 100,000 West Africans perished of hunger in the Sahel between 1968 and 1973 because of drought. How were such figures obtained? Someone calculated the normal death rate for the area, together with the highest death rate in any group of nomads during the drought and estimated an *upper limit* of a hundred thousand. Before we would want to judge the severity of the impact of such droughts, we would like better scientific evidence of the drought's effects.

Summary

In this chapter, we have highlighted a number of ways in which you can catch people "lying" with statistics. Following is a list of the ways we have discussed.

1. Form your conclusion from the evidence. If it doesn't match the writer's, something is probably wrong.
2. Ask about the numbers on which percentages are based, as well as the absolute amounts referred to by the percentages.
3. When you see impressively large or small numbers, determine what percentages would be useful to know before you interpret the statistics.
4. Determine whether it would be important to know if an average is the mean, mode, or median.
5. Determine whether it would be important to know the range and distribution of scores.
6. Check the basis for statistics. Ask, How does the author know?
7. Be alert to faulty statistical comparisons.

Practice Exercises

◊   *Critical Question:* **Are there flaws in the statistical reasoning?**

For each of the four practice passages, identify inadequacies in the evidence supporting the generalization.

Passage 1

Americans in general are spoiled. Most of us tend to judge the times in relative terms—and we have had rich relatives.

Materially, no people on earth have ever been as well off. So, when most of us say "times are bad," we say it in a comfortable home, with a well stocked electric refrigerator, television, and electric laundry equipment.

One in every five households in America in 1980 was affluent (had an income over \$25,00). Twenty-five years ago, only one in 33 households was this comfortable. Our personal income, disposable income, and personal savings have all climbed continuously since 1950.

True, we still have a vast army of poor in the country. One in every 8 Americans is living below the poverty level—one in every four aged 65 or over is poor. But twenty years ago, one in every five citizens was below the poverty line. In seven years, more than 14 million of us have climbed out of the poverty hole.

Any country in which, while population increased 56 percent, home ownership increased 100 percent, car ownership 130 percent, and personal savings 696 percent, is a long way from hard times. All that happened here between 1946 and 1980!

Passage 2

"It just isn't safe to drive anymore," my friend lamented, shaking his head as we tooled through Friday afternoon traffic on the freeway. But the fact is, driving in America is safer than it's been in over 60 years. In 1984, we had 18.4 traffic fatalities per 100,000 population, compared to 25.8 in 1970 and 23.3 in 1950. Today you're a lot safer on the road in your car than you are at home or at work. Twelve out of 100 Americans are laid up or need medical attention during the year because of household accidents. Five out of 100 get hurt at work. But only 2.2 per 100 are injured in automobile accidents.[1]

Passage 3.

Americans are more fit than ever. We are living longer. The average life expectancy at birth of American males climbed from 67.1 years in 1970 to 71.0 years by 1983, and that of American women from 74.7 years in 1970 to 78.3 years in 1983. Also, we are healthier: heart-disease deaths went down 36% nationally between 1978 and 1983 "probably due to reduced smoking, dietary changes, increased physical activity and improved medical care."

Our fitness drive is also paying off in gold at the Olympics. In 1984 Olympic Games track and field competition at Los Angeles, American men and women ran off with 14 gold medals compared to just six in 1976 (the last time we competed). In swimming competition our men and women took 21 gold medals, compared to only 15 in 1976.[2]

———————————————— Sample Responses ————————————————

Passage 1

CONCLUSION: *Materially, times are not bad.*

[1] Michael Bohmbach, *What's Right with America* (New York: Bantam, 1986), p. 36.
[2] Michael Bohmbach, *What's Right with America* (New York: Bantam, 1986), p. 69–70.

REASONS: *1. More households are affluent today.*

One in every five households in 1980 was affluent, with over $25,000 income. Twenty years ago, only one in 33 was comfortable.

2. Our personal income, disposable income, and personal savings have all climbed since 1950.

    a. Fewer Americans—one in every eight rather than one in every five— are below the poverty level. In seven years, more than 14 million of us have climbed out of poverty.

    b. While population has increased 56 percent, home ownership has increased 100 percent, car ownership 130 percent, and personal savings 696 percent between 1950 and 1980.

First, let's look at reason 1. The writer compares ratios—1 in 5 versus 1 in 33. Is this comparison legitimate? No. A very important piece of information has been omitted. What income was needed to be affluent 20 years ago? He has failed to take inflation into account. Using this same logic, probably only 1 in 1,000 would have been comfortable 50 years ago.

The first part of the evidence for reason 2 suffers from the same problem. This evidence cannot be judged until we know how "poverty level" is defined. If the definition has not taken inflation into account or has changed in its basic meaning over time, then these ratios cannot be legitimately compared. Also, in reason 2a, the writer has tossed out an impressively large number—14 million. What percentage does that reflect? Has he taken population growth into account?

Reason 2b presents impressive percentage differences, but what do those percentages mean? Percentages of what? For example, is the home ownership figure based on the percentage of people who own homes, or on the absolute number of homes owned? To judge these percentages, we need to know how they were figured and the absolute numbers on which they were based.

While population has increased 56 percent, what has been the increase in numbers of families or potential homebuyers?

Without the omitted information, the evidence presented does not adequately support the conclusion.

Passage 2

To evaluate this use of evidence, we should first ask ourselves, What would be the most appropriate evidence to address the question, "Is driving in America safer than it used to be?" In our opinion, the best statistic to answer that question is a comparison of the rate of serious accidents per specified numbers of miles driven under certain kinds of conditions, for example city and highway driving, between the present and the past. Those are not the figures given in the essay. The figures given are rates per *100,000 population*; thus the comparison is deceiving. For example, is the per capita mileage driven in 1984 the same as that driven in 1950 and 1970?

The second set of evidence also represents a deceptive comparison because the figures given fail to take into account the fact that we spend much more time in our offices and in our homes than we do in our cars. The appropriate statistic to be used here would be the rate of accidents per hour spent in each setting; note how that rate differs radically from the percentages actually given. (*Note*: The argument presented here is similar to arguing that it's safer for a woman to walk in New York's Central Park than to read in her home, because a larger percentage of rapes occur in the home than in parks.)

Passage 3

The first part of this argument illustrates proving one thing and concluding another. Increased longevity does not necessarily imply increased physical fitness. There is no indication of how "average" was determined, and different averages here might lead to different interpretations of the results. It would be useful here to have comparisons of distributions of the frequency of deaths at various age ranges to get a better sense of whether most people can now expect to live longer or whether a small segment of the population is living much longer than it used to, perhaps because of new medical advances for some disease that used to cause death at an early age. In this particular case, comparisons of the modal age range for dying might be useful.

Comparison of absolute numbers of winners at the Olympics is also potentially misleading because the number of Olympic events has markedly increased over the years and the number of high quality foreign athletes that we compete against also has varied. For example, in 1984 Soviet Bloc Nations did not compete, greatly reducing the quality of competition in some events, including track and field and swimming. Thus, such comparisons are misleading because it cannot be assumed that important characteristics stayed the same over time.

Passage 4 (Self-Examination)

The burdens of age are crushing the young. The old are being enriched at the expense of the young, and the present is being financed with tax money expropriated from the future.

In 1970, an elderly person was more likely to be living in poverty than a child. Today, a child is nearly six times more likely to be poor than is an elderly person. Nearly a fifth of all children today live in households that fall below the official poverty line. About 12.4 percent of all the elderly are poor, but once the value of Medicare and other in-kind benefits are added to their incomes, the poverty rate among the elderly drops to less than 4 percent. Of all Americans living in poverty today, 40 percent are under age 18.

Since 1970, Social Security benefits have increased by 46 percent in real terms, while wages and salaries—the chief source of income for nonelderly adults and their dependent children—have declined by 7 percent after adjusting for inflation. In fiscal 1983 the 11 percent of the population that was elderly received 51 percent of all government spending on social welfare programs. Today's Social Security beneficiary receives, on average, three dollars back for every one dollar that the individual and the employer contributed to the system. A typical young worker entering the labor force today, will not get back even one dollar for the one dollar she and the employer put in.

X

How Relevant Are the Analogies?

Education cannot prepare men and women for marriage. Trying to educate them for marriage is like trying to teach them to swim without allowing them to go into the water. It cannot be done.

Who is responsible for all this unethical behavior in the present Republican administration? It must be the President. After all, a fish rots from the head down. (Paraphrase of argument made at 1988 Democratic National Convention.)

You wouldn't want to ingest a spoonful of arsenic into your system daily. I do not understand why you keep smoking. They both can kill you.

These three arguments use analogies as evidence, a very different kind of evidence from what we have previously been evaluating. How do we decide whether it is good evidence? This chapter addresses that question.

Before reading the rest of the chapter, try to determine the persuasiveness of the three arguments at the beginning of the chapter. When you have completed the chapter, you should be able to evaluate them in a systematic and rewarding fashion.

Instead of relying upon empirical evidence, advocates often attempt to prove a conclusion about something with which they are relatively *unfamiliar* by relying upon its similarity to something with which they are familiar. They use *resemblance* as a form of evidence. They reason in the following way: "If these two things are alike in one respect, then they will probably be alike in other respects as well."

For example, when researchers were first seeking the cause of AIDS, they identified diseases that seemed to share some similarities with AIDS, such as hepatitis, and tried to infer conclusions about the cause of AIDS on the basis of what they knew about the causes of these other diseases. We reason in a similar fashion when we choose to see a movie because a friend recommends it. We reason that because we resemble each other in a number of likes and dislikes, we will enjoy the same movie.

We will refer to an argument that uses a well-known similarity between two things as the basis for a conclusion about a relatively unknown characteristic of one of those things as an *argument by analogy*. Reasoning by analogy is a common way of presenting evidence to support a conclusion.

The Rewards and Risks of Argument by Analogy

Analogies both stimulate insights and deceive us. For example, analogies have been highly productive in scientific and legal reasoning. When we infer conclusions about humans on the basis of research with mice, we reason by analogy. Much of our thinking about the structure of the atom is analogical reasoning. When we make a decision in a legal case, we base that decision on the similarity of that case to preceding cases; thus we reason by analogy. Such reasoning can be quite persuasive.

Analogical reasoning can also be quite deceptive. The Ayatollah Khomeini, for example, used an analogy to defend executing people convicted of adultery, prostitution, and homosexuality:

> If your finger suffers from gangrene, what do you do? You don't let the whole hand and then the body become filled with gangrene. No, you chop the finger off. So it is with corruption. We have to eliminate corruption.

Are gangrene and adultery, prostitution and homosexuality *that* similar? Not at all. Thus, we have a very deceptive analogy. When certain societies burned people as though they were "witches," they acted upon faulty analogical reasoning.

Because analogical reasoning is so common and has the potential to be both persuasive and faulty, you will find it very useful to recognize such reasoning and know how to systematically analyze and evaluate it.

   ◊   *Critical Question:*   **How good is the evidence: How relevant are the analogies?**

Analyzing Analogical Reasoning

Authors use analogies both to *clarify* and to *persuade*. For example, when a writer says of a main character in her novel, "Her eyes were like sparkling diamonds," she is trying to provide us with a vivid picture of the character's eyes; she is clarifying. For our purposes, however, we are more concerned with the use of analogy to support a conclusion, as in the following:

> You would indeed dry up jobs in the restaurant and entertainment business if you took away incentives for business lunch entertainment. More fundamental than that effect is the importance of creating business by using entertainment. Senator Long put it cogently; he said that business entertainment is to the corporate world what fertilizer is to agriculture; it makes for higher yields.[1]

We can use this example to take a close look at the basic reasoning structure of analogical reasoning.

The standard form of reasoning from analogy is as follows:

1. A and B are alike in the following *relevant* respects: W, X.
   (Fertilizer and business entertainment both can be used to stimulate growth).
2. We know it is true of A that Z
   (Without fertilizer, crop yields will probably decrease.)
3. Therefore, it is probably true of B that Z. (Without business entertainment, sales will decrease.)

Note that A refers to something familiar, B to something that we are trying better to understand.

The first statement establishes the basis for analogical reasoning; if the two things being compared in fact are not similar in relevant ways, then there is no reason to expect them to be similar in other ways. The second statement makes very clear what has been observed in A that seems highly relevant to understanding B. The third statement is the conclusion; that what we have observed in A, we will also observe in B.

Note that there is a very important unstated assumption in this reasoning linking (2) to (3): because A and B are similar in some ways, they will be similar in *all* ways. Obviously that assumption is not true! Thus you need to examine analogical reasoning very carefully before you permit yourself to be persuaded.

Given this structure, you can successfully analyze analogical reasoning by asking yourself the following four questions:

1. What are the two things being compared? Of these, which is familiar, and which are we learning about?
2. In what respects are the two things alike?
3. What else is known about the familiar thing?
4. What is the conclusion of the argument?

Let's practice asking these questions, using the following example.

---

[1] Adapted from R. E. Kipling, "Conversation: The Three Martini Lunch," *Politics Today* (May/June, 1978), 5.

Premarital sex is desirable. After all, you wouldn't buy a pair of shoes without first trying them on.

Compare your answers to the four questions with ours.

1. Engaging in premarital sex (B) is being compared to trying on shoes (A).
2. Engaging in premarital sex and trying on shoes are alike in the following respect: they both permit "testing out" something before "buying" it (W).
3. It is true of trying on shoes that it increases the likelihood of making a satisfactory choice (Z).
4. Therefore, it is probably true of premarital sex that it will increase the likelihood of making a satisfactory choice.(Z)

Note that analyzing an analogical argument in this way clarifies all its essential parts. You are now ready to make a judgment about whether the evidence (that is, the resemblance) supports the conclusion.

How to Evaluate Arguments by Analogy

To evaluate the quality of an analogy, you need to focus on three factors:

1. The number of ways A and B are similar.
2. The *relevance* of the similarities between A and B.
3. The *relevance* of the differences between A and B.

In general, the more similarities between A and B, the more confidence you can have that they will be similar in Z. For example, scientific researchers are more willing to infer conclusions about humans based on research with monkeys (similar to humans in many ways) than they are to infer conclusions about humans based upon research with mice.

A word of caution! You can almost always find *some* similarities between any two things. So, analogical reasoning will not be persuasive simply because of many similarities.

In comparing premarital sex and trying on shoes, we determined only one similarity, and we should be very wary of this analogy until we answer our next two questions.

Let's now look at question 2. How do we determine whether the similarities between A and B are relevant? Using our previous symbols, it is likely that W and X will be relevant to Z if they are *causally related* to Z.

Staying with our shoe-fitting analogy, we would want to know whether characteristic W, testing out something before making a decision, is potentially causally related to characteristic Z, making a satisfactory choice. Because W and Z do appear causally related, the analogy has suggested an important principle; now we want to consider further the possible persuasiveness of the analogy by asking our third question: Are the *differences* between A and B *relevant*?

We can follow the same procedure in determining whether the differences are relevant that we followed in determining whether the similarities are relevant. Are the differences *causally related* to Z, the characteristic of interest. Analogies will always differ in *some* respect. But we only weaken analogical reasoning when we find a relevant difference.

Can you think of a major difference between trying on shoes and premarital sex that is causally related to Z, satisfaction with the outcome? There are several relevant differences. For example, a person can develop sexual compatibility with another person through a slow learning process; if a shoe doesn't fit initially, it is highly unlikely that a person will ever feel compatible with the shoe. In addition, sex is only one of many possible dimensions affecting the quality of personal relationships; fit is one of very few dimensions affecting later satisfaction with a shoe.

Because of these major relevant differences, we conclude that this analogy is faulty; it fails to provide strong support for the conclusion that premarital sex is desirable.

Answering the above questions should help you decide whether an argument by analogy supports its conclusion. Strong analogies will be ones in which the two things we compare possess relevant similarities and lack relevant differences.

Let's check out the soundness of the following argument by analogy.

I do not send my son outside when he is sick with flu or measles. Why should parents want to send their youngsters with AIDS to school? Are these children up to going to class? Do they feel like running, jumping and playing when they are ill? You do not let your child go to school with the measles, so keep him at home if he has AIDS. After all, he is sick.

First, let's analyze the reasoning:

1. Measles (A) and AIDS (B) are similar in that they are both illnesses (W).
2. It is true that if a child has measles (A), we don't send him to school (Z).
3. Therefore, if a child has AIDS (B), we should not send him to school (Z).

Next, let's evaluate.

A major similarity between measles and AIDs that is potentially causally relevant to sending children to school (Z) is "having an illness." We note some relevant differences, however. Measles is associated with severe symptoms that gradually disappear, and the measles virus is easily transferred from one person to another. Development of symptoms from AIDS is very unpredictable, and there may be long periods without acute symptoms. It is not highly communicable because it is transferred through the blood. Thus, children with AIDS often feel well enough to want to attend school and, given our present state of knowledge, seem highly unlikely to pass the disease on to others. Because these differences should have some impact upon whether we keep a child out of school (Z), they are relevant; thus, the analogy fails to provide strong support for the conclusion.

Generating Competing Analogies

Another strategy that may help you evaluate reasoning by analogy is to generate alternative analogies for understanding the same phenomenon that the author or speaker is trying to understand. Such analogies may either support or contradict the conclusions inferred from the original analogy. If they contradict the conclusion, they then reveal problems in the initial reasoning by analogy.

For example, when authors argue that alcoholics should be eligible for health insurance, sick leave and other benefits associated with inadvertent disease, they use a particular analogy to infer conclusions about alcoholics: alcoholism is like a biologically caused disease. Others, however, have generated an alternative analogy, arguing that alcoholism is like a "breakdown of the will." Note how thinking about this different analogy may create doubts about the persuasiveness of the original analogy.

Although generating alternative analogies is a difficult process, we highly recommend that you try it. The results can give you many important insights about the phenomenon you are trying to understand, as well as about the strength of the argument you are evaluating.

A productive way to generate your own analogies is the following:

1. Identify some important features of what you are studying.
2. Try to identify other situations with which you are familiar that have some similar features. Give free rein to your imagination. Brainstorm. Try to imagine diverse situations.
3. Try to determine whether the familiar situation can provide you some insights about the unfamiliar situation.

For example, in thinking about alcoholism, you could try to think of other situations in which people repeatedly seek immediate gratification despite potential long-term negative effects. Do smoking, eating, or gambling come to mind? Do they trigger other ways to think about alcoholism?

Summary

You should now be capable of systematically evaluating the three brief analogical arguments at the beginning of the chapter. Ask the questions you need to ask to determine the structure of the argument. Then, ask the questions to evaluate the argument. Look for relevant similarities and differences. Usually, the greater the ratio of relevant similarities to relevant differences, the stronger the analogy. An analogy is especially compelling if you can find *no* relevant difference, and you can find good evidence that the relevant similarities do indeed exist.

We found a relevant difference that weakens each of our three initial sample analogies. Check your evaluation against our list.

(First example) The primary skills required for successful swimming are motor skills; many skills required for a successful marriage are much more complex than motor skills. Such skills as money management and communication can be learned outside the context of marriage.

(Second example) The "parts" of a political administration function much more independently than the parts of a fish. Unethical behavior at lower levels can result from complex and diverse causes.

(Third example) In the case of arsenic, death is immediate and certain; in the case of smoking, death is statistically neither immediate nor certain. Also, smoking provides a great deal of immediate satisfaction; arsenic does not.

Remember: Analogical reasoning can be suggestive only, because we can never assume that A and B are alike in *all* respects.

Practice Exercises

◊ *Critical Question:* **How relevant are the analogies?**

For each of the practice passages, identify and evaluate the relevance of the analogies used as evidence to support the reasoning.

Passage 1

It is important for people to "let their anger out," to ventilate their anger. Energy that is blocked up needs to find release. Any feeling that gets dammed up is dangerous to us because it is likely to "spill over" and possibly flood the rest of our personality system. By expressing your anger, you empty your emotional reservoir, and will feel a gratifying sense of emotional release, freeing up energy to be used for more constructive efforts. In fact, if people could overcome their emotional inhibitions and express their emotions, they would eliminate disturbing tensions and conquer many nagging aches and pains.

Passage 2

Those who support sanctions against South Africa and yet oppose boycotts of erotic magazines sold at neighborhood stores are hypocrites. Pornography enslaves people in the same way Apartheid enslaves them. Nude photography obliterates the emotional, mental and spiritual worth of a person. Those people who support sanctions against South Africa would like nothing better than to impose their morals on the Pretoria government. But here at home, they get squeamish about having to live under someone else's moral code.

Passage 3

We need a system of mandatory, consistent sentences for criminals. Let's assign numbers to each criminal act based upon its severity, then assign penalties accordingly. That is the only fair way to assure that we can get judges to dispense penalties in a just fashion. To assign a numerical value to a particular crime is not unlike equating a touchdown to six points or a field goal to three points.

Passage 1

CONCLUSION: *It is beneficial for people to express their anger.*

REASONS: *Feelings of anger are like water building up in a reservoir; if not released, they will overflow.*

This argument is based upon a comparison. Let's try to determine how much credibility we should give to the comparison by first putting the comparsion into the standard form of an argument from analogy and then applying our evaluation criteria.

Water in a reservoir (A) is like the feeling of anger (B) in the following ways: they both are dammed up (W), one by a dam, the other by some mental mechanism like a dam, and they both can spill over (X), if no mechanism releases them. It is also true of water in a reservoir that when an engineer opens a valve, the release of the water reduces the pressure on the dam and prevents a potentially destructive overspill (Z). Therefore it is probably true of feelings of anger that when a person expresses the anger, its release will reduce the psychic pressure, preventing the anger from spilling over, resulting in some destructive act, such as overt aggression (Z).

Are A and B alike in a number of ways that seem relevant to Z? Yes. We can see that the similarities could be causally related to the need to "ventilate" or to "release." Are there relevant differences? We can think of several. Perhaps anger is more like a "process" than like a "substance", and psychological mechanisms are much more flexible than a dam. Anger may, for example, be like an ongoing experience determined in large part by how we are thinking at the time about external events, and thus controllable by changing our thinking rather than by "releasing the pressure."

Because we see a potentially very relevant difference, we do not view this analogy as strongly supporting the conclusion.

Passage 2

CONCLUSION: *We should support boycotts of erotic magazines sold at convenience stores.*

REASONS: *Nude photography enslaves people in the same way that Apartheid does, and many of us favor sanctions on South Africa.*

Let's again structure this argument in the standard analogical form. The author is asserting that a system that makes available photographs of the naked human body (A) is like Apartheid in South Africa (B) in the following respects: they both demean the emotional, mental, and spiritual worth of a person, and they both enslave the people (W, X). It is true of Apartheid that we impose economic sanctions on those responsible (Z). Therefore, it is probably true of erotic magazines that we should impose economic sanctions upon them (Z).

We find this analogy especially weak for several reasons. First, whether the similarities even exist is questionable. Secondly, there are many relevant differences between selling magazines displaying nude photographs at a local convenience store and Apartheid.

The author talks of "enslavement of people by the pornography industry." But how does pornography enslave the people? And if it does, isn't the enslavement quite different from enslavement in South Africa? Who forces people to view and/or buy sexual magazines? Are not the forces that lead people to participate in nude photography quite different from the forces that prevent some South Africans from self-expression? And isn't the imposing of morals on the Apartheid government quite different from imposing moral rules on those who display magazines. Much of the opposition to the Pretoria government is based on its restriction of freedom of expression, consistent with the government's definition of morality. Such boycotts might also be an attempt to shape society to fit a certain group's definition of morality. Thus, while a person can provide cogent arguments against displaying erotic magazines at convenience stores, we would view this particular argument as a faulty analogy.

Passage 3

CONCLUSION: *Fixed sentences for criminals are desirable.*

REASONS: *Assigning sentences for a crime is like assigning points in a football game.*

The author is trying to demonstrate a relevant similarity: assigning points to a touchdown and assigning points to a crime. Also, a system of points makes a football game fair. But, assigning points to a criminal act is a much more complex process than assigning points to a touchdown. For example, whereas we do not see the circumstances of a football touchdown as relevant to how many points we give it, we might see the circumstances of a crime as highly relevant to how much punishment a criminal should receive. Also, we may desire flexibility and a human element in the very serious business of deciding upon criminal penalties, something we would not desire in a football context—a game. It is possible that judges can better determine which penalty best fits the crime because of their experience and their familiarity with the case. Because of the many relevant differences, we conclude that this analogy is not very relevant.

Passage 4 (Self-Examination)

The point to be made . . . is simply this: if the poor are different in significant ways from the rest of us, are these differences *cultural?* It is easy to be misled and to fall into the easy jargon of the day and call all kinds of minor phenomena cultures or subcultures. Consider a possible analogy: there are several million men who share certain traits, centering around an addiction to alcohol; they work irregularly, for example, show a high arrest rate, and also have high rates of family disorganization; they represent a minority of alcoholics, an even smaller minority of heavy drinkers. On the basis of such findings, would we feel comfortable in talking about a culture, or a subculture, of alcohol. A minority of the rich share many traits of the Sanchez and Rios families, and other families studied by Oscar Lewis—they are alienated from social institutions, tend to be unemployed or irregularly employed, demonstrate high rates of antisocial behavior, and have high divorce rates. Does this small group of the rich constitute a Culture of Affluence?

Poverty is not caused by the "culture of poverty" and the presumed life styles of the poor. It is caused by a lack of money. The overwhelming majority of the poor are poor because they have first: insufficient income; and second: no access to methods of increasing that income—that is, no power. . . . The facts are clear, and the solution seems rather obvious—raise their income and let their "culture," whatever it might be, take care of itself.[2]

[2] Adapted from William Ryan, *Blaming the Victim* (New York: Pantheon Books, 1976).

XI

Are There Any Errors in Reasoning?

In the previous four chapters, you learned questions to ask to decide how well evidence supports factual claims. But good evidence is only part of good reasoning. We also need good logic! We have already learned that authors make logical mistakes in using evidence to prove a factual claim. Authors, however, make many other kinds of mistakes in their reasoning. Let's examine such a mistake:

In the fall of 1988, presidential candidate George Bush responded to the controversy surrounding whether the family of his running mate, Sen. Dan Quayle, helped Quayle get into the Indiana National Guard to avoid the Vietnam draft as follows:

> Dan Quayle served in the National Guard, signing up in a unit that had vacancies at the time and now he is under shrill partisan attack . . . . True, he didn't go to Vietnam, but his unit wasn't sent. But there's another truth; he did not go to Canada, he did not burn his draft card, and he damned sure didn't burn the American flag!

Note that Mr. Bush presents factual claims, and we have no reason to doubt them. But they are *not relevant* to the conclusion! The issue is whether Quayle's family helped him avoid the draft, not whether he is a patriot. As far as we know, Quayle also never bought foreign cars or talked back to his mother. But, these facts are not relevant. We would have to supply an absurd assumption to "fill in the gap" between the reason and the conclusion. Rather than present a relevant reason, Mr. Bush appeals to our emotions and distracts us from the basic issue; he commits an error in reasoning.

This chapter gives you practice in identifying such errors in reasoning. An error in reasoning occurs whenever authors *(a) provide reasoning that requires erroneous or incorrect assumptions,* or *(b) provide support for the conclusion that is actually part of the conclusion "in disguise."*

Evaluating Assumptions

If you have been able to locate assumptions (see Chapters V and VI), you already have a major skill for finding errors in reasoning. The more questionable the assumption, the more erroneous the reasoning. Some reasoning will involve descriptive assumptions that you may reject. Some reasoning will be so irrelevant to the conclusion that you would have to supply blatantly erroneous assumptions to provide a logical link. You should immediately reject such reasoning. Some reasoning will involve value assumptions, and you will have to use your own personal value preferences as a guide to evaluating them.

To demonstrate the process you should go through to evaluate assumptions, we will examine the quality of the reasoning in the following passage. We will begin by assembling the structure.

> The question involved in this legislation is a critical one. It is not really a question of whether alcohol consumption is or is not detrimental to health. Rather it is a question of whether Congress is willing for the Federal Communications Commission to make an arbitrary decision that prohibits alcohol advertising on radio and television. If we should permit the FCC to take this action in regard to alcohol, what is there to prevent them from deciding next year that candy is detrimental to the public health in that it causes obesity, tooth decay, and other health problems? What about milk and eggs? Milk and eggs are high in saturated animal fat and no doubt increase the cholesterol in the bloodstream, believed by many heart specialists to be a contributing factor in heart disease. Do we want the FCC to be able to prohibit the advertising of milk, eggs, butter, and ice cream on TV?

> We all know that no action by the federal government, however drastic, can or will be effective in eliminating alcohol consumption completely. National prohibition of alcoholic beverages was attempted, but the Eighteenth Amendment, after only fourteen years of stormy existence, was repealed by the Twenty-first.

> CONCLUSION: *The FCC should not prohibit alcohol advertising on radio and television.*

> REASONS: *1. If we permit the FCC to prohibit advertising on radio and television, the FCC will soon prohibit many kinds of advertising, because many products present potential health hazards.*

> *2. No action by the federal government can or will be effective in eliminating alcohol consumption completely. National prohibition of alcohol didn't work.*

First, the acceptability of the first reason depends upon an underlying assumption that once we allow actions to be taken on the merits of one case, it will be more difficult to stop actions on similar cases. We do not agree with this assumption, mainly because we believe that there are plently of steps in our legal system to prevent such actions if they appear unjustified. Thus, we judge this reason to be unacceptable.

The credibility of the second reason is questionable because of the weak evidence—an exciting example out of the past. Even if this reason were true, we disagree with an assumption linking the reason to the conclusion, the assumption that the major goal of prohibiting alcohol advertising on radio and television is to *eliminate alcohol consumption completely*. A more likely goal is to *reduce consumption*. Thus we judge this reason to be weakly supported, and judge the reasoning connecting the reason to the conclusion as having questionable validity.

As you search for errors in reasoning, *always keep the conclusion in mind;* then ask yourself, What reasons would be adequate to support this position? If there is a large difference between the reasons presented and what you believe to be strong reasons, there is likely to be an error in reasoning. A further hint we can give you is that, typically, when individuals are claiming that one *action* is more desirable than another, strong reasons will refer to the advantages or disadvantages of adopting a particular position. When reasoning strays from advantages and disadvantages, be especially watchful for errors in reasoning.

Common Reasoning Errors

There are numerous common reasoning errors. Many are so common that they have been given fancy names. Fortunately, it is not necessary for you to be aware of all the common reasoning errors and their names to be able to locate them. If you ask yourself the right questions, you will be able to find reasoning errors—even if you can't name them. Thus, we have adopted the strategy of emphasizing self-questioning strategies, rather than of asking you to memorize an extensive list of possible kinds of errors.

We are now going to take you through some exercises in discovering common reasoning errors. Once you know how to look, you will be able to find most errors. In Exercise A, do the following: First, identify the conclusion and reason. Second, determine whether the reason states an advantage or a disadvantage. Third, identify any necessary assumptions by asking yourself, If the reason were true, what would one have to believe for it to logically support the conclusion, and what does one have to believe for the reason to be true? Last, ask yourself, Do these assumptions make sense? If an obviously erroneous assumption is being made, you have found an error in reasoning, and that reasoning can be judged invalid.

Exercise A

Fluorine is the most toxic chemical on earth; it is so powerful in its corrosive effect that it is used to etch glass. The idea of putting that sort of chemical into our drinking water is just insane. Fluoridation is a menace to health.

Additionally, many medical associations are opposed to fluoridation. For instance, the Texas Medical Association declined to recommend it. It's not hard to explain why some doctors favor fluoridation. For instance, one of its leading advocates has been

Dr. Danger, Dean and Research Professor of Nutrition at the State University Medical School. In the past 6 years, Dr. Danger received over $350,000 from the food processors, the refined-sugar interests, the soft-drink people, and the chemcial and drug interests. Every true nutritionist knows that it is refined sweets, soft drinks, and refined flour that are the basic causes of defective teeth. Is it any wonder that the processors of these foods are so active in helping the chemical interests to cover up for them?

As a first step in analyzing for fallacies, let's outline the argument.

CONCLUSION: *Drinking water should not be fluoridated.*

REASONS: *1. Fluorine is the most dangerous toxic chemical on earth; it is so powerful in its corrosive effect that is used to etch glass.*
2. Many medical associations are opposed to fluoridation. The Texas Medical Association declined to recommed it.
3. Some doctors personally benefit by endorsing fluoridation. Dr. Danger received large sums of money from business groups during the time he endorsed fluoridation.

In the first paragraph, the author tries to prove that fluoridation is very dangerous—a disadvantage. He does this by stating that fluorine is the most toxic chemical on earth; it is so powerful in its corrosive effect that it is used to etch glass. What erroneous assumptions are being made? First, note that the author used *fluorine* to prove something about *fluoridation*. A dictionary will quickly show you that fluorine is not the same as fluoride. The writer has *shifted words* on us. One cannot assume that fluorine and fluoride have the same effect; nor can one assume that any such chemicals when in diluted form will behave as they do in undiluted form. Thus, there is no proof here that fluoridation is dangerous—only that fluorine, in undiluted form, is dangerous.

Now, carefully examine the author's second argument. What assumptions are being made? To prove that fluoridation is bad, he appeals to a personal testimonial; he thus moves away from pointing out factual advantages or disadvantages of fluoridation. A position is not bad just because authorities are against it. What is important in determining the validity of such reasoning is the evidence that the authorities are using in making their judgment.

In addition, in this second argument the writer *shifts words* on us again. He argues that many medical associations "are opposed to" fluoridation and supports this with the fact that the Texas Medical Association "declined to recommend" it. Does *decline to recommend* mean the same as *oppose?* No—*oppose* implies definite disapproval; *decline to recommend* simply signifies an unwillingness to approve. Additionally, is the Texas Medical Association representative of medical associations in general?

What about the third paragraph? Has the writer pointed out advantages or disadvantages of fluoridation? No. He has basically tried to prove that Dr. Danger is biased in his viewpoint. He has attacked Dr. Danger, who favors fluoridation. He has not proven anything about the benefits or dangers of fluoridation. Even if Dr. Danger is biased, his views on fluoridation may still be correct. The issue is whether or not fluoridation is desirable, not whether Dr. Danger is an ethical person. *One does not prove a point by attacking a person.* The assumption that because a person may have undesirable qualities, his ideas are therefore undesirable is clearly a bad assumption. Such an argument diverts attention from the issue. A good argument attacks ideas, not the person with the ideas. Attacking a person, rather than ideas, is frequently called an *ad hominem* argument.

Now, we will look at an argument favoring fluoridation.

Exercise B

Fluoridation is opposed by a crackpot, antiscientific minority. I do not believe that a minority ever has the right to keep the majority from getting what they want. In any city where a majority of us want fluoridation, we should have it; that is the democratic way.

First, let's again keep the structure of the argument in mind as we search for errors. Also, let's once again ask whether the author has strayed from discussing the advantages and disadvantages of fluoridation.

Clearly, the author has not focused on the advantages and disadvantages. First, what do you think about the phrase "crackpot, antiscientific minority"? Obviously, he is giving his opponents a bad name. This is a common practice referred to as *name calling.* For this reason to support the conclusion, it must be assumed that if a group can be labeled with negative adjectives, then their ideas are erroneous. Wrong! Even if opponents of fluoridation deserve their bad name, it is still very possible that fluoridation *is* a bad thing, according to the *facts.* Be wary of name calling!

What about the argument that we ought to do what the majority wants? Certainly it sounds very democratic. But what assurance do we have that the majority are basing their judgments on the *appropriate evidence*? What if there were evidence available that fluoridation caused cancer, but the majority continued to ignore the evidence? We think you get the point. There is no substitute for the facts. Be wary of phrases like, "Most Americans agree that . . ." or "Everybody knows that . . . ." These phrases represent appeals to group-approved attitudes and are frequently referred to as *ad populum* arguments. Again, note that such arguments divert attention from the real issue.

Now let's examine some arguments related to another controversy: Should Congress approve a federally funded child development program that would provide day-care centers for children?

Exercise C

I am against the government's child development program. First, I am interested in protecting the children of this country. They need to be protected from social planners and *self-righteous ideologues* who would disrupt the normal course of life and *tear* them from their mothers and families to make them *pawns* in a universal scheme designed to produce infinite happiness in 20 years. Children should grow up with their mothers, not with a series of caretakers and nurses' aides.

What is at issue is whether parents shall continue to have the right to form the characters of their children, or whether the State with all its power should be given the tools and techniques for forming the young.

Let's again begin by outlining the argument.

CONCLUSION: *I am against the government's child-development program.*

REASONS: 1. *Our children need to be protected from social planners and self-right-eous ideologues, who would disrupt the normal course of life and tear them from their families.*
2. *The parents, not the State, should have the right to form the characters of their children.*

As critical readers, we should be looking for specific facts about the program. Do you find any specifics in the first reason? No. The reason is saturated with undefined and emotionally loaded generalities. We have italicized a couple of these terms. Such terms will typically generate negative emotions, which the writer hopes the reader will associate with the position he is attacking. Again, the writer is engaging in name calling. The use of emotionally charged negative terms serves to distract the reader from the facts.

The writer has tricked us in another way. He states that the program will "tear them from their families and mothers," and the children will be "pawns in a universal scheme." Of course, nobody wants these things to happen to their children. However, the important question is whether *in fact* the bill will do these things. Not likely! The writer is playing two common tricks on us. First, he is appealing to our emotions with his choice of words. Second, he has set up a position to attack which in fact does not exist, making it much easier to get the reader on his side. He has *extended* the opposition's position to an "easy-to-attack" position. The erroneous assumption in this case is that the position attacked is the same as the position actually presented in the legislation. The lesson for the critical thinker is, When someone attacks aspects of a position, always check to see if he is fairly representing the position. If not, you have located the *extension* error. The best way to check how fairly a position is being represented is to get the facts about all positions.

Let's now look closely at the second reason. The writer states that either parents shall have the right to form the characters of their children, or else the State should be given the decisive tools. For statements like this to be true, one must assume that there are only two choices. Are there? No! The writer has created a *false dilemma*. Isn't it possible for the child development program to exist and also for the family to have a significant influence on the child? Always be cautious when controversies are treated as if only two choices are possible; there are frequently more than two. When a writer oversimplifies an issue by stating only two choices, the error is referred to as an *either—or* error. To find *either—or* errors, be on the alert for phrases like the following:

either . . . or
the only alternative is
the two choices are
because A has not worked, *only* B will

Let's shift to a different controversy: Should there be businesses that sell term papers to students?

What's wrong with buying term papers? Most students resort to buying them only because they realize that the system is rotten; the term paper itself has become a farce in the eyes of the students, because they are required to go through the mechanical motions, month after month, of putting things down tediously on paper, writing correct sentences, organizing their paragraphs and ideas, thinking up arguments to use, and all those rituals—surely you aren't going to claim that that is education. Real education is ecstasy, the peak experience.[1]

Again, let's start by outlining the argument.

CONCLUSION: *Buying term papers is defensible.*

REASON: *Term paper rituals are not education; real education is ecstasy, the peak experience.*

The major reason given is "proven" by the "fact" that "real education is ecstasy, the peak experience." Sounds good—but what does it mean? The writer has tried to seduce the reader by using showy terms that have an emotional appeal. He has provided us with glittering generalities, hoping that we will not require a more precise or specific definition of the goals of education and of the appropriate behaviors for obtaining such goals. A position is not good or bad because we can associate it with a good or bad label or a smug phrase. *Good reasons provide specifics!*

Be especially on the lookout for glib phrases or pet slogans. A few common ones follow:

A woman's place is in the home.
Nice guys finish last. (Always?)
Vote for our party—we are for peace and prosperity. (Who isn't?)
Human nature is unchangeable.
Work is what made this country great.
Moderation is everything.

[1]M. Beardsley, *Thinking Straight*, 4th ed. (Englewood Cliffs, N.J.: Prentice-Hall, 1975), pp. 237–38.

Further Diversions

Emotional language is one way that writers and speakers divert our attention from the issue. There is another very common diversionary device. Let's take a look.

> I do not see why people think it is so important to the cause of women's rights that we adopt the Equal Rights Amendment. Why, just look at all the problems we are having with hiring enough women in universities. We hear stories all the time of women not wanting the jobs that are offered.

What is the real issue? Passing or not passing the ERA. But if you are not careful you will get involved in the question of whether there are enough qualified women for academic jobs rather than in the issue of the advantages and disadvantages of the ERA. The writer has diverted the reader's attention to another issue. When a writer or speaker does this, we can say that he has drawn a *red herring* across the trail of the argument. Red herring arguments are very common. Many of us are adept at these, as the following example illustrates:

> MOTHER: Why did you come home an hour late for dinner, when I told you to be on time?
> DAUGHTER: You're always picking on me.

If the daughter is successful, the issue will become whether the mother is picking on her daughter, not why the daughter was out late.

You should normally have no difficulty spotting red herrings as long as you keep the real issue in mind as well as the kind of evidence needed to resolve it.

Appeals to Authority

You encounter appeals to many forms of authority on a daily basis. They are often in the form of of testimonials.

> Movie reviewers: "One of the ten best movies of the year."—Valerie Viewer, *Toledo Gazette*.
> Organizations: "The American Medical Association supports this position."
> Athletes: "Touchdown Beer is a real competitor."—Bill Battle, quarterback.
> Researchers: "Studies show . . ."
> Relatives: "My grandfather says . . ."
> Religion: "The Koran says . . ."
> Magazines: "According to *Newsweek* . . ."

You can easily add to our list. It should be obvious that some appeals to authority should be taken much more seriously as evidence than others. Why? Because some authorities are much more careful in giving an opinion than others.

For example, *Newsweek* and *Time* are much more likely to carefully evaluate the available evidence prior to stating an opinion than is the *National Enquirer*. Athletes are less likely to have evaluated a political candidate than are editorial writers for major newspapers.

We should treat an appeal to authority as good evidence when the authority is any of the following:

1. In a position to have especially good access to pertinent facts.
2. Qualified by training to make these kinds of inferences, or
3. Relatively free of vested interests and biases.

What should you do when you encounter appeals to authority? Be wary! Ask yourself questions concerning the expertise of the authority. Does the authority have special access to objective evidence? Is the authority respected by others in its field? Does it have experience in the field it is discussing? Has it had a history of being reliable? Is it likely to be objective in its judgment? Is it up to date?

Confusing "What Should Be" and "What Is"

> Landlords should clean apartments before they rent them. By cleaning their rental properties, they will be giving their customers what any renter desires—a fresh apartment.

> Being fully aware of this moral obligation, I persuaded my brother to move to a rental unit in Colorado, even though he had never seen it. Now he's mad at me; the apartment was filthy when he arrived. I can't understand what happened?

Do you? The advice to move to Colorado to an unseen rental unit was based on an error in reasoning. That something *should be* true, that is, apartments should be clean when rented, in no way guarantees that what *is* true will conform to the prescription.

Another common illustration of this reasoning error occurs when discussing proposals for government regulation. For instance, someone might argue that regulating advertising for children's television programs is undesirable because parents *should* turn the channel or shut off the television if advertising is deceptive. Perhaps parents in a perfect world would behave in this fashion. Many parents, however, are too busy to monitor children's programming.

When a persons reasons that someone *must be* telling the truth because people *should* tell the truth, he is committing an error in reasoning. We would hope that what should be the case would guide our behavior. Yet many observations convince us that just because advertisers, politicians, and authors *should* not mislead us is no protection against their regularly misleading us. The world around us is a poor imitation of what the world should be like.

Confusing Naming with Explaining

Another confusion is responsible for an error in reasoning that we often encounter when seeking explanations. To explain requires an analysis of why an event occurred. Explaining is demanding work that often tests the boundaries of what we know. It's frequently tempting to hide our ignorance, when asked for an explanation, by labeling or naming what occurred. Then we pretend the name we attached to the event provides adequate insight about causation.

We do so because the naming seduces us into believing we have identified something the person *has* that makes her act accordingly. For example, instead of specifying the complex set of situational factors that lead a person to manifest an angry emotion, we say the person *has* a ''bad temper.''

A couple of examples should be adequate to heighten your alertness to this confusion.

1. In response to Dad's heavy drinking, Mom is asked by her adult daughter, ''Why is Dad behaving so strangely?'' Mom replies, ''He's having a mid-life crisis.''
2. A patient cries everytime the counselor asks about his childhood. An intern who watched the counseling session asks the counselor, after the patient has left, ''Why does he cry when you ask about his youth?'' The counselor replies, ''He's neurotic.''

Perhaps in each case the respondent could have explained but was just in a hurry. But for whatever reasons, neither respondent satisfactorally explained what happened. For instance, the specifics of Dad's genetic inheritance, job pressures, marital strife, and exercise habits would have provided the basis for explaining the heavy drinking. ''A mid-life crisis'' is not only inadequate; it misleads. We think we know why Dad is drinking heavily but we don't.

Be especially alert for this error when people allege that they have discovered a cause for behavior, yet all they have provided is a different name for the behavior.

Searching for Perfect Solutions

1. I cannot support your request for a larger educational budget because there will still be illiterate people even if you received the request.
2. Why try to restrict people's access to abortion clinics in the United States? Even if you were successful, a woman seeking an abortion could still fly to Europe to acquire an abortion.
3. Our city council decided not to hire an additional detective; crime would not cease just because we have another policeperson on the payroll.

All three of these arguments take the same form:

A solution to X does not deserve our support unless it destroys the problem entirely. If we ever find a perfect solution, then we should adopt it.

In each case the error in reasoning is the same. Just because part of a problem would remain after a solution is tried, does not mean the solution is unwise. A partial solution may be vastly superior to no solution at all; it may make a contribution to solving the problem. It may move us a step closer to solving the problem completely. If we waited for perfect solutions to emerge, we would often find ourselves paralyzed, unable to act. A particular solution may be the best we can find.

Begging the Question

Sometimes a conclusion is supported by itself; only the words have been changed to fool the innocent! For example, to argue that dropping out of school is undesirable because it is bad is not to argue at all. The conclusion is "proven" by the conclusion (in different words). Such an argument *begs the question*, rather than answering it. Let's look at one that is a little less obvious.

> Programmed learning texts are clearly superior to traditional texts in learning effectiveness, because it is highly advantageous for learning to have materials presented in a step-by-step fashion.

Again, the reason supporting the conclusion restates the conclusion in different words. By definition, programmed learning is a step-by-step procedure. The writer is arguing that such a procedure is good because it is good.

Let's examine one more example.

> A comprehensive national health insurance plan is wasteful. Thus, passing such a bill would cause a great deal of harm. Because the bill would be so harmful, it is obviously a very wasteful bill.

How does the writer prove that passing the bill will be harmful? By claiming the bill is wasteful. How does he prove it is wasteful? By asserting the conclusion. Thus, the conclusion is used to support the reason that supports the conclusion. This is a special example of begging the question, commonly referred to as *circular reasoning*. The conclusion itself is used as proof for the assertion that is used to prove the conclusion. Thus, the conclusion has not been *proven*; it has been *assumed* in the proof.

Whenever a conclusion is *assumed* in the reasoning when it should have been proven, begging the question has occurred. When you outline the structure of an argument, check the reasons to be sure that they do not simply repeat the conclusion in different words, and check to see that the conclusion is not used to prove the reasons. In case you are confused, let's illustrate with two examples, one argument that begs the question and one that does not.

(1) To allow the press to keep their sources confidential is very advantageous to the country, because it increases the likelihood that individuals will report evidence against powerful people.

(2) To allow the press to keep their sources confidential is very advantageous to the country, because it is highly conducive to the interests of the larger community that private individuals should have the privilege of providing information to the press without being identified.

Paragraph (2) begs the question by basically repeating the conclusion. It fails to point out what the specific advantages are, and simply repeats that confidentiality of sources is socially useful.

Summary of Reasoning Errors

We have taken you through exercises that illustrate a number of ways in which reasoning may be erroneous. We have not listed all the ways, but we have given you a good start. To find errors in reasoning, keep in mind what kinds of reasons are good reasons—that is, the facts and the moral principles relevant to the issue. Reasoning should be rejected whenever erroneous assumptions are found. Reasoning should be rejected when it

> attacks a person or a person's background,
> presents a faulty dilemma,
> oversimplifies,
> diverts attention from the issue,
> appeals to questionable authority,
> confuses "What Should Be" and "What Is,"
> confuses naming with explaining,
> reflects a search for perfect solutions,
> or begs the question.

Reasoning should be approached cautiously when it appeals to group-approved attitudes and to authority. You should always ask, Are there good reasons to consider such appeals as persuasive evidence? A precautionary note is in order here: do not *automatically* reject reasoning that relies on appeals to authority or group-approved attitudes. Carefully evaluate such reasoning. For example, if most physicians in the country choose to take up jogging, that information is important to consider in deciding whether jogging is beneficial. Some authorities do possess valuable information.

Writing and Reasoning

When you write essays, you necessarily engage in reasoning. Because you want your writing to be persuasive, it should be carefully reasoned. The last five chapters can be used as guidelines for your arguments. Awareness of possible errors that writers may commit provides you with warnings to heed. As you become more familiar with statistical and reasoning errors, your writing will improve. A checklist of possible errors will enable you to be your own censor. You can remove reasoning problems before your readers point them out to you.

Practice Exercises

◊ *Critical Question:* ***Are there any errors in reasoning?***

Try to identify the reasoning errors in each of the three practice passages.

Passage 1

The surgeon general has overstepped his bounds by recommending that explicit sex education begin as early as third grade. It is obvious that he is yet another victim of the AIDS hysteria sweeping the nation. Unfortunately, his media-influenced announcement has given new life to those who favor explicit sex education—even to the detriment of the nation's children.

Sexuality has always been a topic of conversation reserved for the family. Only recently has sex education been forced on young children. The surgeon general's recommendation removes the role of the family entirely. It should be up to parents to explain sex to their children in a manner with which they are comfortable. Sex education exclusive of the family is stripped of values or any sense of morality, and should thus be discouraged. For years families have taken the responsibility of sex education, and that's the way it should remain.

Sex education in schools encourages experimentation. Kids are curious. Letting them in on the secret of sex at such a young age will promote blatant promiscuity. Frank discussions of sex are embarrassing for children, and they destroy the natural modesty of girls.

Passage 2

Students should be required to live in college dormitories because college administrators have determined that the benefits outweigh the costs. If students are required to live in dorms, they will be better students.

A most persuasive rationale for this conclusion is provided by remembering that college adminstrators are typically older than college students. Because they are older, they should be more knowledgeable about what is best for students. Recognizing this probability, we should support administrators' advice that student housing in college dormitories should be compulsory.

Passage 3

Behind the Iron Curtain, the athletic system is basically the same as it is in America: the coach runs the athlete's entire life, in which every major decision is made by the coach. This process of decision making has developed the communist athletes into highly disciplined people, loyal to the state. Poets, scientists, and ballet dancers defect in hordes from the Eastern European countries, but communist athletes have chosen almost unanimously to remain in their home countries.

The American athlete, however, has been indoctrinated into the take-order complex of the carbon-copy totalitarian system. The inflexibility of the athletic system in America has turned us into a nation of hypocrites, preaching free will and choice while we produce million of miniature fascists, primed to unleash the same system of law and order they were taught upon another generation of eager-to-please children.

From the first year of Little League to the last year of high school, the supreme status of the coach is impressed upon the athlete. Creativity is suppressed because of its subversive nature, and obedience is demanded. The budding athlete spends six years under the total control of the high school coach, preparing to spend another four years under the control of the college coach. If the athlete is highly successful, he will spend ten additional years bending his knee to a professional coach.

If America is to remain a democracy, its major institutions must become democratic. It is impossible to expect athletes who someday will lead this country to be placed in an environment of oppression and to disregard that oppression. The oppression will surface at a later late. The greatest threat posed to democracy by sports is the graduation of sports figures into politics. Athletes carry their infection of fascism into the political world and turn government into a game, which it is most emphatically not. Nixon could ignore millions of protesters because they were players and he was the coach.

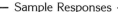

Sample Responses

Passage 1

CONCLUSION: *Sex education should not be taught in schools.*

REASONS: *1. The report reflects hysteria.*
          2. It is the job of parents.
          3. Education encourages promiscuity.

The author begins the argument by attacking the surgeon general rather than the issue. She claims that the recommendation is a byproduct of the AIDS hysteria rather then extensive research. Her suggestion that the surgeon general issues reports in reaction to hot topics in the media undermines his credibility and character and is therefore *ad hominem.*

Her second reason confuses "what is" and "what should be." Just because sex education *should be* up the the parents does not mean that they will provide education.

The third reason presents a false dilemma—either keep sex education out of the schools or face morally loose, value free children. But isn't it possible to have morally loose children with sex education in the home? Isn't it also a possibility that both parents and the schools can play a role in sex education? Might not education result in children who are prepared to handle the issue of sex in their lives rather than morally deficient delinquents?

Passage 2

First, we should note that we have a prescriptive argument. The issue is whether college students should be required to live in college dormitories. The first paragraph states two reasons for supporting such a requirement:

1. College administrators claim the benefits outweigh the costs and
2. Students will be better students if the requirement exists.

Neither reason is very convincing. What is the difference between saying the benefits of X outweigh the costs and saying college administrators favor X? Not much! Thus we can reword the reasons to say college administrators favor the requirement. In this form, we can see the reason as an appeal to authority. There does not appear to be any reason why we should rely on this particular appeal.

The second reason claims that the requirement will make students better. A rewording of the issue might be, would college students be "better" if required to live in college dormitories? It is begging the question to respond that the answer is "yes" because they would be better. We have not advanced the conversation at all.

The third reason, provided in the second paragraph represents a confusion between what should be and what is.

3. Because administrators should be more knowledgeable about students' welfare, they are.

If one accepted the third reason, one would support the requirement if administrators do. Many things should be true, but reality rarely conforms to these prescriptions on our part.

After looking critically at the three reasons and the conclusion, we cannot support the reasoning. We could be convinced perhaps, but not by what was provided in this practice passage.

Passage 3

CONCLUSION: *The American athletic system poses a threat to democracy.*

REASONS: *1. Our athletes are being indoctrinated into a fascist ideology. American coaches exert more oppressive control over the athlete than even communist coaches do. This control suppresses creativity and requires obedience.*

2. *This ideology (the infection) is carried into the political world, turning government into a game. It is impossible to expect athletes placed in an environment of oppression not to reflect that same totalitarian characteristic when they become national leaders.*

You should note several striking deficiencies in this rather complex argument. First, the reasons consist of a number of generalizations, but none of these are supported by any specific evidence. Thus, it is impossible to judge the truth of the reasons.

Second, the writer uses vague, emotionally loaded terms throughout the article. The words "cancer," "infection," "fascism," "oppression," and "carbon-copy totalitarian system" all tend to draw negative emotions from the reader. Until less emotional words are supplied and specific referents are given, it is impossible to judge either the truth of the reasons or the validity of the reasoning. For example, what specifically is meant by "an environment of oppression" or by "carry their infection of fascism into the political world"?

Third, the author of the passage is committing a form of the either-or fallacy. Only two choices are said to be available to us:

(a) Democracy, and a sports program that treats the coach as just one more member of the team, *or*

(b) Fascism, and our current sports program.

Isn't it likely that adjustments could be made in the existing relationship between coaches and their players (here we are assuming that the author's reasons are true) that would enable our democratic political institutions to survive? For example, every coach could be encouraged to remind his team repeatedly that the playing field is in many ways an inadequate model on which to base most important life decisions. The author of the passage does not consider any options beyond (a) and (b). Because of this sloppiness, we cannot accept the author's reasoning.

Passage 4 (Self-Examination)

Higher tuition suggests superior education. These schools called superior by books that rate the quality of colleges and universities are exactly those schools that cost the most to attend. Consequently, you must either pay higher tuition or receive an inferior education.

Higher tuition permits higher salaries for professors. If professors are not kept happy by higher salaries, the quality of the teaching will suffer. The American Federation of Teachers points out that the contented faculty member is repeatedly the same one who is rated superior by supervisors.

The point is that students have a vested interest in paying higher tuition. Those students who gripe about tuition are simply uninformed. We all know that you get what you pay for.

XII

What Significant Information Is Omitted?

Most doctors prescribe Tylenol!

Coke was #1 in recent taste tests!

The purpose of both advertisements is, of course, to persuade you to buy more of the designated product. Even before your critical thinking skills developed to their current level, you knew that such advertisements tell less than the whole truth. This chapter, like the material on assumptions, tries to sensitize you even more to the importance of what *isn't said*. Frequently, we react to an incomplete picture of an argument when we evaluate only the *explicit* components.

You now know a number of good ways to identify weaknesses and strengths in arguments. The ability to spot ambiguities, misuse of evidence, and errors in reasoning is helpful in achieving this goal. We want to devote this chapter to an additional question you must ask in order to make reasonable personal decisions: What significant information is omitted? Sensitivity to missing information has been discussed briefly in several earlier chapters, but it is so important to critical reading that it deserves further emphasis.

Advertisers, teachers, politicians, authors, and parents all want to shape your decisions. It is a natural and highly predictable desire on their part. Typically, therefore, you will encounter only one side of a controversy when there may be dozens of possible conclusions and sets of arguments that would address the controversy. Those trying to persuade you will almost always present their position in the strongest possible light. So when you find what you believe to be strong reasons, it's wise to hesitate and to think about what the author may not have told you. These reasons may not be quite so impressive if you realize that their apparent strength is caused by the author's omission of significant information or of reasons that support different positions.

Interspersed throughout the chapter will be examples of reasoning that are not very convincing, not because of what is said but because of what is omitted. Look carefully at the examples and notice how in each case the failure to look for significant omitted information would have resulted in your making a premature decision.

◊   *Critical Question:*   **What significant information is omitted?**

The Certainty of Incomplete Reasoning

Incomplete reasoning is inevitable. A first explanation for this inevitability is the limitation imposed by time and space. Arguments are incomplete because writers do not have forever to organize them, nor do they have unlimited space in which to present their reasons. Second, the attention span of most of us is very limited; we get bored when messages are too long. Thus, writers often feel a need to get their messages across quickly. Advertising reflects both these factors. The time allotted for presenting the advertising message is short, and the message must both attract and retain your attention. Advertisers consequently engage in many annoying omissions.

For example, a well-known deodorant commercial compares the effectiveness of the advertised brand's roll-on with that for spray versions of several other deodorants. Not suprisingly, the roll-on "lasts longer." Should we then conclude the advertised brand of roll-on deodorant is superior to others? Wait just a minute! What the advertisement neglects to include is any information about the relative effectiveness of roll-ons and sprays in general. A relevant piece of omitted information would be such comparative data. If roll-ons are always more effective than spray deodorants, then the advertisement is persuading us to act in a manner not necessarily consistent with our best interests. Perhaps any roll-on (not necessarily the advertised brand) would last longer than any spray deodorant. The advertiser omitted significant data that you would need if you were to buy wisely.

Another type of missing information is at least as important. Even had there not been missing data in the advertisement, you would still want to consider other possible advantages or disadvantages of different deodorants. The advertiser does not mention price. Why? We can only guess, but he must think you are more interested in the product's effectiveness than in its price. If your values are different, you may not be highly impressed by the longer lasting quality of the advertised deodorant.

A third reason for the inevitability of missing information is that the knowledge possessed by the person making the argument will always be incomplete. For example, no one can know *everything* about the assassination of John F. Kennedy.

Consequently, anyone claiming to know who killed Kennedy must be omitting information that would be helpful to you if you were carefully trying to make up your mind about the identity of the assassin. Similarly, when over half the doctors sampled in a survey of attitudes toward national health insurance fail to complete the questionnaire, it is impossible to know whether or not they differ in significant ways from the doctors who do complete the survey. Yet this is a very important piece of information.

A fourth reason why information may be omitted is because of an outright attempt to deceive. Advertisers *know* they are omitting key bits of information. If they were to describe all the chemicals or cheap component parts that go into their products, you would be less likely to buy them. Experts in every field consciously omit information when open disclosure would weaken the persuasive effect of their advice. Such omissions are particularly tempting if those trying to advise you see you as a "sponge."

A final important reason why omitted information is so prevalent is that the values, beliefs, and attitudes of those trying to advise or persuade you are frequently different from yours. You can expect, therefore, that their reasoning will be guided by different assumptions from those you would have brought to the same question. A particular perspective is like a pair of blinders on a horse. The blinders improve the tendency of the horse to focus on what is directly in front of him. Yet, an individual's perspective, like blinders on a horse, prevents that person from noting certain information that would be important to those who reason from a different frame of reference. Unless your perspective is identical to that of the person trying to persuade you, important omissions of information are to be expected.

Let's review. Omitted information is inevitable. There are at least five reasons for the prevalence of omitted information:

1. Time and space limitations
2. Limited attention span
3. Inadequacies in human knowledge
4. Deception
5. Different perspectives

Do you now see the danger of the sponge model even more clearly? You must actively question expertise and advice if you are to avoid forming opinions based on unnecessarily limited information.

Questions that Identify Omitted Information

If you are now convinced that reasoning will necessarily be incomplete, you may ask, What am I supposed to do? Well, initially you have to remind yourself again and again that regardless of how attractive the reasons supporting a particular decision or opinion may be at first glance, it's necessary to take another look in search of omitted information. How do you search, and what can you expect to find? You ask questions to help decide what additional information you need, and then ask questions designed to reveal that information.

Isn't it silly to ask questions of a writer who cannot answer? Not at all! Although the writer won't answer your questions, asking them has positive results. First, you may be able to supply the missing information because of what you already know. Second, searching for omitted information in written persuasion gives you good practice for when you *are* able to search for omitted information face-to-face with a teacher or anyone else who is trying to persuade you orally. Even more importantly, searching for omitted information prevents you from making up your mind too soon. By asking such questions of written material, you are reminding yourself that the information provided is incomplete. Whatever conclusion you reach on the basis of incomplete information will necessarily be tentative. You cannot be sure about the accuracy of your opinion as long as important information is missing.

The questions you can use to find omitted information are similar to those you have encountered in earlier chapters. Asking critical questions about ambiguity, the use of evidence, and the quality of assumptions usually highlights omitted information.

Important types of missing information include the following:

1. Key definitions
2. Alternative techniques for gathering or organizing the evidence
3. Omitted effects of what is advocated and of what is opposed
4. Missing graphs or data

Take a look at some arguments that have omitted some or all of the types of information listed. Watch how each of the omissions might cause you to form a faulty conclusion. Only by asking that omitted information be supplied in each case could you avoid this danger.

Initially, let's look at an advertising claim. Several cereals are advertised as providing ''part of a balanced breakfast.'' What is meant by the word *part* here? Wouldn't you like to know how large this part is, relative to that in other cereals? Of course, unless you do not mind wasting money. Thus, the advertiser has omitted a key definition. Remember that the goal of the seller is different from yours. The cereal firm wants a sale; you want taste, economy, and nutrition. Consequently, you should expect the advertisement to omit certain information that is crucial to your particular purpose if that omission enlarges sales. One important additional bit of omitted information is the effect on your health of consuming the large amounts of sugar contained in many sugar-coated cereals, an effect that advertisers would prefer not to mention.

Let's now take a look at a more complicated example. Read the following excerpt and ask yourself what has been omitted.

> A young person once had a pretty sure prospect of getting a good job and high salary by going to college. Now that certainty is no longer there.

There has been a big increase in the number of young people graduating from colleges and universities. The demand for college graduates has simply not increased at that pace. One of the sectors where college graduates have traditionally been employed has been in teaching; however, the demand for teachers has fallen. The federal bureaucracy, a major employer of college graduates, has not been expanding in the last several years.

The earnings gap between high school and college graduates has narrowed significantly. Bureau of the Census data indicate that, for the average college graduate aged 25 and over, the advantage declined from about 53 percent to 35 or 36 percent.

What important information was omitted? Did you ask questions that would identify any of the four types of omitted information that we described for you? Let us help you. How did the economist measure what it meant for a college degree to be worth the price? Did his definition of what a college degree is worth reflect a value assumption with which you agree? Did the author of the excerpt examine the most important effects to you of a college education? What useful data are missing? For example, wouldn't it be helpful to know how satisfied college graduates are with their jobs? Obviously, the writer gave you only a partial picture of the value of a college degree. Unless you complete the picture, your decision about whether to go to or continue in college will be very uninformed.

Omitted Information that Remains Missing

Just because you are able to request important missing information does not guarantee a satisfactory response. It is quite possible that your probing questions cannot be answered. Do not despair! You did your part. You requested information that you needed to make up your mind; you must now decide whether it is possible to arrive at a conclusion without the missing information. We warned you earlier that reasoning is always incomplete. Therefore, to claim automatically that you cannot make a decision as long as information is missing would prevent you from ever forming any opinions. The information you need to be perfectly certain that you are right will never be available.

Practice Exercises

◊   *Critical Question:*   **What significant information is omitted?**

In each of the following examples, there is important missing information. Make a list of questions you would ask the person who wrote each passage. Explain in each case why the information you are seeking is important to you as you try to decide the worth of the reasoning.

Passage 1

Doctors and medical experts across the nation need to keep up the effort of urging Americans to reduce their intake of cholesterol and saturated fats. A diet high in cholesterol and saturated fats has been linked to a high incidence of coronary disease.

A survey comparing the food intakes of 1,500 women in 1977 and a similar group in 1985, demonstrates that the warnings of health experts have not been in vain. The findings of the survey reveal that women are consuming 35 percent less whole milk, 34 percent less red meat, and 28 percent fewer eggs. The findings also indicated a 60 percent increase in skim milk consumption and a 29 percent increase in whole grain consumption. Better decisions in the supermarket are resulting in dramatic improvements in the health of American women.

Passage 2

What all the evidence seems to suggest is that some violence portrayed on television could make some TV watchers violent. But consider how many people are killed by tranquilizers. Does that mean we should eliminate them? A generation was raised on westerns and detective shows. If critics are right about the brutalizing effects of television on youth, why didn't young people want to rush off to Vietnam to vent their aggressions? Instead, they did a lot to protest that war and bring it to a stop.

Passage 3

The volunteer service is a failure. The volunteer force could not possible work in a war. What we have now is a peacetime volunteer force, with the inevitability that if we had a war—even a limited war—we'd have to go back to the draft.

The Army is about 100,000 recruits short in its individual Ready Reserve Forces, and projections indicate that it will be about 500,000 short in the early 1990s. The Army itself is experiencing recruiting difficulties; it is about 9 percent under their quota so far in fiscal year '84.

─────────────────── Sample Responses ───────────────────

Passage 1

CONCLUSION: *The warrnings of health experts about high cholesterol and saturated fats have been effective.*

REASONS: *1. Survey data reveals 35 percent less whole milk consumed, 34 percent less red meat, and 28 percent fewer eggs from 1977 to 1985.*

2. Skim milk and whole grain consumption has risen during the same period.

Before you accept the author's conclusion of dramatically improved health for the surveyed women, you should ask questions about what the study did not reveal. For instance, has the decrease in red meat consumption caused deficiencies of iron or other minerals in these women? Are these women selecting low-fat protein rich alternatives to compensate for the decrease in high protein red meat?

Furthermore, fat from other sources should be considered. Whole grain bread is not a wise dietary choice when slathered with butter. Fried fish or chicken is not a healthful alternative to a lean, broiled steak. Decreased fat or cholesterol consumption in a few areas is not a fail-safe indication of improved health. High fat consumption in other areas and possible nutrient deficiencies are important considerations when assessing dramatic health improvements.

Passage 2

CONCLUSION: *We should not place additional restrictions on television violence.*

REASONS: *1. It does not make sense to eliminate something like television violence just because it harms a few people. We have not eliminated tranquilizers, even though they harm some people.*

2. The same young people who watched so much violence on television actively resisted the war in Vietnam. Their actions demonstrate that watching television violence does not make one more violent.

This passage omits important data as well as significant disadvantages of failing to regulate the amount of television violence. For instance, there were many young people who supported the war in Vietnam. How can we know the effects of television violence on attitudes toward war unless we have comparative data on the attitudes of frequent and infrequent television viewers? The author of the passage also omits any reference to the positive correlation shown in many studies between observing violence on television and engaging in violent crimes. What specifically is meant by *some* effect on *some* people? If the effect is mass murders, we would be very concerned.

Passage 3

CONCLUSION: *The volunteer army is a failure.*

REASONS: *1. Too few recruits have been attracted to the volunteer service. We could never fight a war with such a service because we cannot attract enough people even during peacetime.*

2. The current ready reserves are hundreds of thousands short.

As with many arguments, this one does not include any evidence that would weaken its reasoning. Does any evidence exist that would enable us to conclude that the volunteer army is a success? For example, does the composition of the current army provide a more representative cross-section of our population than that prevalent under the draft?

For the first reason to be convincing, we would need to know what the effect of patriotism would be on enlistments during a war. Is it fair to project a shortage of manpower during peace into a prospective period of war (assuming that war has more public support than did the Vietnam War)?

Before responding to the second reason, we would need to know how "short" is determined. Who makes the quotas and on what basis? What are the financial costs of meeting these quotas? What are the advantages of maintaining a small reserve?

Passage 4 (Self-Examination)

The great danger of television is that it requires so little mental effort to watch. Television gives us thousands of images of war, leisure, marriage, police, adolescence, and death, offering its viewers a prepackaged reality that we are asked to absorb rather than evaluate. As a result, we don't have to strive to develop our own understandings of these events or groups. Our brains can relax while the television implants images in them.

Think of the damage television does to our educational system. Teachers increasingly tell us that students cannot concentrate for an extended period. A comparison of college textbooks from 20 years ago with those published now shows an increased use of pictures and simplistic vocabulary and a dramatic decline in the number of words. Distinctions and nuances are ignored in a desperate effort to attract the attention of readers reared on television images. But many of our most valuable ideas are complex. Will future citizens quickly discount these insights as "boring" simply because they require extended concentration to appreciate?

Contrast the mental process that accompanies reading with that which occurs during television viewing. The reader controls the pace of image formation and development. She can reflect on a sentence and even return to earlier sentences in search of a meaning that escaped her the first time through. She may choose to reflect on the extent to which the passage reminds her of her own experiences or enriches her hopes. Television gives little time for such creative use of imagination. The pace continues without pauses—except for the next commercial.

XIII

What Conclusions Are Consistent with the Strong Reasons?

Dr. Palmer received the annual award given by the University Research Association for his classic study of the relationship between marital status and the number of rats in particular residential areas.

Dr. Palmer argued that rats thrive when homes are abandoned during the day. Because a higher proportion of married women than single women remain home during the day, he projected that rats would be less abundant in communities where a higher proportion of residents are married.

His study of three urban suburbs in different parts of the country confirmed in his mind the effectiveness of marriage as a method of controlling rats. He found that every 10 percent increase in married residents resulted in a 5 percent decrease in the number of rats present in the suburb.

Should you urge your local public health officer to spend his budgetary allocation for rodent control on pamphlets praising the joys of marriage? Suppose that you checked Dr. Palmer's data and found it accurate and representative of suburbs in general. Are there other conclusions that might be equally as consistent with Dr. Palmer's data as the conclusion that marriage reduces the rat population? The chapter summary will suggest several alternative conclusions that are possible.

By this stage you should be better equipped to pan for intellectual gold—to distinguish stronger reasons from weaker ones. Strong reasons are those you are least able to criticize.

In descriptive arguments, strong reasons will be persuasive evidence such as findings of a careful research study, a relevant analogy, an appeal to a reliable authority, or compelling examples. For prescriptive arguments, the strong reasons will be principles or descriptive statements you identify as best supported and most relevant.

After you have identified the stronger reasons, one additional step will be useful to you in preparing for a personal decision concerning the controversy in question: identifying the various conclusions that can be based on the strong reasons.

Very rarely will you have a situation in which only one conclusion can be reasonably inferred from the strong reasons. Consequently, you must make sure that the conclusion you eventually adopt is the most reasonable and the most consistent with your value preferences. If you are still undecided about which conclusion is best after you have identified those that can be drawn from the strong reasons, your conclusion will be especially tentative. The recognition that the strong reasons could provide support for conclusions different from yours should heighten your interest in any further tests or studies that would help identify the best conclusion.

You have already encountered in Chapter VIII the benefits of finding multiple conclusions. When writers present a conclusion that is a causal explanation of some evidence, you now know that you should always look for rival hypotheses to explain the evidence. Thus identifying rival causal hypotheses can be one way of identifying conclusions consistent with the strong reasons. Causal explanations to explain empirical evidence, however, are only one kind of conclusion. This chapter helps you to find multiple conclusions for diverse arguments in which writers have presented strong reasons.

◊   *Critical Question:*   **What conclusions are consistent with the strong reasons?**

Assumptions and Multiple Conclusions

Neither evidence attempting to support a factual claim nor a group of strong reasons supporting a prescriptive conclusion can be interpreted in only one way. Reasons do not generally speak for themselves in an obvious way. As we have seen many times, conclusions are reached only after someone makes certain interpretations or assumptions concerning the meaning of the reasons.

If you make a different assumption concerning the meaning of the reasons, you will reach different conclusions. Because we all possess different levels of perceptual precision, frames of reference, and prior knowledge, we repeatedly disagree about which conclusions are preferable. We form different conclusions from strong reasons because our diverse backgrounds and goals cause us to be attracted to different assumptions when we decide to link reasons to conclusions.

Sometimes a writer will mention alternative conclusions that can be reached on the basis of the reasons he has presented. However, *you* will often have to generate possible alternatives. To perform this creative task, try to imagine what different assumptions might enable someone to jump from the strong reasons you have identified to another conclusion. Remember, *many* possible conclusions can be made on the basis of most sets of strong reasons. The next two sections help you recognize the multiplicity of possible conclusions.

Dichotomous Thinking: Impediment to Considering Multiple Conclusions

Very few important questions can be answered with a simple "yes" or an absolute "no." When people think in black or white, yes or no, right or wrong, or correct or incorrect terms, they engage in *dichotomous thinking*. This type of thinking consists of assuming there are only two possible answers to a question that has multiple potential answers.

We encountered dichotomous thinking earlier when we discussed the either-or fallacy. This fallacy, and dichotomous thinking in general, damages reasoning by overly restricting our vision. We think we are finished after considering two optional decisions, thereby overlooking many options and the positive consequences that could have resulted from choosing one of them.

Dichotomous thinkers often are rigid and intolerant because they fail to understand the importance of context for a particular answer. To see this point more clearly imagine this situation:

Your roommate asks you to help plan her ethics paper. The paper is to address the question: Should a person tell the truth? In her mind, the paper requires her to defend a "yes" or "no" position.

You have learned that dichotomous thinking can be avoided by qualifying conclusions, by putting them into a context. This qualification process requires you to ask about any conclusion:

1. *When* is it accurate?
2. *Where* is it accurate?
3. *Why* or for what purpose is it accurate?

You then begin to apply this process to the paper assignment.

Would you be surprised by your roommate's growing frustration as you explained that at certain specified times, in certain situations, to maximize particular values or objectives one should tell the truth? She's looking for "yes" or "no"; you provided a complicated "it depends on . . . ."

Rigid, dichotomous thinking limits the range of your decisions and opinions. Even worse, perhaps, it overly simplifies complex situations. As a consequence, dichotomous thinkers are high-risk candidates for confusion.

The next section illustrates the restrictive effects of dichotomous thinking.

Two Sides or Many?

Before we look at several arguments in which multiple conclusions are possible, let's make sure that you appreciate the large number of conclusions that are possible with repsect to most important controversies. Here are three contemporary questions.

1. Do IQ tests measure intelligence?
2. Is the President's tax proposal desirable?
3. Should judges be elected or appointed?

At first glance, these questions and many like them seem to call for yes or no answers. However, a qualified yes or no is often the best answer. The advantage of maybe as an answer is that it forces you to admit that you do not yet know enough to make a definite answer. But at the same time that you are avoiding a definite answer, you have formed a tentative decision or opinion that calls for commitment and eventual action. Once you recognize that you can never be certain how to answer complex questions, you can better accept the necessity of making decisions even when you know you are missing critical information or understanding. It's wise to seek additional information that would improve the support for your opinions, but at some point you must stop searching and make a decision, even when the most forceful answer you are willing to defend is a "yes, but . . . ."

Glance back at the three questions that preceded the last paragraph. Ask yourself what conclusions would be possible in response to each question, Naturally, a yes or a no answer would be two possible conclusions. Are there others? Yes, many! Let's look at just a few of the possible answers to the first of these questions.

Do IQ tests measure intelligence?

1. Yes, to the extent that intelligence means sequential reasoning.
2. Yes, when they are given to children of the same sociocultural background.
3. Yes, if they are used only for elementary school children.
4. Yes, when the IQ scores are highly correlated with measures of motivation.
5. Yes, but only in terms of the type of intelligence that is useful in schools.
6. No, if you define intelligence as that factor which leads to later success in one's chosen field.
7. No, if they fail to include data gathered orally.

Notice that in each case we added a condition that is necessary before the conclusion can be justified. In the absence of any data or definitions, any of these seven conclusions could be the most reasonable. We would hope to be better able to choose from among these conclusions after analyzing the strong arguments. These seven are just a few of the conclusions possible for the first question. Thus, there may be many possible answers to a question, not just two.

Just for practice, try to suggest five possible conclusions for the third question: Should judges be elected or appointed?

Perhaps this conclusion occurred to you: *Elected, if it can be demonstrated that most of those who would vote understand the tasks of a judge well enough to make a choice consistent with efficient justice.* Or maybe you thought of this one: *Appointed, in those states where the voter turnout in state legislative races has averaged less than 50 percent in the last ten years?* But probably neither of these appears on your list. Why are we so sure? Because there are an enormous number of possible conclusions for this question. It would be an unlikely coincidence if you had chosen either of these two from the huge list of possible conclusions. This great number of answers is what we want you to grasp. Knowledge of the possibility of multiple conclusions will prevent you from leaping to one prematurely.

Searching for Multiple Conclusions

This section contains two arguments that point out multiple conclusions that could be created from the reasons in each argument. The intention is to give you some models to use when you search for conclusions. In each case, we will give you the structure of the argument before we suggest alternative conclusions. One clue to help you in your search is the following: Study the strong reasons without looking at the conclusion, and try to identify as many conclusions as possible that would follow from the reasons. You can always use the when, where, and why questions to help generate alternative conclusions.

CONCLUSION: *Those who refuse to serve in wars should not be pardoned.*

REASONS: *1. They are not sorry for what they did.*

2. A pardon would increase the likelihood that many would refuse to fight in future wars.

3. Our already embattled military would feel even more under attack by this rejection of their past contributions.

Looking at the first reason, we might arrive at entirely different conclusions depending on the definition of *pardon*. The ambiguity in the word permits many conclusions. Each definition might enable us to reach a different conclusion of the following form: *If the writer defines "pardon" as———, then my position would be that———.*

For example, if the writer defines pardon as removing all potential legal penalties in return for which the draft resister must pay no social penalties, then my position would be . . . .

Another way to generate conclusions would be by a careful examination of the three reasons as a group. It is possible to accept the truth of all three reasons and still arrive at several different conclusions. For example: *Because our country does not value international harmony to the extent it should, a pardon is desirable as a stimulus for debate that might reorient our nation's foreign policy.*

CONCLUSION: *Congress should not decriminalize marijuana.*

REASONS: *1. A group of British scientists has shown that smoking marijuana may cause serious brain damage.*
2. Marijuana smokers risk decreasing their fertility.
3. Marijuana smokers often become heroin users.

What conclusions are possible? One would be to decriminalize marijuana in one locale and observe the impact before making a national rule. Alternatively, Congress could sponsor research designed to develop a substance that would produce effects similar to those produced by marijuana without the possible side effects. Another possibility, based on a strong devotion to the value of individual responsibility, would be to permit pot to be sold in stores along with other possibly hazardous materials, the assumption being that those who may misuse the drug have a right to do so. Observe that all three of these conclusions are possible even if we accept the truth of the three reasons. Thus, the same reasons frequently can be used to support several different conclusions.

Productivity of If-Clauses

If you went back over all the alternative conclusions discussed in this chapter, you would notice that each optional conclusion is possible because we are missing certain information, definitions, assumptions, or the frame of reference of the person analyzing the reasons. Consequently, we can create multiple conclusions by the judicious use of *if-clauses.* In an if-clause, we state a condition that we are assuming in order to enable us to reach a particular conclusion. Notice that the use of if-clauses permits us to arrive at a conclusion without pretending that we know more than we actually do about a particular controversy.

When you use if-clauses to precede conclusions, you are pointing out that your conclusion is based on particular claims or assumptions about which you are uncertain. To see what we mean, look at some sample conditional statements that might precede conclusions.

1.   If freedom of religion is meant when the writer speaks of the loss of our basic freedom, then . . . .
2.   If the birth rate continues to rise over the next five years, then . . . .
3.   If we look at his sales record from the FDA's perspective, then . . . .

These if-clauses present you with multiple conclusions that you may wish to assess before making up your mind about the controversy, and broaden the list of possible conclusions from which you can choose your opinion.

Alternative Solutions as Conclusions

We frequently encounter issues posed in the following form:

> Should we do X?
> Is X desirable?

Such questions naturally "pull" for dichotomous thinking. Often, however, posing questions in this manner hides a broader question, What should we do about Y? (usually some pressing problem.) Rewording the question in this way leads us to generate multiple conclusions of a particular form: solutions to the problems raised by the strong reasons. Generating multiple solutions greatly increases the flexibility of our thinking.

Let's examine the following passage to illustrate the importance of generating multiple solutions as possible conclusions.

> Should we outlaw those nudist beaches on the edge of our community? We certainly should. Look at the traffic problems they are causing and the hundreds of cars that have been parking illegally since the beach opened.

Once we change this question to, What should we do about the traffic and parking problems?, a number of possible solutions come to mind, which help us formulate our conclusion to the issue. For example, we might conclude: No, we should not outlaw the nudist beaches, we should have police vigorously enforce the no-parking rules and have the parking service restrict the number of people allowed on the beach.

When strong reasons in a prescriptive argument are statements of practical problems, look for different solutions to the problems as possible conclusions.

Summary

Very rarely do reasons mean just one thing. After evaluating a set of reasons, you still must decide what conclusion is most consistent with the best reasons in the controversy. To avoid dichotomous thinking in your search for the strongest conclusion, provide alternative contexts for the conclusions through the use of when, where, and why questions.

Qualifications for conclusions will move you away from dichotomous thinking. If-clauses provide a technique for expressing these qualifications.

For instance, let's take another look at Professor Palmer's research relating marriage and rodent populations. What alternative conclusions might explain the results he discovered?

PROFESSOR PALMER'S CONCLUSION *An increase in the proportion of married residents is an effective technique for reducing the number of rats in a community.*

ALTERNATIVE CONCLUSIONS   *1. Only when rats have spent their first three months in a relatively rural environment do they react to more contacts with humans by moving elsewhere. (Suppose the three suburbs in the study were relatively new.)*
    2. Only in cultures where married residents usually have more cats than unmarried residents will more married residents mean fewer rats.
    3. If we are interested in merely short-term control of rats, encouraging marriage may be an effective solution.

Many more alternative conclusions are possible in light of Palmer's data. Considering them would improve the quality of our response.

Practice Exercises

◊   *Critical Question:*   **What conclusions are consistent with the strong reasons?**

For each of the following arguments, identify three different conclusions that could be drawn from the reasons.

Passage 1

A recent survey found that more than half of the $50 billion spent annually on automobile repairs was wasted. The survey covered 62 garages in seven cities. The survey found that many unnecessary services were performed and that the work was often of poor quality. In addition, only half the garages visited were judged "fair" in terms of the prices they charged.

What can be done to reduce this waste? A few well-publicized prosecutions might do wonders. Those who take advantage of consumer ignorance are the worst variety of thief. Consumers should make a special effort to see that such garages go broke by not taking sick automobiles to these rip-off artists.

Passage 2

In recent Presidential elections, many more married than unmarried people voted for Republican candidates. This marriage gap is much greater than the more heavily publicized gender gap that favors the Democrats. Among high school students who expected to marry, a recent study found that almost 70 percent planned to vote Republican as soon as they could legally vote. Because most people are married, Democratic Presidential candidates will have an uphill battle in future Presidential elections.

Passage 3

The use of racial quotas for either college admission or employment is wrong. Quotas represent an immoral technique for achieving important objectives. It makes little sense to say that we should create a fair world by unfair means. Equality is desirable, but not at any cost.

In addition, quotas are actually harmful for those whom they are intended to help. It is cruel to place a person in a position where she will be underqualified, because such a person is certain to feel her inadequacy. Many people who receive their positions as a result of quotas will drop out, feeling more unhappy than they felt before the quota was established.

———————————————— Sample Responses ————————————————

Passage 1

CONCLUSION: *Those responsible for automobile repair rip-offs should be prosecuted for fraud.*

REASONS: *1. More than half the annual expenditure on automobile repairs is wasted.*
2. Well-publicized prosecutions of the guilty repair shops will serve as a deterrent and inform consumers as to which garages to avoid.

The author's inference is but one of several that are consistent with the reasons. These include the following:

If the repairs are faulty because of undertrained mechanics, a better solution to the problem would be the licensing of mechanics.

If we assume that mechanics are urged to check automobiles not just for current problems but for impending ones as well, it's possible that the survey data was focusing on a narrow definition of "waste." Perhaps one could thus infer that mechanics should generally be praised for their long-range care of our automobiles.

The automobile is such a complicated mechanism that it's unrealistic to expect repair records any better than those reported in the survey.

Passage 2

CONCLUSION: *Democratic Presidential candidates will have an uphill battle in the future.*

REASONS: *1. In recent elections, more married than unmarried people voted for Republicans.*
2. High school students who expect to marry in the future plan to vote overwhelmingly for Republican candidates.

For purposes of this exercise we will overlook the deficiencies in the reasons. Accepting the reasons, we could infer several conclusions:

When Republicans emphasize family issues, they are especially attractive to married voters.

If Democrats run candidates who rely on the same type of media advisors as those hired by recent Democratic Presidential nominees, they will probably lose.

If prevailing cultural images of home and children remain popular, Democratic Presidential candidates are in trouble.

Passage 3

CONCLUSION: *Racial quotas in colleges and jobs are wrong.*

REASONS: 1. *Racial quotas are immoral and illegal because they violate our standards of equality.*
2. *Quotas harm those who receive jobs or positions, because they are embarrassed and hurt when they fail.*

In this passage there is again a woeful lack of evidence. For purposes of this exercise, however, we simply assume the truth of these reasons. From the reasons, we could reach the following conclusions:

We should encourage affirmative action policies as an alternative to quotas.

Equality of result is more important than equality as the author is defining it. Thus, we should encourage quotas as a means of providing equality of result, especially after we have insured that those who benefit from quotas can, through proper training, succeed at least as often as their white counterparts.

We should enlarge our efforts to teach black history so that more people realize that we need to develop a new standard of equality. With this revised standard, we could create an environment in which quotas would lead to a higher form of equality rather than to failure.

Passage 4

The more expensive a brand of beer, the more convinced purchasers are that the beer is premium quality. This conclusion is an important one for beer distributors because it permits them to enhance sales by increasing price.

This observation stems from research conducted in Dr. James A. Hollister's marketing seminar. The participants in the seminar were told that they would be permitted during class to select a bottle of beer each week to drink at their convenience.

There would be two possible brands of beer from which they could select their beer. They were told that Brand A cost $4 per sixpack and Brand X cost $2.80 per sixpack. In actuality Brand X was a much more expensive beer than Brand A.

At the conclusion of the seminar, students overwhelmingly selected Brand A as the superior beer.

XIV

What Are Your Value Preferences in this Controversy?

This chapter shifts the focus from the search for strong reasons to the quality of value preferences. Even when there are acceptable reasons and no errors in the reasoning, you will not necessarily want to agree with the author. Before you make a decision, you need to consider carefully the major value conflicts and compare your value preferences to those of the writer. Once you have identified the writer's value preferences and your own, you have a basis for accepting or rejecting her conclusion on a rational level. It would make little sense to support conclusions or accept opinions that are supported by reasoning that is inconsistent with your personal value preferences. When you realize that an author's value preferences differ sharply from your own with respect to the controversy in question, you should be very cautious about accepting her reasoning. This chapter encourages you to use value preferences as a proper basis for deciding which opinions to accept.

A word of caution at the outset is needed. Just because a writer has value priorities that resemble yours does not mean that you should automatically agree with her conclusions. For example, you may both agree that the value of public health is greater than that of economic efficiency in the controversy concerning the severity of auto-emission control standards. You may not agree with her conclusion, however, because you may believe that her evidence has failed to show a clear public health risk or because you make different assumptions about how an auto-emission control program can best be implemented.

Thus, determining that a writer has value preferences similar to yours is only one step in critical thinking. Each of the other critical questions must be answered satisfactorily before you can rationally make the author's conclusion yours.

Alternative Ways to Determine Your Value Preferences

If you are to match your value preferences with an author's, you must first identify value assumptions on both sides of the controversy. Chapter V was devoted to helping you identify these assumptions. The next step is a decision about the confidence you should have in your own value preference.

Although we encouraged you to question conclusions that are based on values that you do not see as signficant, we also want to urge you to examine your own values in the process. As you know, there are few universally accepted value assumptions. Maybe the ones you currently hold are simply the result of growing up in a particular family at a particular time in history. Because values play such a predominant role in influencing your behavior and beliefs, you owe it to yourself to think about changing your value assumptions. You cannot in any way *choose* your values unless you have thought seriously about the worth of alternative value assumptions.

By respecting value differences between yourself and others, you give yourself an opportunity to decide which set of values makes the most sense for you. You should ask yourself, Why is this set of values a good one? One way to answer this question is to examine the consequences of these values and to compare them to those of alternative values. Thinking about the consequences of different values permits you to explore the effects of valuing material success more than serenity, for example. It is fair to be dubious about conclusions when they are based on value assumptions you do not share. But as you are questioning these conclusions, spend a little time analyzing the strength of your commitment to the values that stimulated your reaction. Because values have such a powerful influence on your thinking, you must be very certain that you have chosen your values with care. A willingness to listen openly to those whose values differ from yours provides you with the opportunity to question your own value assumptions.

After you have reassured yourself that you indeed should have certain value preferences, there are several techniques you could use to justify these assumptions to yourself and others. It would be reasonable for someone to ask you where you got your value assumptions, suggesting that the quality of these assumptions depends on their source.

Several sources of value assumptions are repeatedly mentioned by those attempting to justify their value priorities:

1. Personal hunch
2. Authority
3. Tradition
4. Moral reasoning

These sources are so commonly used as the basis for value assumptions that we will discuss each one briefly.

When asked why they prefer patriotism to individualism in a particular controversy, many will simply say that it's obvious or common sense. Such an answer suggests that there is no basis for further questioning because the source is a personal hunch. To defend a value assumption based on a personal hunch, you can only assert that you have a strongly felt, unexplainable personal feeling, *period*!

Authority is another frequent source used to justify particular value assumptions. Asserting that one's value assumptions are derived from what one's family, priest, or political heroes believe avoids an explanation of why one has decided to let someone else be the source of these assumptions. The listener is asked to see the value assumption as appropriate solely because an authority approves.

A third way of justifying value assumptions is to base them on cultural or national traditions. The value assumption is deemed appropriate because the speaker has learned it from his community. Because these are the majority values, it is often assumed that they reflect some historical or collective wisdom. Many of those who use this justification would say. "Who am I to argue with the value assumptions of my community?"

The fourth common defense for value assumptions is *moral reasoning*. This view sees value preferences as legitimate to the extent that they are selected after rational argument and reflection. This source of values is based on an implied criticism of the other three sources. Thus, personal hunches, authority, and tradition may be starting points for justifying value assumptions; however, these sources must be examined rationally and critically. If they do not make sense as the source of some of our most fundamental beliefs, then the moral reasoning approach would reject the value assumptions that stem from them.

The first three sources of values preferences share a common problem. The person who accepts them as a proper source of justification tends not to ask himself whether the value assumption is reasonable. Instead, he obeys commands from sources beyond his control. He doesn't really choose value preferences; he accepts those chosen by others or those that pop immediately into his consciousness. Such an approach does not provide a technique for resolving value differences among people. There is no mechanism whereby one reassesses the worth of his value judgments in light of their consequences.

Moral Reasoning and Value Preferences

If you require that each of your value assumptions be justified by moral reasoning, you will always ask, Why is this my value preference in this situation? Is there some rational basis for believing that one value or set of values is any better than the other? Though you have already selected your value preferences, you should make a systematic attempt to justify their reasonableness.

How do you do this? The task is not simple. There are a number of ways to justify value priorities. We believe you will find the following suggestions helpful.

As explained in Chapter V, the basic way to provide reasons for particular value assumptions is to examine the consequences or probable outcomes consistent with the value assumptions. What will be the societal effects of acting on the value preference you have chosen? Answering this question should form the basis for moral reasoning.

Let's look together at an illustration of the use of moral reasoning.

We must legally prevent homosexuals from teaching in the public schools. The scientific evidence that homosexual conduct is caused neither by genes nor by birth defects is overwhelming. The homosexual chooses to be sexually attracted to members of the same sex. Consequently, we should not pity and protect homosexuals, because they knowingly choose to endure the social judgments that are applied to them.

Because homosexuality is learned, we all must be concerned about who is teaching our children. If a child has an openly homosexual teacher, will not the child be attracted to the homosexual life? We do not want our children to see homosexuals in such positions, because they might get the impression that homosexuality is a harmless option.

There is an abundance of evidence that homosexuals recruit young people. Many homosexual periodicals have numerous want ads, complete with nude poses, from homosexuals soliciting partners. Most of these ads are aimed at children under 18. School teachers who are homosexuals are in an ideal position to recruit pupils into a life of homosexuality.

The structure of this argument can be summarized in the following manner:

CONCLUSION: *Homosexuals should not be permitted to teach in public schools.*

REASONS: *1. We should not protect homosexuals because they knowingly choose to endure the negative social judgments applied to them.*

2. Since homosexuality is learned, children might be tempted to adopt this lifestyle if it is presented as a harmless option.

3. Homsexuals recruit young people, and teachers are in an ideal position to engage in such recruitment.

For purposes of the illustration, overlook the sloppy evidence, reasoning errors, and questionable assumptions in the passage. *Imagine* that all three reasons are strong.

A value preference that stands out as very significant to the author of the passage is that tradition is a more important value than toleration of alternative lifestyles. He does not argue that homosexuality is bad; rather his arguments assume that homosexuality, like polio, is something that all people should be protected from. Why? He probably argues in this way because heterosexuality has *traditionally* been the only acceptable lifestyle. Suppose, again for purposes of the illustration, that you agree with the value preference of the author. Then ask yourself what consequences you would expect from acting on this value assumption. You should be able to identify both positive and negative consequences.

On the positive side, a society that emphasizes tradition tends to be more stable. Basic behavior and definitions of right and wrong persist for long periods of time. Those reared in such a society are not faced with choosing from among different roles. They know what is expected of them and can focus their energies on fulfilling that role. Tradition reflects a respect for one's ancestors and elders. Traditions develop over long periods of time, so they are the product not of whim and spontaneity but of historical evolution.

On the negative side, those devoted to tradition tend to resist change. Many useful ideas will probably be rejected in the interests of preserving traditional modes of thinking and behaving. Those who value tradition very highly may engage in harsh forms of repression as a means of restricting change. Such repression endangers the safety and material well-being of those attempting to change traditions.

Next, let's look at the probable consequences of valuing toleration of alternative lifestyles very strongly. Toleration of alternative lifestyles offers encouragement to other people to develop habits and skills in all the variety of ways possible to the human imagination. A world in which such a value is emphasized would be more diverse and would tend to permit human potential the broadest possible fulfillment. Less time and energy would be spent trying to restrict the behavior of others. At the same time, toleration of alternative lifestyles as a value does not lead to a clearly defined set of social and cultural standards. Many people are troubled when faced with numerous choices about what is appropriate or good. Such people need rules as a framework for their lives, and toleration of alternative lifestyles often leads to a rejection of such rules.

What we have attempted to do is suggest some consequences that tend to occur when either tradition or toleration of alternative lifestyles is a dominant value. You should next ask *why* these particular consequences are good or bad. Then you may question the basis for the answer, and so on. At some point you will simply decide that you have traced the rationale for the value preference back as far as your time allows. This chapter, by asking you to justify your value preferences by identifying some of the consequences of acting on them, provides a method for looking at least one level beyond an instinctual acceptance of certain values.

When you anticipate the consequences of acting upon particular value preferences, there are two problems that you will want to recognize. Initially, you need to be able to demonstrate that the predicted consequences are highly probable. It makes little sense to focus on outcomes that are only remotely possible. In the preceding illustration, for example, several historical examples in which groups had been persecuted by those preserving traditions would make it more convincing that valuing tradition very highly may indeed lead to repression. Only those consequences that are very likely should strongly affect your selection of value assumptions. Second, even if you show that the consequences are highly probable, you must present arguments that demonstrate the goodness or badness of particular consequences. If one effect of acting upon your value assumption is the closing of many small businesses, you will still have to form a reasonable argument for why that effect is good or bad as you justify your value assumption. When you can show that the consequences of your value assumption are both highly probable and better than those flowing from alternative value assumptions, *then* you have engaged in responsible moral reasoning.

XV

Judging the Worth of Opinions: Making Tentative Decisions

You now have many of the tools you need to form reasoned personal opinions. The techniques you have learned can save you from sloppy thinking and from being unduly influenced by the thinking of others, but they cannot provide you with a set of indisputably correct answers to the complex dilemmas you will face. They *will* enable you to avoid being a sponge in reacting to other people's attempts to persuade you and will thus permit you to make decisions that are the right ones for you and your value system.

Inappropriateness of Certainty

You can never be sure that your opinions are correct. You can have more confidence in carefully reasoned opinions than you can in other kinds, but the complexity of most important questions requires you to form conclusions before you can be absolutely certain that you are right. Even when we *know* we cannot be wrong, there is some shred of information we have not yet considered or some important implication of our conclusion that we have failed to analyze. Most of us want to be certain that our opinions are accurate, but the limitations of our intellects and the complexities of human dilemmas work together to frustrate this search for certainty. Thus, you should not define a good decision or conclusion as an absolutely correct one, but rather as the best you can achieve given your present limitations.

Making Tentative Personal Decisions

After you have asked the right questions, you are ready to form your reasoned conclusions. You should begin by reminding yourself what the controversy is. In arriving at a decision, it is of utmost importance to do the following:

1. List those reasons that you were least able to criticize.
2. List possible conclusions.
3. Make explicit the personal value preferences and definitions of key ambiguous terms that are relevant to this particular controversy.

Once you have done this, it is time to make your decision.

As you reach decisions, be sure to pay attention to each of these three products of your critical thinking. It may be tempting to use only value assumptions or only evidence in your rush to make a decision. To remind yourself of the need to consider precise definitions, reasons, and value assumptions, ask before each decision, ''Under what conditions would I change my mind?'' For example, you might oppose seat-belt legislation simply because you prefer individualism to public safety. By asking yourself what would have to be true for you to change your mind, you will be forced to consider how many injuries and fatalities would cause you to change your decision.

Your decision will be tentative in most cases. Answers to your questions will not be enough to provide you with certain conclusions. Whatever you decide, you should realize that a different conclusion might be more reasonable if only you knew more about each controversy. But making reasoned tentative decisions is rewarding for those who have gone through the necessary steps.

In many cases, because the reasoning you have encountered may be so weak or so abbreviated, the best tentative decision will be no decision. You will want to wait until you can find the relevant information elsewhere. In such cases, asking the right questions will have been useful to you because you will have been cautious enough not to be led to a premature judgment by a weak argument.

While you may frequently choose to put off making a decision, many issues will require conclusions right away, although it might take a decade to gather all the relevant information. Many of the debates discussed in this book require answers *now*. We need to help persons suffering from schizophrenia *now*. If foods are causing cancer, we need to act *now*. Decisions about building nuclear plants need to be made *now*. Thus, even though you would like to be sure before you form an opinion, you will often have to make a decision without delay.

When Has a Writer or Speaker Done His Job?

One final precautionary note. If you consistently ask the right questions, we will be surprised if you do not have a tendency to judge virtually everything you read as a bad argument, or as a weak argument. Why? Because all of the arguments related to the kinds of issues we have been talking about will be flawed *in some respect*—if only because the writer or speaker does not have sufficient space to present his point of view thoroughly. You will find that it is much easier to find a flaw in someone else's reasoning than to construct your own reasoned arguments. Thus, keep in mind limitations as you judge the writer of a magazine article, a letter to the editor, an editorial, or a textbook. No position will be perfect, but some will be better than others. What you decide to call a well-reasoned presentation will be up to you. You now have the tools to judge the weak from the strong. But we suggest that you do not demand perfection and that you keep the writer's or speaker's purpose in mind.

Look for the *best* argument you can expect, given the writer's purpose and the complexity of the issue.

XVI

Biases that Block Critical Thinking

You are now ready to form your opinions; you have learned a process that results in reasoned opinions. You have no doubt made great progress toward being a better critical thinker. You're aware of several interrelated critical questions that should be asked and answered when evaluating arguments. We suggest that you keep this checklist of critical questions handy as you practice applying the skills you have acquired.

Critical Questions

1. What are the issue and the conclusion?
2. What are the reasons?
3. What words or phrases are ambiguous?
4. What are the value conflicts and assumptions?
5. What are the descriptive assumptions?
6. What is the evidence?
7. Are the samples representative and the measurements valid?
8. Are there rival hypotheses?
9. Are there flaws in the statistical reasoning?
10. How relevant are the analogies?
11. Are there any errors in reasoning?
12. What significant information is omitted?
13. What conclusions are consistent with the strong reasons?
14. What are your value preferences in this controversy?

Still there are a number of mental habits or biases that may prevent you from using the critical skills and attitudes you have worked so hard to develop. This last chapter is an important postscript for a critical thinking text. Its message is, "Beware, we all have biases that stand in the way of critical thinking." Being more aware of these biases gives us a better chance of overcoming them.

The Seductive Quality of Personal Experience

When something happens to us, we experience it directly and intensely. We tend to trust ourselves and our observations. Consequently, in any conversation we have a tendency to stress personal experiences. Furthermore, whenever those experiences differ from those of others, we have an inclination to weigh personal experience more highly, even when it disagrees with the more scientific observations of others.

The average person who cites "personal experience" as a basis for belief is unfortunately running a great risk of several practical errors. Perhaps the most obvious of these errors is captured by checking the sample size of the group claiming to have observed reality. It's *one*, isn't it? While as an individual, you are capable of great insight, would you really want to rely on just one person's observations, even your own?

We can see several dangers of relying on personal experience by imagining how you might answer the following question: Does watching too much violence on television increase the tendency to commit a violent act? Let's take a look at some common errors.

1. *Paying attention only to experience that favors a belief (and ignoring instances that contradict the belief).* You can always find a number of violent people who watch a lot of television. But are you keeping track of the nonviolent people? Perhaps they also watch television often.

2. *Generalizing from only a few experiences.* Maybe you are familiar with a couple of cases in which people committed crimes similar to those committed in a television show. Perhaps they would have committed these crimes anyway.

3. *Failing to "keep track" of events, to count, to control.* How good is your memory? Not as good as careful records!

4. *Oversimplifying.* We sometimes fail to consider that there are other characteristics in addition to those in which we are interested that might be affecting the behaviors under observation. You recall an incident in which a juvenile vandalized a school, just after watching a juvenile gang film on television. But maybe that youth was imitating his violent parents.

Remember: Beware of the individual who says, "My experience proves . . ." or "I can disprove all that because of an experience I had . . . ." The critical thinker is always skeptical of experiences, subjects them to critical analysis, and determines whether they have been adequately confirmed by appropriate observational methods.

Personal Psychological Needs

When an issue arises, our reactions may too often be guided by our deep psychological needs. If certain things are true we feel better. For instance, when someone discusses the relative emotional stability of men and women, intelligence of citizens from various countries, or the impact of aging on competence, each of us has a vested interest in the result of the discussion. We "need" certain conclusions to be true, for we belong to a category of people who look better if certain conclusions are reached.

Because we wish certain conclusions to be true, we may reason as if they are true, despite strong evidence to the contrary. Not only do we want our vested interests to prevail, but we also wish for a comfortable, fair world. The wish for a just world is often transformed in our minds into the belief in a just world.

This belief in a just world can distort our reasoning in numerous regards. Suppose for instance, we bring the belief in a just world to an evaluation of the need for governmentally regulating the amount of radon gas in dwellings. We might erroneously presume that no one would ever build a dwelling that contained dangerous amounts of radon gas; to do so would not be just. Another painful example of the danger of the belief in a just world occurs sometimes when people believe someone who is actually manipulating them with expressions of deep love. In a just world, no one would play with our emotions like that. Thus, some assume we can automatically trust expressions of love. Can we?

Stereotypes

One approach to thinking about biases is to see them as potentially distorting assumptions. You approach any topic with certain preliminary beliefs or habits of mind. The previous section discussed one such habit—a preference for using personal experience to guide choices and adjustments. Another assumption or bias that can distort your decisions is the tendency to stereotype. When we stereotype we allege that a particular group has a specific set of characteristics.

Stereotypes are substitutes for thought. Here are a few examples:

1. Men with beards are wise.
2. Overweight individuals are jolly.
3. Japanese are industrious.
4. Young people are frivolous.
5. Women make the best secretaries for organizations.
6. Welfare recipients are lazy.

All six of these illustrations pretend to tell us something significant about the quality of certain types of people. If we believe these stereotypes, we will not approach people and their ideas with the spirit of openness necessary for strong sense critical thinking. In addition, we will have an immediate bias toward any issue or controversy in which these people are involved. The stereotypes will have loaded the issue in advance, *prior to* the reasoning.

Imagine, for instance, that you considered politicians to be manipulative and greedy. You possess that stereotype and approach political conversations with that assumption. Would you then be able to "pan for gold" with the aid of the critical questions you have learned? Isn't it more likely that you would not give an honest, caring politician a fair chance to convince you of her virtue?

One quick way to sense the danger of stereotypes is to recall how angry it justifiably makes you to hear stereotypes about groups to which you belong. For instance, we've all heard the following stereotypes:

1. Sorority women are silly.
2. College students don't care about society.
3. Business students aren't interested in ideas.
4. Young people are poor drivers.

There seems to be something basically unfair about letting a stereotype prevent our giving someone or his arguments an opportunity to convince us.

Stereotypes are used so commonly because when they are true, they save us lots of time. If all politicians were indeed manipulative and greedy, it would make us more efficient readers and listeners to bring the stereotype with us when participating in a political conversation.

But rarely is a stereotype safe. Nor is it fair! Each person deserves our respect, and their arguments deserve our attention. Stereotypes get in the way of critical thinking because they attempt to short circuit the difficult process of evaluation. As critical thinkers, we want to model curiosity and openness; stereotypes cut us off from careful consideration of what others are saying. They cause us to ignore valuable information by closing our minds prematurely.

The Urge to Simplify

Most of us prefer simplicity to complexity. Decisions and situations with simple answers permit us to move on rapidly and confidently to the next topic or life event. We don't have to wrestle so hard and invest so much mental energy in simple situations.

This bias for simplification was discussed earlier when we introduced dichotomous thinking. One reason for the attractiveness of dichotomous thinking to many of us is its simplicity. We can handle or master two potential alternatives with less anxiety than would emerge were we to see choices in terms of a continuum of possible choices.

Suppose we were to ask you whether drugs should be legalized? If you think of the question as one requiring a "yes" or "no" answer, it appears to be a manageable question you can handle after some initial reflection.

But let's turn back to the section on dichotomous thinking and its dangers and think about the issue in a more realistic vein. There are many types of drugs; legalization takes many forms; potential drug users are various ages; legalization could contribute or detract from many potential social objectives. This issue is so complex it makes our heads hurt to consider it.

Critical thinking, though, forces us to consider an issue as it is, with all the complexity it possesses. To take the easy way out and dichotomize the issue is to miss out on the rich number of possible responses to drugs and other human dilemmas.

The urge to simplify can also limit our search for hypotheses about the meaning of evidence or for alternative conclusions flowing from a set of reasons. Whenever we restrict our perspective we cut ourselves off from potential insight.

For instance, when we choose a spouse, religion, or value assumption, we want to push ourselves to think broadly from alternative perspectives. Consider the obvious deficiencies of choosing your religion solely on the basis of your understanding of what it means to be a Baptist, Methodist, and Presbyterian. The alternatives to these three are incredibly numerous. By not considering these alternatives, by giving in to the desire to simplify the decision, you would have been unnecessarily sloppy in your choice.

While it is frequently realistic to consider all possible alternatives, hypotheses, or conclusions, try to force yourself to resist the bias for simplification. Work on yourself to look further before making important judgments. You cannnot evaluate every possible spouse, for example, but you should look beyond your neighborhood.

Belief Perseverance

As we stressed at the beginning of the book, you bring to any conversation or test a set of preconceptions. You start with opinions. To return to the panning for gold metaphor, *before* you even dip your pan into the gravel you think you have gold in the pan. Your beliefs are valuable because they are yours. Understandably you want to hold onto them.

This tendency for personal beliefs to persevere is a tough obstacle to critical thinking. We are biased from the start of an exchange in favor of our current opinions and conclusions.

If I prefer the Democratic candidate for mayor, regardless of how shallow my rationale is, I may resist your appeal on behalf of the Republican candidate. I might feel bad about myself if I were to admit that my previous judgment had been flawed. This exaggerated loyalty to current beliefs is one of the sources of *confirmation* bias. Because of belief preseverance, we might study the mayoral election in search only for information consistent with our belief that the Democratic candidate is meritorious and the Republican candidate is weak. In this manner, belief perseverance leads to weak-sense critical thinking.

To counter belief preseverance, it's helpful to remember that strong-sense critical thinking requires the recognition that judgments are tentative or contextual. We can never permit ourselves to be so sure of anything that we stop searching for an improved version. The struggle to remain open and full of questions requires us to fight against belief perseverance.

When we change our minds in light of a superior argument, we deserve to be proud that we have resisted the temptation to remain true to long-held beliefs. Such a change of mind deserves to be seen as reflecting a rare strength. Foolish consistency in the face of persuasive counterarguments is intellectually dishonest.

Availability Heuristic

Critical thinking is hard, systematic work. We are always searching for ways to avoid its rigors. Each bias in this chapter can be seen as an attempt to avoid mental effort. I may rely on personal experience, stereotyping, simplification, and my current beliefs because in each case the alternative requires more rigorous "panning."

Another misleading bias that promises to help us reach sound judgments without critical thinking is the availability heuristic. A heuristic is a guide for understanding or discovery. The availability heuristic refers to our tendency to rely on information and memories that are easily retrieved as a basis for our decisions and judgments. The weight attached to a particular piece of evidence therefore depends more on its availability than its appropriateness as a reason.

You can observe the dangers of the availability heuristic all around you. Newspaper headlines about a particularly brutal slaying convince residents that more police must be hired. Reservoirs are built because a recent drought suggested to residents that we may be entering an era with less rainfall. Parents warn their children not to associate with people who dress in a bizarre fashion because the parents vividly remember the trouble caused in their youth by people who wore those kinds of clothes.

To recognize the power of the availability heuristic, imagine that you were asked to compare the safety of airplanes and automobiles. There are volumes of comparative data that you *could* use to form your judgment. Would you consult them or rely on the availability heuristic?

Recent events, for instance, tend to have a disproportionate impact on our perceptions. While the recency of plane crashes in Tokyo, Detroit, or Dallas should not distort your comparison, the resulting tendency to exaggerate the occurrence of plane crashes is common. We may remember better those instances that just occurred even though they may have been exceptions to what normally occurs. The availability of recent events in our memory bank must be consciously checked by asking, "Were those recent events typical?"

Another factor affecting the availability of evidence is its vividness. Striking examples tend to overwhelm typical examples in our memory. One fiery plane crash with dozens of casualties can etch powerful images in our mind. The strength of these images may be totally unrelated to the number of safe flights typically experienced by airlines. Statistics describing what is typical can often be very dry; typical experiences can be dull *and* safe.

Because we have a tendency to remember startling and unusual events, we must struggle to place available information into a broader context. Our desire to engage in strong-sense critical thinking requires us to process "available" information by asking: Is it typical? Answering that question forces us to study evidence, compiled more systematically. "Available" evidence must be diluted with evidence collected from perspectives different from our own.

Panning for Gold in Many Streams

The biases discussed in this chapter can interfere with your search for gold. They can cause you to overlook many possible sources of good arguments. They restrict your panning efforts to a few streams.

How can you avoid these biases? The primary antidote is to adopt the attitudes of a critical thinker. An attitude is a mental stance with which you approach events and issues. Critical thinking is enhanced when you struggle to maintain the following attitudes:

1. *Intellectual Curiosity.* Look for causes and answers every chance you get.
2. *Open-mindedness to Multiple Realities.* Seek out and respect alternative viewpoints and perspectives.
3. *Flexibility.* Be willing to change your mind in the face of strong reasoning.
4. *Humility Concerning Your Beliefs.* Recognize that certainty is almost always an illusion.
5. *Intellectual Skepticism.* Require support for claims or opinions before adopting them.

None of these attitudes is easy to maintain, but the rewards from trying are worth the effort.

For a critical thinker, knowing about these biases is just a first step toward overcoming them. That we tend to stereotype or rely too much on vivid pieces of evidence is a habit of mind that requires conscious resistance.

In a sense, critical thinkers must censor themselves. They must recognize that they will begin conversations or thought with certain tendencies inconsistent with critical thinking. What distinguishes strong-sense critical thinkers is their drive to resist these biases, to keep searching for improved beliefs, and to conduct that search in diverse streams.

Index